# Women and Elective Office

# Women and Elective Office

## Past, Present, and Future

THIRD EDITION

EDITED BY SUE THOMAS
*and*
CLYDE WILCOX

OXFORD
UNIVERSITY PRESS

# OXFORD
#### UNIVERSITY PRESS

Oxford University Press is a department of the University of Oxford.
It furthers the University's objective of excellence in research, scholarship,
and education by publishing worldwide.

Oxford    New York

Auckland    Cape Town    Dar es Salaam    Hong Kong    Karachi
Kuala Lumpur    Madrid    Melbourne    Mexico City    Nairobi
New Delhi    Shanghai    Taipei    Toronto

With offices in

Argentina    Austria    Brazil    Chile    Czech Republic    France    Greece
Guatemala    Hungary    Italy    Japan    Poland    Portugal    Singapore
South Korea    Switzerland    Thailand    Turkey    Ukraine    Vietnam

Oxford is a registered trademark of Oxford University Press
in the UK and certain other countries.

Published in the United States of America by
Oxford University Press
198 Madison Avenue, New York, NY 10016

Library of Congress Cataloging-in-Publication Data
Women and elective office : past, present and future / edited by Sue
Thomas and Clyde Wilcox. — Third edition.
pages cm
ISBN 978–0–19–932873–4 (pbk. : alk. paper)    1. Women in public life—United States.    2. Women—
Political activity—United States.    3. Women political candidates—United States.
I. Thomas, Sue, 1957–    II. Wilcox, Clyde, 1953–
HQ1391.U5W63 2014
320.082—dc23
2013019420

1 3 5 7 9 8 6 4 2
Printed in the United States of America
on acid-free paper

# CONTENTS

*Acknowledgments*   vii
*About the Contributors*   ix

1. Introduction   1
   SUE THOMAS

2. Women's Underrepresentation in U.S. Politics: The Enduring Gender
   Gap in Political Ambition   27
   JENNIFER L. LAWLESS , RICHARD L. FOX , AND GAIL BAITINGER

3. Voter Attitudes, Behaviors, and Women Candidates   46
   TIMOTHY R. LYNCH  AND KATHLEEN DOLAN

4. The Race for the Presidency: Hillary Rodham Clinton   67
   REGINA G. LAWRENCE  AND MELODY ROSE

5. Hillary Rodham Clinton: A Case Study in the Rhetoric of Female
   Political Figures   80
   MOANA VERCOE, RANDALL GONZALEZ, AND JEAN REITH SCHROEDEL

6. Women and Campaigns   97
   REBEKAH HERRICK AND JEANETTE MOREHOUSE MENDEZ

7. Conservative Women Run for Office   111
   RONNEE SCHREIBER

8. Different Portraits, Different Leaders? Gender Differences in U.S. Senators'
    Presentation of Self   126
    KIM L. FRIDKIN AND PATRICK J. KENNEY

9. Female Governors and Gubernatorial Candidates   145
    VALERIE R. O'REGAN AND STEPHEN J. STAMBOUGH

10. Representing Women's Interests in a Polarized Congress   162
    MICHELE L. SWERS

11. Women State Legislators: Women's Issues in Partisan Environments   181
    TRACY OSBORN AND REBECCA KREITZER

12. Entry-Level Politics? Women as Candidates and Elected Officials
    at the Local Level   199
    LAURA VAN ASSENDELFT

13. Judicial Women   216
    SALLY J. KENNEY

14. Indelible Effects: The Impact of Women of Color in the U.S. Congress   235
    LISA GARCIÁ BEDOLLA, KATHERINE TATE, AND JANELLE WONG

15. Lesbian Candidates and Officeholders   253
    DONALD P. HAIDER-MARKEL AND CHELSIE LYNN MOORE BRIGHT

16. Trends in the Geography of Women in the U.S. State Legislatures   273
    BARBARA NORRANDER AND CLYDE WILCOX

17. Women in Elective Office Worldwide: Barriers and Opportunities   288
    PIPPA NORRIS AND MONA LENA KROOK

References   307
Index   347

# ACKNOWLEDGMENTS

We wish to thank Rachel Blum and Patty Baker for their careful, thoughtful, and stellar work on this volume. Their production assistance has been invaluable and has made this third edition of *Women and Elective Office* much better than it would have been otherwise. Thanks also to Shauna Shames for her helpful suggestions and encouragement as the project progressed. Much gratitude also goes to David McBride and Sarah Rosenthal at Oxford University Press for their support of this topic and us. Oxford has been a wonderful home for this series, and we look forward to future collaboration.

# ABOUT THE EDITORS AND AUTHORS

**Sue Thomas** is senior research scientist at the Pacific Institute for Research and Evaluation (PIRE) and director of PIRE–Santa Cruz. Her research specialty is women and politics and, among her books, journal articles, book chapters, encyclopedia entries, and book reviews are *How Women Legislate* and *The Year of the Woman: Myths and Realities*. She is also a coauthor of an award-winning text on American government titled *Understanding American Government*, now in its 14th edition. Prior to joining PIRE, Dr. Thomas served as associate professor of government and director of women's studies at Georgetown University, and her pre-academic career included serving as a legislative advocate in California on behalf of women's issues and as a Title IX specialist in the Los Angeles Unified School District. More recently, Dr. Thomas has also taught courses on women and politics at University of California, Santa Cruz and served as an associate editor and book editor of *Politics & Gender*.

**Clyde Wilcox** is professor of government at Georgetown University. He writes on religion and politics, gender politics, social movements and social issues, interest groups and campaign finance, and science fiction and politics. His latest book is *Religion, Sexuality, and Politics in the U.S. and Canada* (coedited with David Rayside, University of British Columbia Press, 2011).

**Gail Baitinger** is a third-year Ph.D. student in political science at American University. Her research focuses on women and politics, political communication, and public opinion. Her dissertation will examine gender dynamics and agenda setting on the Sunday morning political shows.

**Lisa Garciá Bedolla** is Professor, Social and Cultural Studies, UC Berkeley Graduate School of Education, and chair of Berkeley's Center for Latino Policy Research. She received her Ph.D. in political science from Yale University and her B.A. in Latin American studies and comparative literature from the University of California, Berkeley. She is author of *Fluid Borders: Latino Power, Identity, and Politics in Los Angeles* (Berkeley: University of California Press, 2005), which was the winner of the American Political Science Association's (APSA) Ralph Bunche Award, and the best book award from APSA's Race, Ethnicity, and Politics Section; and *Latino Politics* (Malden, MA: Polity, 2009), winner of a best book award from APSA's Latino Caucus. She is coauthor, with Melissa R. Michelson, of *Mobilizing Inclusion: Transforming the Electorate through Get-Out-the-Vote Campaigns* (New Haven, CT: Yale University Press, 2012). Her work has appeared in numerous academic journals and edited volumes. Dr. Garciá Bedolla's research focuses on how marginalization and inequality structure the political opportunities available to members of ethnoracial groups, with a particular emphasis on the intersections of race, class, and gender.

**Chelsie Lynn Moore Bright** is a Ph.D. candidate in political science at the University of Kansas studying the fields of American government and public policy. Her research focuses on policy analysis, with an emphasis on education policy.

**Kathleen Dolan** is professor in the Department of Political Science at the University of Wisconsin, Milwaukee. Her research focuses on public opinion, elections, and voting behavior. Dolan is the author of the book *Voting for Women: How the Public Evaluates Women Candidates* (Boulder, CO: Westview Press, 2004) and the forthcoming book *Does Gender Matter in Elections* (New York: Oxford University Press). Her work has also appeared in numerous peer-reviewed journals. She has served as coeditor of the journal *Politics & Gender* and is currently a member of the board of the American National Election Studies.

**Richard L. Fox** is professor of political science at Loyola Marymount University. His research examines how gender affects voting behavior, state executive elections, congressional elections, and political ambition. He is author of *Gender Dynamics in Congressional Elections* (Thousand Oaks, CA: SAGE, 1997) and coauthor of *It Still Takes a Candidate: Why Women Don't Run for Office* with Jennifer L. Lawless ( New York Cambridge University Press, 2010) and *Tabloid Justice: The Criminal Justice System in the Age of Media Frenzy* with Robert W. Van Sickel and Thomas L. Steiger (Boulder, CO: Lynne Rienner, 2001). He is also coeditor of *Gender and Elections* with Susan J. Carroll (New York Cambridge University Press, 2010) and *iPolitics: Citizens, Elections, and Governing in the New Media Era* with Jennifer M. Ramos (New York: Cambridge University Press, 2010). His work has appeared in academic journals including *Political Psychology, Journal of Politics, American Journal of Political Science, Social Problems, PS,* and *Politics & Gender*. His op-ed articles have appeared in the *New York Times* and the *Wall Street Journal*.

**Kim L. Fridkin** received her B.A., M.A., and Ph.D. from the University of Michigan. She has contributed articles to the *American Political Science Review, American Journal of Political Science,* and *Journal of Politics*. She is the coauthor (with Patrick J. Kenney) of *The Changing Face of Representation: The Gender of U.S. Senators and*

*Constituent Communications* (Ann Arbor: University of Michigan Press, forthcoming), *No-Holds Barred: Negative Campaigning in U.S. Senate Campaigns* (Upper Saddle River, NJ: Prentice Hall, 2004), and *The Spectacle of U.S. Senate Campaigns* (Princeton, NJ: Princeton University Press, 1999) and is author of *The Political Consequences of Being a Woman* (New York: Columbia University Press, 1996). Dr. Fridkin's current research interests are negative campaigning, women and politics, and campaigns and elections.

**Randall A. Gonzalez** is preparing for his Ph.D. qualifying exams at the School of Politics and Economics at Claremont Graduate University. He has coauthored other publications on political rhetoric and is also conducting researching on judicial behavior when popular sentiments run contrary to established law, which subsumes rulings on gender and racial classes of individuals.

**Donald P. Haider-Markel** is professor of political science at the University of Kansas. His research and teaching is focused on the representation of interests in the policy process and the dynamics between public opinion and policy. He has authored or coauthored over 45 refereed articles, multiple book chapters, and several books in a range of issue areas, including the environment, religion and the culture wars, civil rights, criminal justice, and terrorism. He has been recipient or co-recipient of grants from the U.S. Environmental Protection Agency STAR program, the National Science Foundation, and the American Psychological Foundation.

**Rebekah Herrick** is professor of political science at Oklahoma State University. Her primary research interests concern issues of representation particularly as they relate gender and legislatures. Other areas of interest concern congressional careers and political ambition. She has published three books, and her work has appeared in *Journal of Politics, Social Science Quarterly, Legislative Studies Quarterly, American Politic Research, and State Politics and Policy Quarterly* as well as several other more specialized journals such as *Women and Politics* and *Journal of Homosexuality*.

**Patrick J. Kenney** is dean of social sciences in the College of Liberal Arts and Sciences, associate vice president of the Office of Knowledge Enterprise Development at Arizona State University (ASU), and director of the Institute for Social Science Research. He came to ASU in 1986. He received his B.A., M.A.P.A., and Ph.D. from the University of Iowa. Dr. Kenney has authored and coauthored articles in the *American Political Science Review, American Journal of Political Science, Political Behavior,* and *Journal of Politics*. He has coauthored three books with Kim Fridkin, *The Spectacle of U.S. Senate Campaigns* (Princeton, NJ: Princeton University Press, 1999), *No-Holds Barred: Negativity in U.S. Senate Campaigns* (Upper Saddle River, NJ: Prentice Hall, 2004), and *The Changing Face of Representation: The Gender of U.S. Senators and Constituent Communications* (Ann Arbor: University of Michigan Press, forthcoming). He has received funding from the National Science Foundation to support his research.

**Sally J. Kenney** is the Newcomb College Endowed Chair, executive director of the Newcomb College Institute, and professor of political science at Tulane University. Prior to 2010, she served on the faculties of the University of Minnesota, the University of Iowa, and the University of Illinois. Her research interests include gender and judging, judicial selection, feminist social movements, women and electoral politics, the European Court of Justice, exclusionary employment policies, and pregnancy discrimination. Her latest book is *Gender and Justice: Why Women in the Judiciary Really Matter* (New York: Routledge, 2013). She has produced more than 25 case studies on women and public policy and is currently studying women state Supreme Court justices.

**Rebecca J. Kreitzer** is a doctoral student in political science at the University of Iowa. Her primary research interest is in the adoption of morality policy in the states, with an emphasis on state abortion policies.

**Mona Lena Krook** is associate professor of political science at Rutgers University. Her research analyzes gender and politics in cross-national perspective. Her first book, *Quotas for Women in Politics: Gender and Candidate Selection Reform Worldwide* (Oxford: Oxford University Press, 2009), received the American Political Science Association's 2010 Victoria Schuck Award for the Best Book on Women and Politics. In addition to authoring numerous articles, she is coeditor with Sarah Childs of *Women, Gender, and Politics: A Reader* (New York: Oxford University Press, 2010); with Fiona Mackay of *Gender, Politics, and Institutions: Towards a Feminist Institutionalism* (New York: Palgrave, 2011); and with Susan Franceschet and Jennifer M. Piscopo of *The Impact of Gender Quotas* (New York: Oxford University Press, 2012).

**Jennifer L. Lawless** is associate professor of government at American University, where she is also director of the Women & Politics Institute. Her research focuses on representation, political ambition, and gender in the electoral process. She is the author of *Becoming a Candidate: Political Ambition and the Decision to Run for Office* (New York: Cambridge University Press, 2012) and the coauthor of *It Still Takes a Candidate: Why Women Don't Run for Office* (New York: Cambridge University Press, 2010). Her work has appeared in academic journals including the *American Journal of Political Science, Perspectives on Politics, Journal of Politics, Political Research Quarterly, Legislative Studies Quarterly,* and *Politics & Gender*. She is a nationally recognized speaker on women and electoral politics, and her scholarly analysis and political commentary have been quoted in numerous newspapers, magazines, television news programs, and radio shows. In 2006, she sought the Democratic nomination for the U.S. House of Representatives in Rhode Island's second congressional district.

**Regina Lawrence** holds the Jesse H. Jones Centennial Chair in the School of Journalism. Her books include *The Politics of Force: Media and the Construction of*

*Police Brutality* (Berkeley, CA: University of California Press, 2000); *When the Press Fails: Political Power and the News Media from Iraq to Katrina* (coauthored with W. Lance Bennett and Steven Livingston, Chicago: University of Chicago Press, 2007); and *Hillary Clinton's Race for the White House: Gender Politics and the Media on the Campaign Trail* (coauthored with Melody Rose) (Boulder, CO: Lynne Rienner, 2009). Articles she has authored and coauthored have appeared in *Journal of Communication, Political Communication, Political Research Quarterly, Journalism,* and *International Journal of Press/Politics.*

**Timothy R. Lynch** is a Ph.D. candidate in the Department of Political Science at the University of Wisconsin, Milwaukee. His research interests include political behavior and the role of elections in creating accountability in the U.S. Senate.

**Jeanette Morehouse Mendez** is professor of political science at Oklahoma State University. Her research areas focus on social networks and political information processing of media information. Her recent work includes studying gendered patterns in discussion networks, the effects of facial appearance on perceptions of maturity, competence and vote choice, and the effects of gender on representation when legislative seats change hands. Her work has been published in journals including *Journal of Politics, Social Science Quarterly, Political Psychology, Politics and Gender, Journal of Women, Politics and Policy, PS: Political Science and Politics, Journal of Media Psychology,* and *Journal of Political Science.*

**Barbara Norrander** is professor in the School of Government and Public Policy at the University of Arizona. She and Clyde Wilcox have written about the geography of female state legislators in previous editions of this book. Besides an interest in female legislators, she writes about gender differences in public opinion, the influence of public opinion on state policies, and the presidential nomination process.

**Pippa Norris** is the McGuire Lecturer in Comparative Politics in the John F. Kennedy School of Government at Harvard University and Laureate fellow and professor of government and international relations at the University of Sydney. She has also served as director of the Democratic Governance Group at the United Nations Development Programme in New York. Her work compares democracy, elections and public opinion, political communications, and gender politics in many countries worldwide. A well-known public speaker and prolific author, she has published more than 40 books. Her latest research at http://www.electoralintegrityproject.com includes a forthcoming book, *Why Electoral Integrity Matters,* the first part of a trilogy for Cambridge University Press. In 2011 she was given the Johan Skytte Prize, the most prestigious award in political science.

**Valerie R. O'Regan** is associate professor of political science at California State University (CSU), Fullerton. Her research and teaching focus on women and politics and comparative politics with an emphasis on Latin America and Western Europe.

Her publications include the book *Gender Matters: Female Policymakers' Influence in Industrialized Nations* and several book chapters and articles in leading journals. She is also director of the California State University Intelligence Community Scholars Program at CSU Fullerton.

**Tracy Osborn** is associate professor in the Department of Political Science at the University of Iowa. Her research focuses on women and politics in U.S. state legislatures, Congress, and political behavior. Her recent book, *How Women Represent Women: Political Parties, Gender, and Representation in the State Legislatures* (New York: Oxford University Press, 2012), examines how Democratic and Republican women represent women's issues under different legislative conditions. She has also published articles in journals including *Political Research Quarterly*, *American Politics Research*, and *Politics & Gender*.

**Melody Rose** is chancellor of the Oregon University System. Her recent publications include Executive Women: Pathways and Performance (Boulder, CO: Lynne Rienner, 2012) and Hillary Clinton's Race for the White House: Gender Politics and the Media on the Campaign Trail (Boulder, CO: Lynne Rienner, 2009). She is also professor of political science at Portland State University, where she founded and directed the Center for Women, Politics & Policy.

**Ronnee Schreiber** is associate professor of political science at San Diego State University. Her research interests are in the area of women and American political institutions and women's public policy activism. An updated version of her book, *Righting Feminism: Conservative Women and American Politics*, was published with Oxford University Press in 2012. She has also published in *Political Communication*, *Journal of Urban Affairs*, *Sex Roles*, *Politics and Gender*, and several edited volumes.

**Jean Reith Schroedel** is professor in the School of Politics and Economics at Claremont Graduate University. She has written numerous articles and several books. Her book, *Is the Fetus a Person? A Comparison of Policies Across the Fifty States*, was awarded the American Political Science Association's Victoria Schuck Prize in 2001. In 2009 Schroedel coedited two books on the impact of evangelical Christianity on democracy in America for the Russell Sage Foundation. Over the past several years, she has been collaborating on projects exploring the use of charismatic rhetoric by presidential candidates and just had an article published in *Presidential Studies Quarterly* that examines the partisan differences in presidential candidates' use of such rhetoric.

**Stephen J. Stambough** is professor of political science and chair of the Division of the Politics, Administration, and Justice at California State University, Fullerton. He is coeditor, with David Sanford McCuan, of *Initiative Centered Politics* (Durham: Carolina Academic Press, 2005), a book about direct democracy. He has also published numerous articles related to congressional, presidential, and gubernatorial elections, most recently with a focus on gender politics. He is also the founding director of the Cal State DC Internship program.

**Michele L. Swers** is associate professor in the Department of Government at Georgetown University. She is the author of *Women in the Club: Gender and Policy Making in the Senate* (Chicago: University of Chicago Press, 2013) and *The Difference Women Make: The Policy Impact of Women in Congress* (Chicago: University of Chicago Press, 2002). She is coauthor of *Women and Politics: Paths to Power and Political Influence*, 2nd edition (with Julie Dolan and Melissa Deckman, Upper Saddle River, NJ: Prentice Hall, 2010). Her research on gender differences in legislative behavior has also been published in journals including *Legislative Studies Quarterly, Journal of Women, Politics, & Policy, Politics & Gender*, and *PS: Political Science* as well as several edited volumes.

**Katherine Tate** is professor of political science at the University of California, Irvine. She teaches in the fields of American government, African American politics, public opinion, and race, ethnicity, and urban politics. She is the author and coauthor of several books, including *Concordance: Black Lawmaking in the U.S. Congress from Carter to Obama* (Ann Arbor: University of Michigan Press, 2013).

**Laura van Assendelft** is professor of political science at Mary Baldwin College. She teaches courses on U.S. politics, public policy, and women and politics. Her research interests include women and politics at the state and local level, focusing on the influence of gender on political ambition and leadership style.

**Moana Vercoe** is adjunct lecturer at Loyola Marymount University. In addition to working with a number of community-based nonprofit organizations addressing health and educational disparities, her research focuses on the roles of gender, race, and history in perpetuating the cycle of violence.

**Janelle Wong** is professor of American studies and director of the Asian American studies program at the University of Maryland. She is author of *Democracy's Promise: Immigrants and American Civic Institutions* (Ann Arbor: University of Michigan Press, 2006) and coauthor of two books on Asian American politics. The most recent is *Asian American Political Participation: Emerging Constituents and Their Political Identities* (New York: Russell Sage Foundation, 2011), based on the first nationally representative survey of Asian Americans' political attitudes and behavior. This groundbreaking study of Asian Americans was conducted in eight different languages with six different Asian national origin groups.

# Introduction

SUE THOMAS

> If liberty and equality, as is thought by some, are chiefly to be found in democracy, they will be best attained when all persons alike share in the government to the utmost.
>
> —Aristotle, *Politics*, Book IV, Chapter 4

> There cannot be true democracy unless women are given the opportunity to take responsibility for their own lives. There cannot be true democracy unless all citizens are able to participate fully in the lives of their country.
>
> —Hillary Rodham Clinton, July 11, 1997

In the first and second editions of *Women and Elective Office: Past, Present, and Future* we analyzed the progress women had made in storming statehouses and the national legislature and the impact they made once there. Since the publication of earlier editions, the numbers and diversity of women candidates and office holders have grown and, as the chapters to follow attest, women have made a considerable difference in political debates and policymaking. And several historically significant barriers have been shattered. In 2008, Hillary Rodham Clinton ran for the presidency and gained more than 18 million votes in her quest for the Democratic nomination, a record that far surpasses any woman in U.S. history. In that year, Sarah Palin became the second female vice presidential candidate on a major party ticket. And Nancy Pelosi (D-CA) became the first woman Speaker of the U.S. House of Representatives in 2007 and served until 2011 when she resumed her previous post as House minority leader.

Moreover, as a result of the 2012 election cycle, a number of additional barriers have fallen. In an election season that featured a "war on women" with attacks on reproductive choice, controversy over the meaning of rape, unsuccessful efforts to extend paycheck parity and to reauthorize legislation to prevent violence against women, Tammy Baldwin of Wisconsin became the first open lesbian in the U.S.

Senate; the New Hampshire congressional delegation became the first all-female delegation in history (the state also has a female governor, a female Speaker of the House, and a female chief justice of the state Supreme Court); Mazie Hirono of Hawaii became the first Asian American woman elected to the U.S. Senate; and Oregonian Tina Kotek became the first openly lesbian House Speaker in state-house history. The changes were so impressive that some called 2012 the second "year of the woman." As the first in 1992, it featured opportunities afforded by the once-a-decade redistricting of legislative seats and a political environment in which women issues were front and center.

Thus, the story told by this and earlier editions of *Women and Elective Office* is, in many ways, a story of triumph. The contributing authors chronicle remarkable achievements made even more noteworthy by the struggles to secure them. On the other hand, it has been and, in some ways, still is a story of enduring and evolving challenges to securing full and equal access to and participation in U.S. politics. This introduction provides an overview of forty years of research on women candidates and office holders at the local, state, and national levels, including their historical and current presence, political contributions, and future challenges.

## Does Gender Diversity in Elective Office Matter?

*Women and Elective Office: Past, Present, and Future* rests on the question of whether we ought to be concerned that women are represented among those who make decisions for our government. As long as elected office holders are aware of and care about the interests of all their constituents, does it matter whether legislatures, executives, and judges are predominately male? From broad concerns about the cultivation of healthy democracy to the details of practical policymaking, the answer is yes (Cohen 2002; Dovi 2002, 2007; Hawkesworth 2003; Mansbridge 1999; Phillips 1995, 2012).

The first reason that gender diversity is important is that vibrant and stable democracies derive, in part, from perceptions and experiences of legitimacy. A government that is democratically organized is truly legitimate only when all of its citizens are provided with equal opportunities for full participation. In turn, legitimacy begets trust in and support for government, both of which enhance stability.

If a society is to be successful and healthy, all points of view and the full range of talent must be available for public decision-making. Augmenting the potential for both sexes to contribute to the public sphere ensures access to the range of ideas and perspectives. Increased competition created by a deep talent pool is one way this can be assured.

It is also vital for women to have full access to the public sphere because of their differing life experience from men. Since our society still operates with divisions of labor in the public and private spheres, women and men tend to have some different life experiences and points of reference. These can translate into a distinctive way of seeing existing political issues and can lead to different agendas and priorities. It is important then, that women are included among our political decision-makers so that the concerns with which they are generally more familiar make their way onto policy agendas.

Finally, it is important for women to be included among our public officials for symbolic reasons. If children grow up seeing women and men in the political sphere, each sex will be more likely to choose from the full array of options as they decide how to shape adult lives. U.S. Senator Kelly Ayotte of New Hampshire tells a story about her young daughter, Kate, who told Ayotte that she should *not* run for president. When Ayotte asked her the reason, Kate replied that she wanted to be the first woman president. The likelihood of this kind of ambition among girls increases in a world in which women routinely run for president of the United States.

# History

Women have opened so many doors marked 'Impossible' that I don't know where we'll stop.

Amelia Earhart

Although women were not granted national suffrage until 1920, Elizabeth Cady Stanton, a leading figure in the early women's rights movement, ran for Congress in 1866 and lost. Fifty years later, Jeanette Rankin of Montana became the first woman to win a congressional seat. She served in the House of Representatives twice, from 1917 to 1919 and again from 1941 to 1942, and was also the only representative to vote against U.S. entry into both World Wars. In 1922, Rebecca Latimer Felton of Georgia became the first woman U.S. senator. She was appointed to the position and served for only one day. Ten years later, in 1932, Hattie W. Caraway of Arkansas became the first woman elected to the Senate to a seat to which she was originally appointed. As an indicator of the pace of societal and political change, it wasn't until 1978 that a woman was elected to the Senate without having previously filled an unexpired term. Nancy Landon Kassebaum, a Republican from Kansas, earned that honor. Nine years later, in 1987, Barbara Mikulski of Maryland became the first Democrat to do so (Foerstel and Foerstel 1996).

Several congressional "firsts" occurred fairly recently. For example, in 1968, Shirley Chisholm of New York was the first African American woman elected to the U.S. House of Representatives. She was followed by Floridian Ileana Ros-Lehtinen, who, in 1991, became the first Hispanic woman elected to the House, and Nydia Velasquez of New York, who, in 1992, became the first Puerto Rican woman. It was also in 1992 that Carol Moseley Braun of Illinois became the first African American woman elected to the U.S. Senate (CAWP 2013a). Among the new women of the

113th Congress are two who represent additional firsts: Tulsi Gabbard of Hawaii is the first American Samoan, the first Hindu member of Congress, and, along with new member Tammy Duckworth of Illinois, the first woman combat veteran. Kyrsten Sinema of Arizona is the first openly bisexual member.

Congressional leadership positions were slow to come for women. In 1995, Nancy Landon Kassebaum served as the first female to chair a major U.S. Senate Committee: Labor and Human Resources. In 2007, three women of color became chairs of committees in the U.S. House: Stephanie Tubbs Jones of Ohio (the House Committee on Ethics); Juanita Millender-McDonald of California (Committee on House Administration); and Nydia Velasquez of New York (Committee on Small Business) (CAWP 2013b). In the 113th Congress, Maryland Senator Barbara Mikulski, the longest serving woman in congressional history, became the first woman to chair the influential Senate Appropriations Committee, and Washington Senator Patty Murray served as the first female chair of the Senate Budget Committee.

The first women in state legislative politics broke into office earlier than their counterparts on the federal level. In 1895, Clara Cressingham, Carrie Clyde Holly, and Frances S. Klock won seats in the Colorado statehouse. Their victories came one year after a Colorado constitutional amendment granted women the right to vote. These women won their races, in part, because a record number of women went to the polls: 78 percent of eligible women voted compared with 56 percent of the eligible men.[1] And, foreshadowing a pattern prevalent today, these three representatives made a priority of legislation related to women, children, and families. Together, they ushered legislation through the statehouse that gave mothers equal rights to their children, raised the age of consent from sixteen to eighteen, and created a home for delinquent girls (Cox 1994). In 1896, one year after women's right to vote and hold office was written into the Utah constitution, Martha Hughes Cannon became the first woman elected to a state Senate seat in the United States (CAWP 2013g).

Women of color won state legislative office a good deal later. In 1924, Native American Cora Belle Reynolds Anderson was elected to the Michigan House of Representatives. The first African American women state legislators were Minnie Buckingham Harper, who was appointed to the West Virginia House of Delegates in 1929, and Crystal Dreda Bird Fauset, who was elected to the Pennsylvania House of Representatives in 1938. The first Latinas were elected to the New Mexico House of Representatives in 1930—Fedelina Lucero Gallegos and Porfirria Hidalgo Saiz. More than thirty years later, in 1962, Patsy Takemoto Mink won a seat in the Hawaii Senate, which made her the first female Asian Pacific Islander to serve in a state legislature. Mink later reprised her historically significant status in the U.S. House of Representatives in 1965 (CAWP 2013g). And the first American Indian state legislator, Dolly Smith Akers from Montana, served from 1933 to 1934 (Hirschfelder and Molin 2012).

Elaine Noble, who was elected to the Massachusetts House of Representatives in 1974, served as the first open lesbian state legislator. Thirty-eight years later, in 2012, Susan Allen of Minnesota became the first Native American lesbian to win a seat in a state legislature (*Huffington Post* 2012; Neff 2002).

Ascension of women to state legislative leadership was achieved thirty-nine years after Cressingham, Holly, and Klock joined the Colorado statehouse. In 1933, Minnie Davenport Craig of North Dakota served as the first female Speaker of the House. Consuelo Northrup Bailey of Vermont made history in 1955 as the first female president of a state Senate. Bailey gained that role as a responsibility of her position as lieutenant governor. Prior to that, she served as Speaker of the House of Representatives, which makes her the only woman in the United States ever to preside over both chambers of a state legislature. Thirty-two years later, in 1987, Jan Faiks of Alaska became the first female president of a state Senate independent of gaining the position as a result of holding another office. Not until 2007 did Colleen Hanabusa of Hawaii become the first woman of color to serve as president of a state Senate and in 2008 Karen Bass of California became the first woman of color to serve as Speaker of a state House (CAWP 2013g).

At the executive level, in 1984, Democrat Geraldine Ferraro of New York was the first woman to run for the vice presidency on a major party ticket. In 2008, Republican Sarah Palin of Alaska became the second woman to run. The year 2008 was also when then-senator Hillary Rodham Clinton ran for the presidency. None of these three firsts were successful in their bids. However, state executives have done better: Nellie T. Ross of Wyoming served as the first female governor in the nation. She won a special election to succeed her husband and served from 1925 to 1927. A full fifty years later, the first woman was elected governor without succeeding a spouse: Ella Grasso governed the state of Connecticut from 1975 until 1980. More recently, in 2011, Nikki Haley of South Carolina became the first Indian American woman to serve as governor, and Susana Martinez of New Mexico became the first Latina governor. On the local level, in 1887, Susanna Medora Salter served as the first female elected mayor of an American town in Argonia, Kansas. In 1924, Bertha K. Landes was the first woman to lead a major American city when she became acting mayor of Seattle, Washington. She was later elected to that position. Sixty-three years later, Lottie Shackelford of Little Rock, Arkansas, became the first woman-of-color mayor of a U.S. city. She governed from 1987 to 1991 (CAWP 2013g).

Although many recognize the only four women ever appointed to the U.S. Supreme Court—Sandra Day O'Connor (1981), Ruth Bader Ginsburg (1993), Sonia Sotomayor (2009), and Elena Kagan (2010)—less is generally known about elected and appointed judges and justices at other levels. The first elected woman judge in the United States was Catherine McCullough, who served as a justice of the peace in Illinois in 1907 (Dolan, Deckman, and Swers 2007). In 1920, Florence Ellinwood Allen became the first woman elected to a general jurisdiction court and the first female state appellate judge when she was elected to the Ohio Supreme

Court in 1922. Allen later served as the first female federal appellate judge when she was appointed to the 6th Circuit in 1933. The first African American woman judge, Jane Matilda Bolin, was appointed to the Domestic Relations Court in New York in 1939. In 1963, Lorna Lockwood of Arizona became the first woman to serve as a chief justice of a state Supreme Court. And in another, more recent, set of firsts, the judges on the Northern District of California (federal level) in 2012 were all female. Among the six judges, five were women of color, one of whom was also the first out lesbian on the court (Flatow 2012). In early 2013, the Washington Supreme Court featured a female majority and a newly elected female chief justice, Sheryl Gordon McCloud (*Women's e-news* 1/19/13).

## Women as Candidates for Electoral Office

In the 2012 election cycle, the number of women running for the U.S. Congress surged past previous records: Eighteen women were candidates for the Senate, and one hundred sixty-six women ran for the House of Representatives. The previous records were fourteen Senate candidates in 2010 and one hundred forty-one House candidates in 2004 (CAWP 2012a).

However, progress on other levels was not as encouraging. For example, just one new woman (Maggie Hassan of New Hampshire) ran for governor in the 2012 general elections.[2] And in state legislatures, fewer women entered the general election in 2012 than had done so in 2010 (CAWP 2012b).

U.S. House Minority Leader Nancy Pelosi put the historical progress women have made as successful candidates and the setbacks they have endured in context when she said: "I'm very proud of what we've done, we've increased the number of women in the House, especially on the Democratic side, but it's not enough. We're talking incrementally all the time and I think we need to be talking in a different way; we need to *make our own environment*. We can't just sit back and say, 'Well, we got ten more, and soon we'll have eight more, and in two hundred more years we'll be at parity.' No, I think we say, '*What are the factors that inhibit the increased role of women?*'" (Angyal 2013, italics added).

Indeed, research that has dug deeply into the environment in which women consider and pursue candidacies illuminates the reality that females still face several different challenges than men and bear some disproportionate costs of pursuing politics. The remainder of this section analyzes the ways external challenges and internal decision calculi are reciprocal and reflect a political playing field that is not yet level.

### The Personal and the Political

That women can be as successful as men in pursuing political candidacies is no longer in question. In general, the message is increasingly clear: If women run, they win.[3] But first they must decide to put their hats into the ring. And recent research indicates that women are more reluctant to do so than their male counterparts. In Chapter 2, Jennifer Lawless, Richard Fox, and Gail Baitinger report that, although women's interest in politics equals men's, they are less likely to run for office. This gender gap in ambition is attributed to the facts that women are much less likely to think they are qualified to run for office,[4] even with the same credentials, are less confident and more risk averse than men, are more likely to perceive the electoral environment as highly competitive and biased against female candidates (a finding that has been aggravated by the media treatment of Hillary Clinton and Sarah Palin), and are less likely to receive suggestions to run for office.[5] Critically, these results hold across age group (Lawless and Fox 2005) and across time periods. Buttressing these findings, in Chapter 12 Laura van Assendelft reports that local-level women are less likely than men to run for office, even in the face of lesser demands for fundraising than on the state or national levels, more frequent part-time positions, less intrusive media, and absence of the need to relocate families to capital cities.

One example of national aggregate findings on the ambition gender gap comes from New Hampshire, the state with the first all-female congressional delegation. Although women are very well represented at higher levels of government in the state, they are much more poorly represented at lower levels. In 2012, women were 20 percent of city and town councils and boards of aldermen and selectmen. Compared with two hundred by men, women headed thirty-four cities and towns. Results of a survey to learn the reasons for this disparity showed that women cited the leading and time-consuming role of raising children, aversion to perceived negativity and gender bias in political campaigns, and doubts about their qualifications to run for public office as reasons that they declined to run.[6] Said Sylvia Larsen, a former city councilor, Senate president, and Democratic leader in the state Senate: "Generally, women have to be asked to run. And the evidence shows that unlike men, women are not as likely to wake up one morning and say, 'I'm going to run for office'.... The question is, who is asking women to run for local government? And apparently it's not happening very often" (Leubsdorf 2012).[7]

## Political Challenges: Stereotypes

In Chapter 3, Timothy Lynch and Kathleen Dolan report that, although some citizens are less supportive of women than men candidates, the proportions of the population feeling this way have shrunk dramatically over time. Further, even when such feelings persist, they are often overcome by party loyalty or incumbency status.[8] Yet despite being willing to cast ballots for female candidates, voters still stereotype candidate by sex. Women are seen as more liberal and more competent than men on women's issues, health care, and education, for example, whereas men are seen as more conservative and more competent on crime, agriculture, defense, and the economy (Alexander and Andersen 1993; Fridkin and Kenney 2009; Holman, Merolla, and Zechmeister 2011; Huddy and Terklidsen 1993a, 1993b; Sanbonmatsu and Dolan 2009).[9] An important consequence is that women who run for political office have to calibrate their presentations on the campaign trail to recognize and maximize or counteract these stereotypes. In times and places in which salient issues coincide with women's perceived strengths, female candidates can be advantaged. But when issues related to war, foreign policy, terrorism, or economic decline are uppermost in the minds of the voters, women candidates may be disadvantaged (Herrnson, Lay, and Stokes 2003; Kahn 1994, 1996; Lawless 2004).[10]

Several of the authors in *Women and Elective Office* illuminate the electoral effects of stereotypes on female incumbents and challengers and the efforts they make to address them. Rebekah Herrick and Jeanette Morehouse Mendez explore the interactions among stereotypes, party, and candidate sex in open-seat congressional races in Chapter 6. Comparing women-only races with mixed races, they find that when women run against each other Democrats are advantaged.[11] In Chapter 8, Kim Fridkin and Patrick Kenney demonstrate that U.S. senators use unmediated relationships with citizens, such as their official websites, to counter such stereotypes. To do so, females emphasize experience, decisiveness, and clear positions on public policy matters. Moana Vercoe, Randall Gonzalez, and Jean Reith Schroedel (Chapter 5) and Regina Lawrence and Melody Rose (Chapter 4) analyze the implications of the fact that gender stereotyping matters more in races for the presidency of the United States than any other office. The former set of authors explores the forty-year evolution of Clinton's rhetorical efforts to counter negative stereotypes of female politicians, and the latter set analyzes the gender strategies she used to counteract negative stereotypes of women commanders.

Moving beyond analysis of women as a group, in Chapter 7 Ronnee Schreiber illuminates how female candidates for Congress in 2010 negotiated stereotypes about women and how those responses interacted with party. She finds that Democratic women were more likely to have embraced gendered identities, especially motherhood, compared with Republican women. Schreiber concludes by noting the extent to which masculine norms permeate our political world and how salient they are for women who seek elective office. Another consideration in how women candidates present themselves on the campaign trail in relationship to stereotypes derives from the intersection of gender and sexual orientation. As Donald Haider-Markel and Chelsie Moore Bright discuss in Chapter 15, lesbians running for elective office report that opponents and outside groups sometimes use sexual orientation in a negative manner to undercut their candidacies. Depending on context, however, because lesbian candidates tend to run in districts that are more liberal they can parlay negative attacks into increased campaign funds and volunteer workers.

## Political Challenges: Political and Media Elites

Today, many party organizers and other political elites actively recruit females for elective office. Yet even in places that are most receptive to women candidates, political networks are heavily male dominated and, thus, less likely to turn to women first when encouraging and supporting candidates. The result: In places with the strongest, most powerful parties, women are less likely to run (Sanbonmatsu 2006). Moreover, the two parties are not equal in encouraging women's candidacies: the Democratic Party has been more supportive than the Republican Party, and this has translated into more female Democratic than female Republican candidacies (Elder 2012; Ondercin and Welch 2009; Sanbonmatsu 2002).

Compared with earlier decades, obtaining adequate funds to run quality campaigns is no longer a barrier to women's candidacies. As a group, women are as or more successful than men as campaign fundraisers at every stage of the process from early money through general elections (Adams and Schreiber 2011; Burrell 1998; Darcy, Welch, and Clark 1994; Duerst-Lahti 1998; Duke 1996; Seltzer, Newman, and Voorhees 1997). Yet this is not necessarily because traditional funders are eager to support women, although some certainly are. Rather, women candidates rely heavily on newer, alternative fundraising sources created to overcome historical obstacles. For example, EMILY's List (which stands for "early money is like yeast—it makes the dough rise"), created in 1985, was the first of these innovative political action committees (PACs). Its niche is Democratic pro-choice female candidates. In part, because EMILY's List has been the most successful, it has served as a model for others. WISH List (Women in the House and Senate) supports female Republican candidates; Maggie's List (named after Margaret Chase Smith of Maine, the first woman elected to both houses of Congress) supports fiscally conservative Republican women at the federal level; and LPAC is a bipartisan PAC that supports candidates who champion issues affecting lesbians and their families. These alternate sources of funds help level the playing field for women who run for elective office. But it is important to note that one reason women who are interested in and qualified to run for office perceive disparate fundraising barriers is because women still have a harder time than men raising money from traditional sources and raising large sums. Hence, they often still have to work longer and harder for their campaign war chests.[12]

Although differences are diminishing, media treatment of women is not yet without bias—as highlighted by the reasons given by the Lawless and Fox respondents for avoiding candidacies. The bulk of extant research suggests that female candidates, especially those running for high-level offices, receive less coverage by major news organizations than men, and when they are covered it is often in a negative fashion (Fridkin, Carle, and Woodall 2013; Fridkin and Woodall 2005). Further, minority congresswomen often receive less frequent and more negative media coverage than their counterparts (Gershon 2012). In Chapter 9, Valerie O'Regan and Stephen Stambough illustrate how disparate media treatment of women puts females at a distinct disadvantage compared with men when they pursue governorships.

Across levels and types of offices, media emphasis is also often placed on low probabilities of success rather than on issues or candidate appeals. Further, the press are more likely to cover the policy priorities of men and more likely to highlight the personality traits emphasized by men (Fridkin and Woodall 2005). Finally, the media have tended to concentrate more on women's family responsibilities than on men's similar responsibilities. A recent example is media silence on the family responsibilities of 2012 Republican vice presidential candidate Paul Ryan, who has three young children. This contrasts starkly with the extensive attention to the family responsibilities of the 2008 Republican vice presidential candidate Sarah Palin, who has five children.

Although some studies suggest that, at least in some places, in particular types of media, and at some times,[13] treatment of female candidates is becoming more equitable,[14] most of the literature concludes that different and extra efforts are required by women candidates in to win office (Fowler and Lawless 2009; Meeks 2012).

## Political Challenges: Electoral Rules and Structures

Although not routinely discussed among the challenges faced by female candidates, electoral rules and structures can have disparate effects on women when compared with men as well as among groups of women. For example, in general, female candidates have had more success in multimember districts (multiple representatives in one geographical unit) than single-member districts (Darcy, Welch, and Clark 1994; Hogan 2001; King 2002; Matland and Brown 1992; Nechemias 1985; Rule and Zimmerman 1994; Welch and Studlar 1990). However, African American women are more likely to do better in single-member electoral districts (Darcy, Hadley, and Kirksey 1993; Scola 2006). As Barbara Norrander and Clyde Wilcox discuss in Chapter 16, the trend in U.S. politics has long been toward single-member districts.

Additionally, the once-a-decade redistricting of congressional and state legislative districts may disproportionately affect women. First, As Lisa García Bedolla, Katherine Tate, and Janelle Wong discuss in Chapter 14, the increase in majority minority districts has provided new opportunities for women of color. This is, in part, responsible for why African American women and Latinas are greater proportions of their representative groups in political office than white women. On the other hand, new district maps put in place for the 2012 elections resulted in districts being redrawn to pit female legislators against other legislators, including other women. The result was a reduction in the number of incumbent women who won reelection. In some cases, such as in North Carolina, Colorado, and Georgia, evidence suggests that women legislators and women legislative leaders were disproportionately targeted (Libby 2012).[15] In the international context, in Chapter 17, Pippa Norris and Mona Lena Krook explore structural and rule-based barriers to representational equality, including electoral systems, party rules and procedures, constitutional rights, and legal quotas for candidates. The latter is a popular idea internationally but has not caught on in the United States.

# Women Officeholders

Even with the congressional and state legislative gains that resulted from victories in the 2012 election cycle, women have been and still are vastly underrepresented in elective office compared to their proportion of the U.S. population. In 2013, women hold ninety-eight seats in the U.S. Congress (18.3 percent), the largest number (by eight) ever serving at one time: Twenty are in the Senate and seventy-eight in the House of Representatives. And women of color hold twenty-nine seats and make up 29.6 percent of women and 4.5 percent of all members of Congress (CAWP 2013f).[16]

In 2013, 24.0 percent, of state legislators in the United States are women. They hold 20.3 percent of state Senate seats and 25.3 percent of state House seats. At 340 in number across the nation, women of color are 20.5 percent of women legislators or 4.9 percent of total state legislators (CAWP 2013c).[17]

Five women governors serve as of 2013: Jan Brewer of Arizona; Mary Fallin of Oklahoma; Maggie Hassan of New Hampshire; Susana Martinez of New Mexico; and Nikki Haley of South Carolina. Women hold twelve statewide elective executive offices across the nation, such as lieutenant governor, attorney general, secretary of state, and treasurer (CAWP 2013e, 2013g).

As of 2012, women were 17.4 percent of mayors in cities with populations over 30,000. Of the hundred largest cities in the United States, women of color hold two mayoral positions: Jean Quan in Oakland, California; and Stephanie Rawlings-Blake in Baltimore, Maryland (CAWP 2013d). Women also comprise approximately 28 percent of city councils and 40 percent of school boards (National League of Cities 2012).

At the judicial level, women are 22 percent of all federal judgeships and 26 percent of all state-level judgeships. This compares with the 48 percent of law school graduates and 45 percent of law firm associates who are female (Center for Women in Government & Civil Society 2010).

The comparative perspective shows that out of 190 nations worldwide, there are seven women presidents and ten women prime ministers; additionally, 20.3 percent of parliamentarians are female. The U.S. rates poorly compared with many other nations in that we have never had a woman president, and women's percentage of the federal Congress is below the world average (IPU 2012, 2013).

## Uniformity of Representation

In addition to being underrepresented in elective office generally, women are unequally represented across the nation. They tend to have the greatest presence in northeastern states (and the fewest in southern states), states with high educational levels and high proportions of women in the labor force, and states with part-time legislatures and less expensive races (Hogan 2001; Norrander and Wilcox 2005; Ondercin and Welch 2005; Sanbonmatsu 2002; see also Chapters 9 and 16 in this volume). In the U.S. House of Representatives, women-friendly districts are smaller, more urban, more racially and ethnically diverse, wealthier, and with more educated populations. A similar pattern appears on the state legislative level, and across them representation rates for women range from 41 to 11 percent (CAWP 2013c; Palmer and Simon 2012).

Exploring within group patterns reveals that women of color in state legislatures are more likely to be present in states with higher per capita incomes (Scola 2006). And women-of-color mayors are most often found in cites with small populations and those that are comparatively weak in political power, such as those with mayors elected from within city councils rather elected independently (Lien and Swain 2013).

Parties matter as well. For most of the twentieth century, there have been relatively equal numbers of women across the two parties in Congress and the state legislatures; more recently, Democratic women have outnumbered Republican women in Congress two to one. In 2013, of the twenty women in the Senate, sixteen are Democrats; in the House of Representatives, of the seventy-eight women, fifty-eight are Democrats. The same patterns exist among state legislators[18] and governors as explored, respectively, by Norrander and Wilcox in Chapter 16, and O'Regan and Stambough in Chapter 9. Women of color in Congress are also predominately Democrats as discussed by Bedolla, Tate, and Wong in Chapter 14. And in Chapter 15, Haider-Markel and Bright show that most lesbian candidates run as Democrats in districts where they believe their sexual orientation is more accepted. Overall, the issue is not that Democratic women win their races more than Republican women; it is that the Democratic party has been more welcoming to and more supportive of women candidates (Palmer and Simon 2012).

Leadership positions in legislatures also reflect unevenness in women's representation (Carroll 2008; Darcy 1996; Deen and Little 1999; Rosenthal 1998). Although women have held committee chair positions in proportion to their representation in state legislatures, they are rarer at chamber level. States with female legislative leaders tend to have the highest proportion of women members and the largest and least professionalized legislatures (Arnold and King 2002; Carroll 2004, 2008; Jewell and Whicker 1994; Reingold 2000; Rosenthal 2000; Thomas 1994; Whistler and Ellickson 1999). As is the case with women's legislative presence generally, women leaders have been more prominent in the Democratic Party. Illustratively, in 2008, when California Assembly member Karen Bass was elected Speaker of the Assembly, she became both the first Democratic woman Speaker in state history and, as noted earlier, the first African American woman in the country to serve in that powerful role (CAWP 2013g).

## The Backgrounds of Women Officeholders

Beyond the numbers, what are the backgrounds of women office holders? What are the contours of their public and private lives? What do they seek to achieve in office, and what is their impact? And what challenges do they face based on their status as women and as a minority of office holders? Answers to these questions come mostly from the federal and state legislative levels, but an increasing amount of information is becoming available about local office holders, governors, and judicial women.

To start, women legislators tend to come to their positions from somewhat lesser levels of education than men, from different, usually less high-status and high-paying professions, and from lower-status political experiences. For example, men make up a greater portion of legislators who are college graduates and who complete graduate and professional school (Diamond 1977; Dodson 1997; Gertzog 2002; Kirkpatrick 1974; Thomas 1994, 2002; van Assendelft and O'Connor 1994). They are also less likely to come from professional or business/management positions and are more likely to join legislatures from teaching and social work. With respect to prior political experience, men are more likely to have served on city councils or as mayors, whereas women have served on school boards more than men. At the mayoral level, however, women tend to be as educated as men but are less likely to possess law degrees (Carroll and Sanbonmatsu 2013). While asymmetries between the sexes have diminished over time, the differences have not been eradicated entirely.

These patterns are somewhat different for subgroups of women compared with women as a group. As explored by Bedolla, Tate, and Wong in Chapter 14, Latina representatives in Congress are more educated than their male counterparts. And in state legislatures, women of color tend to be more highly educated than men of color. Only Asian American men are more likely than Asian American women to be highly educated. Comparisons among women of color show that Asian American women have the highest educational rates, followed by African American women, Native Hawaiian and other Pacific Islanders, American Indian and Alaskan Native women, and Latinas (Hardy-Fanta et al. 2006; Lien et al. 2008; Prestage 1991). Former California state senator Gloria Romero is an example of the importance of education in the success stories of women of color. Romero has earned A.A., B.A., M.A. and Ph.D. degrees. She comments: "My mother had a sixth grade education; I have a Ph.D. I understand the transformational power of education and the key it holds to accessing the American Dream."[19]

The private sphere lives of women office holders also reflect gender-based dissimilarities. On the federal, state, and mayoral levels, women have been and still are likely to be older than legislative men, less likely to be married, and more likely to be childless. Of those with children, women tend to have fewer offspring. Further, delayed entry due to childrearing is notably more common for women (Carroll 1989, 1993; Carroll and Sanbonmatsu 2013; Diamond 1977; Dodson 1997; Githens 1977; Kirkpatrick 1974; Mezey 1978; Palmer and Simon 2012; Thomas 1994, 2002; Werner 1968). Many of the patterns found among women as a whole are equally, if not more prevalent, among women of color. For example, Takash (1977) reports that tension between family responsibilities and political service is especially serious for Latinas. And in the U.S. Congress, fewer black women members of

Congress are married than their black male counterparts or white women and men (Bedolla, Tate, and Wong 2005; see also Chapter 14 in this volume).

If women's distinctive life experiences affect their educational and occupational opportunities and choices, does it follow that women office holders have different levels of political ambition for higher office compared with men? Early studies of state legislators indicated that women were substantially less interested than men in higher office (Costantini 1990; Githens 1977; Johnson and Carroll 1978; Sapiro and Farah 1980; Stoper 1977). However, more recent research on legislative women in general and among African American women suggests that ambition level differentials have all but disappeared (Bedolla, Tate, and Wong 2005; Bledsoe and Herring 1990; Carey, Niemi, and Powell 1998; Carroll 1994, 1993; Palmer and Simon 2003; see also Chapter 14 in this volume). Indeed, as Epstein, Niemi, and Powell (2005) note, women office holders are more likely than men to display "careerism." And among state trial court judges, females and non-whites are more progressively ambitious than their white male counterparts (Jensen and Martinek 2009). The same may not be true, however, for all types of elective office and all levels. In Chapter 12, van Assendelft finds that local elective women representatives have low levels of ambition for higher office. Additionally, Lien and Swain (2013) report that most women-of-color mayors have little interest in higher office but rather are interested in focusing on their communities. These authors suggest that research concentrating on political ambition for women as a group obscures the multidimensionality of that attribute.

## Women Officeholders: Their Views and Impact

Scholarly investigation into whether or not female office holders have made a distinctive impact on public policy and political representation has concluded that, over time and on a variety of indicators from agenda creation and definition through policy modification to policy outcomes, the answer is yes. Whether by bringing previously private sphere issues to public agendas (e.g., domestic violence), transforming issues long hidden from public view from whispered conversations to public crimes (e.g., sexual harassment), or expanding the education of men and influencing their policy choices on topics with which they are less familiar (e.g., funding for gender parity in insurance policies),[20] women have created space for public consideration of issues that were not historically accorded much legislative attention.[21] Although institutional structures, rules and norms, party, leadership opportunities and positions, and temporal context all affect the degree to which women can make a difference, their contributions can be felt throughout the political process and in an array of representational activities.[22]

First, women office holders have distinctive political perspectives. Female legislators tend to be more liberal than men and more supportive of women's issues defined either traditionally or from a feminist perspective, such as funding for women's health issues, paid sick leave, child care, medical insurance coverage for pregnancy and mammograms, and prevention of violence against women (Barrett 1995; Dodson 2001; Dodson and Carroll 1991; Epstein, Niemi, and Powell 2005; Hogan 2008; Leader 1977; Lilie et al. 1982; Poggione 2004; Thomas 1990, 1994).

Still, differences across groups of women are evident. African American women state legislators are more liberal than white women or men and feel more strongly than white women about policies that target the specific needs of women (Barrett 1995, 1997, 2001). Illustratively, says Representative Terri Sewell of Alabama, "We bring something unique to the table as women of color, as women generally." Research findings on Latinas support for women's issues are mixed, however. On the local level, Takash (1977) finds that Latinas express clear agreement with feminist goals, but Fraga et al. (2006, 2008) find that Latino/a state legislators show no gender differences in policy priorities.

Party and ideology also matter. As an outgrowth of the more conservative trend of American politics beginning in the mid-1990s, Carroll (2003) found that, while women in state legislatures in 2001 were more liberal than men, Republican women were more conservative and more like their male counterparts than they were in the 1980s. And, in Chapter 11, Tracy Osborn and Rebecca Kreitzer report that, in the late 1990s and early 2000s, although gender differences among state legislators were evident, partisan women held positions on women's issues that were more similar to men in their party than women of the opposite party.

To make a policy difference, issue attitudes and ideological stances must affect lawmaking: women legislators must be active, distinctive in their activity, and successful in pursuing goals. Research suggests that all three requirements are being met. First, legislative women are as participatory as men in legislative activities including bill introduction and passage, committee work, legislative bargaining, and floor presentations (Blair and Stanley 1991a, 1991b; Friedman 1996; Norton 1995; Pearson and Dancey 2011; Shogan 2001; Swers 2002; Tamerius 1995; Thomas 1994; Wolbrecht 2002). And in Chapter 14, Bedolla, Tate, and Wong provide examples of participation by congressional women of color at various stages of the legislative process and discuss how they make a difference to both process and policy outcomes. Second, in the aggregate, women vote for, sponsor, and enact more women's issues legislation than men[23] (Carver 1979; Dodson and Carroll 1991; Frederick 2009, 2010, 2011; Saint-Germain, 1989; Thomas 1990, 1994, 2002). And third, even controlling for the effects of party and ideology, as a group women are as or more successful than men in passing their legislative priorities (Barnello and Bratton 2007; Bratton et al. 2007; Bratton and Haynie 1999; Dodson 1998, 2001; Dodson and Carroll 1991; Dolan and Ford 1997, 1998; Swers 2002; Tamerius 1995; Thomas 1994; Vega and Firestone 1995).[24] The Affordable Care Act (Obamacare) is a good example of how women make a difference. Senator Barbara Mikulski of Maryland introduced an amendment to the act as it was moving through the legislative process that required a comprehensive package of wellness services for women, including counseling for domestic violence and prenatal care (Baker 2012).

### The Conditions of Impact

Unpacking the conditions under which women are most and least likely to make a difference begins with considering groups of women rather than women as a group. African American women are more likely to introduce women-friendly[25] legislation than men (Adams 2007; Bratton, Haynie, and Reingold 2006; Orey et al. 2006). Reingold and Smith (2012) also find that legislative women of color have the strongest countervailing effect on state welfare reform, more so than either other women or men of color. And in Chapter 15, Haider-Markel and Bright report that women's influence on governmental agendas can also matter in terms of preventing measures from achieving an agenda position—as is the case with lesbian office holders who delay or block anti-gay and -lesbian measures from enactment.

Party matters in conditioning women's policy impact in much the same way it does in mediating the relationship between gender and ideology or support for women's issues. There is ample evidence that women cross party lines to support women's issues. A recent example is that, in 2013, all four Republican women in the U.S. Senate voted for the federal Violence against Women Act. Still, this is far from a universal occurrence, and the effects of party can be particularly strong when they interact with political eras, especially eras of polarized politics. In Chapter 10, Michele Swers reports that, during the 2012 election, the war on women gave female congressional Democrats power to develop and execute party strategy to attract coveted women voters by highlighting the party's favorable stances on many women's issues. Conversely, as the party of individual rather than collective opportunity, Republican women did not have the type or level of impact with their party.[26] Similarly, in Chapter 11, Osborn and Kreitzer illuminate the big differences in each party's legislative approach to women's issues and how the positions of majority parties dominate legislative agendas.

Finally, electoral structure matters in the extent to which women can be successful in pursuing women's policy issues in legislatures. By comparing the upper and lower chambers in Arizona (each of which uses different electoral district rules), Clark and Caro (2013) find that both Democratic and Republican women are more active on women's issues in multimember districts than in single-member districts.

Evidence of women's policy difference at the judicial level is substantially more mixed, however, than it is in legislative office. About one-third of studies show that gender makes a difference, one-third feature mixed results, and another third show no pattern. These disparate findings reflect not only the particular constraints on the judicial role compared with executive or legislative roles but also differences across areas of law and levels of the judicial system. For example, gender effects have been found to be strong in sex discrimination in employment cases that come to federal appellate benches (Boyd, Epstein, and Martin 2010). And Moyer (2013) finds that diversity on federal appellate courts is associated with gender differences in civil rights holdings—as is the presence of female chief judges. Summing up such findings, Patricia Wald, former U.S. appellate judge and justice on the International Criminal Tribunal for the Former Yugoslavia, said: "Being treated by society as a woman can be a vital element of a judge's experience.... A judge is the sum of her experiences and if she has suffered disadvantages of discrimination as a woman, she is apt to be sensitive to its subtle expression or to paternalism" (Kalantry 2012:86).

## The Effects of Increasing Representation

Demonstrations of women's influence on political priorities and outcomes invariably lead to questions about whether increasing the proportions of women office holders can accelerate their effects on policy. Studies of critical mass ask whether, all else equal, does the proportion of women in legislative or judicial bodies have a demonstrable effect on policymaking and policy outcomes, particularly with respect to women-friendly policies?

One reason this possibility has earned scholarly attention is that political women subscribe to theories of critical mass. As such, they spend considerable time and effort recruiting and training women candidates, fundraising to increase their chances of success, and mentoring women who win office (Dolan and Ford 1995, 1998; Gierzynski and Burdreck 1995; Thomas 1994, 1997).[27] Research also suggests that African American and white women state legislators both strongly believe that women's policy needs are best served when women legislators are present (Barrett 2001). Illustratively, says former Deputy Speaker of the Indiana House of Representatives Susan Crosby (D): "I'm convinced that having more women legislators will result in more favorable legislation for women" (Mayes 2003).

The evidence to date on the effects of critical mass is somewhat mixed, however. Some studies show that the presence of higher percentages of women in legislatures is associated with higher rates of bill introduction or passage of women-friendly policy (Berkman and O'Connor 1993; Crowley 2004; Hansen 1993; Poggione 2004; Thomas 1994; Thomas, Rickert, and Cannon 2006). For example, a recent study of the U.S. Congress found that "women provided a higher volume of representation on women's interests; however, they do so when they are surrounded with a relatively high proportion of other women in Congress" (MacDonald and O'Brien 2011:482). Research into judicial decision-making also affirms critical mass effects (Collins, Manning, and Carp 2010). However, other studies of legislatures find little or no difference (Bratton 2002, 2005; Caiazza 2004; Reingold 2000; Tolbert and Steuernagel 2001; Weldon 2006).

Part of the discrepancy across research findings is attributable to differences in the number of states, time periods, and issue areas under study. It is also likely that women's impact is mediated by institutional circumstances such as level of majority party control, extent to which committees operate independently, and the degree of professionalism of the legislature (see especially Poggione 2004).[28] Ultimately, the lesson that might be learned from this line of research is that there is much work to be done to deepen our understanding of process and policy-related effects of gender ratios in governmental bodies (Minta 2012).

## Institutional Gendering Challenges

Because nearly forty years of research demonstrates that women individually and collectively make distinctive contributions to politics, questions have naturally turned to their future potential. That women have entered and succeeded in federal, state, and local legislatures, governorships and other executive offices, and in the judiciary indicates that politics in the United States is, to a substantial extent, receptive to their presence and priorities. At the same time, a host of evidence catalogs persistent institutional resistance to women's progress toward parity—up to and including the reality that no U.S. president or vice president has been female.

The first type of evidence of institutional resistance to gender parity is the very slow and nonlinear entry of women into elective offices: progress over the modern era has been neither constant nor irreversible. On the federal level, "... the integration of women into Congress is best described as slow, irregular, and unremarkable" (Palmer and Simon 2012:21). For the first time since the early 1970s, state legislative election cycles produced fewer women as a group in both the 2000 and 2002 election cycles than previously, and from 1994 to 1998 the number of women of color in state legislatures stagnated.[29] The highest level of women in statewide elective executive offices was from 1999 to 2001 (CAWP 2013e). On the local level, the proportion of female mayors was 20.8 percent in 2002 and diminished to 17.4 percent in 2012; of the one hundred largest U.S. cities, fifteen had female mayors in 2002 compared with twelve in 2012 (CAWP 2013d). Rounding out this picture, O'Regan and Stambough show a similarly nonlinear historical pattern for female governors in Chapter 9, and in Chapter 13 Kenney reviews the interrupted progress of female judges. Not only have advances within categories of office holders been elusive, but also progressing from one level of office to another has been more difficult for women. For example, female state legislators are less likely than men to rise to the U.S. Congress (Mariani 2008).

Another type of evidence of institutional resistance is women office holders' concerns about their job quality (Carey et al. 1998; Epstein et al. 2005; Thomas 2002). Elective women feel that they have to produce more, display more patience, pay greater attention to detail, and deliver higher levels of preparation for daily tasks to be perceived as effective and credible and to achieve the same level of success as men.[30] Time has not erased these patterns. In the U.S. House of Representatives, for example, women introduce more bills, participate more vigorously in key legislative debates, and give more of the one-minute speeches that open daily sessions (Stolberg 2011). And among groups of women, the need to produce more may be more intense. Says Redwood City, California, mayor Alicia Aguirre, a Latina, "What I needed to do was work harder than the rest and prove that I had those skills because people don't traditionally see us in those higher up positions" (Carrero 2013).

An additional aspect of differential treatment is straightforward discrimination. Although clearly not as overt as in the past, women across types and levels of office report ongoing concerns. One study of state legislators asked participants about benefits and hurdles experienced in their careers. One-quarter of state legislative women responded by introducing discussions of discrimination, such as confronting an "old boys' club." No men responded similarly (Thomas 2002). Further, the literature on within-group differences indicates that gender-based discrimination is intensified for women of color (Cohen 2002; Sierra and Sosa-Riddell 1994; Simien 2005; Smooth 2006). As Bedolla, Tate, and Wong articulate in Chapter 14, isolation and outright discriminatory treatment makes atmospheric discrimination doubly palpable (see also Cohen 2002). An example comes from the first sisters to serve together in Congress, Latinas Linda and Loretta Sanchez of California, who report that they were dismissed as a "cute novelty act"—despite the fact that numerous brothers have been elected to Congress (Sanchez, Sanchez, and Buskin 2008:197). Another firsthand illustration of discriminatory treatment comes from a female county supervisor in California who spoke to my Women and Politics class in 2008. When asked about gender discrimination, she dismissed it as a thing of the past. Then, one week later, a natural disaster hit her community. When the governor of the state came to the disaster site, he proceeded to address the press and other assembled dignitaries. Opening his remarks, he introduced every male office holder and other notables in attendance but completely ignored this female county supervisor whose constituency was affected. Later, she contacted me to retract her remarks about discrimination and asked that I relay this change of perspective to my students.

A final type of evidence of institutional resistance to women's increased participation and leadership comes from gender difference in legislative styles. Women office holders have long reported feeling out of sync with routine operations. In particular, women operationalize power less as "power over," as men tend to, and more as "power to" (Cantor and Bernay 1992). To fit more closely with their preferences, women envision structures that support long-range planning, consensus building, enhanced communication, cooperation rather than confrontation, improved organization, and putting constituency interests above self-interest (Epstein, Niemi, and Powell 2005; Thomas 1994). These preferences are shared across type and level of office. In Chapter 12, van Assendelft reports similar findings among local women elected representatives. A recent example of women's cooperative stand comes from the relationship of the two female members of Congress from Alabama: Democrat Terri Sewell and Republican Martha Roby. Despite different parties, ideologies, and voting records, they have joined together in a bipartisan caucus to build relationships, to cosponsor bills together, and to socialize outside of work. They view this relationship building as the best way to represent their state and move past the deep polarization of the current congressional environment (Berry 2012). Summing up, U.S. senator Kirsten Gillibrand of New York notes: "We tend to be more results-oriented and less concerned with getting the credit. The female approach is more conciliatory and less combative. We tend to use a more civil tone" (*Economist* 2011).

Cooperative styles are also in evident among women legislative leaders. Overall, they have been found to be more likely to share power rather than using it to dominate their domains, use a consensual rather than a command-and-control style of leadership, and place more emphasis on getting the job done in a team-oriented way (Kathlene 2005; Rosenthal 1998, 2005; Whicker and Jewell 1998). Says former Oregon Senate Leader Kate Brown: "I just don't think there is any question that the women legislative leaders have been much more inclined to stay away from the kind of partisan wrangling that men get involved in.... But because they seem to me to be less interested in confrontation, they have more energy left for direction, for coming up with solutions" (Boulard 1999).

This preference for greater cooperation is replicated among subgroups of women leaders. Female tribal leaders on Indian reservations have been found to be inclusive managers who are more likely than men to compromise (Prindeville and Gomez 1999). Having said that, however, the intersections of gender and race make women leaders' levels of influence and effectiveness complex and contingent (Hawkesworth 2003). Smooth (2006) reports that when African American women serve as chair committees in state Houses they are more likely to be excluded from informal power networks of leaders. When that happens, they possess less influence than any formal title might suggest and less than similarly situated men. As one Southern legislator noted: "The way the process works, if you are one of the big boys—on the Go Team is what we call it—you are going to have influence on just about anything. Basically, four legislators run this place because they have a lot of say" (Smooth 2006:9).

Together, these elements of institutional impermeability can be understood as examples of the effects of gendered institutions. Gender adheres not just to individuals but also to the organizations and institutions to which they belong. As a result, the structures, behaviors, and perspectives that conform to gendered expectations of the institution are rewarded. Those that do not are likely to be devalued and discouraged (Duerst-Lahti and Kelly 1995, 2002; Kathlene 1994, 1998; Kenney 1996). As Duerst-Lahti (2002:380) explains:

> ... [Analysis of gendered institutions] can turn the gaze toward the institution itself if formal and informal structures, practices, norms, rules

tenaciously block congresswomen's desired policy outcomes. Because sometimes women and men do have different policy preferences, cite different life experiences based upon gender, or different assumptions about appropriate behaviors, rules, and practices, institutions predicated upon masculinity are not as responsive to women as to men.

Consistent with this analysis, Mendelberg and Karpowitz (2012) report that unbalanced decision-making groups (80/20, like the current U.S. Senate) result in women speaking less than men and being perceived by themselves and by peers and more quiescent and less effective. Women are also more likely to be interrupted and less likely to perform as strong advocates. But when women are 60 to 80 percent or more of a group, they speak as much as men, advocate for their issue positions more, and are less often interrupted. In a related study of school board members, conducted by the same authors, gender gaps equal to those found in the first study were reduced significantly when women's presence reached parity.

## Societal Gendering

Deeply interwoven with institutional gendering is a wider phenomenon that may be called societal gendering. That is, attitudes about women and men's proper roles, dominant characteristics, or expected divisions of labor affect women's public sphere participation and effectiveness. This affects women candidates and office holders no less than others. Indeed, masculinized understandings of political leadership flow from societal gendering.

One way societal gendering affects political women is that, despite their considerable professional responsibilities, they are expected to also be primarily responsible for private life. For example, state legislative women are much more likely than men to be in charge of everyday household tasks such as cleaning, cooking, shopping, dishes, and laundry. Most centrally, those with children are much more likely to serve as primary caretakers of the family (Thomas 2002). It may not be surprising, therefore, that among married legislators a supportive spouse is a much more prominent feature of women's career path than men's (Carroll 1989; Mezey 1978; Sapiro 1982; Stoper 1977; Thomas 2002).

Thus, socialized roles, including gendered divisions of labor, affect the politics of women's presence, their level of accomplish in office, and their ability to lead. Because of them, women ambitious for elective office delay entry into politics, decline to enter at all, or enter on a limited basis and stay for shorter periods of time than men. The result: women's chances of reversing their minority status, obtaining sufficient collective experience, and maximizing their impact are reduced. Illustratively, at a press conference in 2013 at which Nancy Pelosi announced her decision to stay on as Minority Leader for the 113th Congress, one journalist suggested she step down to make room for younger members. In addition to pointing out that the journalist was not offering men in leadership the same advice, she added: "I knew that my male colleagues...had a jump on me because they didn't have children to stay home [with].... You got to take off about 14 years from me because I was home raising a family" (Dittmar 2013).

Overall, the result of societal and institutional gendering is a political playing field that is not yet level. Although women office holders can and do win office and achieve policy success and institutional effectiveness, the need to prove their qualifications and competence, negotiate political and societal expectations and stereotypes, and fit public sphere activity around private sphere responsibilities constitutes a higher cost to serve. Further, when costs are assessed among groups of women, especially women of color, the effects are likely to be even more complex and disproportionate (Cohen 2002; Lien et al. 2008; Sierra and Sosa-Riddell 1994; Simien 2005; Smooth 2006).

## Shaping the Future

The remaining question is whether institutional and societal gendering can be overcome, particularly when it comes to the ultimate glass ceiling: the presidency and vice presidency of the United States. Say scholars Heldman, Carroll, and Olson (2005:316), "[There is] perhaps no political position where gender stereotypes work more to women's disadvantage than the highly masculinized office of the U.S. presidency."

Conventional answers to how institutional obstacles can be reduced tend to focus on representational parity—with the hope that, with equal or nearly equal proportions women and men in office, these obstacles will decline substantially. Conventional answers to unbalanced societal divisions of labor tend to focus on remedies, such as governmentally mandated child care, that provide women with an enhanced ability to achieve professional and private balance. It is possible, however, that, although increasing the number and diversity of women in office and reaping the benefits of improved policy are necessary conditions to transforming institutions, they may not be sufficient. One reason this may be so is that, despite more than fifty years of the second wave of the feminist movement, women's representation at all levels of elective office has not increased commensurate with increases in educational attainment or occupational success. Women have made up almost half of law school classes for some time, for instance, but men are still three-quarters of elective office holders.

Another reason that transformation may be necessary to eliminate or substantively reduce gendered obstacles to equal participation is that young women's political ambitions and opportunities remain truncated. A Princeton University report details a decline in the number of female students in campus leadership positions since 2000. Indeed, only one woman has been elected to the presidency of the student government since 1994. Further, the backsliding is not a Princeton-specific occurrence (Marcus 2011). Confirming this pattern, a recent survey of college students between the ages of eighteen and twenty-five shows that young women are less likely than young men to have considered running for office, express interest in a future candidacy, or perceive elective office as desirable (Lawless and Fox 2013). This youth gender gap is comparable to the gap among potential adult candidates discussed in Chapter 2.

A last reason that routine operations may have to be reconceptualized and that business as usual may need to be transformed for women's political parity to be achieved is that remedies concentrating on isolated elements of women's disparate responsibilities and challenges, such as increased provision of child care, do not change the fundamental foundation of inequality. For example, more child care does not necessarily equalize men's presence in the private sphere, a necessary condition for accelerating women's increased presence in the public one.

## Conclusion

This chapter's review of the research on women candidates and office holders explored their historical and current presence as well as their contributions and future challenges. On one hand, women's presence in the U.S. Congress is higher than it has ever been in our history. On the other, the same is not true for state legislatures, gubernatorial positions, and statewide elected executives, judges, and mayors. And enduring evidence suggests that, although women who chose to run are, as a group, as successful as men in winning office, they face particular challenges and pay a higher cost for their success.

The good news is that, even in the face of the challenges examined in this chapter, many women have found ways to succeed around them to both participate and make distinctive and meaningful contributions to the work of representation. The key question for the longer term is whether women of the twenty-first century can make more rapid and more linear progress than has been true in the past. Will the 2012 electoral cycle example of the all-female congressional delegation from New Hampshire and the new levels of inclusion among groups of women in local, state, and national offices spur accelerated levels of participation and success? Or will slow, small augmentations with occasional reversals continue? Whatever the answer, to forge ahead is the only sensible course. For women candidates and office holders, much remains to be done. As Aristotle asserted in the fourth century, liberty and equality depend on it.

## Notes

1. In 1893, Colorado became the first state to approve women's suffrage in a popular election. It was not until 1920 with the ratification of the 19th Amendment to the U.S. Constitution that women across the nation gained the right to vote in all elections.

2. Her victory brought the number of female governors to five. The record serving simultaneously is nine and was achieved first in 2004 and again in 2007 (CAWP 2013e).

3. That women win races at equal rates to men has not always been the case. Historically, they have faced overt discriminatory barriers from three groups. It was not uncommon for party elites to fail to recruit women, to decline to support candidacies of those who ran, and to direct women interested in running toward sacrificial lamb seats. Taking their cues from party organizers, campaign contributors were also reluctant to back women candidates. Voters too exhibited hostility toward female candidates at every level of office (Gertzog 1995; Mandel 1981; Tolchin and Tolchin 1973; Van Hightower 1977).

4. Female mayors are also much more likely than men to say that having sufficient prior political experience is central to decisions to run (Carroll and Sanbonmatsu 2013).

5. Women mayors indicate that, by more than two to one, they were recruited to run rather than being self-starters and were encouraged by personal sources more than professional ones (Carroll and Sanbonmatsu 2013).

6. Female mayors are more likely than men to indicate that having children who are old enough is a primary consideration in running for office (Carroll and Sanbonmatsu 2013).

7. Several organizations both recruit and train women candidates, including EMILY's List Political Opportunity Program for pro-choice Democratic women; the 2012 Project of the Center for American Women in Politics; and party organizations, such as Women Lead of the Democratic Congressional Campaign Committee; HOPE (Hispanas Organized for Political Equality); and myriad state and local organizations such as Ready to Run Pittsburgh, Real Women Run (Utah), and California Women Lead. To address disparate perceptions of young females, Running Start encourages and trains high school and college women to consider and plan candidacies for elective office.

8. Yet some voters still question whether women are truly qualified (Dolan 2010). One manifestation of comfort levels with women candidates is discussed by Stout and Kline (2011), who find that preelection polls for Senate and gubernatorial races from 1989 to 2008 consistently underestimate support for female candidates. Further, the phenomenon is more common in states that are culturally conservative.

9. Bos (2011) also finds that gender stereotypes affect delegates' to political conventions likelihood of supporting female candidates.

10. Research suggests that it is necessary for female candidates to emphasize their qualifications for office, especially having economic expertise, cultivating and maintaining a confident presentational style without being seen as abrasive, demonstrating proactive approaches to issues, and obtaining third-party validations (Barbara Lee Family Foundation 2012).

11. Palmer and Simon (2012) find that female congressional incumbents are reelected at slightly higher rates than men and have higher voting margins. But they are challenged more often in primary races. Women incumbents also draw more female challengers than male incumbents.

12. Carroll and Sanbonmatsu (2013) report that women mayors echo these sentiments.

13. One study suggests that this disparate treatment may be lessening among some types of media. Hayes and Lawless (forthcoming) find no gender bias in local media treatment of women and men candidates for the House of Representatives in the 2010 midterm elections.

14. Including among women who run in mayoral races (Atkeson and Krebs 2008).

15. Term limits have exacerbated this trend. Carroll and Jenkins (2001) find that the interaction of term limits on seats held by women and the drop-off in the number of women running for office results in fewer women in the lower chambers of statehouses. However, the impact of term limits on female African American state legislators is complex. In one of two years investigated, their numbers went down; in the second year, they increased by one (Carroll and Jenkins 2005).

16. Women are also represented in congressional leadership at low levels—particularly in the Republican Party. These positions include chamber leaders, such as Speakers of the House and presidents of the Senate, committee chairs, vice chairs, and ranking members, party or caucus leaders, and fundraising committee leaders. In the 113th Congress, women hold four chamber leadership positions in the Senate, all for the Democratic minority: Patty Murray (WA) is the Democratic Conference secretary; Debbie Stabenow (MI) is vice chair of the Democratic Policy committee; Jeanne Shaheen (NH) is the Steering and Outreach Committee vice chair; and Barbara Boxer (CA) is Democratic Chief Deputy Whip. In the House of Representatives, in addition to Minority Leader Nancy Pelosi (CA), female Democratic leaders include Chief Deputy Minority Whips Maxine Waters (CA), Jan Schakowsky (IL), Diana DeGette (CO), and Debbie Wasserman Schultz (FL) and Steering and Policy Committee co-chair Rosa DeLauro (CT). For the Republican majority, Cathy McMorris Rodgers (WA) is chair of the Republican Conference; Lynn Jenkins of (KS) is the conference vice chair; and Virginia Foxx (NC) is the conference secretary (CAWP 2013b).

17. Ten females are presidents of state Senates, and six are Speakers of state Houses, a record by two (CAWP 2013c).

18. In state legislatures, Democratic women hold 63.5 percent of the seats; Republicans hold 35.6 percent. Democrats are 94 percent of women of color state legislators compared with the 6 percent held by Republicans. Among statewide elected executives, women hold seventy-six positions, with Republicans and Democrats equally divided. However, among the twelve women-of-color statewide elected executives, eight are Democrats and four are Republicans.

19. From California State Senator Gloria Romero's website: http://dist24.casen.govoffice.com/index.asp?Type=B_BASIC&SEC=%7B762B701F-34D8-4FCB-88A3-14E3653382B7%7D (February 12, 2009).

20. Examining the evolution of discourse in congressional debates over abortion, Levy, Tien, and Aved (2002) find that the way female legislators talk about abortion has influenced the substance and style of their male colleagues' floor speeches.

21. One recent example of how bring more women to the U.S. Senate has made a difference concerns Senator Kirsten Gillibrand (D-NY), the newly appointed chair of the Senate Committee on Armed Services Subcommittee on Personnel, who, amid widespread reports of rape of service women by servicemen, held the first hearing on sexual violence in the military in a decade.

22. Women office holders also focus differential attention to constituency work and are particularly concerned with the women of their constituencies and beyond (Carroll 2002, 2003; Diamond 1977; Dodson 2006; Epstein et al. 2005; Reingold 2000; Richardson and Freeman 1995; Rosenthal 1998; Thomas 1992, 1994). Additionally, Takash (1977) and Prindeville and Gomez (1999) find, respectively, that Latinas and Indian women pay particular attention to women constituents.

23. When women legislators represent the same party and the same districts as men who preceded them, they sponsor more women's issues bills (Gerrity, Osborn, and Mendez 2007). And Griffin and Wolbrecht (2012) find a sizeable dyadic representation (congruence of legislators' views and their districts) gender gap favoring men in districts represented by Republicans and similar gap favoring women in districts represented by Democrats.

24. Anzia and Berry (2011) show that congresswomen secure roughly 9 percent more spending from federal discretionary programs than congressmen.

25. Women-friendly policies are operationalized differently among scholars. Each definition shares the underlying agreement that women's issues or women-friendly policies are those meant to address inequalities of power between the sexes and to increase women's autonomy.

26. Volden, Wiseman, and Wittmer (2013) find that minority party women in the U.S. House of Representatives are better able to keep their sponsored bills alive through later stages of the process than are minority party men. The opposite is true for majority party women, but they make up for this by introducing more legislation. Moreover, while the legislative style of minority party women has served them well consistently across the past four decades, majority party women have become less effective as Congress has become more polarized.

27. A good recent example is Gillibrand's extensive fundraising for women candidates for Congress in the 2012 electoral cycle. Another example is Maine's retiring Republican Senator Olympia Snowe, who has transferred campaign committee funds in an effort to encourage young women to participate in public service (Stone 2012). The Sanchez sisters of Congress also report that they emphasize mentoring to increase the proportion of women and women of color in politics (Sanchez et al. 2008).

28. The validity of the concept itself is contested. Skeptics point out that no magic number at which women's behavior is likely to change dramatically is likely to exist; critical actors championing legislative action are likely to be more important; the influence of the women's movement may affect legislative outcomes to a greater degree; the concept suggests that women are monolithic; the influence of feminist legislators of either sex is likely to be more important than larger numbers of ideologically diverse women; and increased numbers of women in legislatures may even result in backlash to women's presence.

29. The high-water mark for women's state legislative representation was 2010, with 24.5 percent.

30. These perceptions hold true regardless of party identification, ideology, or region from which women are elected (Dodson and Carroll 1991; Main, Gryski, and Schapiro 1984; Thomas 1994, 1997).

# 2

# Women's Underrepresentation in U.S. Politics: The Enduring Gender Gap in Political Ambition

JENNIFER L. LAWLESS, RICHARD L. FOX, AND GAIL BAITINGER

As of the 1970s, women occupied almost no major elective positions in U.S. political institutions. Ella Grasso, a Democrat from Connecticut, and Dixie Lee Ray, a Democrat from Washington, served as the only two women elected governor throughout the decade. Not until 1978 did Kansas Republican Nancy Kassebaum become the first woman elected to the U.S. Senate in her own right. By 1979, women comprised fewer than 5 percent of the seats in the U.S. House of Representatives and only about 10 percent of state legislative positions across the country.

Today, if we glance at the television screen, peruse the newspaper, listen to the radio, or scan the Internet, we might be tempted to conclude that women have made remarkable gains. Nancy Pelosi currently serves as the Minority Leader in the U.S. House of Representatives. Former secretary of state (and former U.S. senator) Hillary Clinton not only received 18 million votes when she sought the Democratic nomination for president but also achieved the highest favorability ratings of any member of the Obama Administration. In 2011, polls repeatedly placed former vice presidential candidate Sarah Palin in the top tier of potential candidates for the Republican presidential nomination. And Michele Bachmann garnered serious and sustained attention as a candidate for the GOP nomination for president in 2012.

But these famous faces obscure the dearth of women who hold elective office in the United States. When the 113th Congress convened in January 2013, 82 percent of its members were men. The percentages of female office holders presented in Table 2.1 demonstrate that it is not only at the federal level that women are numerically underrepresented. Large gender disparities are also evident at the state and local levels, where more than three-quarters of statewide elected officials and state

27

*Table 2.1* **Women Officeholders in the United States (2013)**

| Office | Percent Women |
|---|---|
| U.S. Senators | 20.0 |
| Members of the U.S. House of Representatives | 17.8 |
| State Governors | 10.0 |
| Statewide Elected Officials | 22.4 |
| State Legislators | 23.7 |
| Mayors of the 100 Largest Cities | 12.0 |

Sources: Women & Politics Institute, American University; Center for American Women and Politics, Rutgers University.

legislators are men. Further, as of January 2013, men occupy the governor's mansion in 45 of the 50 states, and they run City Hall in 88 of the 100 largest cities across the country.

The low numbers of women in politics are particularly glaring when we place them in context. Whereas the 1980s saw gradual but steady increases in the percentage of women seeking elected office and the early 1990s experienced a sharper surge, the last several election cycles can be characterized as a plateau. Indeed, the 2010 congressional elections resulted in the first net decrease in the percentage of women serving in the U.S. House of Representatives since the 1978 midterm elections. The number of women elected to state legislatures, which act as key launching pads to higher office, also suffered the largest single year decline in 2010. Although the 2012 elections did not represent a net loss as far as women's numeric representation is concerned, the gains represented only a 2 percent overall increase.

It should come as no surprise, therefore, that women's underrepresentation in American politics raises several normative concerns regarding fundamental issues of political representation and democratic legitimacy. As discussed in the introduction to this volume, many scholars have uncovered evidence, at both the national and state levels, that male and female legislators' priorities and preferences differ (Burrell 1996; Dodson 1998; Gerrity, Osborn, and Mendez 2007; Swers 2002; Thomas 1994).[1] Women's presence in positions of political power, therefore, reduces the possibility that gender-salient issues will be overlooked. Further, women's inclusion in the top tier of political accomplishment also infuses into the legislative system a distinct style of leadership, which is the second reason that women's underrepresentation is worrisome. Women are more likely than men to adopt an approach to governing that emphasizes congeniality, cooperation, and participation, whereas men tend to emphasize hierarchy (Weikart et al. 2006; Kathlene 1994, 1995; Tolleson-Rinehart 1991).[2] Finally, political scientists point to symbolic representation and the role model effects, political efficacy, and political engagement that women's presence in positions of political power confers to female citizens (Atkeson 2003; Atkeson and Carrillo 2007; Campbell and Wolbrecht 2003; Mansbridge 1999; Pitkin 1967/1972).[3] Together, the literatures on substantive and symbolic representation suggest that the inclusion of more women in positions of political power would change the nature of political representation in the United States. Moreover, the government would gain a greater sense of political legitimacy, simply by virtue of the fact that it would be more reflective of the gender breakdown of the national population.

In light of the importance of women's presence in politics, it is critical to understand why so few women hold public office in the United States. In this chapter, we argue that the fundamental reason for women's underrepresentation is that they do not run for office. There is a substantial gender gap in political ambition, and it is persistent and unchanging. We arrive at this conclusion by analyzing data we collected in 2001 and 2011 from thousands of male and female "potential candidates"—lawyers, business leaders, educators, and political activists, all of whom are well situated to pursue a political candidacy. In addition to highlighting the persistent gender gap in political ambition, we identify three central factors that continue to hinder women's full entrance into electoral politics. In the end, we document how far from gender parity we remain and the barriers and obstacles we must still overcome to achieve it.

## Conventional Explanations for Women's Underrepresentation: A Brief Review of the Literature

Scholars have devoted the last few decades to gaining a better understanding of why so few women occupy positions of political power in the United States. Much of the earliest research in the women and elections subfield asserted that overt discrimination accounted for the gender disparities in office holding (Githens and Prestage 1977; Kirkpatrick 1974). Electoral gatekeepers all but prohibited women from running for office in the 1970s. And those women who did emerge as candidates often faced sexism and a hostile environment (Boxer 1994; Witt, Paget, and Matthews 1994).

In the contemporary electoral environment, the degree to which the political system remains rife with gender bias is more difficult to determine. At the candidate level, individual accounts of women who face overt gender discrimination once they enter the public arena are increasingly uncommon (Woods 2000). Indeed, studies of campaign fundraising receipts and vote totals, often considered the two most important indicators of electoral success, demonstrate that women fare just as well as, if not better than, their male counterparts (Cook 1998; Fox 2010; Lawless and Pearson 2008; Smith and Fox 2001).[4]

In light of the growing contradiction between a political system that elects few women and a body of research that identifies the electoral environment as increasingly unbiased against female candidates, political scientists have turned to two institutional explanations for women's numeric underrepresentation. First, and perhaps most notably, they point to the incumbency advantage (Darcy, Welch, and Clark 1994; Nixon and Darcy 1996; Palmer and Simon 2008). Not only do the overwhelming majority of incumbents seek reelection in both state legislative and congressional elections, but also their reelection rates are very high (Jacobson 2012). Second, women's historic exclusion from the professions that tend to lead to political careers contributes to the gender disparities in office holding (Clark 1994; see also Lawless and Fox 2010). The basic implication of the "pipeline" explanation is that as more and more women come to occupy the careers that are most likely to lead to political candidacies, more and more women will acquire the objective qualifications and economic autonomy necessary to pursue elective office. In a leading American government textbook, Fiorina and Peterson (2002, 340–1) state that the underrepresentation of women "will naturally lessen as women's career patterns become more like those of men."[5]

The conventional assessment that emerges from the current explanations for gender disparities in elective office is that, overall, we are on a steady course toward equity in women's numeric representation. Certainly, overcoming institutional inertia is slow going, but the horizon looks bright. When women run for office, they perform at least as well as men. As women's presence in the candidate eligibility pool approaches men's, we should see the number of female elected officials approach the number of men as well. The problem with these explanations and the rosy prospects for women's representation they offer, however, is that they cannot account for the plateaus that have come to characterize women's presence in U.S. political institutions.

## The Political Ambition Explanation

We argue that missing from the conventional prognosis is an understanding of the gender dynamics underlying the process by which individuals move from the eligibility pool into elective office. Prospects for gender parity in our electoral system cannot be evaluated without an in-depth assessment of the manner in which gender interacts with and affects levels of political ambition. Put simply, if women and men are not equally likely to express interest in running for office, then women's presence in the political pipeline and open-seat opportunities that arise are insufficient for bolstering women's candidate emergence. To investigate this proposition, we developed and conducted the Citizen Political Ambition Study, a series of mail surveys and interviews with women and men in the pool of potential candidates. Our goal was to conduct a nuanced investigation of how women and men initially decide to run for all levels and types of political office, either now or in the future.[6]

The original survey, carried out in 2001, served as the first national study of the initial decision to run for office. Based on mail survey responses from 1,969 men and 1,796 women, we concluded that women were less likely than their male counterparts to consider running for office and that, across generations, men expressed more comfort and felt greater freedom than women when thinking about seeking office.[7]

But a lot has happened in the U.S. political arena since our initial survey. The events of September 11, 2001, wars in Iraq and Afghanistan, Nancy Pelosi's election as the first female Speaker of the House, Hillary Clinton and Barack Obama's 2008 battle for the Democratic presidential nomination, Sarah Palin's vice presidential candidacy, and the rise of the Tea Party movement are among only the many recent developments that might affect interest in running for office. For some people, the current political climate might motivate them to take action. For others, the effect might be increased cynicism and disengagement from politics. In either case, the altered political landscape, coupled with the continuing need to understand why women do not run for office, motivated us to conduct a new wave of the Citizen Political Ambition Study.

In 2011, we completed a survey of a new sample of potential candidates. The samples of women and men are roughly equal in terms of race, region, education, household income, profession, political participation, and interest in politics. Thus, our sample of 1,925 men and 1,843 women allows us to shed new light on the gender gap in political ambition.[8]

## The Persistent Gender Gap in Political Ambition

Men and women do not have equal interest in seeking elective office. In the 2001 survey, we found strong evidence that gender plays a substantial role in the candidate emergence process. Overall, more than half of the respondents (51 percent) stated that the idea of running for an elective position had at least "crossed their mind." Turning to the respondents who considered a candidacy, though, the data presented in Figure 2.1 highlight a significant gender gap among the 2001 respondents: men were 16 percentage points more likely than women to have considered running for office.[9] Notably, this gender gap persisted across political party, income level, age, race, profession, and region.[10] When we turn to future interest in office holding, the prospects for women's full inclusion in electoral politics are even bleaker. The gender gap in future interest in running for office has grown over the course of the last 10 years. More specifically, while men's interest in a future candidacy remained virtually unchanged across the last decade (it held steady, with approximately 23 percent of men expressing interest in running for office at some point in the future), women's interest dropped; 18 percent of women in 2001, compared with 14 percent of women in 2011, expressed interest in a future candidacy.

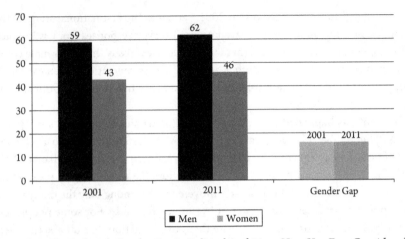

*Figure 2.1* The Enduring Gender Gap in Political Ambition: Have You Ever Considered Running for Office?. *Notes:* Bars represent the percentage of women and men who responded that they had "seriously considered" or "considered" running for office (this includes respondents who actually ran for office). The gender gap is significant at $p < .05$ in both the 2001 and 2011 comparisons.

Our measures of whether a respondent ever considered a candidacy—retrospectively or prospectively—capture even the slightest inclination of running for office. Because men might be more cavalier than women when assessing whether they ever thought about pursuing an elective position (see Lawless and Fox 2010), we also asked members of our eligibility pool sample whether they ever investigated how to place their name on the ballot or ever discussed running with potential donors, party or community leaders, family members, or friends. Even when we turn to these concrete steps that are often required to mount a political campaign, though, we uncover gender gaps of at least the same magnitude. Figure 2.2 reveals that, across professions, men are significantly more likely than women to have engaged in each of these fundamental campaign steps.

Establishing a complete understanding of the gender gap in political ambition, however, requires that we look beyond broad levels of interest in running for office and steps taken en route to an eventual candidacy. We must also assess whether men and women in the candidate eligibility pool are equally open to seeking high-level positions. After all, in many cases, politics is a career ladder; politicians often move from local to state to national office. More than 70 percent of the members of the U.S. Congress, for instance, held office prior to running for the House or Senate (Malbin, Ornstein, and Mann 2008). Yet among office holders, evidence suggests that women are less likely than men to climb the political career ladder (Fulton et al. 2006; Lawless and Theriault 2005). In fact, school boards, which comprise the offices with the highest ratio of female office holders (estimated at about 40 percent), are not typically utilized by politicians who harbor ambition to

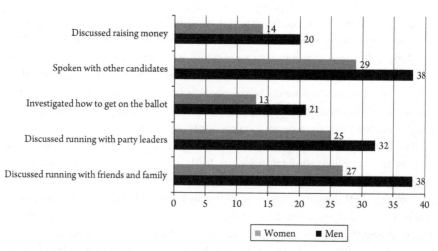

*Figure 2.2* The Gender Gap in Steps Taken that Typically Precede a Candidacy. *Notes:* Bars represent the percentage of women and men who answered affirmatively for each activity. The gender gap is significant at *p* <.05 for all comparisons.

launch political careers at higher levels of office (Deckman 2007; see also Bullock et al. 1999; Hess 2002). The gender disparity in progressive ambition—or interest in climbing the political career ladder—could be a result of differences in the level of office at which women and men enter politics in the first place.

To determine where potential candidates focus their office-specific interests, we asked the members of the sample to state the first office they would seek should they enter a political contest. We then presented them with a list of several local, state, and federal positions and asked whether they would ever consider running for any of those posts. The data reveal that women are less likely than men to consider running for high-level elective offices.

Let us begin with an analysis of the first office for which respondents would consider running. Many potential candidates seem well aware of career ladder politics. Most respondents who are willing to consider running for office at some point in the future would get involved at the bottom rung of the ladder. A total of 76 percent of the women and 60 percent of the men select a local office—school board, city council, district attorney, or mayor—as the first office for which they might run. The gender gap in interest reverses itself with increases in the stature of the level of office. Men are significantly more likely than women to identify a state office (25 percent of men compared with 18 percent of women) or federal office (15 percent of men compared with only 6 percent of women) as their first choice. The gender gap in ambition for high-level office is wider when we consider that 31 percent of women, but only 23 percent of men, stated unequivocally that they have ruled out any consideration of a future run for office.

The magnitude of the gender gap in interest in high-level office is even greater when we turn to the positions in which respondents might ever be interested in seeking. Table 2.2 presents the percentages of potential candidates who would entertain a candidacy for 10 elective offices. At the local level, women are more likely than men to report interest in a school board position, but men are approximately 40 percent more likely than women to consider running for the state legislature and are roughly twice as likely as women to express interest in a federal position.

Based on a variety of measures, the 2011 gender gap in political ambition is roughly the same magnitude as it was in 2001. That is, women today remain just as unlikely, relative to men, as women 10 years ago to consider running for office. Moreover, even though they have risen to the top ranks within often male-dominated professions, and despite the fact that they yield from the management and leadership positions that tend to position candidates for the highest public offices, women express far less ambition than men to enter the upper echelons of the political arena. Our evidence suggests that the context of gender dynamics in the United States and historic patterns of career segregation continue to influence the decision to run for office. The remainder of this chapter sheds light on why this may be the case and

Table 2.2  **Gender Differences in Office Preferences**

|  | Women | Men |
|---|---|---|
| *Local or Community Office* | | |
| School Board | 35%* | 26% |
| City Council | 30 | 32 |
| Mayor | 7* | 11 |
| District Attorney | 3 | 2 |
| *State-Level Office* | | |
| State Legislator | 25* | 35 |
| Statewide Office | 2 | 3 |
| Governor | 3* | 6 |
| *Federal Office* | | |
| House of Representatives | 9* | 19 |
| Senate | 6* | 11 |
| President | 1* | 2 |
| Sample Size | 1,766 | 1,848 |

*Notes:* Entries indicate the percentage of respondents who would ever consider running for each position. Percentages do not add up to 100 percent because respondents often expressed interest in more than one position. * indicates that the gender gap is significant at $p < .05$.

speaks to a series of gender dynamics in the political arena that work to women's detriment.

# Three Central Barriers to Women's Candidate Emergence

We focus on three of the central factors that contribute to the difficult road ahead as the United States moves toward gender parity in elective office. The first factor highlights gender differences in women and men's perceptions of themselves as candidates and of the electoral environment. The second factor focuses on women's support from and interactions with electoral gatekeepers. The third factor identifies the complex role that family dynamics play in the decision to run for office. All of our findings, though, reveal the perpetuation of deeply embedded patterns of traditional gender socialization, whereby men have much greater comfort than women in thinking of themselves as candidates.

## Gendered Perceptions of Qualifications to Run for Office and of the Electoral Environment

Our 2001 study revealed that one of the biggest barriers keeping women from emerging as candidates centered on self-perceptions of qualifications to run for office. In 2011, the same dynamic emerges. Consistent with the findings from 10 years ago, the data presented in Table 2.3 indicate that men remain almost 60 percent more likely than women to assess themselves as "very qualified" to run for office. Women in the sample are more than twice as likely as men to rate themselves as "not at all qualified."

Importantly, the gender gap in perceptions of qualifications to run for office does not stem from gender differences in direct political experiences or exposure to,

*Table 2.3*  **Self-Assessment of Qualifications to Run for Public Office**

*How qualified are you to run for public office?*

|  | Women | Men |
| --- | --- | --- |
| Very Qualified | 22% | 35% |
| Qualified | 35 | 38 |
| Somewhat Qualified | 31 | 21 |
| Not at All Qualified | 12 | 5 |
| Sample Size | 1,745 | 1,846 |

*Note:* The gender gap is significant at $p < .05$ for all comparisons.

or familiarity with, the political arena. A total of 23 percent of women and 26 per-cent of men have conducted extensive policy research; 69 percent of women and 74 percent of men regularly engage in public speaking; and 75 percent of women and 70 percent of men report experience in soliciting funds. In addition, more than 80 percent of the women and men in the sample have attended political meetings and events, two-thirds have served on the boards of nonprofit organizations and foundations, and roughly three-quarters have interacted with elected officials in some professional capacity.

Women's self-doubts are important not only because they speak to deeply embedded gendered perceptions but also because they play a much larger role than do men's in depressing the likelihood of considering a candidacy. More specifically, among women who self-assess as "not at all qualified" to run for office, only 39 per-cent have considered throwing their hats into the ring. Among men who do not think they are qualified to run for office, 55 percent have given the notion of a can-didacy some thought. Because gender differences in perceptions of qualifications correlate with respondents' assessments of their own electoral prospects, women are significantly less likely than men to think they would win their first campaign. Compared with 38 percent of men, 31 percent of female potential candidates think it would be "likely" or "very likely" that they would win their first race if they ran for office. Alternatively, women are approximately 50 percent more likely than men to think the odds of winning their first race would be "very unlikely."

Why do women think they are unqualified to run for office when similarly situated men voice far less hesitation? Although fully explicating the gender gap in potential candidates' perceptions of their qualifications is beyond the scope of this chapter, we offer two explanations. First, entering the electoral arena involves the courageous step of putting oneself before the public, often only to face intense examination, loss of privacy, possible rejection, and disruption from regular rou-tines and pursuits. This decision, even for experienced politicians, requires charac-ter traits such as confidence, competitiveness, and risk-taking—characteristics that men have traditionally been encouraged to embrace and women to eschew. As the data presented in Table 2.4 reveal, women are significantly less likely than men to report that they have the traits generally required of candidates for elective office. In terms of thick skin, an entrepreneurial spirit, and a willingness to take risks, men are at least 25 percent more likely than women to believe that they possess the political trait in question. Women are less likely than men to perceive themselves as possess-ing key ingredients required to be "qualified" to run for office.

Second, the reality of gender-neutral election outcomes does not mitigate the gendered perceptual lens through which women view the electoral process. To shed light on gender differences in perceptions of the electoral system, we asked respondents the extent to which they regard their local and congressional elec-tion landscapes competitive. Because the women and men are geographically matched, differences in responses reflect perceptual, not true, differences in levels of

*Table 2.4* **Self-Assessment of Politically Relevant Traits**

| Do you consider yourself....? | Women | Men | Advantage for Men |
|---|---|---|---|
| Confident | 66% | 73% | +7 |
| Competitive | 64 | 74 | +10 |
| Risk-Taking | 31 | 39 | +8 |
| Entrepreneurial | 26 | 36 | +10 |
| Thick-Skinned | 24 | 33 | +9 |
| Sample Size | 1,745 | 1,846 | |

*Notes:* The gender gap is significant at $p < .05$ for all comparisons.

competition. The data presented in the top half of Table 2.6 indicates that a majority of women judge their local and congressional elections as "highly competitive."
Women are roughly 25 percent more likely than men to assess the political landscape this way. Further, more than half the women in the sample do not believe
that women who run for office fare as well as their male counterparts. Seven out
of 10 women doubt that female candidates raise as much money as similarly situated men. Men are significantly more likely than women to perceive lower levels of
both electoral competition and gender bias against women in politics (see bottom
of Table 2.5).

There may be no systematic bias against female candidates on Election Day, but
gender differences in potential candidates' perceptions of themselves and of the
electoral environment are striking, and perceptions in this case trump reality. These
findings suggest that men's longer presence and success in top positions in the professions from which candidates tend to emerge may result in (or reinforce) levels of
confidence about entering the political arena, also a male-dominated environment.
Because women are more likely than men to view the electoral process as biased
against them, self-doubt regarding their qualifications and more pessimistic perceptions of the likelihood of winning may simply be a rational response to what women
perceive as a more challenging political context.[11]

## Gendered Patterns of Political Recruitment

Recruitment and encouragement lead many individuals who otherwise might never
consider running for office to emerge as candidates. Ten years ago, women were far
less likely than men to report being recruited to run for office. Over the course of
last decade, however, many women's organizations burst onto the political scene.
In 2007, the Women's Campaign Forum launched its "She Should Run" campaign,

*Table 2.5*  **Gender Differences in Perceptions of the Electoral Environment**

|  | Women | Men |
|---|---|---|
| *Perceptions of the Electoral Environment* | | |
| In the area I live, local elections are highly competitive. | 55 % | 39 % |
| In the area I live, congressional elections are highly competitive. | 62 | 50 |
| *General Perceptions of Bias Against Women in Politics* | | |
| Women running for office win as often as men. | 47 | 58 |
| Women running for office raise as much money as men. | 27 | 40 |
| Sample Size | 1,753 | 1,833 |

*Notes:* Entries indicate the percentage of respondents who answered affirmatively. The gender gap is significant at $p <.05$ for all comparisons.

a nonpartisan, online effort to build the pipeline of Democratic and Republican pro-choice women and inject them into the networks that can promote eventual candidacies. Emerge America, founded in 2002, trains Democratic women across the country to develop networks of supporters so that they can successfully run for and win elective office. The EMILY's List Political Opportunity Program, which began in 2001, trains and supports pro-choice Democratic women to run for all levels of office. Many statewide and local women's organizations have also recently launched aggressive campaigns to bring more women into political circles and positions of power. Thus, although they vary in mission and target group, collectively these organizations endeavor to move more women into the networks from which candidates emerge. Indeed, 22 percent of the women in our sample report some contact with a women's organization whose mission is to promote women's candidacies.

To assess the degree to which gender continues to affect patterns of political recruitment, we asked respondents whether they ever received the suggestion to run for any political office from a party leader, elected official, or political activist (including nonelected individuals working for interest groups and community organizations). Figure 2.3 illustrates that the gender gap in political recruitment remains substantial; women remain less likely than men to receive the suggestion to run from each type of electoral gatekeeper. It is likely that these gender gaps are smaller than would be the case if women's organizations did not strive to facilitate women's candidate emergence. But their efforts can do only so much. Party leaders, elected officials, political activists, and nonpolitical actors continue to encourage far more men than women to enter the electoral arena. And these patterns persist across party lines.

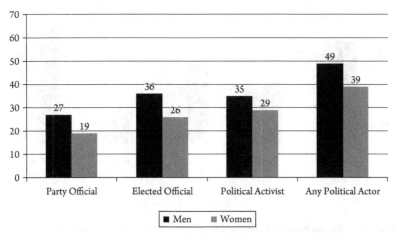

*Figure 2.3* Encouragement to Run for Office from Political Actors. *Notes:* Bars represent the percentage of women and men who were recruited to run for office by each political actor. For all categories, women are statistically less likely than men (at $p <.05$) to report receiving the suggestion to run for office.

We also asked respondents if they ever received the suggestion to run for office from "nonpolitical actors," defined as colleagues, spouses/partners, family members, and religious connections. The data presented in Figure 2.4 reveal that on this dimension, too, women remain less likely than men to have been encouraged to run for office, regardless of the source.

The lack of recruitment is a particularly powerful explanation for why women are less likely than men to consider a candidacy. A total of 67 percent of respondents who have been encouraged to run by a party leader, elected official, or political activist have considered running, compared with 33 percent of respondents who report no such recruitment (difference significant at $p <.05$). The same pattern holds for nonpolitical actors; whereas 78 percent of the potential candidates in our sample who have not received encouragement to run from a colleague, spouse, or family member have not considered a candidacy, 72 percent of respondents who have received such a suggestion have considered throwing their hats into the ring (difference significant at $p <.05$). Importantly, women are just as likely as men to respond favorably to the suggestion of a candidacy. They are just less likely than men to receive it.[12]

Certainly, not all political offices are alike, and patterns of recruitment vary across level of office (although our data suggest that they always work to women's disadvantage). But at the aggregate level, the gender gap is noteworthy, especially in light of the fact that the women and men in this sample of potential candidates exist in the same tier of professional accomplishment and express comparable levels of political interest. The recruitment patterns reported by the potential candidates we surveyed corroborate studies finding that gatekeepers more actively seek men than

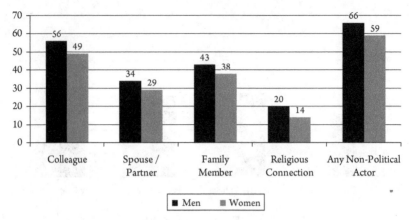

*Figure 2.4* Encouragement to Run for Office from Nonpolitical Actors. *Notes:* Bars represent the percentage of women and men who were recruited to run for office by each nonpolitical actor. For all categories, women are statistically less likely than men (at $p < .05$) to report receiving the suggestion to run for office.

women to run for office (Sanbonmatsu 2006; Niven 1998). Considering the heavy weight potential candidates place on recruitment and the degree to which support for a candidacy bolsters levels of political ambition, both major political parties will continue to field an overwhelming majority of male candidates unless they make conscious efforts to recruit more women.

## Gendered Household Roles and Responsibilities

The results of our 2001 survey revealed that women were much more likely than men to be responsible for the majority of household work and childcare. Despite women's substantial movement into high-level positions in the professional arena, women and men continued to conform to traditional gender roles at home. Our 2011 survey data demonstrate that little has changed over the past 10 years.

Table 2.6 provides a breakdown of the respondents' family arrangements and distribution of household and childcare responsibilities. Women in the sample are significantly less likely than men to be married and have children. This suggests that some women who choose to become top-level professionals are more likely than men to deemphasize traditional family structures and roles. Those women who are married and who do have children, however, tend to exhibit traditional gender-role orientations. In families where both adults are working (generally in high-level careers), women are roughly 6 times more likely than men to bear responsibility for the majority of household tasks, and they are about 10 times more likely to be the primary childcare provider. Notably, these differences in family responsibilities are not merely a matter of gendered perceptions. Both sexes fully recognize this

*Table 2.6* **Gender Differences in Family Structures, Roles, and Responsibilities**

|  | Women | Men |
|---|---|---|
| *Marital Status* | | |
| Single | 15%* | 8% |
| Married or Living with Partner | 72* | 86 |
| Separated or Divorced | 13* | 6 |
| *Parental Status* | | |
| Has Children | 73* | 83 |
| Has Children Living at Home | 41* | 45 |
| Has Children under Age 7 Living at Home | 15 | 15 |
| *Household Responsibilities* | | |
| Responsible for Majority of Household Tasks | 43* | 7 |
| Equal Division of Labor | 45* | 41 |
| Spouse/Partner Responsible for Most Household Tasks | 12* | 52 |
| *Childcare Responsibilities* | | |
| Responsible for Majority of Childcare | 60* | 6 |
| Equal Division of Childcare | 35* | 40 |
| Spouse/Partner Responsible for Majority of Childcare | 6* | 54 |
| Sample Size | 1,766 | 1,848 |

*Notes:* Number of cases varies slightly, as some respondents omitted answers to some questions. The household tasks data do not include respondents who are not married or living with a partner; and the childcare arrangements data do not include respondents who do not have children. * indicates that the gender gap is significant at $p < .05$.

organization of labor. More than 50 percent of men acknowledge that their spouses are responsible for a majority of household tasks and childcare, while only 7 percent of women make the same claim. This division of labor is consistent across political party lines.

We also asked respondents how many hours they spend per day on various activities, including work, childcare, housework, and hobbies. Women and men work the same number of hours (roughly 9 hours per day), but women devote significantly more of their nonworking time than men to household tasks and childcare. Whereas women report spending about 2.1 hours per day on household tasks, men report spending about 1.6 hours per day. Among respondents with children, women spend roughly two-thirds more time each day than men on childcare (women spend 2.8 hours per day, compared with men, who spend 1.7 hours per day). Men spend more time exercising and pursuing their hobbies and interests (all of these gender differences are significant at $p < .05$). Hence, the data certainly suggest that women's lives are more hectic and confined than those of most of their male counterparts.

The degree to which traditional family dynamics continue to prevail in American culture is, in and of itself, remarkable. But surprisingly, women's disproportionate familial responsibilities do not dramatically affect whether they have considered running for office or express interest in running for office in the future. Of women who are responsible for the majority of the household tasks and childcare, for instance, 48 percent have considered running for office. Forty-five percent of women who shoulder no such burdens have thought about a candidacy. In another example, 43 percent of women with children at home have considered a candidacy, compared with 46 percent of women without children at home. Neither of these small differences approaches conventional levels of statistical significance. Our data suggest that the struggle to balance family roles with professional responsibilities has simply become part of the bargain for contemporary women. Of course, even if family structures and arrangements do not preclude women from thinking about a full range of lifetime career options, the circumstances under which such thoughts cross potential candidates' minds might differ for women and men. As one gender politics scholar so aptly characterized political ambition in the contemporary environment, "Women may now think about running for office, but they probably think about it while they are making the bed."[13] What emerges from this analysis of family roles and structures is the fact that women, though no longer directly impeded from thinking about a candidacy just because they have certain familial responsibilities, face a more complex set of choices than do their male counterparts.

## Where Do We Go from Here? Summary and Conclusion

The findings from the Citizen Political Ambition Study cast a cloud over future prospects for gender parity in U.S. political institutions. Our 2011 survey data reveal a large and enduring gender gap in political ambition—one that is virtually unchanged from 2001. The findings suggest that the gender gap stems from the fact that women are more likely than men to doubt their qualifications and perceive a biased and highly competitive electoral environment and less likely than men to receive support and encouragement to run for office, both from political gatekeepers and personal contacts. In addition, women's more demanding household and family roles add complexity to the decision to run for office. Our findings highlight the importance of deepening our understanding of the manner in which women and men in contemporary society are socialized about politics, the acquisition of political power, and the characteristics that qualify individuals to seek it.

The gender gap in political ambition, coupled with the stagnation in the number of women serving in elected offices throughout the last decade, makes the road ahead look quite daunting. Indeed, many barriers to women's interest in running for office can be overcome only with major cultural and political changes. But future prospects for women's broader representation are further dampened by the lack of a coherent women's movement. Hillary Clinton's presidential campaign—particularly the media coverage she garnered—certainly elevated issues of sexism and gender consciousness into the national discourse.[14] But her candidacy did not bring with it the kind of rallying cry to elect more women that accompanied the Equal Rights Amendment or the Clarence Thomas confirmation hearings (see Kornblut 2010). In fact, Clinton's candidacy was frequently cited as evidence of the dramatic strides the United States has made toward attaining gender equity. Perhaps the only issue that motivates some degree of unified political action for women's rights focuses on reproductive freedom. A broad network of pro-choice groups—such as Planned Parenthood Action Fund, NARAL Pro-Choice America, National Women's Political Caucus, and EMILY's List—enjoy considerable influence in political circles, especially among Democrats. But motivating activism even on this issue can be difficult.

Barring radical structural change in the institutions of politics and the family, achieving gender parity in U.S. government is not on the horizon. But our findings provide direction for a future research agenda aimed at determining the specific factors that might spur ambition among female potential candidates. What types of recruitment messages are particularly effective in encouraging women's candidacies? Can the dissemination of information showing that women perform as well as men at the polls combat women's negative attitudes and pessimistic expectations about the electoral process? What specific steps can political parties, electoral gatekeepers, and political activists take to improve women's self-assessments of themselves as candidates? While this type of research carries clear normative implications for organizations and individuals working to increase the number of women candidates in electoral politics, it will also shed even more light on the nuances of how women are socialized to think about the electoral process. Only then can we close the gender gap in political ambition.

### Notes

1. For additional evidence of substantive representation at the congressional level, see Paolino 1995; Swers 1998. At the state level, see Berkman and O'Connor 1993; Carroll, Dodson, and Mandel 1991; Kathlene, Clarke, and Fox 1991; Saint-Germain 1989; Thomas 1994; Thomas and Welch 1991. It is important to note, however, that with the growth of party polarization came the disappearance of moderate Republican women in recent Congresses. As the GOP has moved to the right, Republican women have become ideologically indistinguishable from their male counterparts (Frederick 2009). This finding holds even when the analysis focuses strictly on "women's issues."
2. For additional political science studies pertaining to gendered political styles and the public policy ramifications that ensue, see Alexander and Andersen 1993; Fox and Schuhmann 1999; Rosenthal 1998; Thomas 1994. Not all studies uncover such gender differences, though (see, e.g., Blair and Stanley 1991; Dodson and Carroll 1991; Duerst-Lahti and Johnson 1992).

3. On the other hand, Dolan (2006) and Lawless (2004a) find little empirical evidence—based on National Elections Studies data—to support the assumption that the presence of women candidates translates into any systematic change in women's political attitudes or behaviors.

4. Of course, the role of gender and discrimination in the electoral process is more complex than scholarship that focuses on aggregate vote totals might suggest. Under the right circumstances, women can compete evenly against men, but such is not always the case. As discussed in the introduction to this volume, female congressional candidates face more primary competition than do their male counterparts (Lawless and Pearson 2008), and they must raise more money to perform as well as men at the polls (Fiber and Fox 2005). In addition, geographic differences facilitate women's election in some congressional districts but reduce their chances of success in others (Palmer and Simon 2008; see also Norrander and Wilcox in this volume). In-depth examinations of campaigns also reveal the manner in which gender remains relevant in the electoral process. Gender stereotypes play a role in how the media cover candidates (Fowler and Lawless 2009; Fox 1997; Hayes 2011; Kahn 1996). Party recruiters invoke stereotypes when identifying potential candidates for political contests (Sanbonmatsu 2006; Niven 1998). And voters rely on stereotypical conceptions of women and men's traits, issue expertise, and policy positions when casting ballots (Dolan and Sanbonmatsu 2009; Lawless 2004b; Koch 2000; McDermott 1997, 1998). As women have achieved parity on some dimensions, then, other barriers remain deeply embedded in the institutions that shape political competition.

5. Although many political scientists whose research focuses on women's underrepresentation might not arrive at such an adamant conclusion, they do agree that women's increasing proportion in the candidate pipeline will work to promote greater gender balance in U.S. political institutions (Conway, Ahern, and Steuernagel 2004; Darcy, Welch, and Clark 1994; Duerst-Lahti 1998; Thomas 1998).

6. This was an endeavor to which virtually no research had been devoted. When we embarked on this project and conducted the first wave of our study, there were two exceptions: the National Women's Political Caucus's (Newman 1994) poll of potential candidates; and a mail survey of potential candidates in New York state, which served as a pilot for our national study (Fox, Lawless, and Feeley 2001).

7. For a book-length treatment of the results of the 2001 study, see Lawless and Fox 2005.

8. We drew a national sample of 9,000 individuals from the professions and backgrounds that tend to yield the highest proportion of congressional and state legislative candidates: law, business, education, and political activism. In assembling the sample, we created two equal-sized pools of candidates—one female and one male—that held the same professional credentials. Turning specifically to the four subsamples, we obtained a random sample of 2,000 lawyers from the 2009 edition of the *Martindale-Hubble Law Directory*, which provides the names of practicing attorneys in all law firms across the country. We stratified the total number of lawyers by sex and in proportion to the total number of law firms listed for each state. We randomly selected 3,000 business leaders from *Dun & Bradstreet's Million Dollar Directory, 2009–2010*, which lists the top executive officers of more than 160,000 U.S. public and private companies. Again, we stratified by geography and sex and ensured that men and women held comparable positions. For the sample of educators, we compiled a random sample of 800 public and private colleges and universities from the University of Texas's list of roughly 2,000 institutions that grant at least a four-year bachelor's degree. We selected 400 male and 400 female professors and administrative officials. We then compiled a national sample of 600 male and 600 female public school teachers and principals from a list of all public schools throughout the country from the Department of Education's website. Our final eligibility pool profession—"political activists and professionals"—includes 1,200 state branch and local chapter executive directors and officers of organizations that focus on the environment, abortion, consumer issues, race relations, civil liberties, taxes, guns, crime, social security, school choice, government reform, and "women's issues," 200 congressional chiefs of staff and legislative directors, and 600 local party leaders.

We employed standard mail survey protocol in conducting the study. Potential candidates received an initial letter explaining the study and a copy of the questionnaire. Three days later, they received a follow-up postcard. Two weeks later, we sent a follow-up letter with another copy of the questionnaire. We supplemented this third piece of correspondence with an email message when possible. Four months later, we sent another copy of the questionnaire. The final contact was made the following month, when we sent a link to an online version of the survey.

From the original sample of 9,000, 1,661 surveys were undeliverable. From the remaining members of the sample, we received 3,953 responses. After taking into account respondents who left the majority of the questionnaire incomplete, we were left with 3,768 completed surveys, for a usable response rate of 51 percent. Response rates within the four subsamples were lawyers, 54 percent; business leaders, 38 percent; educators, 56 percent; political activists, 58 percent and did not differ by sex.

9. Women are not only less likely than men to consider running for office but are also less likely to do it. Overall, 12 percent of the respondents had run for some elective position. Men, however, were 40 percent more likely than women to have done so (9 percent of women, compared with 14 percent of men; difference significant at $p$ <.05). Although there was no statistically significant gender difference in election outcomes, women were less likely than men to reach this seemingly gender neutral "end stage" of the electoral process.

10. All of the comparisons we present here and throughout the remainder of the report are based on the overall sample of potential candidates. When we break the data down into professional subsamples (i.e., lawyers, business leaders, educators, political activists), in almost all cases the magnitude of the gender gaps and levels of statistical significance remain unchanged.

11. For a thorough empirical analysis of the gender gap in potential candidates' perceived qualifications, see Fox and Lawless 2011.

12. For a thorough, multivariate explication of the gender gap in political recruitment, see Fox and Lawless 2010; Lawless and Fox 2010.

13. We thank Georgia Duerst-Lahti for this comment.

14. For a discussion with prominent scholars and feminists about the role gender plays in political life, see Fortini 2008.

# 3

# Voter Attitudes, Behaviors, and Women Candidates

TIMOTHY R. LYNCH AND KATHLEEN DOLAN

Before women can hold local, state, or federal elective office in the United States, they have to stand as candidates. Although office holders make policy and represent their constituents, candidates campaign and attempt to secure votes from members of the general public. For all candidates then, the crucial relationship is with the voters whose support or rejection make or break a candidacy. However, for women candidates the issue of their relationship with voters is somewhat more complex than it is for men candidates (Lawless 2008; see also Chapter 2 in this volume).

In American politics, the vast majority of candidates, past and present, are men. For this reason, since they first appeared on the scene women have stood out. And this uniqueness has colored their relationship with the public. For much of our nation's history, women candidates were met with hostility from voters who saw women's proper place as in the home. Slowly, as the United States experienced social, cultural, and economic change, acceptance of women candidates became more common. The steady rise in the number of women candidates since the early 1990s has mirrored a steady increase in the positive attitudes and behaviors people display in their interactions with these women. But if we are to understand how and when women are successful office holders, we must continue to explore the dynamics of their relationship with the voters as candidates. In this chapter, we outline three aspects of the public's relationship with women candidates: (1) attitudes toward women in politics; (2) stereotypes people hold about women candidates; and (3) whether people vote for women candidates.

# Attitudes about Women

Key to the chances of women candidates' success in seeking office is a set of positive attitudes among the public toward a political role for women. One of the major roadblocks to women candidates in earlier times was the widespread belief that politics was not an appropriate activity for women. A public believing that a woman's place is in the home is unlikely to vote for any women candidate with the courage to run. However, if voters feel that women have an equal role to play in political life, they can use these attitudes as a baseline against which to evaluate individual women candidates and decide if they are worthy of support. Holding more egalitarian attitudes about women in politics doesn't guarantee that a voter will choose a woman candidate, but it is essential to that voter's willingness to *consider* voting for a woman. As we will see, the increased success of women candidates during the last 30 years or so has been mirrored by a gradual shifting in attitudes about women's place in political life.

There are two ways to explore public attitudes about women in the political world: first, to take stock of beliefs about the proper role of women in society; and, second, to directly examine people's attitudes about women in elective office. We begin first with an examination of the evolution of attitudes toward women in the political world by relying on several long-standing sources of information about politics. Then we turn to the results of a 2010 public opinion survey of attitudes and behaviors toward women candidates and office holders to gain an understanding of the status of the contemporary relationship between women candidates and voters.

Since 1972, the American National Election Studies (ANES) has explored public attitudes about women's place in the world. One question asks whether women should have an equal role with men in running business, industry, and government or whether their place is in the home. The question is asked with a seven-point scale, with a score of 1 indicating strong belief that women should have an equal role with men and a score of 7 representing a strong belief that women's place is in the home. Figure 3.1 presents the data for the percentage of people who say that they support women having an equal role in society. Over the years, there has been consistent movement in the direction of people expressing support for an egalitarian position. In 1972, 47 percent of people believed women should have an equal role, 29 percent said women's place was in the home, and 19 percent put themselves in the middle of these two positions. By 2008, support for women's equal role in society has increased to 84 percent of U.S. adults, with 8 percent taking the middle position and only 7 percent saying women's place is in the home. Again, change has occurred in favor of more egalitarian attitudes toward women in politics, but about 15 percent of Americans still may see the political world as an inappropriate place for women.

Over the same time period, the General Social Survey (GSS) has asked respondents whether they believe that women have the right temperament to be in politics.

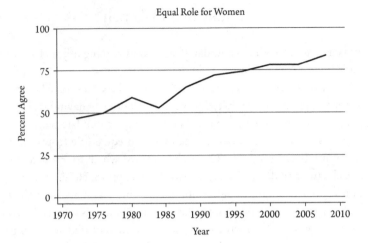

*Figure 3.1* Equal Role for Women. *Source:* National Election Study, 1972–2008, http://www.electionstudies.org/.

The question dealing with emotional characteristics asks respondents to "Tell me if you agree or disagree with this statement: Most men are better suited emotionally for politics than are most women." As Figure 3.2 demonstrates, agreement with this perspective has run from 47 percent of survey respondents in 1974 to about 26 percent in 2008. Although this question also demonstrates significant evolution in the public's thinking about women, it is important to note that today approximately one-fifth of the public willingly express concern about the abilities of women in the political arena. At the same time, while we note the trend in liberalization of attitudes toward

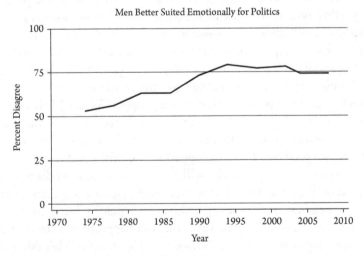

*Figure 3.2*  Men Better Suited Emotionally for Politics. *Source:* Generally Social Survey, 1972–2008, http://www3.norc.org/gss+website/

women in the public sphere, some respondents may mask bias against women candidates by providing an answer they think is more socially acceptable.

We have a good sense of the public's support (or lack thereof) for women in political office going back to the 1930s, when the scientific study of public opinion was getting its start. One of the earliest of these surveys was conducted by the American Institute for Public Opinion, later the Gallup organization, on people's attitudes on the question of a woman president. In 1936, in response to a question that asked, "Would you vote for a woman for president if she was qualified in every other respect?," 65 percent of the public said no (Smith 1975). Readers should note that the wording of the question reveals much about the way women's political role was perceived at this point in time. The phrase "if she was qualified in every other respect" clearly implies that the major way she isn't qualified is as a woman. The question wording has changed over time, reflecting a move away from an automatic assumption that a woman's sex was her disqualifying trait to the present form that asks, "If your party nominated a generally well-qualified person for president who happened to be a woman, would you vote for that person?" Figure 3.3 traces responses to the question about a woman president through the present day. The data clearly show that the American people have gradually changed their thinking about whether they would vote for a woman candidate for our nation's highest office, starting with a minority of people being will to do so in 1937 to the vast majority (95 percent) in the contemporary period indicating they would. However, as recently as 2000, when asked, all else being equal, would a woman or a man make a better president, 42 percent of survey respondents chose a man, 31 percent a woman, and 22 percent said candidate sex would not matter to performance in office (Simmons 2001). Of course, a woman major-party candidate

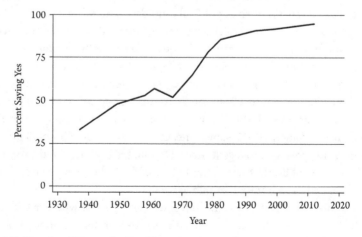

*Figure 3.3* Vote for a Woman for President. *Source:* Gallup Organization, 1937–2012.

for president in the United States has been a hypothetical situation during the entire period in which this question has been asked. Levels of support, already high, have not changed much since the high-visibility candidacies of Hillary Rodham Clinton and Sarah Palin in 2008, when their quests for the presidency and vice presidency, respectively, stimulated broad societal conversations about the possibility of a woman in the White House. Indeed, in 2009 after these historic candidacies 92 percent of Americans said they would vote for a woman, but 56 percent said that they thought "America was not ready for a woman leader" (Pew 2008). For this reason, it seems reasonable to suspect that these questions about a woman president probably overestimate support for women candidates to some degree (Streb et al. 2008).

## 2010 Survey of Public Perceptions of Women Candidates

Although these figures represent the clear evolution in support among U.S. adults for a larger role for women in public and political life, we are still left with relatively little understanding of how people feel about women candidates outside of the somewhat limited and episodic public opinion polling that takes place. With support from the National Science Foundation, we carried out an extensive public opinion survey of 3,150 U.S. adults with the goal of learning about a range of attitudes and behaviors that people exhibit when they evaluate women and men candidates for office. The respondents in this survey were drawn from 29 states in which women ran against men for U.S. House, Senate, governor, attorney general, and state education leader. Approximately half of the respondents experienced elections in which women ran against men, and the other half experienced more traditional elections in which both candidates for office were men. The primary goal of the project was to examine the impact of candidate sex in elections with and without women candidates. But these data also allow us to get a sense of contemporary public attitudes toward women as political candidates and office holders.

To address a common concern about women's suitability for office, we can examine responses from the 2010 survey to the question of whether women or men are better suited emotionally for politics. As Figure 3.4 demonstrates, respondents in this sample have similar evaluations to the contemporary respondents from the GSS data cited in Figure 3.2. In the 2010 survey, approximately 70 percent of respondents disagreed with the notion that men are better suited emotionally for politics than are women. At the same time, this leaves us with about 30 percent of the sample who agree with that sentiment. Despite the evolution in thinking about women's place in public life, there seems to be a fairly sizable group that still considers women to be less well suited for public life than are men.

To look more closely at these attitudes, we can examine whether the sex and party identification of the respondents shapes their thinking about this issue. Figure 3.4 also offers the sex and party breakdown of sample respondents who agree

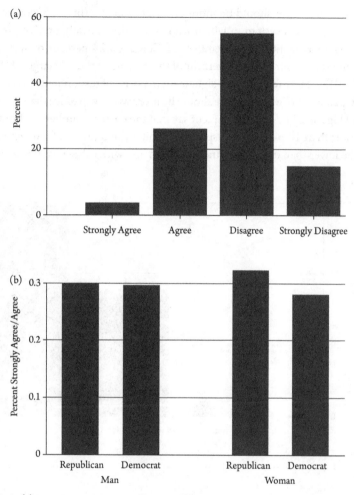

*Figure* 3.4 (a) Men Better Emotionally Suited for Politics. (b) Men Better Emotionally Suited by Respondent Sex and Party

that men are better suited for politics than women. Among this 30 percent, we see that women and men are equally likely to take this position, as are Democrats and Republicans. Republican women are slightly more likely to take this position than are Democratic women, but the differences among women here are not large. In general, we might expect that these factors could shape these attitudes about women's suitability, but there is no evidence of that in this survey. Instead, it may be that traditional stereotypes about women's emotionality may still resonate with some segment of the U.S. population.

Another measure of peoples' acceptance of women having a role in political life asks people to consider whether the number of women currently in office is about right or whether there should be more or fewer women. This is, of course, in the context of a political system in which women are dramatically underrepresented, comprising 18 percent of the members of Congress, 24 percent of state legislators around the country, and 12 percent of the mayors of the 100 largest U.S. cities (CAWP 2013). Here we see that a significant majority of respondents in our survey, about 60 percent, believe that there should be more women in office than is currently the case (Figure 3.5). About 32 percent say that the current number is "about right," while fewer than 10 percent of respondents think the number of women in office should be lower than it is. These findings are in line with other recent research that

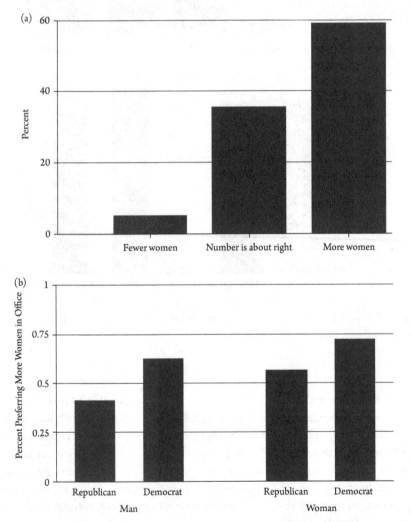

*Figure 3.5* (a) Number of Women in Office. (b) Number of Women in Office by Respondent Sex and Party. *Source:* 2010 Voting for Women Survey.

shows support for more women in office and for the notion that the United States would be governed better with more women leaders (Dolan and Sanbonmatsu 2009; Simmons 2001). In looking further at these attitudes, we see that respondent gender and party have an impact here. Figure 3.5 also presents responses for women and men based on their political party attachments. It is clear here that party is as important as gender. While women Democrats are the most likely to prefer more women in office (about 75 percent of this group), men Democrats are second most likely to support an increase in the number of women in office (about 65 percent), more likely than either Republican women (55 percent) or men Republicans (40 percent). So while we might expect women as a group to be the most supportive, the generally more liberal gender attitudes held by Democrats can positively influence male attitudes as well. Support for this notion among women can be more limited among those with more conservative political views.

Another way of thinking about the possible link between respondent sex and attitudes toward women in office is by asking about what Sanbonmatsu (2002) calls a *baseline gender preference* for candidates or office holders of one sex or another. Her evidence suggests that many people have an underlying preference to be represented by a woman or a man. This preference can combine with issue position preferences to move voters toward or away from a woman or man candidate. Rosenthal's (1995) findings support the notion that people often favor candidates of one sex or the other based on their assumptions about what those candidates are like or what they will do in office. Our survey asked respondents to consider whether, if all else were equal, they had a preference for candidates and leaders who were women or men. As Figure 3.6 shows, respondents in the survey were equally likely to indicate that they prefer women and men. However, it also suggests that this preference is shaped more by respondent sex than party. Again we see that Democratic women in the sample are much more likely to have a baseline preference for women candidates and office holders, with about 75 percent of these women taking that position. But slightly more than 50 percent of Republican women respondents prefer women candidates to men. Male respondents, on the other hand, are more likely to prefer men candidates, with about 60 percent of Democratic men and 75 percent of Republican men taking this position.

A follow-up question asked respondents whether it was important to them that they be represented in elected office by someone of the same sex. Figure 3.7 demonstrates that only 10 percent of respondents said that this was "very important," while 40 percent said that it was "somewhat important." However, we again see women's greater interest in same-sex representation. A majority of all women in the sample say that same-sex representation is "somewhat" or "very important" to them, with Democratic women more likely to take that position than Republican women. Men are less likely to say that same-sex representation is important, and the differences between Republican and Democratic men are negligible, with Republican men being slightly more likely to prefer same-sex representation than Democratic men.

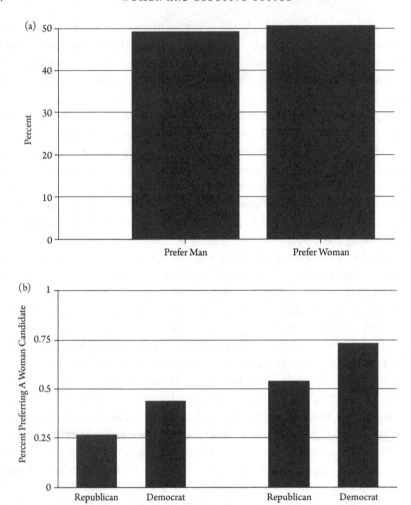

*Figure 3.6* (a) Baseline Gender Preference. (b) Baseline Gender Preference by Respondent Sex and Party. *Source:* 2010 Voting for Women Survey.

Given that men are used to having same-sex representation simply as a by-product of a system dominated by male office holders, it makes sense that men are less likely to value this than are women. Women respondents probably desire what they are much less likely to experience, while men may take this representation for granted.

## Stereotypes about Women

Another key to our understanding of the relationship between women candidates and voters is the notion of gender stereotypes, which involve ideas, shaped by gender

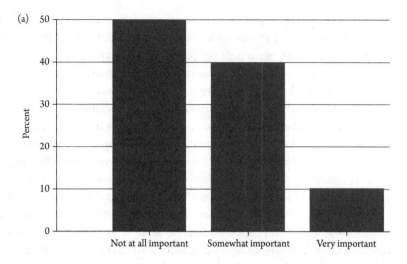

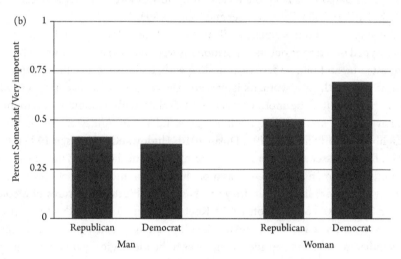

*Figure 3.7* (a) Importance of Same-Sex Representation. (b) Importance of Same-Sex Representation by Respondent Sex and Party. *Source*: 2010 Voting for Women Survey.

considerations, about what is proper or expected from women and men. Over the course of a lifetime of experiences, people develop a set of expectations about how women think and behave. These same stereotypes applied to family, workplace, and social interactions are often transmitted to the political world. Indeed, there is significant evidence to suggest that voters look at women candidates and women office holders from a gendered perspective, ascribing certain stereotyped issue position competencies and personality characteristics to them. In developing an extensive literature on women candidates for elective office, political scientists have demonstrated that the public look at women and men in politics in predictably stereotypic ways. These stereotyped assessments of political leaders and candidates focus on three major areas: personality traits, issue specialization, and ideology.

In terms of gender-linked personality traits, women candidates and office holders are generally viewed as more compassionate and honest than men, warmer and more expressive, and better able to deal with constituents than men. Men, on the other hand, are viewed as more competent, decisive, stronger leaders, and possessing a greater ability to handle a crisis (Alexander and Andersen 1993; Burrell 2008; Huddy and Terkildsen 1993a; Kahn 1996; King and Matland 2003; Lawless 2004; Leeper 1991; Paul and Smith 2008; Sapiro 1981–82). Trait stereotypes are relevant for candidates since several studies have found that people evaluate the stereotyped masculine traits (experience, leadership) as more important in politics than the feminine traits (honesty, compassion), particularly as the level of elected office being considered rises from the local to the national level (Huddy and Terkildsen 1993b; Lawless 2004; Rosenwasser and Dean 1989).

Assumptions about women candidates and office holders generally conform to stereotyped thinking about issue positions as well. Women are assumed to be more interested in, and more effective at dealing with, issues such as childcare, poverty, education, health care, women's issues, and the environment than are men, while men are thought to be more competent at dealing with economic development, military, trade, taxes, and agriculture (Alexander and Andersen 1993; Brown, Heighberger, and Shocket 1993; Dolan 2010; Huddy and Terkildsen 1993a; Koch 1997; Rosenwasser and Dean 1989). In terms of political ideology, numerous studies find that women are perceived as more liberal than men and that they are often perceived as more liberal than they are, based on objective measures of ideology (Koch 2000, 2002; McDermott 1997). Koch makes the argument that these inaccurate assessments of women candidates' ideology can have consequences at the polls. Given that most voters consider themselves to be ideologically moderate, the perceived liberalism of Democratic women candidates moves them further away from the average voter, reducing the chances that they would receive votes. However, the exaggerated liberalism of Republican women candidates moves them closer to the average voter, who might then be more likely to choose that woman candidate.

Perhaps the most important aspect of stereotypes of women candidates is that ideas about the abilities and competencies of female and male candidates may serve as a basis for voters to choose or reject a particular candidate. Much of the earlier literature on stereotypes and candidate sex raises concerns that the presence of gender stereotypes could mean that people would fail to see women candidates as having the right set of skills or policy interests to be viable leaders (Fox and Smith 1998; Huddy and Terkildsen 1993; Lawless 2004). However, there is conflicting evidence from the literature on whether stereotypes will generally hurt or help women candidates. For example, in an experimental study, Brooks (2011) found that women and men candidates were equally penalized for emotional displays of anger and tears, countering the notion that there is a double standard in the emotional expectations that people have about women's traits. At the same time, Lawless (2004) suggests that since September 11 women candidates may face more scrutiny from voters whose primary issue concerns involve terrorism and military issues. Other research finds that the stereotypes of women being more honest and concerned with ethical government can work to increase their support among voters who value these traits and can even "soften the blow" to a woman candidate's image in the context of negative campaigns (Dolan 2004; Fridkin, Kenney, and Woodall 2009; McDermott 1998). Fridkin and Kenney (2009; see also Chapter 8 in this volume) find that voters evaluated women U.S. Senate candidates as more honest and caring and more competent on health-care issues than their male opponents. Male Senate candidates, however, did not get the same positive boost from stereotypes about masculine traits, such as policy competence on economic issues. Clearly, while stereotypes can often be active in public evaluations of women and men candidates, the current status of the literature is unsettled as to the positive or negative impact of these trait and issue stereotypes.

## Gender Stereotypes and Political Party

An additional thing to consider when discussing voter stereotypes of women candidates is the role of political party. People hold partisan stereotypes in the same way that they hold gender stereotypes (Rahn 1993). Since we know that party identification is a powerful influence on evaluations of candidates and vote choice, we must consider how and when candidate sex is relevant once we have considered political party. It may be that candidate sex, while an important influence on political decisions in isolation, loses some of its impact when it is measured against other important political variables. Acknowledging this potential interaction is necessary because the majority of women candidates for national and state office in the past 20 years have run as Democrats. From 1990 to 2012, 65 percent of the women candidates for the U.S. Senate and 66 percent of the women candidates for the U.S. House of Representatives have run as Democrats (CAWP 2013). Given that people's stereotypes of the Democratic and Republican parties correspond in many ways to thinking about women and men (Democrats and women are thought to be better able to address social issues and poverty whereas Republicans and men are assumed to be more well suited for economic and military policies), it may be the case that gender and party stereotypes can work to reinforce each other (as in the case of a woman Democrat) or offset each other (as with a woman Republican). While attention to these important possibilities is still limited, recent studies tend to support the idea that, in most instances, partisan cues overwhelm other sources of information about candidate beliefs and positions and limit the influence of gender stereotypes. In an experimental study, Huddy and Capelos (2002) find that only on handling of women's issues did candidate sex exhibit any impact on people's evaluations of candidates. Hayes (2011) found that voter party stereotypes are more powerful than gender stereotypes when voters evaluated U.S. Senate candidates, although Sanbonmatsu and Dolan (2009) discovered evidence that the public perceive gender differences within political parties, leading to different experiences for women Democrats and Republicans. It is clear that learning more about the evaluations people make of women, in light of their party identification, is an important step in understanding how candidate sex affects elections.

## 2010 Survey Data

One of the goals of the 2010 survey was to examine whether people hold stereotypes about women and men while considering their political party as well as their sex. For a series of issues, we asked respondents to think about whether they saw a Democratic woman or man member of Congress as being more capable of handling that issue. We then posed the question a second time, asking them to think about whether a Republican woman or a Republican man would be better. It is clear from the findings of the 2010 survey that people hold clear policy competence stereotypes of women and men even in the light of political party. Figure 3.8 offers the evaluations that people made when they were asked to think about whether women or men who share a party would be better at handling a series of traditional female issues. The top of the figure illustrates the comparison between Republican women and men in Congress, and the bottom illustrates the same issues for Democratic women and men—abortion, health care, and education—all of which people generally stereotype as areas of female competence. But they are also issues that people see Democrats as being better able to handle than Republicans. When faced with this potential conflict between party and gender stereotypes, it is clear that on female issues women are given greater credibility regardless of party. In fact, the evaluations are quite similar—Republican women are seen as much better able to handle all three issues than are Republican men, and Democratic women are seen as superior on all three to Democratic men.

Interestingly, when we look at evaluations of male policy competence (Figure 3.9), we see that men in each party are assumed to be more competent than women, but by much narrower margins. Here the male issues are the war in Afghanistan, crime, and budget deficits. Republican men and Democratic men are assumed to be better able to handle each of these three issues than their women party counterparts. But on two of the three issues—Afghanistan and the deficit—men's advantage is relatively narrow. This is surprising given that military and economic issues are traditional areas of presumed male policy superiority. In this sample, however, women are given almost as much credibility as men. It is only on the issue of crime that we see the large margin in favor of men in each party that

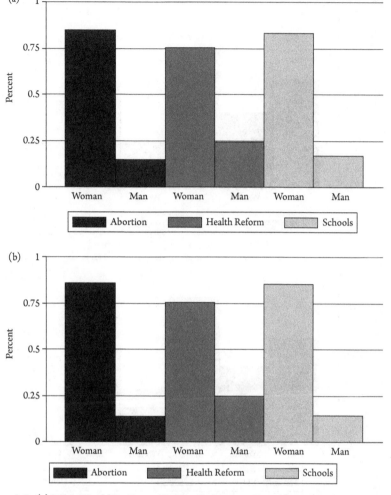

*Figure 3.8* (a) Who Would Be Better To Handle Issues—Republican Woman or Man? (b) Who Would Be Better To Handle Issues—Democratic Woman or Man?. *Source:* 2010 Voting for Women Survey.

we would typically expect. And, interestingly, Republican men appear to have no particular advantage over Democratic men or Republican women on issues where the gender and party stereotypes should advantage them. Although party stereotypes are important, gender stereotypes appear to be preeminent in the minds of these voters, with women clearly holding an advantage. These findings may give us some interesting insights into intraparty contests between women and men, as in primary elections.

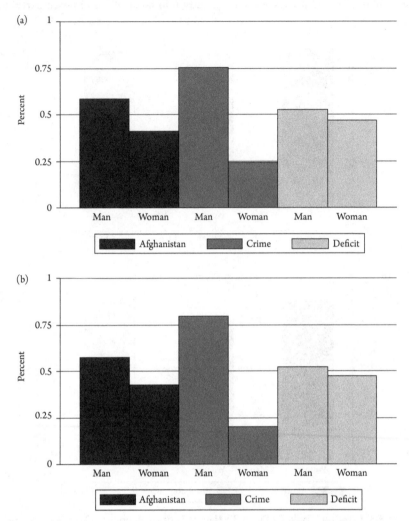

*Figure 3.9* (a) Who Would Be Better To Handle Issues—Republican Woman or Man?.
(b) Who Would Be Better To Handle Issues—Democratic Woman or Man? *Source:* 2010
Voting for Women Survey.

## Voting for Women

Implicit in any study of voting for women candidates is the idea that their sex
matters, that voters are choosing a *woman* candidate as opposed to choosing a
candidate without any consideration of his or her sex. Of course, voting for a
woman candidate can be an "accidental" act: a voter may choose a candidate who
shares his or her political party or policy position on an important issue without

the candidate's sex- or gender-related issues coming into play. Indeed, we know from countless works that political party is the strongest predictor of vote choice at every level of elected office. But some research suggests that voters often do seek out particular types of candidates, candidates with certain characteristics (e.g., sex, race, age) for a host of reasons. Most of those focus on questions of representation.

In her classic work on representation, Hannah Pitkin (1972) discusses representation as a complex concept with more than one meaning. In terms of political representation—when a voter chooses a candidate to hold some decision-making office—she describes two approaches. First, representation can be *descriptive*, "the making present of something absent by resemblance or reflection." Second, representation can involve activity, acting on behalf of others. This form of representation is known as *substantive* representation. Both forms of representation are relevant for the study of voting for women candidates. Despite the gains made by women elected officials in the contemporary period, women are still largely "absent" from the halls of government. Their underrepresentation at all levels of office is obvious and undeniable. Thought of this way, descriptive representation occurs when voters choose women candidates because they see the absence of women in office and seek to change that status quo. Elected women officials then serve the function of "standing for" women in the larger society in a very literal way that male representatives cannot.

While important, descriptive representation by women candidates and office holders is not necessarily sufficient as an explanation for why people vote for women candidates. We do not elect government officials merely to stand (or sit) in office and reflect who we are demographically. Instead, we expect them to govern, to act in our best interests. So people choosing women candidates may also do so because they want these women to pursue a particular set of policies once in office. Part of the argument in favor of electing women to achieve substantive representation is the idea that women candidates are better suited than men to address concerns of particular interest to women in the larger society. Given the degree to which the public sees the abilities of women and men candidates in gender-stereotyped ways, we should not be surprised if many people assume that women candidates would be more effective in dealing with issues and policies of concern to women.

## Do Voters Support Women Candidates?

The first and most basic question facing women candidates in American politics is whether they can garner sufficient vote support from the public to win elections. For many years, the answer to this question was no. In general, women running for office failed to conform to the public's stereotyped ideas about women's proper role in society, leading to ambivalence at best and hostility at worst toward their candidacies. For a long time in the United States, women's electoral success was limited to a relatively small number of offices in certain areas of the country (Dolan 2004). Indeed, the disadvantage women candidates faced because of their sex continued until relatively recently. However, since the 1970s, evidence of the increasing electoral viability of women candidates has steadily emerged. One of the most significant studies of the success of women candidates, produced by the National Women's Political Caucus, examined success rates of women and men candidates based on their incumbency status (Newman 1994). The results clearly showed that, when similarly situated women and men candidates are compared (e.g., women incumbents and men incumbents, or women and men challengers), women win election as often as men do, and more often in some circumstances. The NWPC report concluded that the primary reason for the low number of women in elected office in the United States was the small number of women who ran for office and not because voters refused to consider them. These findings have been confirmed by other studies that examine the vote share won by women candidates in both primary and general elections (Burrell 1994; Fox 1997; Herrnson, Lay, and Stokes 2003; Seltzer, Newman, and Leighton 1997). So while it is clear that every woman candidate is not successful in every election, there does not appear to be systematic or widespread bias against women candidates because of their sex.

## Do Women Support Women Candidates?

The second and perhaps most obvious question to ask when examining voting for women candidates is, "Do women vote for women?" This so-called affinity effect has been an implicit, and sometimes explicit, assumption underlying much of the research done on women candidates. Past research indicates several reasons for the assumption that women voters will be more likely to vote for women candidates than men will. First, some expect that a sense of group identity will draw women voters to women candidates. Indeed, several experimental studies demonstrate that voters are most likely to choose candidates like themselves. For example, black voters are more likely to choose black candidates than are whites (Sigelman and Welch 1984). Other researchers refer to the impact of a "gender consciousness" at work, suggesting that women voters have positive feelings toward women candidates beyond a simple shared demographic similarity. Here these positive feelings toward women candidates "as women" are shaped, perhaps, by an acknowledgment of the underrepresentation of women in elected office or a sense that women's political fortunes are bound up with other women (Tolleson-Rinehart 1992). This finding has been supported by numerous other studies, whether they involve women simply preferring women candidates in some hypothetical situation or voting for them in an election (Dolan 1997, 1998; Plutzer and Zipp 1996; Rosenthal 1995; Seltzer, Newman, Leighton 1997).

Important too is the role of political issues in the relationship between women voters and women candidates. It is possible that there are "group-salient" issues that draw women voters to women candidates. Issues like sexual harassment, abortion, or childcare tend to be of greater importance to women voters, and they may see women candidates as uniquely suited to dealing with these issues (Paolino 1995). Finally, a linkage between women voters and women candidates may not be based on gender or gender-based issues per se but instead on a shared partisan identity. Currently, women in the United States are more likely to identify with the Democratic Party than the Republican Party, and more women candidates run for office as Democrats than as Republicans. Women voters, who are more likely to be Democrats, may simply be choosing candidates of their party, many of whom are women (Cook 1994). Democratic women candidates often do much better in garnering votes from women than do Republican women (Cook 1998; King and Matland 2003), although Brians (2005) offers evidence that Republican women are willing to cross party lines to support women candidates.

At the same time, there is significant evidence to suggest that it is overly simplistic to say that women vote for women. Women voters do not always vote for women candidates, and some never do. Instead, women may be more likely to choose women candidates than men voters would be, but this dynamic is often shaped by other factors such as race, political party, and level of office. For example, studies have demonstrated that certain subgroups of women—African Americans, liberals, feminists, and those who are well educated—are more likely to choose women candidates than are other women (Eckstrand and Eckert 1981; Lewis 1999; Philpot and Walton 2007; Sigelman and Welch 1984; Smith and Fox 2001). Other work has shown that women voters may be influenced by the level of office involved, being more likely to choose women candidates for the House of Representatives but no more likely than men to do so in Senate elections (Cook 1994; Dolan 2004).

## 2010 Survey Data

The same survey data used to examine the attitudes and stereotypes people hold about women and men candidates also allows us to examine who votes for them. Since these data were gathered from people who took part in elections in which women ran against men, we can test the hypothesis that voter characteristics will be related to deciding to vote for a woman or a man candidate. The findings presented here scrutinize the vote choice decisions of respondents who voted in U.S. House races in which a woman ran against a man and focus on three variables known or thought to be important to vote choice: party identification; incumbency; and voter sex.

The notion that an affinity effect makes women voters more likely to choose women candidates than men voters does not appear to have much support in the 2010 election. As Figure 3.10 demonstrates, women and men voters were equally

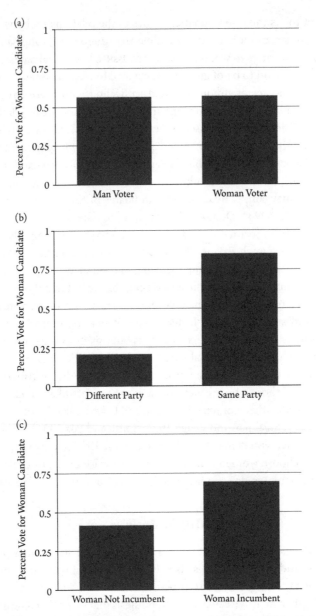

*Figure 3.10* (a) Impact of Gender on Vote for Woman Candidate. (b) Impact of Party Identification on Vote for Woman Candidate (c) Impact of Incumbency on Vote for Woman Candidate. *Source:* 2010 Voting for Women Survey.

likely to choose the woman candidate in their House race. About 55 percent of both women and men voted for a woman candidate for the House, which, while not evidence of a gender affinity effect, is certainly evidence that people have no concerns about choosing women candidates in general.

One of the primary reasons that the affinity effect is not stronger in voting for women candidates is the power of two other important political variables: political party identification and incumbency. In the 2010 analysis, the most important variables in determining whether a voter would choose a woman candidate were whether the voter and the woman candidate shared the same party identification (second panel of Figure 3.10) and whether that woman candidate was an incumbent (third panel of Figure 3.10). The impact of each of these variables is significant. About 85 percent of respondents chose the woman candidate when she shared their party, but only 20 percent did so when she was the candidate of the opposite party. Women incumbents were chosen almost 70 percent of the time, while nonincumbent women were chosen only about 40 percent of the time.

Elections scholars have long understood that these two variables are the most important in shaping vote choice, and this dynamic is no different when women candidates are involved (Campbell et al. 1960; Jacobson 2004). Voters approach elections predisposed to vote for the candidate of their party or the incumbent and often need a strong reason to deviate from that choice. For many, probably most, voters, candidate sex is not sufficient to pull someone toward a candidate of the other party. In the current time period, when women voters are more likely to identify with Democrats than Republicans and women candidates are more likely to run as Democrats than Republicans, what appears to be an affinity based on sex may really be an overlap of partisan preferences. Given the power of party identification, it is hard to imagine that many Democratic women voters would choose a Republican candidate simply because she was a woman or vice versa. Given the power of incumbency in American elections, in general, it is important to see that women incumbents accrue the same advantages in terms of vote support that male incumbents do.

## Conclusion

Women candidates for political office in the United States have come a long way since the days when their candidacies were unthinkable, when they were met with skepticism or outright hostility from the public. Yet even in 2012 they are still rare enough on the political scene that we refer to them as "women candidates." Certainly, most evidence suggests that bias against women candidates is largely a thing of the past. But that doesn't mean that a candidate's sex is irrelevant in the electoral arena. Instead, hostility toward women has been replaced by a more complex set of considerations that involve people's social and political reactions to candidate sex and gendered issues.

The research reviewed in this chapter clearly demonstrates that people express high levels of verbal support for women candidates. But this support in the abstract can be colored in the real world by the stereotypes that people hold about women and men. Voters sometimes extend their social stereotypes about women to women in the political world, assuming that they will be more liberal, gentler, and better able to handle the compassion issues than men. These evaluations can cut both ways, helping women candidates when voters value attention to compassion issues and potentially hurting them when the focus in on economic or military concerns.

While positive public attitudes toward women candidates are important, willingness to vote for them is crucial. Here again, we have seen an evolution from a time when a woman's sex was a clear detriment to the present day when being a woman is, at best, a positive and, at worst, a largely neutral consideration. All in all, voters are supportive of women candidates, but the reasons for their support often involve more traditional influences like party identification and incumbency. And complexity is evident here too in that we cannot assume that women voters will always be a natural voter base for women candidates. All things being equal, many women would probably like to support women candidates. But all things are rarely equal in politics. Voters are influenced just as strongly by political party identification and the power of incumbency when women candidates are on the ballot as when they are not. Women candidates are not simply women and they present voters with a complex mix of sex, party, and experience considerations that those voters must weigh when deciding their vote. In the end, women candidates have a relationship with the public that is colored by their sex but not controlled by it.

# 4

# The Race for the Presidency: Hillary Rodham Clinton

REGINA G. LAWRENCE AND MELODY ROSE

A televised debate held in Ames, Iowa, in August 2011 among contenders for the Republican presidential nomination featured eight candidates—including one woman. During the debate, moderator Byron York of the *Washington Examiner* asked Congresswoman Michelle Bachmann (R-MN) about remarks she made in 2006 that she had studied tax law because her husband told her to, even though she disliked the idea. "But the Lord said, 'Be submissive. Wives, you are to be submissive to your husbands,'" Bachmann said at the time. York asked, "As president, would you be submissive to your husband?"—a question booed by some in the studio audience. According to one news account, "Bachmann paused for a few moments before quipping, 'thank you for that question, Byron.' She continued, "Marcus and I will be married for 33 years this September 10th. I'm in love with him. I'm so proud of him. And both he and I—what submission means to us, if that's what your question is, it means respect. I respect my husband. He's a wonderful, godly man, and a great father. And he respects me as his wife. That's how we operate our marriage. We respect each other. We love each other."[1]

In many ways, the trail to the White House was cleared by Hillary Rodham Clinton and Sarah Palin in 2008. Clinton's near nomination to the Democratic ticket and Palin's historic role as the first female Republican candidate for the vice presidency (and second woman on a major party ticket) offered American voters new images of executive gender politics on a national scale. And though that electoral cycle may have answered some questions about the viability of female candidates in presidential campaigning, the number of questions raised was perhaps larger. Within months of the 2008 election, which produced neither a female president nor vice president, speculation began about the future of women in executive office: Would Clinton's near miss encourage or discourage future candidates? Was Palin sufficiently prepared for the vice presidency, and would she go on to mount a presidential effort in 2012? Would Clinton run again? These questions were shortly answered, and the field of potential female thinned quickly leaving, if only briefly, Bachmann.

Bachmann's short-lived bid for the presidency in 2011 and 2012 reminded the country both that women are not done running for the highest office and that obstacles remain for those who make the effort. More importantly for our purposes here, Bachmann's effort calls to mind our earlier research on the Clinton candidacy (Lawrence and Rose 2009), in which we concluded by quoting journalist Gail Sheehy (2008), who had observed that in the end "nobody knew how to run a woman as leader of the free world."

Bachmann's brief run illustrates that that Sheehy's (2008) observation continues to ring true. She struggled to create what we call a gender strategy: a presentation of herself and her candidacy that navigates deeply held and often contradictory expectations for women's "appropriate" place in public life and especially executive office. Bachmann fumbled on numerous occasions in speaking to perceived women's issues. Some will recall her awkward remarks regarding the human papillomavirus (HPV), or cervical cancer, vaccine, in which she repeated the speculation that the vaccine would be harmful to women's well-being.[2] And as this chapter's opening paragraph demonstrates, she struggled to defend an earlier statement that she was biblically obligated to submit to her husband. One writer for *Vanity Fair* responded to Bachmann's debate performance by asserting, "A woman who pursues an entire career she hates the idea of, just because her husband told her to, is not a woman who should be occupying the Oval Office—or anything remotely near it." A commentator on a conservative radio talk show argued, however, that "in the era of 'women's liberation,' Bachmann's past remark regarding submission to her husband 'is worthy of note.' "[3]

These controversial moments from the most recent presidential campaign reveal that women candidates for the nation's highest office will be dogged by gender-infused expectations and tensions, media coverage practices, and personal context. But they also demonstrate that, as we consider these variables in the study of a woman's candidacy, we must also consider the interplay of these variables with both the gendered features of the office of the presidency and the norms and expectations of her political party. In this chapter, we describe some of the challenges of *gender strategy* and *gender–office congruency* faced by American women who seek national executive office and how those challenges played out in the particular case of Hillary Rodham Clinton's candidacy. We conclude by arguing that there is a rich field awaiting scholars to include analysis of party affiliation in their gender and politics research: as more women seek national executive office, the nuances between Republican and Democratic gender strategies can be more carefully assessed.

# Female Candidates and Their Obstacles

Though it may now be easy to forget, Clinton came very close to securing the Democratic nomination in 2008. She entered the race as the presumptive Democratic nominee, enjoying particular strengths in fundraising and name recognition. She suffered from the outset, though, from low "likeability" ratings in public opinion polls, questions regarding her experience, and some mishandled election strategy decisions. Still, she came far closer to the White House than any woman before her, earning 18 million votes. Had a few key factors played out differently—the specific timing of particular state primaries, for example, or the Democratic party's decisions about how to award delegates in some contested circumstances—we might have witnessed a general election contest between Clinton and Republican nominee John McCain, which could well have played out in Clinton's favor. In other words, it is important to remember that Hillary Rodham Clinton was far from a long shot and to recall her candidacy not just in terms of its failures but also its near success.

In our previous research (Lawrence and Rose 2009), we attempted to place the 2008 Clinton campaign in context by focusing on an interlocking set of variables that, we argued, shape *any* female candidate's attempt to gain the White House. Those variables include long-standing gender stereotypes, media norms and routines that shape news coverage of all candidates (male or female, though with special inflections for women), and the candidate's own persona along with the particulars of the electoral context in which she competes (e.g., party rules governing each election year's primary calendar, methods for allocating delegates).

Lawrence and Rose (2009) argued that gender stereotypes are crucial factors shaping the female presidential candidate's fortunes but that other factors are equally important (see also Fowler and Lawless 2009). It is important to remember that Clinton's campaign also stumbled against more benign and less gendered barriers. So careful to check all the boxes a female candidate must check along her route to the White House, such as demonstrating fundraising prowess and assembling an experienced campaign team, Clinton appeared cavalier in some tactical choices that would prove decisive: her choice to run essentially a general election campaign during the primary season by speaking to the ideological center rather than the more liberal Democratic base; her campaign's decision to work toward a Super Tuesday sweep of key primary contests rather than preparing for a longer, broader fight including organizing in caucus states; and her campaign's reliance on old-style fundraising and communications against an opponent exploiting new technologies to their fullest (Cottle 2008; Kuhn 2008; Sheehy 2008; Smith 2008.) All proved missteps in hindsight. Moreover, the Clinton campaign suffered from poor press relations. Unfortunately for Hillary Clinton, her characteristic discomfort with self-disclosure, sealed into place by her scorching experiences with the press as first lady, set media scripts in motion that would haunt and perhaps deeply undermine her presidential campaign.

As Clinton's case suggests, gender stereotypes are not by themselves an adequate explanation for the United States' failure so far to elect a female president. Instead, stereotypes must be understood in relation to other factors that help determine a candidate's success. Importantly, the female candidate's own personal history will matter to her bid for office. While Clinton faced many of the predicted challenges for a female presidential candidate, her campaign for the presidency held great promise because she had overcome barriers that had held other women candidates back: she had attained international name recognition, a high-profile Senate seat that gave her foreign policy credentials, and a large campaign war chest. By the same token, her candidacy was undone not just by the generic dynamics of gendered politics but also by Clinton's particular path to power. Her former role as First Lady and her marriage to a famous and politically polarizing president—as well as the particular way she embodied the First Lady role—all created complicated challenges when she sought to occupy the West Wing herself. As political scientist Kathleen Dolan (a contributing author to this volume) observed, "For all the post-mortems we do on 2008, I don't think we'll ever be able to separate out what is gender stereotypes from what is Hillary Clinton" (quoted in Toner 2008). The variety of reactions her candidacy evoked are directly related to her role as an ambitious, complicated woman first entering the White House as the equal political partner of her president-husband and then attempting to reenter as president herself. This is a professional and personal profile Hillary Rodham Clinton shares with no other woman in American history, and she may, in that sense, be a poor test case for the question of whether Americans are ready to elect a woman as president. Then again, given the paucity of women on the presidential stage, any one female candidate may be too rare to test general propositions about women and politics.

We argue that because of these interlocking constraints of gender stereotypes with other features of the electoral context, every female presidential candidate needs a *gender* strategy: a way of presenting herself and her candidacy to the media and voters that negotiates the double binds (Jamieson 1995) that still tie women to contradictory expectations. Any female candidate who enters presidential politics will be presented with tactical choices that either stabilize or topple her balance between competing gravitational pulls: demonstrating proper "femininity" along with the required "toughness" for the Oval Office (see also Thomas and Schroedel 2007).

Gender strategies are not always well thought out or evenly consciously considered. Evidence from inside the 2008 Clinton campaign suggests that some running her campaign did not think about their candidate's challenges in gendered terms, while others assumed that Clinton's gender would produce more or less automatic support for her candidacy among women voters. In the aftermath of Clinton's loss, and of Sarah Palin's, there may be more deliberate consideration of gender by campaign insiders in subsequent election cycles. But gender strategy is likely still a little understood dynamic, as are the particular challenges women who seek different types of political office face.

# Gender and Office Congruency

Women have become increasingly successful in seeking elected office, as this volume and the results of the most recent round of U.S. elections demonstrate. But as we also learn in this text, their success is uneven. We argue here that both office and party matter in thinking through the complexities of women in politics. The specific features of executive offices, particularly the U.S. presidency, present female candidates with significant structural and attitudinal hurdles, while female candidates' party banner lends specific symbolic resonances to candidacies in ways not accounted for when we look only at her gender.

An emerging theory of gender–office congruency contends that certain political offices align more readily with still-existing gender stereotypes, making those offices easier for women to obtain (Rose 2013). Accordingly, voters' beliefs about candidate traits, which have been shown to influence voter choice (Bishin, Stevens, and Wilson 2006; Goren 2002, 2007) could make election to executive offices more challenging for women because those offices are associated in the public's mind with leadership traits more readily attributed to men, such as assertiveness and decisiveness (Alexander and Andersen 1993; Fowler and Lawless 2009; Schaffner 2005). Real or presumed candidate traits may also weigh more heavily in executive office elections. For example, Hayes (2010, p. 7) suggests that because legislators "are not unitary actors, voters may be less concerned with their leadership abilities." Huddy and Terkildsen's (1993) experimental research found that perceived leadership traits were a stronger predictor of voter choice in executive than legislative contests. Moreover, legislative roles may align with female gender because the job is considered collaborative, and the legislator is one of many actors in the chamber. Executive office positions its occupant as the "only" veto authority over a larger, more deliberative legislative body and often oversees security or military authorities (Rose 2013).

For example, governorships could be *more* attainable for women because the policy arenas associated with state executive office involve domestic issues like education and health care with which women are stereotypically thought to be more at home (Falk 2007; Kahn 1996; Schaffner 2005; Witt et al. 1994). But it is also reasonable to hypothesize that winning executive office, such as state governor, is harder for women precisely because of the nature of the role: Executive authority by definition contrasts with deeply entrenched notions of female collaboration and deference. Smith, Paul, and Paul (2007) find much less gender incongruence in experiments presenting women as U.S. Senate candidates than in experiments positing female presidential candidates, despite the fact that increasing percentages of Americans report that they would vote for a female presidential candidate. In short, the emerging evidence suggests that executive office may be less aligned than legislative office with female gender expectations.

Among executive offices, the American presidency presents particular challenges for female candidates. Structurally, history teaches that the office can be reached only by a handful of career paths, but those pathways, including multiterm service in the Senate, in governorships, in the vice presidency, and in the military, have not been as open to women (Lawrence and Rose 2009, chapter 1). The presidency is also among the most "macho" offices imaginable because, as "leader of the free world," the president presides over the world's most formidable military and carries a potential veto power over congressional action. Moreover, attaining the presidency—unless one assumes the office through succession when the sitting president dies or is incapacitated—requires unmatched political ambition. Given the considerable financial and strategic challenges to winning the U.S. presidency, no one who is not deeply ambitious can hope to win the prize. But Western culture has historically treated ambition in women as suspect and even dangerous (Lawrence and Rose 2009, chapter 3).

Indeed, enduring public prejudices form key attitudinal barriers to female presidential candidates in the United States. Overall, the public opinion data reveal a striking and significant dilemma: over the past several decades, increasing numbers of Americans report that they would vote for a woman, *if she were qualified* for the job. What do these responses mean? The very fact that pollsters have phrased the question in this way reveals a presumption that most women are not qualified. Clearly, more is at stake in the mind of the pollster and the voter than the basic constitutional requirements of the job.

The "resonance" model of voting (Iyengar et al. 1997) sheds additional light on those unspoken qualifications. Research indicates that women candidates are generally perceived as more credible on issues stereotypically associated with women's competence in caring, such as education, health care, and protecting the environment; according to this theory, the public may be less accepting of female candidates who venture into "male" turf of national security, crime, and economics (Iyengar et al. 1997; Kahn and Gordon 1997; also see Lynch and Dolan in this volume). The apparent lesson of this research is that women should stick to "their" turf—something a woman running for the White House, especially during a time of war and terrorist threats, simply cannot do.[4]

Therefore, the challenge for female candidates lies in fitting (when possible) the policy issues and duties associated with the particular political offices they seek with deeply held gender stereotypes (Kahn 1996) and establishing "gender issue ownership," using voters' dispositions toward gender as an asset (where possible) rather than a liability (Herrnson, Lay, and Stokes 2003). For a woman seeking the presidency, the considerable challenge is to convince the public that she is indeed "tough enough" for the job while not running afoul of deeply held injunctions against appearing "strident" or emasculating (Jamieson 1995). The literature predicts that, to be successful, a female candidate would need to emphasize masculine traits and themes because, as Duerst-Lahti (2007, p. 91) puts it bluntly, "Women are expected to be feminine, but presidential candidates are judged by the quality of their masculinity." The first woman to achieve the presidency will have successfully strategized within the confines of this complicated double bind.

## Gender and Party in the Presidential Context

This gender strategizing is made more complicated by partisanship: how women establish gender issue ownership as they seek a specific office will also be affected by their party affiliation. Because all candidate messages (both male and female alike) are voiced through a party filter (see Osborn 2012; also Osborn in this volume), the field of women and politics must begin to account for ways women craft gender strategies based not only on the office they seek but also on the party label they bear. As more female candidates for the office of the presidency present themselves, we may well find that Republican women will adopt different gender strategies than Democratic women to satisfy partisan expectations for policy and even perhaps for gender attributes. And given the two-staged process of presidential elections, it stands to reason that female candidates will shape their primary election strategies with the voting base in mind and will adjust that message in the general election as their male counterparts do.

For example, some literature demonstrates that the public assume female politicians to be more liberal than male politicians (Koch 2000). This assumption could create a particular challenge for any woman candidate facing a mixed constituency of voters—and most certainly for a female presidential candidate in a general election. An interesting possibility is that women Democrats are hindered by the double whammy of party–gender ideological assumptions (Democrats are liberal–women are liberal), while Republican women may be helped by gender as a moderating factor in voter assessment during a general election (women may be presumed liberal, but Republicans are not)—though by the same token, these assumptions could be problematic for Republican women courting more conservative voters during primary campaigns.

Again, these patterns are far from certain, and much remains to be discovered through empirical research as more female candidacies materialize. In executive office, we have not seen a systematic accounting of how party interacts with office in the ways that female candidates establish their gender strategy. An intriguing area for further research remains how the party identity of female executive candidates, particularly for the presidency, shapes their gender strategies. In 2008, we saw Hillary Rodham Clinton present herself in pastel pantsuits and launch a "listening tour," while the campaign of vice presidential hopeful Sarah Palin, in contrast, associated her with rural interests by disseminating pictures of the candidate in hunting gear. These differences could of course reflect personal style, but they also reveal underlying realities of each party's base: Democrats appealing to a more urban, broad coalition and Republicans associating more closely with rural interests concerned with local control and personal freedoms. In the end, the female candidate must choose her gender strategy carefully, and she is guided in those decisions by party considerations.

## A Case Study: Clinton versus Palin

Hillary Rodham Clinton's gender strategy in 2008 involved a complicated mix of both feminine and masculine messaging (Lawrence and Rose 2009). In the main, Clinton's campaign took a stance of gender neutrality: "I'm not running because I'm a woman," she would often say. "I'm running because I'm the most qualified candidate." Clinton thus did not run "as a woman," nor did she couch most of her appeals to voters in gendered terms. Yet in particular venues and at particular moments in the campaign—especially in the lead-up to crucial primary contests in which female voters were thought to be decisive—the Clinton campaign deployed more overt appeals to women voters. At other moments, particularly as the close contest between Clinton and Barack Obama wore on well past Super Tuesday and the remaining delegates were to be found in blue-collar states, the campaign veered into heavily masculinized appeals.

One illustration of the more feminine aspects of this strategy is found in the campaign's "Dorothy" ad, produced in mid-December 2007 as the crucial Iowa caucuses approached.[5] The ad begins with a black-and-white photo marked, "Dorothy and Hillary 1948," featuring a toddler Clinton in a bonnet, apparently taking her first baby steps. The ad's audio track features Clinton's mother, Dorothy Rodham, describing her daughter: "What I would like people to know about Hillary is what a good person she is. She never was envious of anybody. She was helpful. And she's continued that with her adult life, with helping other women." At this moment, the words "Hillary's mom lives with her" appear at the foot of the screen in a font that looks handwritten. "She has empathy for other people's unfortunate circumstances," Rodham's voice continues, while the camera cuts to footage of her and her daughter talking and smiling together. "I've always admired that because it isn't always true of people. I think she ought to be elected even if she weren't my daughter."

The campaign made no secret that Dorothy (both the ad and the person) was being deployed to mobilize female voters, particularly older women who, in the words of one reporter, "might feel an emotional bond with Mrs. Clinton—seeing her like a daughter or seeing something of themselves in her" (Healy 2007). Not coincidentally, both Chelsea Clinton and Dorothy Rodham were brought to Iowa on the heels of Oprah Winfrey's high-profile Iowa event on behalf of Barack Obama—part of the Obama team's own explicit effort to win over women voters (Toner 2007).

In vivid contrast to the Dorothy ad, "3:00 a.m." was released in late February, prior to the Texas and Ohio primaries.[6] In this ad a gravelly male voice establishes Clinton's credibility in the arena of national security: "It's 3 a.m. and your children are safe and asleep. But there's a phone in the White House and it's ringing." The narrator continues, "Your vote will decide who answers that call, whether it's someone who already knows the world's leaders, knows the military—someone tested and ready to lead in a dangerous world."

The Clinton campaign's gender strategizing was thus premised on a mix of toughness and feminine appeal. According to internal campaign documents (Green 2008), Clinton's lead consultant, Mark Penn, argued that "most voters in essence see the president as the 'father' of the country.... They do not want someone who will be first mama...[But] they are open to the first father being a woman." Penn's "Overall Strategy for Winning" included themes of "the infusion of a woman and a mothers' sensibilities into a world of war and neglect" (Green 2008). As the campaign wore on, Clinton began telling campaign audiences that "the choice we face" was that "one of us is ready to be commander in chief in a dangerous world" (Healy and Zeleny 2008), repeating on the campaign trail the admonition earlier deployed to call attention to Clinton as the only woman on the presidential stage—"if you can't stand the heat, get out of the kitchen"—but that now carried a more complicated connotation. Clinton's Indiana campaign appearances were widely noted (and, by some, derided) for featuring the candidate in a series of manly postures, including drinking shots with union workers in a local bar.

Viewed in isolation as the nation's first female candidate with a strong chance of winning the White House, Clinton's campaign exhibits a complex gender strategy that mixed claims of gender neutrality with sometimes overt appeals to both stereotypically feminine and masculine traits. Viewed in comparison with another high-profile female candidacy, an even greater range of available gender strategies is revealed.

In an analysis of selected speeches, interviews, and advertisements from the campaigns of Hillary Clinton and Sarah Palin in 2008 (Lawrence and Rose 2013; see also Chapter 5 in this volume), we found clear differences in the way Clinton and Palin presented themselves and their candidacies. Clinton talked much more openly and directly about "women's issues" such as health care and education, while Palin largely avoided these disfavored Republican topics. While Clinton talked about women's equality, sometimes (for select audiences) recalling the unequal playing field she had faced as a young law school graduate or invoking the global struggle for women's rights, Palin rarely if ever addressed the latter and emphasized instead her status as a member of the Title IX generation for whom gender discrimination is "irrelevant." Clinton positioned herself on the equality-based twin platforms of political experience and policy expertise and often deemphasized her own sex, while Palin self-consciously displayed traditional femininity. Often clad in stiletto heels, silk skirts, and a trademark beehive hairdo, Palin embraced that most traditionally feminine justification for power—motherhood—as she showcased her large family, including her infant son, in her campaign appearances. Indeed, in her acceptance speech at the Republican Convention, Palin spent nearly a third of her speaking time introducing her husband and children, implicitly underscoring her values as a conservative woman and symbolically embracing the traditional role of women in the family. She commonly introduced herself to audiences herself by explaining that she "never really set out to be involved in public affairs," and she described herself as having been an "average hockey mom" who went from the PTA to the governorship (Palin 2008). Yet Palin also famously presented herself as an avid, camouflage-draped hunter—a contrast that few Republican voters seemed to have found jarring but that many Democratic voters may have viewed with disdain.

Yet Palin also gestured toward feminine solidarity, at least on one occasion, in terms more stark than Clinton employed. Speaking in California, she invoked the words of former secretary of state Madeleine Albright, the first woman to serve in that office, to suggest that gender loyalty should cross party lines: "there's a place in Hell reserved for women who don't support other women" (Pitney 2008).[7] Palin also overtly highlighted her feminine "difference," perhaps most famously when she called on Clinton's own language to draw attention to her historic role on the Republican Party's ticket, offering to finish the fight Clinton had begun. "It was rightly noted in Denver this week that Hillary left 18 million cracks in the highest, hardest glass ceiling in America," she told the crowd who attended the announcement of her selection, "but it turns out the women of America aren't finished yet, and we can shatter that glass ceiling once and for all" (Eilperin and Kornblut 2008). Defending his running mate's credentials, Republican presidential nominee John McCain burnished Palin's gender qualification during the final presidential debate, announcing that she was "... a role model to women and reformers all over America" (CNN Political Ticker 2008).

In other words, both women ran "as women" by some definition of that phrase, but each emphasized different aspects of gender—their own gender, the gender of voters, and gendered policy issues—in ways that make sense given their different party allegiances. Of course, some of these differences undoubtedly reflect the personalities and life stories of two very different women. Given her own limited time in public office, for example, Palin could not have hoped to have laid claim to the same mantle of "experience" with which Clinton cast her own bid for office. And some contrasts are due to the differences between running for the White House versus occupying second place on a presidential ticket; indeed, significant differences of gender–office congruency would seem to make the vice presidential post, with its "running mate" expectations, somewhat easier for a more traditionally feminine woman to persuasively embody. After all, one does not run independently for the vice presidency but rather is called to service. But the point here is simply that the different expectations of Republican versus Democratic voters opened different avenues of policy emphasis and personal presentation to Palin as a Republican candidate.

In the final analysis, any presidential candidate's gender strategy is likely to be complicated, given the mutual demands today for candidates to display both toughness and some degree of human empathy. As the candidacies of Hillary Clinton and Sarah Palin demonstrate, those strategies can be quite complex and even somewhat contradictory; Palin's pearls and camouflage contrast was at times matched by the Clinton's campaign's allusions to both machismo and motherhood.

It seems premature to predict what kinds of gender strategies will be most successful for candidates of opposing parties seeking the presidency. Ultimately, while toughness is a leading unstated credential for the presidency and Clinton was obliged to demonstrate it, in her particular case it seems to have backfired to some extent because preexisting narratives about her already framed her as overly ambitious (Lawrence and Rose 2009). Though the campaign attempted to create a message conveying both "masculine" strength and "feminine" caring, the balance tipped as the campaign wore on to a much tougher fighter image infused with hypermasculine imagery, leaving us to wonder whether a campaign more grounded in a distinctly feminine voice might have succeeded. Meanwhile, Palin's candidacy raises the question of whether Republican women—particularly of Palin's generation and beyond—will find it possible, as Palin did, to occupy a longer stretch of the gender continuum.

Duerst-Lahti (2006, p. 28) notes that "much of the heat around gender performances, or the way individuals 'do gender,' derives from contests to make one version of gender the hegemonic form, the form that is recognized as right, just, proper, and good. It is the form most able to control all other forms, and therefore it becomes most 'normal.'" In this vein, we suggest that Sarah Palin's entrance onto the national stage did not simply usher another woman to within striking distance of the White House. Palin brought with her an almost utterly different "version of gender" that signals a contemporary struggle for the "proper" articulation of female power. Palin's gender strategy was clearly enormously appealing to some voters, especially social conservatives, who lauded her stand on abortion and her personal decision to carry her Down's syndrome baby to term; and to some Republican men, who could be seen at campaign events carrying signs reading "Palin is a Fox." Yet just as clearly, Palin came in for heavy criticism and negative media coverage (Center for Media and Public Affairs 2008), at least in part, it seems, because of her highly feminine style.

The case of Clinton in 2008, meanwhile, also leaves open a fundamental question of gender strategy: Should she have run more explicitly "as a woman"? Should she have more consistently highlighted her history-making candidacy and what that might mean for American politics? Clinton did not make the case that America needed a woman president, though she did at times suggest that there are hurdles to women who seek that post (see Sheehy 2008). In fact, Clinton tended to raise gender at times and in ways that played right into the news media's obsession with campaign strategy and Clinton's ambition, so that gender talk during campaign 2008 became mostly talk about whether Clinton was benefiting politically from being a woman. Whether the country might benefit from electing a woman was rarely discussed.

## Conclusion: The Future Female Presidency

Our argument here is that scholars should begin to analyze gender strategies more seriously and rigorously and to bring considerations of both office and party to bear. This research seems particularly needed in light of recent election patterns. At the U.S. Senate level, women have been steadily—albeit very slowly—making inroads. As a result of the 2012 election, fully 20 percent of U.S. senators are now women, a historic high (16D; 4R). In contrast, women have struggled to gain a foothold in governors' mansions and have lost ground since reaching nine gubernatorial seats in 2004 and 2007. In 2013, the number of female governors will slip from six to five as a consequence of the 2012 election (1D; 4R).

Though Hillary Rodham Clinton and Sarah Palin, each in her own way, helped clear women's future path to the White House, an opening Michelle Bachmann exploited briefly and haltingly in 2011, female presidential candidates may be few and far between for the foreseeable future. With no women vice presidents or five-star generals and the ranks of women governors and U.S. senators still relatively thin, "...there is no Hillary waiting in the wings. Except, of course, Hillary" (Zernike 2008). As we consider the future candidacies that may emerge, however, we do well to remember that the candidate and her context profoundly affect any woman's race for the White House. The highly gendered aspects of the presidency and the particular opportunities and constraints of party matter, and as more female candidacies materialize we continue to learn how.

In all, the candidacy of Hillary Clinton, or of any female presidential hopeful, must be understood against a constellation of variables that shape the political opportunity structure and the candidate's strategic choices. Clinton's run for the White House was indelibly shaped not only by society's deeply held gender stereotypes and biases but also by her particular gender strategy, which itself was indelibly shaped by the party banner she carried. Given the backdrop of androcentric notions of the presidency, gender strategy and gender–office congruency loom as crucial but underexplored aspects of how women run for high office. In a very real sense, perhaps the biggest lesson of Clinton's 2008 quest for the White House—and our analysis of it—was to prove that "nobody knew how to run a woman as leader of the free world" (Sheehy 2008).

## Notes

1. Stephanie Condon. 2011. "GOP Debate Moderators Defend 'Submissive' Question Aimed at Bachmann." *CBS News.* August 12. http://www.cbsnews.com/8301-503544_162-20091816-503544.html.

2. Rachel Weiner. 2011. "Bachmann Claimed HPV Vaccine Might Cause 'Mental Retardation.'" *Washington Post Online.* September 13. http://www.washingtonpost.com/blogs/the-fix/post/michele-bachmann-continues-perry-attack-claims-hpv-vaccine-might-cause-mental-retardation/2011/09/13/gIQAbJBcPK_blog.html (November 12, 2012).

3. Condon 2011.

4. Interestingly, recent research has begun to challenge assumptions about "male" and "female" issues. Bystrom, for instance, finds that "a 1999 study of spot ads from the 1996 mixed-gender U.S. Senate and gubernatorial races found a new trend emerging: females stressed male traits such as toughness even more than male candidates, ran more negative ads, and actually stressed warmth and compassion less than male candidates" (102).

5. Kate Phillips. 2007. "Clinton Ad: Dorothy Speaks." *New York Times.* December 13. http://thecaucus.blogs.nytimes.com/2007/12/13/clinton-ad-dorothy-speaks/ (accessed March 8, 2013).

6. Hillaryclinton.com. 2007. "Hillary's Mom Ad." December 13. http://www.youtube.com/watch?v=FSlmpIFr2wQ (accessed March 12, 2013).

7. Much was made in the media of the observation that Palin learned of the Albright quote by reading it from her Starbucks cup and that she misquoted the former secretary of state, who said, "There's a place in Hell reserved for women who don't *help* other women" (Pitney 2008).

# 5

# Hillary Rodham Clinton: A Case Study in the Rhetoric of Female Political Figures

MOANA VERCOE, RANDALL GONZALEZ, AND JEAN REITH SCHROEDEL

> ...I'm always rather nervous about how you talk about women who are active in politics, whether they want to be talked about as women or as politicians, but I want you to know that we are grateful to have you as both today.
>
> —John Fitzgerald Kennedy remarks to a
> U.N. Delegation of Women, December 11, 1961

> Words have a funny way of trapping our minds on the way to our tongues, but they are a necessary means even in this multi-media age for attempting to come to grasps with some of the inarticulate maybe even inarticulable things that we're feeling.
> —Hillary Rodham Clinton, Wellesley College Commencement Address,
> May 30, 1969

> ...In democracies in the television age, female leaders also have to navigate public prejudices—and these make democratic politics far more challenging for a woman than for a man.
> —Nicholas D. Kristof, *New York Times*, February 10, 2008

From student body leader in the late 1960s to First Lady of Arkansas and in the White House, senator from New York, presidential candidate, and finally secretary of state, Hillary Rodham Clinton's life has been one of firsts. Clinton's long public career can be viewed as reflecting both the promise and limitations of second-wave feminism. While Clinton is an extraordinary individual, her four-decade-long career sheds light on how women must negotiate an often hostile political landscape. As amplified in several chapters in this volume, women in public life face a double bind in that they must balance perceptions of warmth and competence, often viewed as feminine, and masculine qualities reflected in communalism and agentism (the orientation toward power versus the orientation toward the group) in a way that is not expected of men (Eagly 1987, 1997; Eagly, Wood, and Diekman 2000; McGinley 2009).

At the time when Clinton graduated from college, women occupied very few elected political positions. Only 2 percent of the members of Congress were female, less than 5 percent of state legislators were women, and several states did not even have a single woman serving in any elected office. These numbers gradually increased throughout the 1970s and 1980s. A sharp upswing in the numbers of women running for and elected to office in 1992, the vaunted "year of the woman," led many to think we had entered a new era. The optimism evaporated with a return to incremental gains in the rest of the 1990s, followed by a plateau and then stagnation during the first decade of the 2000s, when women's representation in state legislatures hit a high of just under a quarter female before dropping slightly. At this time, 12 percent of the country's governors are women, as are 12 percent of mayors in the nation's 100 largest cities, and after the 2012 elections for the first time 18 percent of the membership of Congress are female (Center for the American Woman and Politics 2012a, 2012b, 2012c, 2012d).

In this chapter, we begin by tracing the arc of Clinton's public career, highlighting ways that she has tried to negotiate gender expectations while pursuing an active professional and political career. Then we turn to an in-depth analysis of how these competing demands are reflected in her public discourse—from her 1969 commencement address at Wellesley College to her statements as secretary of state up to the 2012 election. Using textual analysis, we plot strategies employed by Clinton that are reflected in her rhetoric over a forty-year period in relation to the changing political context in which she operated. We pay particular attention to her use of stereotypical masculine and feminine rhetorical phrasing (e.g., communal and agentic language). We believe that the study of her rhetoric not only provides insights into her extraordinary career but also illuminates the gendered nature of political discourse across time.

## Clinton's Career: Activism While Negotiating Gender Expectations

Although Clinton was raised in a staunch Republican family and as a high school student campaigned for the 1964 Republican presidential candidate Barry Goldwater, she also reached adulthood at the height of the second wave of the women's movement. During her first year at Wellesley College in 1965, Clinton served as president of the Young Republicans, but by her junior year she was campaigning for Democratic presidential challenger Eugene McCarthy. Following Martin Luther King, Jr.'s assassination, Clinton organized a two-day student strike and worked with black students to pressure the administration to recruit more African American students and faculty. In 1969, the student body lobbied for Clinton to become the first student in Wellesley's history to give the commencement address (Gerth and Van Natta 2007).

This accolade brought Clinton her first taste of national attention when she appeared on a nationally syndicated talk show and was featured in *Life* magazine.

While at Yale Law School, Clinton worked at a public interest law firm associated with the Children's Defense Fund, a nonprofit child advocacy organization, and interned for the U.S. Senate Subcommittee on Migratory Labor researching housing, health, and education issues as well as working on several political campaigns (Bernstein 2007; Gerth and Van Natta 2007). Following graduation, Clinton took a position as staff attorney for the Children's Defense Fund, joined the Richard Nixon impeachment inquiry staff advising the House Judiciary Committee, and published several well-regarded law journal articles of children's issues, all of which led historian Garry Wills (1992) subsequently to describe her as "one of the most important scholar-activists of the last two decades."

## The Arkansas Years

After moving to Arkansas and getting married, Clinton taught at the University of Arkansas Law School, became a partner in the Rose Law Firm, and was appointed by President Jimmy Carter to the board of directors of the Legal Services Corporation, a nonprofit organization that promotes legal assistance for low-income people. Clinton's decision to keep her maiden name Rodham drew criticism during her husband's 1978 Arkansas gubernatorial campaign (Frandina 2009), and her choice of whether or not to use her maiden name in defining herself in the public arena continues to draw scrutiny from some (Associated Press 2007; Kelly 1993; Preston 2006). It became an issue in Bill Clinton's 1980 failed reelection bid when his opponent accused the couple of undermining traditional family values. To defuse critics, she dropped Rodham during Bill Clinton's successful 1982 gubernatorial campaign. As First Lady of Arkansas, Clinton promoted "activist" state programs in childcare, health, and education (Wills 1992). This balancing of feminist leanings, professional aspirations, and political realism worked, and Clinton subsequently was named Arkansas' Woman of the Year in 1983 and Arkansas' Young Mother of the Year in 1984 (National Archives and Records Administration 1994), in addition to twice being placed by the *National Law Review* on its list of "The 100 Most Influential Lawyers in America" (Gerth and Van Natta 2007: 85).

## The White House Years

Clinton's activism as First Lady of Arkansas and her husband's 1992 presidential campaign claim that voters were getting "two for one" (Kiely 2008) were clear signals that she was going to be a political force in the White House. This perception was reinforced by Clinton's immediate decision to take an office in the West Wing, which housed the president's staff, rather than in the East Wing where previous First Ladies located their offices (Burrell 1997: 171–172). Instead of solely fulfilling the public hostess role expected of First Ladies, Clinton clearly functioned as a trusted advisor to the president. She was not the only First Lady to fill this sort of role, but she was also much more open about her policy role than previous First Ladies (Black 2001).[1] Her highest-profile policy position, as head of the Task Force on National Health Care Reform, initially was given high marks, but those plummeted after opponents launched a massive public relations assault on the proposal. (That assessment is likely to be revised upward as historians come to view the reforms proposed by Clinton as an important precursor to the Barack Obama Administration's Affordable Care Act.) Throughout her tenure as First Lady of the United States, Clinton not only continued to be a strong voice for children[2] but also became an outspoken women's rights advocate for the first time after the failure of health-care reform. In the aftermath of this policy failure, Clinton began to travel abroad extensively[3] and strongly argued that "human rights are women's rights and women's rights are human rights" (Healy 2007). At the 1995 United Nations Conference on Women in Beijing, she gave a powerful speech attacking the many forms of violence that women and girls face throughout the world and contending that women's rights are an essential component of human rights (Burrell 1997: 176).

From the beginning of her time in the White House, Clinton's nontraditional approach to her role as First Lady generated criticism.[4] One needs to think only of the stir created by her offhand comment made during her husband's 1992 presidential campaign that "I suppose I could have stayed home and baked cookies and had teas, but what I decided to do was to fulfill my profession which I entered before my husband was in public life." Clinton was pilloried as denigrating stay-at-home-wives and mothers (Bernstein 2007: 109). She also had to endure heavy criticism for investments she and her husband made in a real estate ventured called Whitewater; for the suicide death of friend, former law partner, and Deputy White House Counsel Vincent Foster; and for the decision to stand by her husband after his philandering became public. Yet Clinton persevered and then confounded her critics by moving her legal residence to New York and running for the Senate during her husband's waning days in the Oval Office.

## Hillary's Senate Career

Despite being labeled a carpetbagger, a derogatory term originally describing those from northern states who moved to the South after the Civil War to exploit the opportunities of Reconstruction, Clinton was elected to the Senate in 2000 with 55 percent of the vote. Although she had not previously lived in New York, she built a base of support during her Senate campaign by visiting every county in the state and engaging small groups in a "listening tour" (Gerth and Van Natta 2007: 204). Upon entering the Senate, Clinton also dampened down fears of Senate colleagues that she was a radical feminist through actions such as getting them coffee at Democratic caucus meetings (Barone and Cohen 2007: 1130) and being a regular attendee at the Senate Prayer Breakfast (Bernstein 2007: 548). After the September 11 attacks in 2001, Clinton worked with New York's senior senator, Charles Schumer, to obtain funding for the recovery effort. Her leadership in advocating for 9/11 first responders resulted in investigations into the long-term health implications of surviving the attacks on the World Trade Center (Gerth and Van Natta 2007: 349).

During her first term, Clinton not only worked hard to master the nuances of New York state politics but also earned kudos for being a "work horse" rather than a "show horse" in the Senate. In spite of the track record she earned during her first term, her opponent in her 2006 reelection campaign, John Spencer, tried to discredit her by charging that she had undergone cosmetic surgery. Clinton's response was to laugh and suggest that reporters look closely at her face to see if they could see any scars (Barone and Cohen 2007: 1132). Clinton was returned to the Senate with 67 percent of the vote in 2006, carrying all but four of New York's sixty-two counties and reinforcing the inappropriateness of suggesting plastic surgery as a criterion for judging the performance of anyone in elected office, let alone someone with her record. Clinton's legislative history includes measures to improve prescription drug safety for children, support for foster and adoptive families, and increased benefits for military families. Her efforts on the Senate Armed Services Committee led Republican Senator Lindsey Graham of South Carolina to describe Clinton as "…very reasonable" on defense issues (Barone and Cohen 2007: 1130).

## Running for President

Few were surprised when Clinton announced her intention to run as a presidential candidate in January 2007. Throughout the first half of that year, she was the clear front runner, leading in fundraising and the opinion polls of likely Democratic voters. However, the race tightened in fall 2007, and by early 2008 Clinton had fallen behind Obama in the polls. Although there are many possible reasons Obama prevailed rather than Clinton, there is absolutely no disputing that Clinton was subjected to an unprecedented degree of hostile and sexist attacks during the campaign that came from both the right and the left (Lawrence and Rose 2011; Uscinski and Goren 2011). Moreover, when it began to appear as if Clinton might not gain the Democratic nomination, she was pressured to prematurely withdraw her candidacy and was subsequently criticized for failing to immediately support Obama (Jaffe 2008). In short, Clinton was chastised for behaving just like an ambitious politician and fighting to the end, something that is viewed positively as "having fire in his belly" when the candidate is a man but is unseemly in a woman.

## Serving as Secretary of State

Although Obama and Clinton were fierce competitors during the primary season, Obama clearly had developed respect for Clinton's expertise and political instincts, and he asked her to become secretary of state less than a week after he was elected. Clinton described her decision to accept the appointment thusly: "I'm pretty old-fashioned and it's just who I am. So at the end of the day, when your president asks you to serve, you say yes, if you can" (Barr 2009). And it does not seem that Obama's respect for Clinton was misplaced as she has proven to be an innovative leader of the State Department. For example, few people are aware of the existence of the Quadrennial Diplomacy and Development Review, a blueprint for elevating American civilian power to advance national interests and better partner with the U.S. military (LaFranchi 2010; Lemmon 2011), which Clinton instituted shortly after taking office. This may be her most lasting State Department legacy.[5] Prior to her tenure, the State Department had lacked a procedure for regularly reviewing its priorities, policies, and programs. Central to Clinton's approach is humanitarianism and human rights. Clinton's vision of these clearly encompasses advocating on behalf of women, and she made women's issues a central component of U.S. foreign policy by creating a new role for a U.S. ambassador-at-large for global women's issues. And in late 2011, in a speech before the United Nations Human Rights Council, Clinton stated unequivocally that "gay rights are human rights" (BBC News Online). During the Arab Spring and the persistent turmoil throughout the Middle East, Clinton has continued to be a strong voice for human rights. Under her leadership the State Department has expanded its use of social media to empower and provide support to citizen protesters (Calabresi 2011), but this has not come at the expense of traditional diplomacy. By mid-2012, Clinton has set a new record for the number of secretary of state trips to foreign countries (Klapper and Lee 2012).

While not opposed to the strategic use of military power—as is evident in her presence as the only woman in the White House picture of those involved in observing the mission to take out Osama bin Laden—Clinton has sought to position the United States as a "smart power," willing to use force when necessary but not as the dominant means of pursuing foreign policy goals (Calabresi 2011).

## Hillary Clinton: The Case of a Woman in Politics

Given the many and varied political and leadership roles she has taken and aspired to over the span of her career, Hillary Clinton offers a case study of women's political leadership. Case studies are generally an accepted methodological choice for research when the subject under review is either new or had previously been unavailable to researchers. Clinton meets both of these criteria because of the unprecedented nature of her achievements as well as the documentation of them. From her 1969 commencement address onward, many of her speeches have been recorded. The accessibility of Clinton's rhetoric over time allows for the intensive examination of an individual, including developmental factors, in relation to its context that characterize a case study (Flyvberg 2011). In this instance, the examination focuses on the development of an individual in relation to a dynamic and often hostile political context. By focusing on her rhetoric we can examine the way Clinton used language in negotiating the changing political landscape with its inherent expectations of women in power over time.

## Gender Stereotypes

Over the past four decades, scholars have sought to understand how gender as a social construct affects all aspects of human life. *Gender* encompasses the ways that social roles, behaviors, and character traits are interpreted as appropriate or inappropriate based on the biological sex of the individual. As Duerst-Lahti (1997: 12) notes, gender is "*relational*: To understand feminine requires understanding masculine." With respect to this project, two areas of gender-related research are particularly relevant: (1) political science research on the relationship between gender stereotypes and leadership; and (2) social psychology research on gender, language, and perceptions of leadership ability.

## Gender Stereotypes and Leadership Assessments

Political scientists have identified two types of gender stereotypes that affect male and female leaders: belief stereotypes and trait-based stereotypes. The first refers to stereotypes about the ideology and issue stances of individuals with women in general being viewed as more liberal than men and as better able to handle issues such as education, health, and social welfare but as less capable of handling foreign affairs, crime, the economy, and defense (Dolan 1998; Huddy and Terkildsen 1993a; Koch 2000, 2002; Matland and King 2002). The second, trait-based stereotypes, is the assumption that women are more compassionate, trustworthy, willing to compromise, and empathetic but that men are stronger leaders and are more assertive, active, and self-confident (Burrell 1996; Huddy and Terkildsen 1993a; Matland and King 2002). A more in-depth analysis of the impact of attitudes toward women on voter behavior is provided by Dolan and Lynch in Chapter 3. Although gender stereotypes do occasionally advantage women, they generally have been found to make it more difficult for women to gain high political office, because those are thought to require more of the "masculine" issue competencies and character traits (Fox and Oxley 2003; Huddy and Terkildsen 1993b).

Within social psychology, leadership studies are an important subfield of research, some of which focuses on the relationship between trait-based stereotypes and perceptions of leadership. While both warmth and competence are generally viewed as positive attributes in a leader, these evaluations are influenced by gender stereotypes. Male leaders almost always gain an advantage by getting high marks on both of these dimensions. Competent females, however, often receive lower evaluations because competence among women can be perceived as coldness, which violates the gender stereotype requiring women to be warm (Cutler 2002; Fiske et. al. 1999, 2002).[6] This is compounded by the findings of experimental studies combining cognitive psychology and political science showing that when evaluating candidates on characteristics unrelated to job performance, such as facial features, female candidates are judged as less mature and less competent than their male counterparts (Herrick et al. 2012; Todorov et al., 2005). This research suggests that women with leadership ambitions must try to find a means of conveying the gender-expected warmth while at the same time overcoming perceptions of lesser maturity and competence without projecting coldness (Eagly and Carli 2007: 83–118; O'Neill and O'Reilly 2011; Rosette and Tost 2010).

## The Importance of Rhetoric in Assessing Leaders

Most people do not have opportunities to directly observe leaders carrying out their tasks, so their evaluations of leadership ability must be based on other criteria. Public speeches, debates, and other media engagements are the predominant means of indirectly assessing leadership potential and ability (Shamir 1995). There is an inherent subjectivity in evaluations of the public utterances of leaders because their language is mediated by followers' perceptions and attributions, with the most effective leaders being labeled as "charismatic" (Bligh, Kohles, and Meindl 2004). Moreover, charisma is an ambiguous concept, first identified by Weber (1947: 333) as "a certain quality of an individual personality, by virtue of which he is set apart from ordinary people and treated as endowed with supernatural, superhuman, or at least exceptional powers or qualities."

Researchers have sought to "demystify" charismatic leadership by identifying the types of rhetoric most often associated with leaders being labeled as charismatic (Emrich et al. 2001; Schroedel et al. 2013; Seyranian and Bligh 2008; Shamir, House, and Arthur 1993). Visionary rhetoric, where the leader creates a linkage between core aspects of his or her vision and core aspects of followers' self-concepts, has been found to be positively associated with the leader being labeled as charismatic. Somewhat surprisingly, there has been only minimal research on gender and charisma (Bligh et al. 2010). This is interesting given that charismatic constructs are often labeled as *feminine* or *masculine* based on their relationship to gender trait characteristics. Yet we would strongly suggest that the types of charismatic constructs that are labeled as feminine and masculine are closely tied to the issues and character traits typically associated with women and men.

## Feminine Constructs

Communal constructs are rhetorical phrases that enhance the sense that the speaker and listeners are part of the same community. These constructs strengthen collective identity. They are gendered as feminine because they stress the empathetic bonds between the speaker and the audience. The four communal rhetorical constructs are as follows:

a. *Collective focus* language builds consensus and trust. It affirms a shared social identity (Hogg, Hains, and Mason 1998). One way of measuring this is through the use of words such as *humanity* and *team*.
b. *Followers' worth* involves language that demonstrates the leader's confidence in her or his followers and enhances their sense of efficacy (House, Spangler, and Woycke 1991). Words that praise the audience as well as terms that are associated positive emotional states are included by this construct.
c. *A leader's similarity to followers* is enhanced by the use of language that highlights her or his status as a member of the same in-group as the followers (Bligh, Kohles, and Meindl 2004). This is measured by the use of language that focuses on familiarity with followers and builds rapport while downplaying individual differences.
d. *Cooperation* language signals commitment to a shared vision and collective outcomes. The use of this type of language is considered part of the feminine leadership ethic (Marshall 1993; Rosenthal 2000). Words denoting friendship, teamwork, and self-sacrifice are included in this construct.

## Masculine Constructs

The agentic charismatic constructs emphasize character traits that have been strongly associated with male leaders, such as strength, competence, and decisiveness. The agentic constructs fall into three general categories:

a. *Action*-oriented rhetoric is a bold and purposeful articulation of a vision. It often involves a call to action (Conger 1991). Words reflecting movement, speed, and physical processes are associated with this construct.
b. *Adversity* rhetoric typically involves a call to rebel against conditions that are presented as intolerable and that the leader, with the support of followers, will overcome (Conger 1991). Words describing situations as unacceptable typify this construct.
c. *Competition* rhetoric goes beyond calls to action and involves goal direction. Dominance and force exemplify this masculine leadership construct (Marshall 1993; Rosenthal 2000), which is measured by language associated with personal triumph, excess energy, and resistance.

A fuller description of each construct and more examples of the words that typify each are included in Appendix A.

# Methodology

## Sample

Our primary data set is composed of nearly 700 speeches given and statements made by Clinton from her 1969 commencement address at Wellesley College through to the November 6, 2012, election. To focus on prepared statements where Clinton is presenting herself to a larger audience rather than interacting with one or more individuals, the data set deliberately excludes interviews. Using her graduation from college as our starting point, the data set spans six key periods of her political development and public engagement: before becoming First Lady of Arkansas; First Lady of Arkansas; First Lady of the United States; senator of New York; presidential hopeful in the 2008 primaries; and secretary of state.

## Computer-Aided Content Analysis

Using computer-aided content analysis allows us to examine Clinton in her own words and analyze choices made in her rhetoric in relation to the political context. The goal of content analysis is to make inferences from texts to context objectively and systematically (Krippendorff 1980; Neuendorf 2002). Computer-aided content analysis permits examination of subtleties within a text that might not be evident to even the most sophisticated and informed reader without the bias that can result "when something as volatile and emotional as politics is examined by something as volatile and emotional as a human being" (Hart 1984: 101). Additionally, distinguishing rhetorical style from the subject matter of particular speeches allows the identification of trends in linguistic orientation over time. Inherent in this approach is the assumption that words matter and the choice of words in framing an argument may reveal as much about the speaker as might the argument itself.[7] A brief description of each construct and sample words are included in Appendix A.

A possible limitation of this type of textual analysis is that it conflates word frequency with salience—it assumes that the frequency of word use reflects their importance. This limitation is not a major factor in studying Clinton's use of agentic and communal rhetorical constructs over time. A more important limitation is that it analyzes texts independent of context. This is of greater concern due to the range of roles played by Clinton over time, the variety of topics on which she has spoken, and differences in the audiences she has addressed. We counter this challenge by considering the context within which she spoke in our analyses.

In examining changes in Clinton's rhetoric over time, we looked at both her position in the political system and the issues under discussion. We compared the seven rhetorical constructs over the aforementioned six time periods, using the 1969 Wellesley Commencement Address as our starting point. Acknowledging that the prevalence of masculine and feminine charismatic constructs may vary according to the subject matter of a speech and the context, we divided the statements analyzed into three masculine and five feminine issue domains and two gender-neutral issue domains. The topics included in the feminine issue domain were women's issues, children and families, health issues, education, and human rights. The masculine issue domain included commerce, defense, and international relations. We also identified two gender-neutral categories. The first category is composed of topics such as climate control, history, and American heritage, which are equally the domain of men and women. The second we labeled as inspirational and include commencement speeches (aside from the Wellesley Address) and statements to State Department staff and families.

# Results

The means, standard deviations, and correlations for the rhetorical constructs under examination are provided in Table 5.1. Although the four feminine rhetorical constructs correlate positively with each other and negatively with the masculine construct of action, the variables do not breakdown along strictly gendered lines, suggesting a more complex interplay between gender expectations and Clinton's use of language over time and across issues. Table 5.2 breaks down the statements analyzed by period and the gendered nature of the subject matter. During Clinton's years in the White House, over half of her speeches addressed topics that can be classified as feminine in orientation, such as adoption, health, and education. This proportion has progressively decreased throughout her career, and as secretary of state approximately two-thirds her statements relate to commerce, international relations, conflict, and defense, which are more masculine in orientation.

Given the change in the gender nature of the issues addressed by Clinton, it might be expected that her rhetoric changed over time to favor the masculine aspects of charisma; however, this has not been the case. We used pairwise t-tests (a statistical technique that determines if a data pair differs from each other in a significant way), that compare the average use of a particular rhetorical construct, to identify changes in Clinton's use of the seven rhetorical constructs over time. Table 5.3 compares the means of each construct from 1969 to November 2012. Due to data availability, the analysis focuses on her time in the White House as First Lady and beyond. Over time, there were no significant changes in Clinton's use of *Adversity* and *Similarity to Followers*. Clinton has not employed the mechanisms that unite people through the feminine construct of similarity and the masculine construct of common challenges differentially in negotiating her various leadership roles and the expectations of women in power.

Interestingly, over time and as she has become more involved in stereotypically male political and issue domains—as presidential candidate and as secretary of state—Clinton has used more of the feminine charismatic rhetorical constructs and less of the masculine. *Collective Focus* has steadily increased; *Similarity to Followers*

*Table 5.1* **Means, Standard Deviations, and Correlations for Clinton's Language**

| | Mean (s.d.) | Collective Focus | Followers' Worth | Similarity to Followers | Cooperation | Action | Adversity |
|---|---|---|---|---|---|---|---|
| | | | | Correlations | | | |
| Collective Focus | 8.89 (3.59) | | | | | | |
| Followers' Worth | 6.45 (3.22) | 0.057 | | | | | |
| Similarity to Followers | 2.81 (2.17) | 0.069 | 0.011 | | | | |
| Cooperation | 6.18 (4.51) | 0.190** | 0.171** | 0.186** | | | |
| Action | 2.64 (2.30) | −0.199** | −0.037 | −0.105** | −0.088 | | |
| Adversity | 3.48 (3.36) | −0.069 | 0.009 | 0.030 | 0.045 | −0.066 | |
| Competition | 3.77 (3.05) | 0.075 | −1.000* | 0.137** | 0.064 | -0.054 | 0.307** |

$N = 671$. $^*p < 0.05$; $^{**}p < 0.01$.

*Table 5.2* **Breakdown of Statements Analyzed by Period and Subject Category**

| | Arkansas | White House | Senate | Campaign | State Department |
|---|---|---|---|---|---|
| Commencement | | 4% | 19% | 29% | 13% |
| Feminine | 100% | 59% | 31% | 15% | 14% |
| Masculine | | 27% | 38% | 43% | 66% |
| Indeterminate | | 10% | 13% | 13% | 6% |
| Total | 4 | 239 | 16 | 84 | 299 |

dipped during her time in Senate but has subsequently increased; and after showing little change *Cooperation* has increased markedly during her time as secretary of state. In contrast, Clinton's use of the masculine aspects of charismatic rhetoric has decreased. Her use of the rhetoric of *Competition* peaked during her time in Senate, and *Action*-oriented language has decreased in frequency since Clinton became

*Table 5.3* **Comparison of Means and Standard Deviations of Rhetorical Elements over Time**

| | Wellesley | Arkansas | White House | Senate | Campaign | State Department |
|---|---|---|---|---|---|---|
| Collective Focus | 5.14 | 7.18 | 8.25 (3.40) | 8.81 (4.37) | 9.40 (5.99) | 9.24 (3.66) |
| Followers' Worth | 8.98 | 7.92 | 6.09 (2.53) | 5.24 (2.90) | 5.89 (3.64) | 6.96 (3.53) |
| Similarity to Followers | 1.25 | 2.21 | 2.41 (1.65) | 1.53 (1.20) | 2.93 (2.43) | 3.16 (2.41) |
| Cooperation | 4.05 | 4.20 | 4.18 (2.43) | 4.51 (2.05) | 4.20 (2.66) | 8.44 (5.21) |
| Action | 1.25 | 1.95 | 2.25 (1.68) | 3.69 (2.82) | 4.06 (2.96) | 2.50 (2.33) |
| Adversity | 6.73 | 5.68 | 3.36 (3.24) | 5.25 (2.91) | 3.57 (2.25) | 3.44 (3.70) |
| Competition | 2.00 | 2.31 | 2.95 (2.39) | 5.74 (3.84) | 4.62 (3.20) | 4.08 (3.27)* |
| Number of Speeches | 1 | 4 | 239 | 16 | 84 | 299 |

*$p < 0.05$; **$p < 0.01$.

secretary of state. Bligh et al. (2004) show that Clinton's use of the *Action* rhetorical construct in the 2008 presidential primaries did not differ significantly from Barack Obama or Mitt Romney's use of that construct. They further demonstrate that when compared with the language used by Obama, John McCain, and Romney in the primaries Clinton did not score significantly higher on the feminine constructs than her male counterparts and was outscored by Obama on both *Collective Focus* and *Followers' Worth*. Thus, it may be that Clinton responded to the context of contestation in the primaries by adjusting the balance of her rhetoric.

In examining Clinton's rhetoric in relation to issues that are generally gender stereotyped, we again used pairwise t-tests to compare the means of the seven charismatic constructs according to subject matter. This allows for a more nuanced analysis of Clinton's negotiation of gender in language and context. Within the data set, approximately one-third of the statements relate to the stereotypically feminine issues of children, families, health, education, and human rights. Almost half of the data set relates to the stereotypically masculine issues of business, international relations, and conflict, with the majority of these coming in the latter periods of Clinton's career. The remaining statements are split between inspirational statements made at commencements or to staff and family members and those that are gender neutral and include topics such as climate change, history, and heritage.

*Table 5.4* **Comparing Means and Standard Deviations of Rhetorical Elements across Issues**

|  | *Inspirational* | *Feminine* | *Masculine* | *Indeterminate* |
|---|---|---|---|---|
| Collective Focus | 9.97 (6.12) | 8.24 (3.38) | 9.05 (3.65) | 8.92 (3.73) |
|  | ** |  |  |  |
| Followers' Worth | 6.45 (2.84) | 6.14 (2.53) | 7.35 (5.46) | 7.92 (5.59) |
| Similarity to Followers | 2.27 (1.85) | 2.27 (1.91) | 3.06 (2.40) | 2.50 (2.01) |
| Cooperation | 5.15 (2.89) | 4.58 (2.80) | 7.72 (5.46) | 5.19 (2.87) |
| Action | 3.47 (2.36) | 2.43 (1.83) | 2.54 (2.57) | 2.78 (1.20) |
| Adversity | 2.66 (1.86) | 3.65 (3.74) | 3.51 (3.43) | 3.80 (2.98) |
| Competition | 3.26 (2.37) | 3.28 (2.74) | 4.02 (3.23) | 3.91 (3.60) |
| Number of Speeches | 81 | 205 | 301 | 57 |

$^*p < 0.05$; $^{**}p < 0.01$.

The results of this analysis of speeches according to the gendered breakdown of the issues covered are shown in Table 5.4.

While we maintain that the gendered charismatic constructs are tied closely to issues and character traits, Clinton shows how fluid these ties can be when navigated by a skilled leader and communicator. Although there is no significant difference in the usage of the *Action, Adversity,* and *Followers' Worth* rhetorical constructs, it is interesting to note that the lowest average scores for *Followers' Worth* occur in the feminine issue category. *Similarity to Followers,* another feminine rhetorical construct, is significantly higher for masculine issues than for either feminine issues or inspirational statements, as is *Cooperation.* For each of the stereotypically feminine rhetorical constructs, the lowest average is recorded in a feminine issue category. The only masculine rhetorical construct with a significant difference between issue categories is *Competition,* which is higher for masculine issues than feminine issues.

These results suggest that Clinton employs the masculine rhetorical structure of *Competition* according to traditional expectations in relation to gendered issue areas—highlighting conflict when discussing stereotypically masculine issues and downplaying it in stereotypically feminine domains. However, she deviates from traditional expectation in her use of the feminine rhetorical structures. Clinton uses feminine aspects of charisma more than masculine ones in speaking about stereotypically masculine issues. She brings the strengths of both masculine and feminine charisma to these statements. This counterintuitive result validates the choice of single rather than composite measures in exploring Clinton's use of gender in her rhetoric, since, like her career, her rhetoric does not follow established or expected patterns.

## Discussion and Conclusion

In examining Clinton's rhetoric during the 2008 presidential primaries, Bligh et al. (2010: 18) conceived of her voice as "the particular leadership style expressed in Clinton's speeches" and demonstrated her manipulation of masculine and feminine charismatic constructs over the course of the primaries. They concluded that they could not sufficiently assess if Clinton had found her voice during the primaries. In examining Clinton's rhetoric, "her voice" as it may be, over a longer period, we sought to examine her development as a charismatic and unprecedented woman leader over time, according to her own words. In her confirmation hearings before the Senate Foreign Relations Committee on January 13, 2009, Clinton expressed her philosophy as the nominated secretary of state:

> I believe that American leadership has been wanting, but is still wanted. We must use what has been called "smart power": the full range of tools at our disposal—diplomatic, economic, military, political, legal, and cultural—picking the right tool, or combination of tools, for each situation.

Although she was speaking about the role of American leadership in the international system at a particular point of time, Clinton's words can be seen as reflecting part of her own leadership philosophy. Throughout her political career and in the various roles in which she has served, Clinton has used the full range of tools at her disposal. We found changes in her rhetoric over time and in response to the political context and her subject matter. The balancing between masculine and feminine charismatic constructs across issue areas we found underscores how Clinton demonstrates that "to understand feminine is to understand masculine" (Duerst-Lahti 1997: 12). Documenting Clinton's understanding and mastery of gendered rhetorical constructs challenges stereotypes and reveals that the development of a voice, while fluid in using gendered language in unexpected ways, remains distinctively feminine and in control.

# Appendix A: Overview of Charismatic Structures

| Construct | Description | Sample Words |
|---|---|---|
| Collective Focus | Singular nouns connoting plurality that function to decrease specificity, reflecting a dependence on categorical modes of thought. Includes social groupings, task groups, and geographical entities. | Crowd, choir, team, humanity, army, congress, legislature, staff, county, world, kingdom, republic |
| Follower's Worth | Affirmations of a person, group, or abstract entity. | Dear, delightful, witty, mighty, handsome, beautiful, shred, bright, vigilant, reasonable, successful, conscientious, renowned, faithful, good, noble |
| Similarity to Followers | Attitudinal similarities among groups of people. Includes terms of affinity, assent, deference and identity. | Congenial, camaraderie, companion, approve, vouch, tolerance, willing, consensus, resemble, equivalent |
| Cooperation | Behavioral interactions among people that often result in group outcomes. Includes relationships from formal work and informal associations to more intimate interactions, job-related tasks, personal involvement, and self-denial. | Unions, schoolmates, caucus, chum, partner, cronies, sisterhood, friendship, consolidate, mediate, alignment, network, detente, exchange, public-spirited, care-taking, self-sacrifice, teamwork, sharing, contribute |
| Action | Human movement, physical processes, journeys, speed, and modes of transit. | Bustle, job, lurch, leap, circulate, momentum, revolve, twist, barnstorm, jaunt, wandering, travels, lickety-split, nimble, zip, ride, fly, glide, swim |

| Construct | Description | Sample Words |
|-----------|-------------|--------------|
| Adversity | Natural disasters, hostile actions, censurable human behavior, unsavory political outcomes, and human fears. | Earthquake, starvation, killers, bankruptcy, enemies, vices, infidelity, despots, betrayal, injustices, exploitation, grief, death |
| Competition | Human competition and forceful action including physical energy, social domination, and goal-directedness. Includes words associated with personal triumph excess human energy, disassembly, and resistance. | Blast, crash, explode, collide, conquest, attacking, violation, crusade, command, challenging, overcome, master, defend, rambunctious, prod, poke, pound, shove, dismantle, demolish, overturn, prevent |

## Notes

1. When asked by pollsters in 1993 whether they preferred a more traditional First Lady, 70 percent of respondents concurred (Burrell 1997: 181).

2. Clinton played a major behind-the-scenes role in crafting and building support for the Children's Health Insurance Program that provided health coverage for children whose families' incomes exceeded the levels for eligibility of Medicaid coverage but that were still too low to be able to afford health insurance (Jackson 2008).

3. During her eight years in the White House, Clinton traveled to 79 countries, more than any previous First Lady (Healy 2007).

4. More than 20 articles in the popular press compared Hillary Clinton to Lady Macbeth (Burns 2008: 142).

5. While serving on the Senate Armed Services Committee, Clinton had become familiar with the Defense Department's review process and used it as a model for the State Department's new review process (Wolfson 2009).

6. With specific regard to Clinton, see Gaffney and Blaylock 2010.

7. We employ DICTION 5.0 as our primary tool in examining Clinton's negotiation of the stereotypically gendered communal and agentic rhetorical constructs over time. Developed explicitly for examining American political rhetoric and grounded in linguistic theory, DICTION uses the words most frequently encounter in U.S. political discourse in enumerating patterns in language choices, clusters of lexical and contextual associations in thinking, the epistemological assumptions of the speakers' communicative cultures, verbal tone, proportionality, and intertextual "continuities and discontinuities" in language usage (Hart 2001: 44). As a lexical program, DICTION concentrates solely on word choice and the frequency of predefined families of words. It uses 33 predefined dictionaries containing over 10,000 search words in analyzing text. DICTION chunks texts into 500-word passages for analysis and then averages the characteristics of each of the individual passage to yield a composite score for each text. This allows for easy comparison of speeches regardless of their length. For the same of consistency and comparability, we included statements only 500 words or longer in our data set.

# 6

# Women and Campaigns

REBEKAH HERRICK AND JEANETTE MOREHOUSE MENDEZ

Elections are gendered in that candidates' gender affects the nature of campaigns. Men and women candidates tend to bring distinctive attributes to campaigns and often differ in their backgrounds, reasons for running, and the issues they prioritize. Voters' responses to candidates, too, are affected by candidate gender. For example, voters tend to stereotype women as liberal and men as conservative. The media also often cover men's and women's campaigns differently. To say that elections are gendered does not mean that men and women differ in every respect, however. And, indeed, men and women candidates are remarkably similar in their electability and use of campaign strategies and techniques. In this chapter, we will briefly summarize some of the differences and similarities in the campaigns of men and women state and federal legislative candidates. Also, we examine how the gender mix of the candidates within individual elections affects the results. We ask whether campaigns with only men candidates are different from those that have men and women (mixed-gender races) or those that have only women. Specifically, we are interested in whether Republican women are advantaged when they run against women compared with when they run against men.

## Differences in the Candidacies of Men and Women

Differences between men and women candidates exist at the beginning of campaigns. Their political ambition and backgrounds tend to differ. As Lawless, Fox, and Baitinger note in Chapter 2, women are less likely than men to run for office in the first place, even if they are equally qualified by objective measures, although once in office they have similar levels of ambition. Compared with men, women are more likely to consider the wishes of their family in making the decision to run and to run because of policy concerns above personal ambition (Thomas, Herrick, and Braunstein 2002).

Perhaps because of this the background of men and women candidates varies (Dolan, Deckman, and Swers 2007). For example, forty-seven congresswomen have been widows/widowers[1] who replaced their spouses in office. Women candidates are also less likely to be lawyers or have previous electoral experience but are more likely to be teachers, nurses, and social workers and have experience in interest groups or as volunteers. Women are also more likely to be Democrats. In 2013, the percentage of women who are Democrats in the U.S. Senate is 80, and for the U.S. House the figure is 74.4 percent; for state representatives, it is 63.7 percent, and it is 62.8 percent for state senators.[2] However, many of these differences started to dissipate at the end of the twentieth century and are likely to continue to do so. Gertzog (2002, 106), for example, documents the rise in women running for Congress as strategic politicians (which he defines as having previous elective office and running in an open seat) from 21 percent of women House candidates prior to 1940 to 67 percent from 1984 to 2000.

Geography also matters. Although men candidates run throughout the nation, women are more likely to run and win in what have been referred to as "women-friendly" districts (Palmer and Simon 2006, Chapter 6). Women tend to run and do well in northern states, in nontraditional political cultures, in urban areas, and where voters have high levels of socioeconomic status or high numbers of minorities (Hogan 2001; Ondercin and Welch 2005, 2009; Palmer and Simon 2006; see also Chapter 16 in this volume). Table 6.1 lists the states and the number of women running as major party nominees in the general election for state legislature and Congress in 2012. As it indicates, western states and New England states tend to have more women candidates than southern states.

There are some differences too in the campaigns of men and women candidates. Men are more likely to campaign on issues such as the economy and foreign affairs and women on social policies and women issues (Bystrom and Kaid 2002; Fox 1997; Kahn 1993; Dabelko and Herrnson 1997; Panagopoulos 2004; Robertson et al. 1999; but see Dolan 2005). Women may also be more likely to campaign on policy than personal traits (Panagopoulos 2004). Although as "the gentler" sex, one may expect that women would be less likely to run negative ads, but they are more likely to run negative or attack ads than are men (Bystrom and Kaid 2002; Fox 1997; Herrnson and Lucas 2006; Kahn 1993; Panagopoulos 2004; Robertson et al. 1999). A key reason for this is that negative ads against women are thought to be less successful than those run by women. Men may be reluctant to run attack ads against women for fear of not appearing gentlemanly or fear that the attacks will be seen as unfair, while for women going negative is a way to counter stereotypes and appear tough (Fox 1997; Fridkin, Kenny, and Woodall 2009).

Not only do men and women candidates differ, but also voters react differently to women candidates than to men candidates. As Lynch and Dolan explore in Chapter 3, women candidates are stereotyped as liberal and competent on issues related to women, health care, and education while men are stereotyped as

Table 6.1 **Number of Women Candidates for Legislative Positions by State**

| State | State Legislature | U.S. Congress | State | State Legislature | U.S. Congress |
|---|---|---|---|---|---|
| Alabama | N/A | 4 (7)N/A | Montana | 51 (100) | 1 (1) |
|  |  |  |  | 15 (26) | 0 (1) |
| Alaska | 24 (40) | 1 (1) | Nebraska | N/A | 0 (3) |
|  | 8 (19) | N/A |  | 11 (26) | 1 (1) |
| Arizona | 30 (60) | 4 (10) | Nevada | 20 (42) | 1 (4) |
|  | 18 (30) | 0 (1) |  | 9 (12) | 1 (1) |
| Arkansas | 29 (100) | 0 (4) | New | 205 (400) | 2 (2) |
|  | 11 (35) | N/A | Hampshire | 19 (24) | N/A |
| California | 33 (80) | 24 (53) | New Jersey | N/A | 4 (13) |
|  | 13 (20) | 2 (1) |  |  | 0 (1) |
| Colorado | 41 (65) | 1 (7) | New Mexico | 35 (70) | 3 (3) |
|  | 12 (20) | N/A |  | 16 (42) | 1 (1) |
| Connecticut | 73 (151) | 2 (5) | New York | 55 (150) | 12 (27) |
|  | 17 (36) | 1 (1) |  | 22 (63 or 62) | 2 (1) |
| Delaware | 15 (41) | 0 (1) | North | 50(120) | 5 (13) |
|  | 9 (21) | 0 (1) | Carolina | 8 (50) | N/A |
| Florida | 42 (120) | 12 (27) | North | 21 (50) | 1 (1) |
|  | 22 (40) | 0 (1) | Dakota | 8 (25) | 1 (1) |
| Georgia | 62 (180) | 1 (14) | Ohio | 43 (99) | 8 (16) |
|  | 9 (56) | N/A |  | 7 (17) | 0 (1) |
| Hawaii | 25 (51) | 2 (1) | Oklahoma | 24 (101) | 1 (5) |
|  | 10 (25) | 2 (1) |  | 3 (24) | N/A |
| Idaho | 39 (70) | 1 (2) | Oregon | 29 (60) | 3 (5) |
|  | 16 (35) | N/A |  | 8 (14) | N/A |
| Illinois | 53 (118) | 7 (18) | Pennsylvania | 56 (203) | 5 (18) |
|  | 21 (59) | N/A |  | 8 (25) | 0 (1) |
| Indiana | 30 (100) | 4 (9) | Rhode Island | 24 (75) | 0 (2) |
|  | 8 (25) | 0 (1) |  | 11 (38) | 0 (1) |
| Iowa | 39 (100) | 0 (4) | South | 26 (124) | 4 (7) |
|  | 13 (26) | N/A | Carolina | 5 (46) | N/A |
| Kansas | 58 (125) | 1 (4) | South Dakota | 27 (70) | 1 (1) |
|  | 21 (40) | N/A |  | 7 (35) | N/A |
| Kentucky | 29 (100) | 0 (6) | Tennessee | 28 (99) | 3 (9) |
|  | 2 (19) | N/A |  | 6 (16) | 0 (1) |

(Continued)

| State | State Legislature | U.S. Congress | State | State Legislature | U.S. Congress |
|---|---|---|---|---|---|
| Louisiana | N/A | 0 (6) | Texas | 47 (150) | 15 (36) |
| | | N/A | | 7 (31) | 0 (1) |
| Maine | 84 (151) | 1 (2) | Utah | 32 (75) | 2 (4) |
| | 16 (35) | 1 (1) | | 4 (16) | 0 (1) |
| Maryland | N/A | 4 (8) | Vermont | 73 (150) | 0 (1) |
| | | 0 (1) | | 12 (30) | 0 (1) |
| Massachusetts | 54 (160) | 1 (9) | Virginia | N/A | 1 (11) |
| | 14 (40) | 1 (1) | | | 0 (1) |
| Michigan | 54 (110) | 3 (14) | Washington | 44 (98) | 5 (10) |
| | N/A | 1 (1) | | 16 (26) | 1 (1) |
| Minnesota | 73 (134) | 2 (7) | West Virginia | 35 (100) | 2 (3) |
| | 38 (67) | 1 (1) | | 2 (17) | 0 (1) |
| Mississippi | N/A | 1 (4) | Wisconsin | 46 (99) | 1 (8) |
| | | 0 (1) | | 12 (16) | 1 (1) |
| Missouri | 57 (163) | 5 (8) | Wyoming | 19 (60) | 1 (1) |
| | 6 (17) | 1 (1) | | 1 (15) | 0 (1) |

In each cell, the top number is number of women candidates in the lower house, and the numbers in the second row are senate seats. AL, LA, MD, MS, NJ, and VA did not have state legislative races in 2012. Numbers in parenthesis are the number of seats up for election. N/A means there were no elections for that office in 2012.

*Sources*: Information for this table comes from Book of States 2011, http://ballotpedia.org, http://www.cawp.rutgers.edu/fast_facts/elections/canleg2012.php.  http://cawp.rutgers.edu/fast_facts/elections/candidates_2012.php and CAWP Election Watch: Women State Legislative Candidates by Office and Party 2012.

conservative and competent on issues related to agriculture, crime, and defense (Alexander and Andersen 1993; Dolan 2004a, 2004b; Fridkin and Kenney 2009; Huddy and Terkildsen 1993a, 1993b; Leeper 1991; Sanbonmatsu and Dolan 2009; Sapiro 1981, 1982). Men candidates are also perceived as having more masculine traits (e.g., instrumentality) and as more knowledgeable, and women candidates are perceived as having more feminine traits (warmth and expressiveness) and as more honest (Alexander and Andersen 1993; Fridkin and Kenney 2009; Huddy and Terkildsen 1993a, 1993b; Sapiro 1981–82). These stereotypes may be reinforced since women legislators are more likely to work on these issues than men (Poggione 2004; Swers 2002; Welch 1985). However, as Republican women such as Michele Bachmann increase their numbers in office, these stereotypes may weaken.

There has been much debate about whether these stereotypes harm the electability of women. Although voters often prefer candidates with masculine traits and issue competencies (Huddy and Terkildsen 1993a), other research has found that women who highlight their gender and focus on the stereotypes do well in elections (Herrnson, Lay, and Stokes 2003). What is likely is that the effects of the stereotypes are contextual. In places and times when voters want nontraditional candidates or candidates concerned with compassion issues, women do well to capitalize on stereotypes but at other times do best by countering the stereotypes.

Relatedly, the media tend to treat men and women candidates differently. Research has shown that the media are more likely to report on women's appearances and family than men's appearances and family and tend to focus more on the issues on which men run than on issues on which women run. However, in more recent times, and for some levels of office, especially lower-level offices, these differences have sometimes been eradicated.

## Similarities between Men and Women's Campaigns

One of the main, yet surprising, ways men and women candidates are similar is their electability. Between 1992 and 2010, among candidates who ran against a major party challenger, 93.4 percent of women incumbents seeking reelection to the U.S. House of Representatives won compared with 94.1 percent of men incumbents. Among challengers, 5.7 percent of women won and 5.7 percent of men won their races. Table 6.2 further breaks these results down by party.[3] Although we present figures on the outcome of House races, research at other levels as well as those using experimental designs have similar conclusions (Darcy, Welch, and Clark 1994; Dolan, Deckman, and Swers 2007; Leeper 1991; Sapiro 1981–82). For example, Dolan, Deckman, and Swers (157) found that between 1972 and 1994, 56 percent of women state senate candidates won their races compared with 55 percent of men. The figures for state house/assembly candidates are 52 percent and 53 percent, respectively.

Another way men's and women's campaigns are similar today is in fundraising (Dolan, Deckman, and Swers 2007; Fox 2000; Dabelko and Herrnson 1997). For example, between 1992 and 2010, on average each woman U.S. House of Representatives incumbent raised $1,230,908, and each man incumbent raised $1,157,918. For challengers, the figures were $438,034 for women and $320,785 for men. Although women appear to have a slight advantage, this may be caused by women running in women-friendly districts, which are likely to be more expensive areas to run. When examining mixed-gender races, Fiber and Fox (2005) found that men raise more money in open-seat races.

A final similarity is that, aside from issues and negativity of campaigning, the campaigns of men and women candidates are remarkably similar. Dabelko and

*Table 6.2* **Electoral Victories by Gender, Party and Race Type**

*Male Incumbents*

|  | *Total* | *Incumbent Win* | *Percentage Winning* |
|---|---|---|---|
| Democrats | 1,418 | 1,319 | 93.0 |
| Republicans | 1,437 | 1,368 | 95.2 |
| Total | 2,855 | 2,687 | 94.1 |

*Female Incumbents*

|  | *Total* | *Incumbent Win* |  |
|---|---|---|---|
| Democrats | 326 | 303 | 92.9 |
| Republicans | 143 | 135 | 94.4 |
| Total | 469 | 438 | 93.4 |

*Male Challengers*

|  | *Total* | *Challenger Win* | *Percentage Winning* |
|---|---|---|---|
| Democrats | 1,240 | 56 | 4.5 |
| Republicans | 1,518 | 102 | 6.7 |
| Total | 2,758 | 158 | 5.7 |

*Female Challengers*

|  | *Total* | *Challenger Win* | *Percentage Winning* |
|---|---|---|---|
| Democrats | 330 | 18 | 5.5 |
| Republicans | 216 | 13 | 6.0 |
| Total | 546 | 31 | 5.7 |

Herrnson (1997) discovered that men's and women's campaigns for the U.S. House of Representatives are similar in their resources, strategies, and techniques (e.g., both use radio, TV, direct mail, and get-out-the-vote campaigns). Similarly, Sapiro et al. (2011) found little difference between men and women campaign ads in casting and setting, policy, traits and tone, and purpose.

Some of these similarities may mask differences, however. For example, although men and women raise similar levels of funds, there is some evidence that they have different sources of money, that women may have to work harder to get the same level of funding, and that women may have to spend more per vote received (Fiber and Fox 2005; Herrick 1996). Additionally, if women ran equally throughout the nation instead of focusing on women-friendly districts, their success rates are likely to be lower.

# Gender Mix of Candidates

Most of the literature on women campaigns has examined differences and similarities between men and women candidates, ignoring how the gender mix of candidates in a campaign affects the election. That is, it may be that when a man runs against a man the fundamentals of the election differ from women-only or mixed-gender races. Since women and men candidates act differently and are perceived differently on the campaign trail, it seems likely that the candidate mix will affect the campaign. For example, since men and women campaign on different issues, it is likely that more issues will be discussed in mixed-gender races than men- or women-only races. Additionally, gender mix may affect the campaigns because candidates adjust their strategies to their opponents (Carsey et al. 2011). If candidates use gender-based stereotypes or rely on gender differences to forecast their opponents' behavior, then the gender mix may affect the campaign. If a man candidate, for example, expects his woman opponent to focus on compassion issues, he may be more likely to address them than if he were running against a man whom he does not expect to address these issues.

Although there has not been research focusing directly on the gender mix in campaigns, some research touches on the topic. Bystrom and Kaid (2002, 167) state, "...Men's discussion of such 'feminine' issues as health care and elderly issues; their emphasis on such 'feminine' traits such as honesty, sensitivity, and trustworthiness; and their use of touch in ads may have been prompted by competing against women." Panagopouos (2004) also suggests that campaigns differ depending on the gender mix. He found that men tend to have a more negative tone when running against men than against women,[4] and men also tend to assert their status as an experienced leader when running against men. On the other hand, when men run against women, they run more policy ads and more ads on children issues. When women campaign against men, they portray their opponents as less honest, themselves as tough, and run more ads dealing with personal themes and social policies. And when women run against women, they run more ads dealing with education and social security.

Also suggesting that the gender mix of campaigns affects elections is a growing body of literature indicating that gender and party stereotypes interact to affect the electability of Republican or Democratic women. Voters often lack the information they need to evaluate candidates so they infer the needed information, such as issue positions, based on known characteristics (Conover and Feldman 1989). One such characteristic is party. Voters infer issue positions based on candidate's party, such that Democratic candidates are seen as having liberal positions and Republicans as having conservative positions (Conover and Feldman 1989; Matland and King 2002; Northpoth 2009; Rahn 1993). And, as noted earlier, women politicians are stereotyped as more liberal or competent on issues associated with liberals than men politicians. Studies combining party and gender stereotypes find that since Democrats are stereotyped as liberal and Republicans conservative and that women are stereotyped as liberal and men conservative, voters stereotype Democratic women as the most liberal, followed by Democratic men, Republican women, and Republican men (Dolan 2004; Koch 2002; Matland and King 2002; Sanbonmatsu and Dolan 2009).

These conclusions are nuanced. Gender stereotypes are larger when there is more, not less, information; voters have to know enough to be able to know which categories to use and how to use them (Koch 2002). Thus, Koch found an interaction with incumbency such that stereotypes are stronger in races with incumbents. Koch also discovered that reinforcing stereotypes are stronger than conflicting stereotypes such that stereotypes about Democratic women are more likely to cue voters than those for Republican women because party and gender stereotypes are reinforcing for Democratic women but not Republican women.

The previous literature has relied on experiments and has not examined the outcomes of real elections. In contrast, here, we examine whether there is a partisan effect caused by the gender mix based on election results. We chose to look at partisan effects of gender mix because of the importance of party. Which party controls Congress in this highly partisan era has incredible influence on the nature of our politics. Specifically, we expect that women-only races will advantage the Republican Party. Since Republican women are stereotyped as moderates and Democratic women as very liberal, we expect that Republican women's positions will be seen as in line with a higher percentage of voters than will be the case for Democratic women. Although this line of reasoning suggests that when men run against men Democratic men may be advantaged, we are less sure of this expectation based on the findings of existing literature. Koch (2002, 455) found that the novelty of candidates prompts stereotyping or inference formation. Thus, since women candidates are still more novel than men candidates, gender stereotyping may be stronger for women candidates. Specifically, the gender stereotype of men candidates as conservative may have little effect on Democratic men when running against a man. In mixed-party races, we do not expect either party to be advantaged.

## Data and Results

To estimate the effects of the gender mix on campaigns, we divide U.S. House races between 1992 and 2010 into gender-mix categories. Of the 3,792 House of races with two major candidates running against one another, 94 were women only, 1,003 were mixed, and 2,694 were men only. Since incumbency plays such a strong role in elections,[5] we further divide the cases by incumbency, which results in 12 categories as follows:

- Open-seat mixed gender (Republican women)
- Open-seat mixed gender (Democratic women)
- Open-seat women only
- Open-seat men only
- Democratic incumbent women only
- Democratic incumbent men only
- Democratic incumbent mixed gender (woman Democrat)
- Democratic incumbent mixed gender (woman Republican)
- Republican incumbent women only
- Republican incumbent men only
- Republican incumbent mixed gender (woman Republican)
- Republican incumbent mixed gender (woman Democrat)

To measure how well the Republican Party performs in a race, we used the Congressional Quarterly (CQ) Voting and Elections database to calculate the percentage of the Republican vote shares. CQ compiles all election data from each state and county and gives information on the candidate's name, party affiliation, and votes received. Our expectation is that the Republican Party will pick up a greater share of the vote in women-only races and that the effect will be greatest when there is an incumbent.

Since factors other than gender mix of candidates and incumbency can affect the Republican share of the vote, we control for district traits, levels of Republicanism (Republican mood), and financial advantage. The district controls include income level, education, and race, all using census data arranged per congressional district for the years of interest. Education was calculated as the percentage of the population over the age of 25 who obtained a bachelor's degree or higher. Income is the median household income. And for race we used percentages of African Americans and Hispanics in the district. We do this since district traits affect party vote, and we want to try to isolate the effect of gender mix on the Republican vote.

We also control for the level of Republicanism in time and place by using the Cook Report's partisan voting index (PVI). PVI measures the average distance of a district compared with the nation as a whole over the previous two presidential elections. These data are widely respected for representing how likely a congressional district is to lean toward one political party.[6] To control for whether or not it was a good Republican year, we created a variable coded 1 if the Republican Party gained seats in the House compared with the Democratic Party. Finally, we controlled for a Republican financial advantage with campaign finance data. We took the difference between the money raised by the Republican candidate and that raised by the Democratic candidate. Higher values indicate that the Republican candidate raised more money than the Democratic candidate.

# Findings

Using a multivariate statistical analysis called regression, we modeled how well the Republican Party does in the election as a function of our 12 gender dyads. We were interested in how gender dyads affect our dependent variable which is the Republican vote share (or the percentage of vote) a Republican receives in the election. Because of the way the statistical technique works, we must exclude one gender dyad to model this equation. The excluded category is the open-seat mixed-gender (Republican women) category. This means that the coefficients for the gender dyads are measured in relationship to this category. Since this comparison is a bit awkward when there are 12 dyadic combinations, to simplify analysis we estimated the Republican Party's share of the two-party vote and present the results in Table 6.3.

Complete tables with the results for the House model can be found in Appendix A. They indicate that the model performs well and is consistent with our expectations. The $R^2$ in the equation in the table is .80, indicating that the model explains 80 percent of the variance in Republican vote percentage. Also, the control variables have the expected relations with Republican vote. That is, consistent with past research the Republican Party increases in districts with higher PVI scores (the score indicates a more Republican leaning district) as well as when Republicans

*Table 6.3* **Estimated Republican Vote Share Based on Regression Equations**

| Type of race | % Republican | Type of Race | % Republican |
|---|---|---|---|
| Mixed-Gender Open Seat (Republican Women) | 50.16 | Mixed-gender Democratic incumbent (woman Democrat) | 40.60 |
| Mixed-Gender Open Seat (Democratic Women) | 50.58 | Mixed-gender Democratic incumbent (woman Republican) | 40.43 |
| Women-Only Open Seat | 47.97 | Women-only Republican incumbent | 59.82 |
| Men-Only Open Seat | 51.47 | Men-only Republican incumbent | 63.06 |
| Women-Only Democratic Incumbent | 41.96 | Mixed-gender Republican incumbent (woman Republican) | 61.91 |
| Men-Only Democratic Incumbent | 31.85 | Mixed-gender Republican incumbent (woman Democrat) | 61.38 |

nationwide are winning (capturing a Republican mood). Similarly, the higher the levels of college education, and the more African Americans and Hispanics in a district, the lower the Republican vote share.

Most important for our purposes, the results offer support for our expectations, although they are contextual. First, the results reinforce Koch's (2002) findings that gender effects are greater when there is an incumbent. In open seat races, there is very little effect of candidate gender mix. In such races, the Republican Party averages 47.97 points when there are two women; this rises slightly to about 50 points when there are mixed-gender races and to 51.47 points in men-only races. The differences are not large but suggest that, if anything, the Republican Party is slightly disadvantaged in women-only races.

The other factor that conditions the effect of candidate gender mix is the party of the incumbent. The largest effect of gender mix of candidates is when there is a Democratic incumbent, and here the effects are consistent with our expectations. In men-only races with a Democratic incumbent, the Republican Party averages only 31.85 percent of the vote, and in mixed-gender races with a Democratic incumbent the average Republican vote share is just over 40 percent, regardless of the incumbent's gender. Most importantly, the Republican share of the vote grows to 41.96 percent in women-only races with a Democratic incumbent. However, the effects of gender mix when there is a Republican incumbent mirrors that of open-seat races—there is a slight disadvantage for the Republican Party in women-only races. In women-only races with a Republican incumbent, the Republican Party averages 59.82 percent of the vote, but when there is a Republican man the Republican Party average raises to 63.06 percent. The Republican Party also does better in mixed-gender races with a woman Republican incumbent than in women-only races with a Republican incumbent. It averages a little over 61 percent of the vote regardless of whether the women was the incumbent.

We suspect that the effects of women-only races are largest when there is a Democratic incumbent because Democratic women present the clearest ideological picture. As Koch (2002) found, the effects of gender stereotypes are largest for incumbents because voters have enough information to access stereotypes and for Democratic women because the stereotypes of their party and gender are reinforcing. Women Democrats are not only the easiest to stereotype but are also among the most liberal members of Congress and campaign as such.

## Conclusion

Congressional races are gendered. Men and women candidates behave in a gendered manner before and during the campaign and are treated differently based on their gender by the media and voters. Another way elections are gendered is that the gender mix of the candidates affects partisan prospects. These effects are mitigated by context. Our research shows that in open-seat races there is little difference between Republican vote share by gender mix of candidates, but to the degree that there is a difference the Republican Party is disadvantaged in women-only races. Similarly, when there is a Republican incumbent, the Republican Party is slightly disadvantaged in women-only races by about 3 percent of the vote compared with men-only races. However, when there is a Democratic incumbent, the Republican Party picks up an additional 10 percent of the vote in women-only races compared with men-only races. That the effects are largest for Democratic women is consistent with the findings of Koch (2002), who discovered that gender stereotypes are strongest in races with incumbents and for Democratic women since party and gender stereotypes are reinforcing.

There are a couple of implications of our findings. One is that if the Republican Party wants to increase its numbers in the House, and presumably other offices, they will do well to identify Democratic women incumbents to run against. The other implication is more academic. Any effort to understand gender differences in campaigns need to consider not just the gender or sex of each individual candidate but also the gender or sex of individual candidates' opponents. Here, we focused on partisan effect of gender mix, but in other work we examine the effect of gender mix on the nature of campaign issues and voter engagement in the election.

# Appendix A. House

| | |
|---|---|
| Women-Only Republican Incumbent | 9.66*** (1.78) |
| Women-Only Democrat Incumbent | −8.20*** (1.47) |
| Women-Only Open Seat | −2.19 (2.37) |
| Mixed-Gender Woman Democratic Challenger | 11.22*** (1.10) |
| Mixed-Gender- Woman Democratic Incumbent | −9.56*** (1.11) |
| Mixed-Gender Open Seat, Woman Democrat | 0.42 (1.26) |
| Mixed-Gender Woman Republican Incumbent | 11.75*** (1.24) |
| Mixed-Gender Woman Republican Challenger | −9.73*** (1.17) |
| Men-Only Republican Incumbent | 12.90*** (1.03) |
| Men-Only Democrat Incumbent | −10.31*** (1.03) |
| Men-Only Open Seat | 1.31 (1.10) |
| Income | 0.0002*** (0.00002) |
| College Educated | −0.21*** (0.01) |
| Black | −0.18*** (0.01) |
| Hispanic | −0.11*** (0.01) |

| | |
|---|---|
| PVI | 0.42*** (0.01) |
| Republican Financial Difference | –2.46e-9 (2.15e-08) |
| Republican Mood | 4.19*** (0.28) |
| Constant | 48.32  (2.30) |
| N | 3,790 |
| $R^2$ | 0.80 |

*Note*: regression analyses.

***$p < 0.001$; **$p < 0.01$; *$p < 0.05$; +$p < 0.10$.

Dependent variable: Republican Party vote share.

Women-Only Republican Incumbent: 1 if woman only race with Republican incumbent, 0 otherwise.

Women-Only Republican Democrat: 1 if women only race with Democratic incumbent, 0 otherwise.

Women-Only Open Seat: 1 if women only race with no incumbents, 0 otherwise.

Mixed-Gender Woman Democratic Challenger: 1 if Woman Democratic challenger versus Man Republican incumbent, 0 otherwise.

Mixed-Gender Woman Democratic Incumbent: 1 if Woman Democratic incumbent versus Man Republican challenger, 0 otherwise.

Mixed-Gender Open Seat, Woman Democrat: 1 if open seat race; Democratic woman versus Republican man, 0 otherwise.

Mixed-Gender Woman Republican Incumbent: 1 if Republican woman incumbent versus Democratic man challenger, 0 otherwise.

Mixed-Gender Woman Republican Challenger: 1 if Republican woman challenger versus Democratic man incumbent, 0 otherwise.

Men-Only Republican Incumbent: 1 if Republican man incumbent versus Democratic man challenger, 0 otherwise.

Men-Only Democrat Incumbent: 1 if Democratic man incumbent versus Republican man challenger, 0 otherwise.

Men-Only Open Seat: 1 if men only race with no incumbents, 0 otherwise.

College Educated: Percentage of district/state over age 25 with bachelor's degree.

Black: Percentage of district/state who identify as black.

Hispanic: Percentage of district/state who identify as Hispanic.

Open Seat: 1 if the race is open seat, 0 if an incumbent is running for reelection.

PVI: Cook Report's partisan voting index for district/state; higher scores indicate less competitive district/state.

Competition: Republican vote share minus Democratic vote share.

Republican Finance Differential: Money raised by the Republican candidate minus the money raised by the Democratic candidate.

Republican Mood: 1 if Republicans gain sets in the House (years 1994, 2002, 2004, 2010), 0 otherwise.

*Notes*

1. The current number is only three. See Center for American Women and Politics (CAWP). 2005. "Fact Sheet: Women Who Succeeded Their Husbands in Congress." http://www.cawp. rutgers.edu/fast_facts/levels_of_office/documents/widows.pdf (accessed August 1, 2012).
2. State figures come from CAWP. 2013. "Fact Sheet: Women in State Legislatures 2013." http://www.cawp.rutgers.edu/fast_facts/levels_of_office/documents/stleg.pdf (accessed March 8, 2013). National figures were calculated from CAWP. 2013. "Fact Sheet: Women in the US Congress." http://www.cawp.rutgers.edu/fast_facts/levels_of_office/documents/cong.pdf (accessed March 8, 2013).
3. These figures were calculated by authors using data from the CAWP, Congressional Quarterly Elections Data, and the Federal Election Commissions campaign finance data reports.
4. Fox (1997) too finds that men are more likely to go negative against a man opponent than a woman opponent.
5. Since World War II just under 94 percent of incumbents who have sought reelection won (Davidson, Oleszek, and Lee 2011, 62).
6. Since the PVI started in 1997, we calculated the PVI for 1992 through 1996. Given redistricting after 1990, we could find past presidential voting numbers per district only from *The Almanac of American Politics,* and only 1988 was included in the 1992 book. As such, for 1992 we created PVI scores based only on the 1998 election.

# 7

# Conservative Women Run for Office

RONNEE SCHREIBER

Leading up to the 2010 general elections, former Republican vice presidential nom-inee Sarah Palin laid claim to helping generate a movement among conservative women. In an ad touting the political salience of "Mama Grizzlies" she contended that "it seems like it's kind of a mom awakening in the last year and a half, where women are rising up and saying, 'No, we've had enough already."[1] Palin suggests an emergence of political participation among conservative women, but her comments belie the fact that women have long been engaged in conservative movement poli-tics. This activism includes organizing national opposition to constitutional amend-ments like the Equal Rights and Women's Suffrage Amendments as well as women's advocacy aimed at challenging laws in favor of legal abortion, same-sex marriage, and government-funded family leave (Hardisty 1999; Klatch 1987; Mansbridge 1986; Marshall 1997; Rymph 2006; Schreiber 2012a). Conservative women have also founded political action committees, public policy groups, and organizations that raise money and train women to run for office.[2] There is one realm, however, in which conservative women's participation has been significantly lacking—in elected, especially nationally elected, office.[3] Compared with Democratic women and Republican men, Republican women lag behind in representation in state and national legislative bodies.[4] Myriad factors, having to do both with their gendered and partisan identities, shape Republican women's political fortunes in this arena and influence how they run for office as well.

I begin this chapter with a review of scholarship that evaluates the challenges Republican women encounter as they seek office, putting this group in the context of all women candidates as well as comparing them with their male counterparts. The second part of the chapter examines data from websites of women who ran for Congress in the 2010 general elections, noting where partisan and gender identities are salient or where other factors rendered these variables relatively insignificant.

I note that 2010 provided an uncommon electoral environment for these candidates and explore the extent to which this context mattered as well.

Exploring Republican women's fate in electoral politics reminds us that not all politically engaged women are liberal and/or feminist. Indeed, a full understanding of women's political participation is incomplete without recognizing the ways conservative women are active in politics and the factors that influence their quest for political power and stature.

## Gender, Party, and Running for Office

Overall, when women run, they win their races as often as men (Thomas 2005). However, all women still face challenges as they seek office. On a range of factors, voters evaluate men and women candidates differently (Dolan 2010; see also Chapter 3 in this volume). This holds true for personality traits, leadership skills, and issue competency. Women are thought to be more liberal and compassionate than men and better able to handle and promote "women's issues" like education (Dolan 2010; Huddy and Terkildsen 1993; Sanbonmatsu and Dolan 2009), while men are viewed as being strong, intelligent, and more conservative, with perceived competency on issues like defense and crime (Lawless 2004; Sanbonmatsu and Dolan 2009).

Despite voters' views, studies do show more similarities than differences between men and women in terms of campaign styles, issue priorities, and presentation of self (Dolan 2009; Bystrom et al. 2004). That is, gender may factor into voter perception, but the candidates themselves actively work against these perceived differences as they seek their support. While voter assessments can sometimes help women (e.g., if the campaign environment is one in which voters preferred a more "compassionate" approach to politics), most women running for office face a double bind and thus may be concerned about voter stereotyping. Women are viewed through a more "feminized" lens (whereby they are perceived to be more communal and compassionate than men), and voters prefer women in general to behave this way (Carroll 2009; see also Duerst-Lahti 2005 for a related argument). However, because voters typically associate leadership with more "masculine" or agentic qualities, women must navigate among these competing expectations. Thus, for women candidates a feminized projection of self has risks—voters expect women to be more communal and caring but do not think that those are qualities that make for effective leaders. Men are especially likely to think that women should not hold national leadership positions (Carroll 2009).[5]

Republican women, on the basis of their gendered identities, are certainly not exempt from these challenges, but they also encounter a special set of voter expectations that differ from Democratic women. Several scholars have demonstrated that sex and party intersect in candidate evaluations by voters and thus shape their primary and general election campaigns (Dolan 2005; King and Matland 2003; Sanbonmatsu and Dolan 2009; Winter 2010). As Winter (2010, 609) notes, "Gender and party categories may each derive their meanings in part from their relationship with the other." This is due in part to the fact that voters assess the two major political parties through a gendered lens. That is, voters think of the Democratic Party as being relatively feminized compared with a masculinized interpretation of the Republican Party. In turn, with an eye toward party as a cue, this influences how voters evaluate candidates' skills and competency. Additionally, being a woman candidate may mean something different depending on the corresponding party affiliation, suggesting that gender identity in electoral contexts must be considered in light of how it intersects with partisanship and ideology. For example, Republicans are less likely to vote for Republican women in primaries because they perceive of them as being too liberal (King and Matland 2003) and less emotionally suited for political leadership positions (Sanbonmatsu and Dolan 2009). King and Matland found, for example, that "Republican partisans are much less likely to support a female candidate relative to an otherwise identical male candidate" (604). Indeed, compared with their Democratic female counterparts, Republican women did not fare as well in the 2010 and 2012 primaries where, in most cases, they had male Republican opponents. In 2010, 36 percent of Republicans won their primaries versus 65 percent of Democratic women. The percentage of Republican women winning their primaries in 2012 rose to 44 percent, but it was still much lower than the 62 percent of Democratic women who won their primaries.[6]

The picture is not entirely bleak, however, for Republican women. Democrats and Independents may be willing to cross over and vote for Republican women, giving them an edge against a male opponent (King and Matland 2003). This is in part because "Republican women are thought to provide voters with a mixed message: a liberal cue—gender—and a conservative cue—party" (Sanbonmatsu and Dolan 2009, 7). Additionally, party and gender cues are dependent on electoral context and a candidate's specific constituency, meaning that other factors may overwhelm a candidate's partisan affiliation or gendered identity (Gershon 2009). Being a Republican woman might be an advantage or might matter very little depending more on the race itself.

Conservative ideology about gender roles also factors into voter assessment as well as women's decisions to run for office. Premised on theological beliefs about the need for male leadership in (heterosexual) families and gendered values about women as caretakers, social conservatives believe that women should prioritize their roles as mothers when their children are young (see, e.g., LaHaye and Crouse 2001; Lewis and Yoest 1996; Schlessinger 2008). Indeed, many conservatives opposed the Equal Rights Amendment because of its alleged threat to women's status as wives and stay-at-home mothers (Foss 1979; Mansbridge 1986; Schlafly 1972). Even economic conservatives, who do not tend to espouse traditional views about gender roles, have argued that due to gender differences women are better suited than men to be primary caretakers and have advocated for policies that reflect this sentiment (Schreiber 2012a). Greenlee (2010) also found that in some cases, for some women voters, motherhood produces conservative shifts in issue priorities.[7]

On the other hand, conservative women have long argued that their status, or potential status, as mothers means that women can offer different but valuable insights in the political realm compared with their male counterparts (Nickerson 2012; Schreiber 2011). And Republican voters prefer women candidates who are mothers to those who do not have children (Stalsburg 2010). Palin herself invoked her "hockey mom" status and promoted women in the 2010 elections as "Mama Grizzlies." Interviews recently conducted with conservative women leaders also speak to the shifting beliefs among conservatives about mothers in politics. Most interviewees invoked a liberal "choice" frame to support women's decisions to have families in addition to their professional lives. Alyssa Cordova (2011) of the Clare Boothe Luce Policy Institute (CBLPI) summed it up this way:

> We think that as a woman you have the right, [as] an American, you have the right to choose whichever you'd like. And if that means a combination of both or one or the other that's fine...Maybe you'll be a stay-at-home mom for a while, and then you'll go on maybe later when your kids are maybe a little bit older and have a career. And then of course some of them work while their kids are little, and they just do whatever they can. I think it's a personal decision that should be made between you and your family, and nobody else should be telling you that one makes you a stronger woman than another....So I would say that's probably our position. It's a very personal decision.

It is important to note that although organizational actors like Cordova promote flexibility for women, they rarely talk about men in the context of parenting or having work–family conflicts. Implicitly then, they are still highlighting the salience of parenting roles for women and minimizing them for men.

There is a growing consensus among these women not only that maternal duties should not preclude women's entrance into political activism or electoral politics (Schreiber 2011) but also that this can lead to candidates better suited to representing conservative women. Marjorie Dannenfelser (2011), president of the Susan B. Anthony List, a political action committee that raises money for pro-life women candidates, articulated this sentiment about the 2010 elections:

> I really believe this past election was a tipping point in the type of woman that was running. Not only do I believe it, but [also] the numbers back it up. It was what it was. The dominant woman running was a pro-life conservative woman. It was the one getting through the primaries, it was the one doing the best in elections, and the women that did poorly, especially

challengers, were women who were of the old model. There really is now a new model. At the very minimum there is room for both.

Confirming this perspective in a more lively fashion, Tea Party Patriot Shelby Blakely (2011) spoke to why Republicans needed more mothers in office:

> [T]here are actually several reasons. Number one, conservatism in America has been painted as rich old white men that hate everyone else and have had it easy for too long. You can't say that with women. Do you really think you're going to come up to me in public and say you're just a rich person that doesn't care about people, when I just recently caught someone's puke that morning?

Conflicting conservative values about women's roles and gendered norms, then, present an additional test for Republican women candidates as they decide whether or not their candidacies are viable and also how to frame their messages as they campaign. Emphasizing traditional gendered attributes like motherhood may help them garner votes from social conservatives but also might cast them as being too feminized for leadership duties by some male Republican voters.

Another challenge for Republican women is that of their party's increasing conservatism, including its elite. Republican women candidates must grapple with how well they "fit" their party's image and how this affects their party leadership's willingness to support their candidacies. Thomsen (2012) argues that we should expect more moderate Republican women selecting out of running for office due to their lack of "party fit" with this relatively conservative group. "Party reputation," she argues, "sends messages about the types of candidates that belong in the party" and Republicans who are less conservative (e.g. are pro-choice) will assume their candidacies are not viable (3). Relatedly, scholars have found an inverse correlation between the numbers of social conservatives in a state and the amount of women who serve in their respective state offices (Merolla, Schroedel, and Holman 2007). Elder (2012) also found that states with more Republican voters have less women in their state legislatures. As noted, Republican voters also shy away from Republican women candidates because they perceive them as being too liberal (King and Matland 2003).

Finally, another factor related to women's electoral fortunes is the support of women's organizations (Sanbonmatsu, Carroll, and Walsh 2009; Thomsen 2012). Research shows, for example, that women state legislators report organizational encouragement from a women's group as one reason they decided to run for office (Sanbonmatsu, Carroll, and Walsh 2009). However, there is also a partisan gap here, with Democratic women more likely than Republican women to report such encouragement. Since 2008, however, conservative women's organizations like Smart Girl Politics and Voices of Conservative Women have formed and have joined forces with older conservative women's groups such as Clare Boothe Luce Policy Institute, Susan B. Anthony List, Concerned Women for America, and Independent Women's Forum to more actively promote Republican women's bids for office. This includes recruiting and training women for leadership positions and raising money for their campaigns (Schreiber 2012a). Organizational efforts are likely to be aimed at more conservative women, as these groups generally represent the ideologically extreme base of the Republican Party. In addition to encouraging and supporting conservative women office seekers, women's groups can influence the Republican Party's willingness and comfort level  with promoting more women in office. This shapes how voters think about Republican women candidates. As noted, Republican voters expect women to be more liberal, and conservative women themselves may not feel that their party is a good fit for them. However, as women's groups that have legitimacy among conservatives and voters support women candidates, this could help shift how voters and the public think about conservative women candidates.

Given these varied and sometimes competing influences on conservative women running for office, Republican women face unique challenges as they seek and campaign for their seats. In the next part of the chapter I explore data gathered from websites of women who ran for Congress in 2010. These elections set a new record for the number of Republican women running for Congress[8] and provide a distinctive opportunity to examine if ideological and partisan differences among women matter in terms of how they present themselves and what factors influence their political fortunes. As noted, both gender and partisan affiliation provide cues to voters. How did these identities intersect and influence women's campaigns in the 2010 elections?

## Data and Methods

I conducted an extensive systematic content analysis of campaign websites from the 2010 general elections assessing how women candidates for Congress present themselves and discuss their policy priorities. In addition, I coded for incumbency, previous experience, whether or not they won their elections, and if they were married or had children, since candidates' marital or parental status factors into voters' perceptions about candidates' priorities, leadership skills, and ability to do their jobs. Most of the candidates' personal information was presented in their biographies, and their policy priorities were frequently available on their issues pages or front pages. I also examined every other text section of their website (e.g., "Media," "Events," "Endorsement") to confirm that my information was accurate.[9]

Of the 153 women candidates running in 2010, I was able to archive ninety-two of their websites, which were downloaded in October 2010 and subsequently coded after the election. The sample conforms to the party ratio of the full population of women running for office that year (36 percent Republican, 64 percent Democrat) and is split evenly between incumbents and challengers. Of the candidates examined, 51 percent were incumbents (forty-seven incumbents and forty-five challengers); 18 percent were endorsed by the Tea Party and 25 percent running against Tea Party–endorsed candidates.[10] A total of 13 percent of them ran against other women. Like the population running for office, the sample was mostly white (76 percent). The rest represented these racial and ethnic groups: 6 percent Latina; 10 percent African American; and 1 percent Asian/Pacific Islander. There were a few cases in which I could not determine the candidate's racial or ethnic identity.

Candidates have many opportunities to go public. They can organize rallies and community events, run advertisements, and use other social media. These data reflect a segment of these activities and are thus limited to this particular form of campaign communications. Websites, however, provide an unmediated source of information for voters and lack the external stereotyping common when candidates are presented to the public by other media (Dolan 2005; Gershon 2009). They offer rich information about candidates' "presentation of self" (Bystrom et al. 2004) what characteristics and issues the candidates view as important to garner votes and credibility and how the intersection of partisan and gendered identities factors in. Over half of the voting public use the Internet for campaign information, suggesting that websites have some influence in shaping voter choice and perception (Smith 2011).

## Electoral Context

As noted, the electoral context for Republican women in 2010 was uncommon and must be considered when examining these data. Tea Party activism, support from conservative women leaders and organizations, and Palin's push for Mama Grizzlies generated momentum for Republican women and brought national attention to their campaigns (Feldman 2010; McManus 2010).

In some ways, however, factors that produced enthusiasm for conservative women also presented them with challenges. The presence of the Tea Party, for example, added a twist. Organizations that represent Tea Party groups do not officially prioritize "social issues";[11] thus, their organizational agendas align more closely with established economic conservative groups and leaders. For example, Tea Party Patriots describe three "core values": fiscal responsibility; constitutionally limited government; and free markets. The organization adds that although "we do not take stances on social issues ... [we] urge members to engage fully on the social issues they consider important and aligned with their beliefs."[12]

Nonetheless, several studies indicate that while Tea Party organizations list economic conservative issues as their policy priorities, many adherents are also socially conservative religious Republicans (Clement and Green 2011; Deckman 2011; Williamson, Skocpol, and Coggin 2011), complicating how all candidates had to understand and speak to this visible voting bloc in 2010 (Wilson and Burack 2012).

To attract the widest range of Republican voters, candidates must balance between social and economic conservative values and policy goals.

As noted, women's organizations were more publicly supportive of conservative women candidates in 2010. However, like the broader base of the Republican Party, there is not ideological congruency among conservative women leaders. Broadly, these organizations represent social or economic conservatives (Schreiber 2012a). Social conservatives will more likely be concerned with women candidates' marital and maternal status as they favor traditional heterosexual families where women are the primary caretakers. And while economic conservatives are not immune from favoring these social and domestic arrangements, they care more about where candidates stand on the economy when evaluating them for office. These distinctions were clearly illustrated in commentary about Palin's Mama Grizzly theme as articulated by leaders of conservative women's organizations. For the economic conservatives of Independent Women's Forum (IWF), former president Michelle Bernard argued that issues trump gendered expectations when considering candidates:

> Today, you see women campaigning on the economy, on education, on poverty, on prosperity, national security and terrorism...And we have finally gotten to a point in time when most of the American public sees that women's issues are no different than men's, and we see that in the candidates that are at the top of the tickets in state and national ballots across the country...[I] firmly believe that all of these women would have run and were probably thinking about running long before Sarah Palin was on the vice presidential ticket with Senator McCain (as quoted in Saine 2010).

Alternatively, the social conservatives of Concerned Women for America (CWA) rallied around Palin's Mama Grizzly theme:

> These Mama Grizzlies are simply not going to sit by silently while the forces of Big Government socialism tear their families apart. So Mama Grizzlies are showing up at town hall meetings, running for office, organizing through the Internet and letting their voices be heard like never before. I believe this awakening of Mama Grizzlies across our nation is the most important and most powerful political story of 2010. In fact, pollsters are confirming that Mama Grizzlies like you and me will likely play the deciding role in next month's elections.... Thousands of Mama Grizzlies are taking a stand....With just a few days until Election Day, Concerned Women for America is inviting Mama Grizzlies who understand the threats facing our families and our society to make a bold declaration.... I'm a woman, I'm conservative and I WILL VOTE! (Nance 2010; emphasis in original).

Keeping these tensions and context in mind, in the following section I assess how women campaigned for Congress through their websites.

## Website Data Analysis

### Motherhood and Partisanship

Republican women candidates are faced with a quandary. How do they appeal to social conservatives who may be wary of women who eschew traditional female/ maternal roles by opting for professional careers? Complicating this assessment is that the broad base of Republican voters and activists are not necessarily ideologically congruent on social issues, presenting women candidates with a dilemma about how to evaluate the salience of gendered norms for potential voters, even from those within their own party. Given these tensions, and considering data indicating that generally Republican voters prefer women candidates who have children over those who do not, I examined whether the candidates mentioned their parental status and articulated that this status mattered to them in terms of their policy priorities or solutions.

Of the candidates who are mothers (73 percent of all candidates in my sample—71 of Democrats and 77 percent of Republicans), 80 percent specifically noted on their websites that they were mothers. However, only 26 percent of them articulated that being a mother matters in terms of their issue priorities or positions.[13] Examining the link between party and salience of motherhood, 22 percent of Democratic women and only 15 percent of Republican women candidates mentioned that being a parent related to their issue priorities or policy solutions. Republican women candidates, then, are less likely than Democratic women to articulate a connection between their maternal identities and their policy goals.

What accounts for these partisan differences? Republican women might be deemphasizing gendered characteristics to work against stereotyping from voters within their own party about their leadership skills. Although highlighting maternalism might garner support from social conservatives, candidates are unwilling to do so and risk being constructed as too feminine for national leadership. Studies show that Democratic voters are generally more supportive of women who articulate such concerns, so they may risk less by invoking their maternal status (Elder and Greene 2012; Sanbonmatsu and Dolan 2009).

Pushing this analysis, I examined whether candidates who mentioned their maternal status were more or less likely to win their elections. The results indicate mentioning parental status proved to be a tremendous detriment for all women. An incumbent who has children but does not mention them had a 97 percent chance of being reelected. Mentioning children dropped her chances to 82 percent. Nonincumbents who did not mention their maternal status had a 55 percent probability of being elected. Mentioning their motherhood, however, dropped that chance to a mere 13 percent.[14] Although the data could not be disaggregated by party due to sample size, this is a significant and troubling finding. Democratic women supposedly represent open-minded constituents comfortable with mothers pursuing career paths. These data suggest a different story. As previously discussed, the picture has been less clear for Republican women as to whether or not mother-hood renders them appealing or not to potential voters. Social conservatives expect a focus on the maternal, however, perhaps not so much in the realm of national, professional politics. Mama Grizzlies can rise up as long as they take care to keep their cubs close by.

## Gender, Partisanship, and Issue Priorities

Voters value different traits between men and women who run for office, but they also believe that men and women differ in terms of issue competency (Dolan 2010; Lawless 2004; ; Sanbonmatsu and Dolan 2009; see also Chapter 3 in this volume). Scholars argue that it would benefit women candidates, for example, to emphasize issues like the economy, defense, and taxes in an effort to "neutralize the stereo-types" about women's competencies (Dolan 2010, 85). To assess how women can-didates in 2010 framed their issue competencies and priorities, I scored the top five policy goals for each candidate.[15] Taking the group as a whole, the top five issues were economy, health care, education, energy, and the budget. Parsing out by party affiliation, Republican candidates cited health care,[16] the economy, budget, taxes, and energy as their priorities, whereas Democratic women favored economy, educa-tion, health care, environment, and energy policies. The major differences between Republican and Democratic women is that Republican candidates do not list edu-cation and the environment among their top priorities as frequently as Democrats do. However, all women candidates mention the economy and health care with great regularity (Table 7.1).

These findings show that electoral environment, voter concerns, and voter expectations about competent leaders all played into candidates' priorities. An exit

*Table 7.1*  **Top Five Policy Priorities**

| All Candidates | Republicans | Democrats |
| --- | --- | --- |
| Economy | Health Care | Economy |
| Health Care | Economy | Education |
| Energy | Budget | Health Care |
| Budget | Tax Cuts | Environment |
| Environment | Energy | Energy |

poll of 2010 voters on issue salience found that the "economy was by far the most crucial issue." About 90 percent claimed being "worried about the direction of the economy in the coming year, and a majority said the country was seriously on the wrong track."[17] Deckman (2011) confirms these data and finds that for women voters overall the economy was paramount in the 2010 elections. In addition, passage of the Obama-endorsed health care plan Affordable Care Act of 2010 was a major point of dispute among Democrats and Republicans in this election, making it a salient campaign issue.[18]

Regardless of party, this is not a group of candidates who exhibited expected gendered norms on issue priorities. Both Republicans and Democrats shied away from talking about "women's issues" in favor of those that allegedly have more broad-based appeal. For example, the gendered and salient issue of abortion was mentioned by only 6 percent of all candidates—four Republican and two Democratic candidates. To the extent that women generally, and especially those seeking Republican backing, wish to cast themselves as competent on masculinized issues, these candidates followed that path. Since Democratic voters are more likely to cite supporting candidates on issues like the environment and education (Sanbonmatsu and Dolan 2009), it follows that the Democratic women in this sample were more likely than Republican women to mention these as concerns.

## Gendered Identities, Incumbency, and Partisanship

Despite lack of attention to women's issues on their websites, most studies of women elected officials find that once in office women are more likely than men to spend time representing women's interests. Research also demonstrates that within their respective parties women place a higher priority and spend more time on gender equity issues as well as policies related to women's traditional roles as nurturers and caregivers. Women vote differently than their male colleagues, feel a special responsibility to represent women, and work together to advance a collective agenda (Carroll 2002; CAWP 2001; Dodson 2006; Swers 2002).

Given this behavior and that the gendered identities of Republican candidates were part of the election story in 2010, I examine if women make explicit references to their gender as they campaign. For example, if a candidate noted that she was the "first woman" to run or hold a professional position or articulated that being a woman mattered in terms of her issue positions, I coded that as the candidate invoking her gendered status. Overall, almost half of the candidates noted their gendered status, and there was no difference among the women by party in terms of who did so. But this also means that half of the candidates did not explicitly construct themselves as "women candidates." As with their relative inattention to women's issues, this suggests that gender and the media hype about 2010 being the "Year of the Woman" was not something that candidates felt was especially valuable as they sought victory.

Once in office, both Republican and Democratic women act as representatives for women's interests. Thus, I examined if the incumbents in my sample were more likely than challengers to note their gendered status. Due to the myriad advantages incumbency confers, women already holding office may feel more secure articulating a relationship between descriptive and substantive representation, especially if they have a track record of doing so in Congress. Indeed, when controlling for partisan identity, all incumbents were twice as likely to talk about their gendered statuses—66 versus 31 percent[19]—confirming the salience of incumbency in campaigns regardless of other factors. This finding also suggests that as more women win and hold onto their national seats, gender-based surrogate and descriptive representation could continue to increase.

### Previous Experience, Partisanship, and Electoral Success

Although women, especially Republican women running in 2010, were heralded for bringing much needed outsider perspectives to Washington, many had prior political experience. Almost 60 percent of the candidates under study had previous political experience, and there were no partisan differences among them: 59 percent of Democrats and 58 percent of Republicans held prior elected or appointed offices. And when controlling for incumbency, both Republican and Democratic women had significantly greater chances of winning their elections if they held previous elected or appointed office. Democrats had 61 percent chance of being elected versus 21 percent chance for those without it. Despite being lauded for their relative newness, Republican women without previous experience had a 49 percent chance of being reelected versus an 85 percent chance for those who were not new to electoral politics.[20] Although this was touted as the "Year of the Conservative Woman" (McManus 2010), candidates were not immune from factors that all office seekers encounter in general elections.

# Conclusions

Republican women fared relatively well in the 2010 elections. However, it is not obvious that their being Mama Grizzlies mattered in terms of their electoral fortunes. Indeed, these findings suggest otherwise. Although there are some evident partisan differences in terms of campaign styles and outcomes,[21] what is also salient are the similarities between Republican and Democratic women among the factors examined. Being challengers or inexperienced or mentioning their maternal status influenced their campaigns and whether or not they won their races. General elections for all candidates usually require appealing to a broad base of supporters, and many challengers in these races faced incumbents who typically have an upper hand in reelection campaigns. The most startling finding from these data is the significance of motherhood for these candidates. First, although most of these women are mothers, very few articulated that this was relevant to their issue positions, likely due to voter expectations about women's capabilities and priorities. The large discrepancy in campaign outcomes for women related to their mentioning being mothers is especially noteworthy. Women candidates may believe that gender can sometimes be an asset or liability but prefer to make this cue subtle. Studies do show that once women enter elective office they behave differently than men in terms of issue priorities, but these candidates did not provide many clues that they intended to behave that way. Democratic women are more likely to embrace their gendered identities, suggesting that Republican women may consider it a liability in their quest for office. And this research shows that they might be right. Highlighting a focus on "equality" versus gender role differences is likely a wise strategy for women running for office. This also confirms that gender conformity and masculine norms are still salient for women as they seek positions of institutional power.

The extent to which motherhood should matter for women is not new but does reveal the challenges that all women, regardless of partisan affiliation, face as they seek political influence as elected officials. Feminist and conservative women activists have long invoked their identities as mothers in politics, in part because it gave, and continues to give, women legitimacy to act in the public sphere. Whether or not this holds true for women running for office is less clear. The cases examined in this study indicate that despite women's increasing presence in state houses and Congress, debates about the status of motherhood are not likely to diminish and are central to the realm of electoral politics.

While this study shows that Democratic and Republican candidates share some experiences as women running for office, feminist activists are not necessarily eager to support conservative women's bids. Since feminists have called for increasing the number of women in elective office, however, their opposition requires that they clearly differentiate between women candidates who promote feminist goals over those who do not. Feminist groups faced this challenge in 2008 when they endorsed Barack Obama and Joe Biden over John McCain and Sarah Palin in the presidential race and needed to clarify why they did not back a woman running for vice president (Schreiber 2012b). In 2010, the feminist National Organizational for Women political action committee also reminded its backers that "as feminists, we cannot allow right-wing candidates (not even the 'mama grizzlies') to take control of Congress."[22] Given such institutionalized feminist opposition, the aforementioned advocacy for Republican women by conservative women's groups could be especially critical for these office seekers.

Republican women's representation in office is growing slightly, but candidates are not explicitly delineating themselves based on gendered characteristics. We should continue to pursue why this is the case and if partisan differences factor into the campaign process. Can Republican women transform the party and its base, or will these candidates and elected officials have to oblige masculinized behavior and issues to fit in? How Republican women candidates grapple with their own party's perceived sexist image and policy goals will also be something for scholars and activists to watch in the future.

### Notes

1. Palin's ad can be found at http://www.youtube.com/watch?v=oF-OsHTLfxM.
2. For example, Susan B. Anthony List supports pro-life women candidates.
3. Of the ninety women serving in the 2012 Congress, sixty-one were Democrats and twenty-nine were Republican. Of the 1,750 women serving in state legislatures in 2012, 679 were Republican. Data available from the Center for American Women and Politics (CAWP).
4. For the purposes of this analysis, I use *conservative* and *Republican* interchangeably.
5. Here I am using *feminine* and *masculine* to refer to stereotypical understandings of men and women's behaviors and characteristics. Carroll cites myriad studies supporting the idea that the public does view men and women through these gendered and narrow lenses.
6. CAWP. 2012. "Face Sheet: Women Candidates in 1992–2012." http://www.cawp.rutgers.edu/fast_facts/elections/documents/canprimcong_histsum.pdf (accessed March 8, 2013).
7. Elder and Greene (2012) do find an opposite effect, concluding that being a mother makes a voter more liberal.
8. Of the ninety women serving in the 112th Congress (2011–2013), twenty-nine were Republican. This represents an increase from the twenty-one Republican women serving in the previous Congress. Data obtained from the Center for American Women and Politics at http://www.cawp.rutgers.edu.
9. I published another study using this data set (Schreiber 2012c). Parts of that study are reproduced and referenced in this chapter as well.
10. This measure is a bit tricky since there is no official Tea Party organization and one of the main Tea Party groups (Tea Party Patriots) does not endorse candidates. However, the national Tea Party Express endorsed candidates, as did Sarah Palin, who was linked to the Tea Party in this election. Their endorsements made national news according to a sweep of news stories found on Nexis/Lexis. If the candidate had an endorsement from either of these sources (or if her opponent was endorsed by either), she was considered Tea Party endorsed. Given that the media did little to distinguish among Tea Party organizations and Sarah Palin, these endorsements likely provided cues to voters about Tea Party support.
11. Of course, economic policies affect social relations and social relations factor into citizens' economic well-being and status. Here, this term distinguishes among social or cultural issues like abortion, gay rights, family structures, and those that focus on policies targeting economic structures, institutions, and regulations.
12. Tea Party Patriots. 2011. "About Tea Party Patriots." http://www.teapartypatriots.org/about/ (accessed March 8, 2013).
13. For example, if a candidate said, "As a mother, health care reform is important to me," I coded that as articulating a connection between maternal status and issue position/priority. If it was not clear from their campaign Web pages whether or not candidates had children, I looked at their Wikipedia pages, newspaper stories, and online bios to gather that information.
14. In the regression model that generated these probabilities, the mentioning parenthood dummy variable was significant at a $p = .053$ level, with sixty-four cases.
15. Issue priorities were usually found on the "Issues" section of the Web page or on their home pages if they did not have an "Issues" page.
16. The meaning of *health care* as discussed by these candidates varied. Some explicitly referenced the Affordable Care Act of 2010 (a.k.a. "Obamacare"), while others just discussed the need to provide health care to a broader range of the U.S. public.
17. Jackie Calmes and Megan Thee-Brenan. 2010. "Independents Fueled G.O.P Gains." *New York Times*. November 3, A8. http://www.nytimes.com/2010/11/03/us/03exit.html.

18. This analysis originally appeared in Schreiber 2012c.
19. A chi-square test indicates that this is significant at $p = .001$.
20. Significant at $p = .006$ level with ninety-two cases.
21. For more in-depth analysis of how these candidates presented themselves during this campaign see Schreiber 2012c.
22. This comment can be found at National Organization for Women's email blast list: http://salsa.wiredforchange.com/o/5996/blastContent.jsp?email_blast_KEY=87580.

# 8

# Different Portraits, Different Leaders? Gender Differences in U.S. Senators' Presentation of Self

KIM L. FRIDKIN AND PATRICK J. KENNEY

## Introduction

Representative governments use a form of democratic rule, typically elections, to provide accountability between leaders and the people. Representatives spend a considerable amount of time, energy, and resources communicating with constituents between elections and during campaigns. A fundamental problem for U.S. representatives is communicating with hundreds of thousands, if not millions, of constituents. Most congressional districts include over 700,000 constituents, while state populations range dramatically from approximately a half million to over 30 million citizens. Members of Congress employ a number of different approaches to communicate with citizens. These approaches are diverse and include mailings, telephone calls, small meetings in towns and cities, large gatherings in parades and athletic events, pamphlets, interviews with reporters and editors, press releases, official and campaign websites, and advertisements in newspapers, on TV, on radio, and on the Internet (see, e.g., Fenno, 1978, 1996; Herrnson, 2004; Jacobson, 2009; Kahn and Kenney, 1999). The messages embedded in these mediums are dynamic, changing in response to political events and the ebb and flow of electoral cycles.

These communication strategies have many goals, but chief among them is for representatives to make strong claims for why they should remain in office. At a minimum, representatives must demonstrate that they are "responsive" to citizens' preferences (Manin, Przeworski, and Stokes, 1999). Communicating responsiveness requires representatives to "present" themselves to their constituents (Fenno, 1978) and to "explain" their Washington activity (Pitkin, 1967).

Scholars have been trying to understand representatives' communications for at least thirty years (for a review see Herrnson, 2004). However, across this time frame, the descriptive face of the U.S. Congress has changed dramatically. Currently, 20 women serve in the U.S. Senate, representing well over 100 million constituents (CAWP, 2012). In contrast, following the 1986 elections only 22 years ago, only two women held seats in the U.S. Senate (i.e., Kansas and Maryland), representing 6.7 million citizens (CAWP, 2010). These dramatic changes raise new and interesting questions for students of representation. For example, do women and men legislators "present" themselves differently to constituents? Do women and men representatives "explain" Washington activity differently with citizens? Surprisingly, we do not know the answers to these basic questions.

To be sure, there is evidence that women and men "act" differently in office. For example, female policymakers, like women in the electorate, are more likely to take liberal positions on a wide variety of issues, including gun control, social welfare, civil rights, and environmental protection (e.g., Burrell, 1994/1996; Dodson and Carroll, 1991; Epstein, Niemi, and Powell, 2005; Poole and Zeigler, 1985; Schumaker and Burns, 1988; Welch, 1985). Women legislators are also more likely than men to take the lead on issues of special interest to women (e.g., Boles, 2001; Diamond, 1977; Reingold, 2000; Thomas, 1994).

Similarly, women and men seem to approach policymaking differently, with men taking a more formal, hierarchical, coercive approach and women approaching policymaking and leadership by emphasizing openness, consensus building, and egalitarianism (see, e.g., Kathlene, 1995, 1998; Kirkpatrick, 1974; Thomas, 1994). And some researchers have found that female representatives believe they place more emphasis on constituency service, that they are more approachable, and that they are more trusted than their male colleagues (e.g., Flammang, 1985; Richardson and Freeman, 1995; but also see Reingold, 2000).

With clear differences in how women and men legislate, we expect to see similar variance in how women and men communicate with constituents. A straightforward approach to the examination of the communication process between representatives and constituents is to examine legislators' "controlled communications." These are the messages legislators deliver to citizens and the news media to demonstrate how they are responding to constituent demands and preferences. Mayhew (1974) referred to these communications as legislators' efforts to "advertise" their responsiveness to citizens as a way of securing their reelection. The most easily accessible controlled communication from U.S. lawmakers is press releases.

Although senators yearn for press coverage, it is often difficult to isolate the specific impact that news coverage has on constituents' evaluations of legislators. However, there is mounting evidence that politicians who "advertise" their representational messages and activities are able to generate more favorable assessments among constituents. Scholars examining political pamphlets (see, e.g., Lipinski, 2001; Lipinski and Neddenriep, 2004; Yiannakis, 1982), websites (see, e.g., Bickers et al., 2007), and press stories (see, e.g., Arnold, 2004; Druckman, 2004; Schaffner, 2006) have found that constituents, on balance, know more about legislators and are more likely to think their legislator is doing a good job when they are exposed to media messages. The U.S. Senate is an ideal laboratory for our study. Currently, 20 percent of U.S. senators are women. Several of these women senators are quite senior, elected in the early 1990s or earlier. In addition, women senators represent a variety of states ranging from very small (e.g., Maine) to the largest in the nation (i.e., California). The U.S. Senate, because of its staggered six-year terms, provides variability in the electoral cycle. In the next section, we present the underlying theoretical explanations for our expectations that women and men senators will communicate differently with constituents.

# Expectations and Hypotheses

We expect men and women legislators to act strategically, emphasizing messages that will generate favorable images among constituents. More specifically, men and women politicians are likely to recognize the pervasiveness of gender stereotypes and adopt messages to take advantage of perceived strengths while downplaying or compensating for perceived weaknesses.

## Senators' Communications about Legislation

U.S. senators must develop a communication strategy targeting the important issues of the day. We theorize that senators' policy messages will focus, to a large degree, on issues that highlight and emphasize a senator's stereotypical strengths. People, a priori, expect male politicians to be better at issues where the primary goal is to defeat the competition (e.g., economy, business, defense), while people expect female politicians to be more effective with communal issues, where the main goal is to help others, such as health care or caring for the environment (e.g., Huddy and Terkildsen, 1993; Lammers, Gordijn, and Otten, 2009; see also Chapter 3 in this volume). These attitudes follow directly from gender expectations: men are seen as competitive and assertive, and women are perceived as communal and socially oriented. Therefore, women politicians are viewed as more capable at handling social issues, while male politicians are expected to be better equipped to handle economic, defense, and foreign policy issues (see, e.g., Alexander and Andersen, 1993; Falk and Kenski, 2006; Kahn, 1996; Lawless, 2004b; Matland, 1994; McDermott, 1998; Rosenwasser and Dean, 1989; Sapiro, 1982).

We expect both men and women senators to highlight their stereotypical strengths regarding issues for two reasons. First, we know that when men and women run for office they often emphasize different sets of issues, with male candidates focusing more on international affairs and budget policy and women emphasizing social-oriented issues like education and social welfare (Dabelko and Herrnson, 1997; Herrnson, Lay, and Stokes, 2003; Kahn, 1996; but also see Bystrom et al., 2004; Dolan, 2005). We expect that candidates, once elected, will remain faithful to their issue priorities or risk facing negative electoral consequences (Arnold, 1992; Pitkin, 1967).

Furthermore, men and women emphasize different issues as candidates and as officeholders because they have distinct policy priorities. Research examining the issue agendas and legislative initiatives of men and women officeholders consistently demonstrate that women are more likely to work on issues of special concern to women (see, e.g., Swers, 2002; Thomas, 1991). Senators, by emphasizing their "preferred" issues in their communications, hope to set the public's agenda regarding the pressing issues of the day (see, e.g., Erbring, Goldenberg, and Miller, 1980; Iyengar and Kinder, 1987; McCombs, 1993). Furthermore, by focusing on their policy strengths, senators hope to increase the salience of these issues and to "prime" the public to consider these policy dimensions when thinking about their sitting senators (e.g., Iyengar and Kinder, 1987).

## Senators' Communications about Personal Traits

Legislators want citizens to know who they are, where they came from, and what they are like. And citizens want to know about the character of their representatives. According to Fenno (1978, 1996), House members and senators want citizens to consider them to be "good" people. While being viewed as a good person or trustworthy is important, representatives also want their constituents to view them as strong leaders, competent, effective, and empathetic.

Legislators strive to enhance people's views of their personality characteristics in their representational messages. In deciding the types of traits to highlight in their representational messages, men and women face different obstacles. Research in social psychology demonstrates that people hold leadership prototypes, and these prototypes organize how information is processed and how leaders are evaluated (see, e.g., Lord and Maher, 1991; Scott and Brown, 2006).

Furthermore, there is considerable evidence that the traits associated with the leadership prototype are agentic traits, like intelligence, dominance, and decisiveness (see, e.g. Lord, de Vader, and Alliger, 1986). And research in political science demonstrates that traits associated with the prototypical political leader, such as experience, competence, and strength, are also agentic in nature (see, e.g., Huddy and Terkildsen, 1993; Kinder, 1986; Kinder et al., 1980; Markus, 1982).

Given the salience of agentic traits for the evaluations of leaders, U.S. senators need to assure their constituents that they embody these characteristics. Since there is a clear overlap between men's stereotypical strengths and the prototypical characteristics of leaders, women senators need to revise constituents' views regarding their possession of agentic traits. Women senators, more than their male colleagues, need to highlight their experience, strength, and competence in their representational messages.

Male senators, on the other hand, do not need to highlight their agentic traits. People's adherence to gender stereotypes leads them to see men as more decisive, stronger, and knowledgeable. Instead, male senators may feel more of a need to shore up their communal qualities in their communications. Since gender-role stereotypes lead people to view male senators as less empathetic, less helpful, and less caring than their female counterparts, male senators may spend time trying to improve their constituents' views of their communal credentials. Demonstrating empathy is an important quality linked with electoral success (Fenno, 1978, 1998).

While press releases often highlight policy matters, these controlled communications rarely discuss the senators' personal traits. Instead, the press releases may emphasize certain legislative actions that signify or imply that the senator possesses certain personal characteristics. To begin, senators spend time allocating federal dollars and brining home projects to their states. In the senators' press releases, they may advertise these efforts at "allocation responsiveness." Men and women senators may differ in how they advertise their allocation responsiveness. Since men need to revise perceptions that they are not as caring or empathetic as their female counterparts, male senators may be more likely to advertise their successes at "taking care" of the state as a way of improving constituents' views of their connectedness and concern. Highlighting successful projects such as saving jobs at a local plant or improving the state's water quality may encourage people to view these senators as more concerned about the lives of their constituents.

In addition to allocation responsiveness, senators may advertise their "symbolic responsiveness" in the press releases. Symbolic responsiveness refers to actions focused on building trust and confidence with constituents (Eulau and Karps, 1977; Fenno, 1978; Wahlke, 1971). Senators routinely take part in symbolic activities (e.g., participating in a parade) and make symbolic statements (e.g., formally thanking veterans for "maintaining America's freedom").

Since male senators need to improve constituents' views of their empathy and trustworthiness, men may spend more time highlighting their symbolic activities as a way of increasing confidence and rapport with their constituents and ideally revising citizens' stereotypical views of their empathetic qualities. Women, in contrast, may not want to allocate resources and space on something where they have a natural advantage.

In his classic book *The Electoral Connection*, Mayhew (1974) discusses the importance of position taking as a way for representatives to use roll call votes to stake out popular positions on issues. However, position taking may also be used to highlight a senator's decisiveness or resolve. By highlighting a specific position on an issue or a set of issues, a senator may be demonstrating his or her ability to make hard decisions, even though these decisions may sometimes be unpopular. In other words, position taking may signal to constituents that the senator is tough and not afraid of making difficult choices. Given this line of reasoning, we expect that women senators may have a greater desire to take clear positions on issues as way of highlighting their decisiveness and changing people's stereotypes of women as weak.

Just as women senators may be more likely than male senators to advertise clear policy positions as a way of demonstrating their tenacity, women senators may be more likely than their male colleagues to highlight their leadership positions within the U.S. Senate. By emphasizing their "chairmanship" of an important subcommittee or by discussing their party leadership posts, women are attempting to revise potentially damaging stereotypes constituents may hold about women's leadership abilities. By stressing leadership positions, women senators may also be sending a message about their experience and effectiveness. Since women senators need to dispel worries about their possession of these types of agentic traits, we expect women to be more likely than men to mention their leadership positions in their press releases.

Finally, Mayhew (1974) explains that representatives often engage in credit claiming, where a member of Congress asserts responsibility for desirable policy outcomes (e.g., lower taxes, improved social security benefits, better economy) or claims credit for bringing a popular project back to the state. By claiming credit for helping constituents, senators are trying to demonstrate how much they care for the citizens of their states. Given gender-role expectations, people may view men senators as less caring than women senators. Therefore, male senators may feel more compelled to explicitly claim credit for legislative successes benefiting their constituents. By claiming credit in their press releases, male senators may be trying to revise potentially damaging stereotypes regarding their communal qualities.

However, credit claiming is an electorally advantageous strategy for incumbent senators. And while women senators may be more reluctant than male senators to claim credit overall, women may be more likely to claim credit for issues and projects highlighting their stereotypical strengths. [1] More specifically, women may be more likely to claim credit on "female" issues (e.g., education) or "female" projects (e.g., projects related to the care of children). In contrast, male senators will highlight their successes for all projects and issues, regardless of content.

In the end, we expect men and women to communicate differently with constituents in their press releases. Men and women senators will attempt to highlight their perceived stereotypical strengths with regard to issues and revise perceptions of their stereotypical weaknesses when it comes to personal traits.

# Design

We drew a sample of 32 U.S. Senators from the 109th Congress (2005–2006) to examine how men and women senators communicate with their constituents. We included all of the sitting female senators ($n = 14$) in our sample and then sampled male senators who matched the female senators in terms of Americans for Democratic Action (ADA) scores and seniority.[2] See Appendix A for a list of the senators included in the sample, along with the senator's party affiliation, seniority, and ADA score in 2006.[3] For each senator, we collected all press releases from the senator's official website for January–April 2006 and August–November 2006. Given the large number of press releases posted on Senate websites, we sampled every other day.[4] We coded 1,920 press releases with an average of 50 press releases per senator.

In coding the press releases, we attempted to measure three different types of responsiveness: legislative responsiveness (e.g., discussion of policy, bill sponsorships); allocation responsiveness (e.g., discussion of federal projects in states); and symbolic responsiveness (e.g., discussion of "nontangible" actions such as participating in a parade or touting the state's National Football League football team).[5] For the discussion of issues, coders counted the number of paragraphs discussing an issue or policy matter, the senator's specific position on the policy, and whether the senator claimed credit for a successful policy outcome.

Overall, the majority of the press releases discussed policy (58 percent), while almost one-quarter of the press releases announced a new or ongoing federal project (24 percent). Approximately one-tenth of all the press releases (11 percent) focused on a symbolic action, such as creating "National Milk Day" or renaming a bridge in honor of a military hero. Finally, 6 percent of the press releases focused on something other than policy, projects, or symbolism, for example, announcing a visit by a national or state leader.[6]

# Findings

## Press Releases on Public Policy

We begin by examining policy discussion in press releases. We look at the substance of the issue emphasis in senators' controlled communications. The data in Figure 8.1 indicate that men and women senators emphasize their stereotypical policy strengths in press releases. Men mention competitive issues more than communal issues (57 percent v. 43 percent, $p < .01$). Similarly, women senators tend to prefer discussing communal issues compared with competitive issues (53 percent v. 47 percent, $p < .01$). Furthermore, men senators are more likely than women senators to discuss competitive issues in their press releases (57 percent v. 47 percent, $p < .01$).

We examine whether these gender differences persist in a multivariate model, controlling for additional factors. To begin, we need to control for the party of the senator since Democrats will be more likely than Republicans to focus on "compassion" issues, like health care, the environment, and education. And we want to make

Proportion of Women Partisans in Selected State Houses

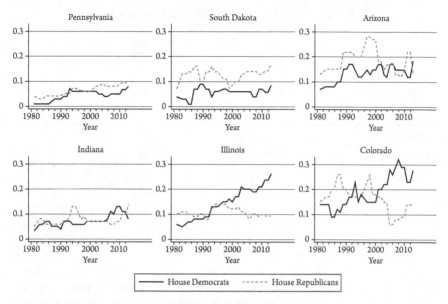

Compiled from data from the Center for American Women in Politics (CAWP)
Common scale for all state legislatures

*Figure 8.1* Gender Differences in Policy Emphasis in U.S. Senators' Press Release
*Note:* Competitive issues include defense, foreign policy, business, inflation, economy, budget, energy, farm, taxes. Communal issues include health care, elderly, welfare, childcare, education, the environment.

sure that women's greater focus on compassion issues is not driven by the fact that women senators are more likely to be Democrats than Republicans.

We also control for three additional factors: the seniority of the senator; the senator's proximity to reelection; and the length of the senators' press releases. Senior senators, who may be "safer" electorally, may be less likely to focus on policy matters—communal or competitive issues—in their press releases. Second, the senator's proximity to the upcoming election could affect how often senators communicate with constituents about issues. In particular, as senators approach election they may be more likely to discuss issues, both competitive and communal issues compared with senators whose reelection is two or four years away. Third, we control for the number of paragraphs in each press release so that specific foci are not simply a function of the length of the senators' press releases.[7]

The findings in Table 8.1 demonstrate that the gender of the senator does indeed shape the focus of the issue discussion in press releases. Women senators are more likely to talk about communal issues like education, health care, and the environment in their press releases and male senators spend significantly more time focusing on competitive issues like the economy and foreign policy, even when we

*Table 8.1*  **Logistic Regression Predicting Discussion of**
**Competitive and Communal Issues in Press Releases**

|                              | Communal Issues | Competitive Issues |
| ---------------------------- | --------------- | ------------------ |
| Gender of Senator            | .22 (.13)*      | −.37 (.13)***      |
| Party of Senator             | .24 (.11)**     | .40 (.11)***       |
| Election Year                | .10 (.13)       | .39 (.13)***       |
| Seniority                    | −.012 (.009)    | −.012 (.008)**     |
| Number of Paragraphs         | .025 (.007)***  | .02 (.007)***      |
| Constant                     | −1.56 (.14)***  | −1.10 (.13)***     |
| % of Cases Correctly Predicted | 76%          | 71%                |
| N                            | 1,920           | 1,920              |

*Notes:* Unstandardized logit coefficients are followed by standard errors in parentheses. The dependent variable is whether the press release mentioned competitive or communal issues. Competitive issues are defense, foreign policy, business, inflation, economy, budget, energy, farm, taxes. Communal issues are health care, elderly, welfare, childcare, education, and environment. Gender of the senator is coded 1 for female senators, 0 for male senators. Party of the senator is coded 1 for Democratic senators, 0 for Republican senators. Election year is coded 1 for senators up for reelection in 2006, 0 for other senators. Seniority is coded as years in office. Number of paragraphs is the number of paragraphs per press release.

***$p < .01$; **$p < .05$; *$p < .10$.

control for the senator's party, seniority, proximity to election, and the length of the press releases.

In addition, and as expected, the party of the senator influences the issue content of press releases. We find that Democratic senators spend significantly more time focusing on communal issues compared with Republican senators. Furthermore, Democratic senators are more likely to discuss competitive issues compared with Republican senators. The greater emphasis on competitive issues may reflect the political context of 2006. One of the most important issues, according to public opinion polls in 2006, was President George W. Bush's handling of the Iraq War (Preston 2006). Democratic senators, in their press releases, spent substantially more time focusing on the Bush Administration's handling of the war in Iraq compared with Republican senators.[8]

The electoral context also matters, according to the results in Table 8.1. Senators who are approaching reelection (compared with two or four years away) are significantly more likely than other senators to talk about competitive issues. These senators may want to stake out positions on issues or to demonstrate their ability to deal with these salient issues as they approach their reelection bids. In addition, and as expected, senior senators are less likely to mention competitive and communal issues in their press releases. Finally, the probability of discussing competitive and communal issues increases with the length (in paragraphs) of the press releases.[9]

## Press Releases Highlighting Projects

Senators discuss the federal projects they have brought back to their state in about one-quarter of their press releases. Since men need to revise perceptions that they are less caring and empathetic, we expect male senators will be more likely to advertise their successes at "taking care" of the state as a way of improving constituents' views of their empathy and connections to the state.

We examined the number of projects mentioned in press releases and found that men senators are significantly more likely to mention projects compared with women senators. In particular, male senators average around two mentions per press release, while their female counterparts average one mention per press release.[10] We explored whether the gender difference in discussion of projects remains statistically significant in a multivariate model. As in the analysis in Table 8.1, we controlled for differences in the senator's seniority, the senator's position in the election cycle, the senator's party, as well as the length of the senator's press releases.

The results of the multivariate analysis are presented in Table 8.2.[11] The negative and statistically significant coefficient for the gender of the senator indicates that men are significantly more likely than women senators to mention specific federal projects, such as the opening of a new post office or funding aimed at revitalizing an urban community. The greater emphasis on messages about projects may be an attempt by male senators to demonstrate their empathy for citizens of their states. In contrast to the gender of the senators, Democrats and Republicans do not differ in their emphasis on federal projects, senior senators are not more or less likely to focus on these types of projects, and proximity to reelection does not influence the likelihood a senator discussing projects in their controlled messages.

## Press Releases on Symbolic Activities and Statements

Symbolic activities and statements are aimed at fostering trust and empathy between citizens and legislators (e.g., Fenno, 1978). Since male senators need to improve constituents' views of their empathy and trustworthiness, they may spend more time highlighting their symbolic activities as a way of increasing confidence and rapport with their constituents and ideally revising citizens' stereotypical views of their communal qualities.[12]

Senators do not advertise their symbolic activities nearly as often as their policy priorities or their distributive activities. Only about 1 in 10 press releases mention the senator's symbolic actions, for example, naming a library after a local hero or

*Table 8.2* **Negative Binomial Regression Estimates**

| | Predicting Allocation Responsiveness in Press Releases Mentioning Federal Projects |
|---|---|
| Gender of Senator | −.29 (.15)* |
| Party of Senator | −.10 (.14) |
| Election Year | −.23 (.16) |
| Seniority | .01 (.01) |
| Number of Paragraphs | .03 (.01)** |
| Constant | .12 (.17) |
| Likelihood Ratio χ2 | 23.27*** |
| Degrees of Freedom | 5 |
| Number of Observations | 1920 |

*Notes*: Standard errors are in parentheses, followed by levels of significance. The dependent variable is the number of paragraphs claiming credit for an issue or policy outcome. Gender of the senator is coded 1 for female senators, 0 for male senators. Party of the senator is coded 1 for Democratic senators, 0 for Republican senators. Election year is coded 1 for senators up for reelection in 2006, 0 for other senators. Seniority is coded as years in office. Number of paragraphs is the number of paragraphs per press release.

***$p < .01$; **$p < .05$; *$p < .10$.

cutting a ribbon at a ceremony commemorating the opening of a new federal courthouse. In the bivariate case, we found that male senators are somewhat more likely to mention these symbolic activities compared with women senators.[13] However, when we ran a multivariate model, we discovered that the gender of the senator is unrelated to whether or not symbolic communications appear in press releases.[14] Therefore, our expectation that male senators would emphasize symbolic statements to shore up their "communal" disadvantage is not supported by the data. Men and women senators are equally unlikely to emphasize these symbolic connections with constituents in their press releases.

## Press Releases on Position Taking and Leadership Credentials

Since position taking may signal to constituents that the senator is tough and not afraid of making difficult choices, we expected women senators to have a greater desire to take clear positions on issues as way of highlighting their decisiveness and changing people's stereotypes of women as weak. Women senators may also seek to emphasize their agentic qualities by spending more time discussing their legislative positions (e.g., committee chair, leadership position). By emphasizing their "chairmanship" of an important subcommittee or by discussing their party leadership posts, women attempt to revise potentially damaging stereotypes that constituents may hold about women's leadership abilities. Since women senators need to dispel worries about their possession of agentic traits, we expected women to be more likely than men to mention their leadership positions in their press releases.

When we compared men and women senators, we found that nearly half (47 percent) of women's press releases mention their leadership positions, while men cite their positions of power only 37 percent of the time.[15] Similarly, women are more likely than their male counterparts to take clear positions on policy positions in their press releases. In fact, in more than 25 percent of their press releases, women senators take a specific stance of an issue, whereas male senators take unambiguous stands on issues 18 percent of the time.[16]

We examined the impact of gender in models predicting two dependent variables: (1) the number of times senators mention their leadership positions; and (2) the number of times senators stake out specific positions on issues. The results of this analysis are presented in Table 8.3.[17] As with the previous analyses, we controlled for the party and seniority of the senators as well as the senator's proximity to election and the number of paragraphs in the press releases.

The findings in Table 8.3 suggest that women senators do indeed emphasize their leadership positions in Congress more than men senators. In particular, women senators are more likely to mention their position on important committees and subcommittees as well as to advertise their leadership position in the chamber. We also found, as expected, that female senators are clearer when talking about matters of public policy than their male counterparts. Women senators are more likely to stake out a clear position on an issue in their press releases compared with male senators. Even controlling for a series of political factors, the gender of the senator significantly influences how often senators mention their positions of leadership and how often senators take specific positions on policy matters.

A look at the additional variables in the models revealed that senior senators are more likely to talk about their leadership positions and are more likely to discuss issues in a clear manner compared with their more junior colleagues. Also, GOP senators, who controlled the Senate in 2006, were more likely to talk about leadership positions compared with Democrats. These senators are also more likely than their Democratic colleagues to take clear sides on issues. And, not surprisingly, senators who are nearing reelection are less likely to take clear stands on issues compared with senators whose electoral campaigns are two or four years away.

## Press Releases on Credit Claiming

Representatives often engage in credit claiming, where a member of Congress asserts responsibility for desirable policy outcomes (e.g., lower taxes, improved social security benefits, better economy) or for bringing a popular project back to

*Table 8.3* **Negative Binomial Regression Estimates Predicting Discussion of Leadership Positions and Clarity of Issue Positions in Press Releases**

|  | Leadership Positions | Clarity of Issue Positions |
|---|---|---|
| Gender of Senator | .37 (.13)*** | .35 (.09)*** |
| Party of Senator | −.68 (.11)*** | −.31 (.08)*** |
| Election Year | −.05 (.13) | −.28 (.10)*** |
| Seniority | .02 (.007)*** | .01 (.005)** |
| Number of Paragraphs | .03 (.006)*** | .03 (.005)*** |
| Constant | −2.133 (.15)*** | −1.38 (.11)*** |
| Likelihood Ratio χ2 | 66.14*** | 68.11*** |
| Degrees of Freedom | 5 | 5 |
| Number of Observations | 1,920 | 1,920 |

*Notes:* Standard errors are in parentheses, followed by levels of significance. The dependent variable, leadership position, is measured by the number of paragraphs discussing the senator's leadership positions (e.g., committee or subcommittee chair, party leadership position) in the U.S. Senate in the press release. The dependent variable, clarity of issue positions, is measured by the number of paragraphs in the press release stating an explicit position on an issue. Gender of the senator is coded 1 for female senators, 0 for male senators. Party of the senator is coded 1 for Democratic senators, 0 for Republican senators. Election year is coded 1 for senators up for reelection in 2006, 0 for other senators. Seniority is coded as years in office. Number of paragraphs is the number of paragraphs per press release.

***$p$ <.01; **$p$ <.05; *$p$ <.10.

the state (Mayhew, 1974). Given gender-role expectations, people may view men senators as less caring than women senators. Therefore, male senators may feel more compelled to explicitly claim credit for legislative successes benefiting their constituents. To test our expectation, we began by looking at whether men and women differ in their likelihood of claiming credit on issue matters. We examined the number of paragraphs in a press release where a senator claims credit for an issue or policy outcome. In addition, we distinguished between credit claiming for competitive issues and credit claiming for communal issues. The findings for the three models are presented in Table 8.4.[18] Turning to the findings in the first column, male senators are significantly more likely than female senators to claim credit for favorable policy outcomes. Even controlling for the senator's party, seniority, proximity to the election, and the number of paragraphs in the press releases, men are found to be more likely than women to praise their own accomplishments.

*Table 8.4* **Negative Binomial Regression Estimates**

|  | *Predicting Credit Claiming for Policy Outcomes* | | |
|---|---|---|---|
|  | *Credit Claiming* | | |
|  | *Overall* | *Competitive Issues* | *Communal Issues* |
| Gender of Senator | −.47 (.15)*** | −.89 (.39)** | −.15 (.29) |
| Party of Senator | −.003 (.13) | −.63 (.31)** | .70 (.25)*** |
| Election Year | .74 (.15)*** | .91 (.38)** | 1.06 (.28)*** |
| Seniority | .007 (.009) | −.03 (.03) | .009 (.02) |
| Number of Paragraphs | .009 (.008) | .02 (.01)* | .001 (.01) |
| Constant | −1.62 (.15)*** | −3.82 (.41)*** | −2.25 (.25)*** |
| Likelihood Ratio $\chi$2 | 26.19*** | 16.06*** | 37.55*** |
| Degrees of Freedom | 5 | 5 | 5 |
| Number of Observations | 1,920 | 1,920 | 1,920 |

*Notes:* Standard errors are in parentheses, followed by levels of significance. The dependent variable is the number of paragraphs claiming credit for an issue or policy outcome. Competitive issues are defense, foreign policy, business, inflation, economy, budget, energy, farm, taxes. Communal issues are health care, elderly, welfare, childcare, education, and environment. Gender of the senator is coded 1 for female senators, 0 for male senators. Party of the senator is coded 1 for Democratic senators, 0 for Republican senators. Election year is coded 1 for senators up for reelection in 2006, 0 for other senators. Seniority is coded as years in office. Number of paragraphs is the number of paragraphs per press release.

***$p$ <.01; **$p$ <.05; *$p$ <.10.

A look at different types of issues shows that men are significantly more likely than women to claim credit for competitive issues (see column two in Table 8.4). Male senators are more likely to tout their policy achievements for issues corresponding to their stereotypical strengths compared with women senators. However, when examining communal issues, we found that men and women senators do not differ in their likelihood of claiming credit. The results in Table 8.4 suggest that the content of policy discussion does influence whether men and women senators claim credit for policy outcomes. Women are less likely than men to claim credit in general (for all issues), and they are significantly less likely to claim credit on competitive issues. However, women are not more or less likely than men to claim credit for issues that correspond to women's stereotypical strengths.

An examination of the rival explanations in the three models indicates that senators approaching reelection are much more likely to claim credit for policy successes than senators two and four years away from their next reelection bid. Proximity to reelection is powerfully related to credit claiming in each of the three models in Table 8.4. We also see that Democrats and Republicans are equally likely to claim credit on policy matters in general. However, the substance of the issues is important for Democratic and Republican senators. GOP senators are more likely to claim credit on competitive issues, and Democratic senators are more likely to stress communal issues. This is an interesting finding and resonates with the theory of "issue ownership" (Petrocik, Benoit, and Hansen, 2003–). Republicans are seen as able to keep taxes low and government small and to maintain a strong national defense, while Democrats are expected to help the elderly, protect social security and the environment, and provide health care for citizens.

Senators also claim credit for bringing popular projects back to their states. Therefore, we replicated the analysis in Table 8.4, but we examined press releases

*Table 8.5* **Logistic Regression Predicting Credit Claiming for Federal Projects**

|  | Credit Claiming | | |
|---|---|---|---|
|  | Overall | "Male" Projects | "Female" Projects |
| Gender of Senator | −.86 (.39)** | −2.36 (1.26)* | .29 (.60) |
| Party of Senator | −.90 (.37)** | −.49 (.87) | −1.25 (.67)* |
| Election Year | .46 (.43) | 1.62 (.99) | −1.75 (1.08) |
| Seniority | .06 (.02)** | −.10 (.09) | .08 (.04)** |
| Number of Paragraphs | .03 (.03) | .12 (.05)** | .02 (.04) |
| Constant | −2.44 (.37)*** | −3.73 (.72)*** | −3.94 (.67)*** |
| % of Cases Correctly Predicted | 91% | 98% | 97% |
| N | 463 | 463 | 463 |

*Notes*: Unstandardized logit coefficients are followed by standard errors in parentheses. The dependent variable is the number of paragraphs claiming credit for federal project. "Male" projects are related to the following areas: defense, jobs, farm, and business. "Female" projects are related to the following areas: health care, the poor and elderly, childcare, education, and the environment. Gender of the senator is coded 1 for female senators, 0 for male senators. Party of the senator is coded 1 for Democratic senators, 0 for Republican senators. Election year is coded 1 for senators up for reelection in 2006, 0 for other senators. Seniority is coded as years in office. Number of paragraphs is the number of paragraphs per press release.

***p <.01; **p <.05; *p < .10.

mainly about federal projects. We looked at credit claiming overall and then distinguished between credit claiming on projects corresponding to "male" policy domains (e.g., a project creating jobs by building a new highway) and "female" policy domains (e.g., funding a methamphetamine taskforce).[19]

The results presented in Table 8.5 demonstrate that the gender of the senator does indeed shape credit claiming on federal projects. Just as with issues, men are more likely to claim credit for projects generally and are more likely than women senators to claim credit for projects corresponding to their stereotypical strengths. However, with regard to projects relating to "female" issues, there is no relationship between the gender of the senator and claiming credit for federal projects related to women's stereotypical strengths.

We also found that party and seniority are related to credit claiming on projects, with senior senators and Republican senators spending more time claiming credit for bringing projects back to their states compared with junior and Democratic senators. Republicans, who were in the majority in 2006, and senators with more seniority are more likely to have the clout and political power required to bring more projects back to their states.

# Conclusion

Scholars studying representation have been increasingly interested in whether men and women legislators conduct their jobs differently. As the number of women legislators has climbed, so has research aimed at examining these types of questions. Conspicuously missing from this research agenda are efforts to explore how men and women legislators communicate with their constituents. If men and women behave differently but these differences are not communicated to their constituents, then democratic accountability is incomplete. In this chapter, we advanced our understanding of how male and female U.S. senators communicate with constituents through their official press releases.

We developed a two-pronged theoretical framework based on gender stereotypes citizens hold about men and women politicians. On one hand, we expected men and women senators to produce press releases that highlight positive gender stereotypes about policy matters. And on the other hand we predicted that senators would generate press releases aimed at counteracted potentially damaging gender stereotypes about personal characteristics. Our expectations regarding reinforcing positive gender stereotypes and revising negative gender stereotypes were confirmed.

We found that the gender of the senator predicted the types of issues senators discussed in press releases. For example, male senators played to their strengths and focused on "male" issues in their press releases, and they also took "credit" for policy outcomes, especially those related to "male" issues. In addition, senators worked hard to offset citizens' negative views of their personal traits. Male senators provided evidence of their caring and empathy by sending out press releases focusing on the federal projects they helped deliver to their states and by emphasizing their symbolic responsiveness. Women senators, on the other hand, strove to tell citizens that they were experienced and decisive by focusing press releases on the important positions they hold in the U.S. Senate and by pronouncing clear positions on matters of public policy.

This study, based on a snapshot of U.S. senators in 2006, suggests that men and women deliver distinct representational messages. The gender differences in communications are stable and persist, even when we control for the party of the senator. However, we need to explore whether these gender differences are stable across time and across difference modes of communication. For example, when senators rely on Facebook, Twitter, and Instagram to reach out to their constituents, are men and women senators delivering different messages? As communication mechanisms change and evolve, scholars need to assess whether men and women senators continue to deliver distinct messages when using new media.

## Appendix A: Sample of Senators

| Name of Senator | Class[1] | First Elected | ADA Score[2] |
|---|---|---|---|
| **1. Murkowski, Lisa** (R-AK) | III | 2002 | 20 |
| 2. Stevens, Ted (R-AK) | II | 1966 | 5 |
| **3. Lincoln, Blanche** (D-AR) | III | 1998 | 95 |
| 4. Pryor, Mark (D-AR) | II | 2002 | 90 |
| **5. Boxer, Barbara** (D-CA) | III | 1992 | 100 |
| **6. Feinstein, Dianne** (D-CA) | I | 1992 | 95 |
| 7. Allard, Wayne (R-CO) | II | 1992 | 0 |
| 8. Salazar, Ken (D-CO) | III | 2004 | 100 |
| 9. Martinez, Mel (R-FL) | III | 2004 | 5 |
| 10. Nelson, Bill (D-FL) | I | 2000 | 55 |
| 11. Durbin, Richard (D-IL) | II | 1996 | 100 |
| 12. Obama, Barack (D-IL) | III | 2004 | 100 |
| **13. Landrieu, Mary** (D-LA) | II | 1996 | 95 |
| 14. Vitter, David (R-LA) | III | 2004 | 15 |
| **15. Mikulski, Barbara**(D-MD) | III | 1986 | 90 |

| 16. Sarbanes, Paul (D-MD) | I | 1976 | 100 |
|---|---|---|---|
| **17. Collins, Susan** (R-ME) | II | 1996 | 65 |
| **18. Snowe, Olympia** (R-ME) | I | 1994 | 65 |
| 19. Levin, Carl (D-MI) | II | 1976 | 100 |
| **20. Stabenow, Debbie** (D-MI) | I | 2000 | 100 |
| 21. Burr, Richard (R-NC) | III | 2004 | 5 |
| **22. Dole, Elizabeth** (R-NC) | II | 2002 | 5 |
| 23. Sununu, John (R-NH) | II | 2002 | 10 |
| **24. Clinton, Hillary** (D-NY) | I | 2000 | 100 |
| 25. Schumer, Charles (D-NY) | III | 1998 | 100 |
| 26. Smith, Gordon (R-OR) | II | 1996 | 20 |
| 27. Wyden, Ron (D-OR) | III | 1994 | 95 |
| 28. Chafee, Lincoln (R-RI) | I | 1998 | 75 |
| 29. Cornyn, John (R-TX) | II | 2000 | 10 |
| **30. Hutchison, Kay** (R-TX) | I | 1993 | 15 |
| **31. Cantwell, Maria** (D-WA) | I | 2000 | 95 |
| **32. Murray, Patty** (D-WA) | III | 1992 | 95 |

[1] Class 1: 2006 election, Class 2: 2008 election, Class 3: 2010 election.

[2] ADA scores are for 2005.

## Notes

1. Dolan and Kropf (2004), looking at newsletters of members of Congress, found that male legislators are more likely to claim credit on "male" issues (e.g., defense), while women legislators are more likely to claim credit on "female" issues (e.g., health care).
2. More specifically, we relied on a modified stratified sampling procedure.
3. Currently, there are 17 women in the U.S. Senate: 5 Republicans and 12 Democrats. All of the women senators in our sample and all of the women currently serving in the U.S. Senate are Anglo, and none of these women are members of the Tea Party.
4. To avoid any periodicity problems, we sampled every odd day in the first month (e.g., January) and then every even the day the following month.
5. We did not measure service responsiveness since the discussion of casework did not appear in the senator's press releases.
6. In conducting our content analysis, we followed the procedures described by Neuendorf (2002). A team of eight research assistants (political science graduate and undergraduate students) coded the press releases. Coders were provided with the code sheet and a codebook containing detailed instructions for coding each variable. The comprehensive guidelines in the codebook helped to reduce individual differences among coders. During the content analysis training sessions, the coders completed a pilot coding of 10 press releases. Differences among coders were discussed, if necessary, adjustments were made to the code sheet and codebook. The pilot procedure helped standardize the coders' techniques so that all coders were assessing the content in the same way. Given the comprehensiveness of the training procedures,

maturation effects by coders during the content analysis process were reduced. In addition, coders were kept blind to the purpose of the study as a way to reduce potential bias. Cohen's kappa was used to assess intercoder reliability, with a resulting score of .93 ($p < .001$), indicating a high level of agreement among coders.

7. We rely on logistic regression because we are examining the probability of mentioning competitive issues (1 = mentioning these issues, 0 = not mentioning these issues) or communal issues in the senators' press releases.

8. This difference is statistically significant ($F = 7.31, p < .01$). (All statistical tests are two-tailed tests unless otherwise specified.)

9. We also looked at whether committee assignments were related to a senator's emphasis on competitive and communal issues since committee assignments often drive legislative priorities (see Hall, 1996; Schiller, 1995). Standing committees in the U.S. Senate were easily classified as dealing with competitive or communal issues or both. Given the large number of committees focused on competitive issues, all the senators in the sample sat on at least one of these committees. However, not all senators sat on a committee devoted to communal issues. We looked at whether senators sitting on committees devoted to communal issues were more likely to mention these types of issues in their press releases. However, committee assignment failed to significantly influence the senator's likelihood of mentioning communal issues. Similarly, senators sitting on communal committees were not significantly less likely to focus on competitive issues.

10. The gender difference in allocation emphasis is statistically significant ($F = 24.157, p < .01$).

11. Since we are examining count data (i.e., the number of times a senator mentions federal projects in his or her press releases), we rely on negative binomial regression since the data are not normally distributed around the mean.

12. Some researchers have found that female state legislators believe they devote more time than men to keeping in touch with constituents and helping constituents with their problems (e.g., Carey, Niemi, and Powell, 1998; Richardson and Freeman, 1995). However, Reingold (2000) found that few gender differences in perceived constituency service efforts.

13. The gender difference in symbolic emphasis reaches statistically significance ($F = 2.152, p < .10$, one-tailed test).

14. The binomial regression coefficient for gender in the model predicting the number of references to the senator's symbolic activities is −.12 with a standard error of .22. The control variables included in the multivariate model are the party of the senator, proximity to an election, seniority of the senator, and the number of total paragraphs in the press releases.

15. This difference is statistically significant ($F = 9.42, p < .05$).

16. This difference is statistically significant ($F = 7.30, p < .05$).

17. As in our earlier analysis, we rely on negative binomial regression since we are examining count data here (i.e., the number of times a senator takes a clear position in his or her press releases).

18. Since we are examining count data here (i.e., the number of times a senator claims credit in his or her press releases), we rely on negative binomial regression since the data are not normally distributed around the mean.

19. The dependent variable is 1 if the senator claims credit in the press release and 0 if the senator does not claim credit. Given the binary dependent variable, we rely on logistic regression in this analysis.

# 9

# Female Governors and Gubernatorial Candidates

VALERIE R. O'REGAN AND STEPHEN J. STAMBOUGH

Although women make up approximately 53 percent of the population in the United States, when it comes to leadership men are the ones who have historically made the decisions for the country. Whether it is at the national or subnational levels, government has been viewed as a man's job. This is especially apparent as we look at the office of governor in the fifty states that make up this country. It is also apparent during the election cycles for these state leadership positions when female candidates' names on the ballots are no longer a rarity. This chapter will examine what we know about women running for governor and governing based on party, geography, and other political factors with a special focus on the new class of ideologically conservative women governors. We begin with a look at the history of women who have sought and held the office of governor and the state of the research on women and gubernatorial politics.

## History and Context of Female Gubernatorial Candidates and Governors

It has taken many years for women to become part of the governing landscape of the United States. During most of that time, women were either absent or held token status within the government. For example, since 1922 there have been only thirty-nine female senators in the history of this country, and 237 women have held seats in the House of Representatives since 1917 (CAWP 2013a).

At the state level, women have been more successful getting elected to state legislatures, with 23.7 percent of these seats currently being held by women. In fact, the percentage of female state legislators has surpassed 30 percent in eight states currently, with other states coming close to the 30 percent mark. In South Carolina and Louisiana, the percentage of female representation lingers around the 10 percent level. However, since 1971 the number of female state legislators has increased more than fivefold (CAWP 2013c).

When examining the chief executive position at the state level, we find that women's success in reaching the governors' office is also a relatively recent occurrence. As of 2012, only thirty-four women have served as governor of a state, six of them holding the position currently.[1] Eleven of the female governors gained their seat by either succeeding their husbands for different reasons, standing in as an interim governor, or finishing their predecessors' terms; three of these women (Jane Hull of Arizona, Jodi Rell of Connecticut, and Jan Brewer of Arizona) were later elected to a full term (CAWP 2013e).

The first female governor was Nellie Tayloe Ross of Wyoming, who won a special election to fulfill her deceased husband's term. She was inaugurated on January 5, 1925. Fifteen days later, the second female governor took office in Texas; Miriam "Ma" Ferguson was elected as a surrogate for her controversial husband who was forbidden from seeking office due to his impeachment and removal from office. The first female governor to get elected based on her own credentials and support was Ella Grasso of Connecticut in 1974 (CAWP 2013e).

Over the years Texas, New Hampshire, Kansas, Connecticut, Washington, and Arizona have had more than one female governor. Besides Ma Ferguson, Ann Richards was elected and served in Texas from 1991 to 1995. In New Hampshire, the voters elected Jeanne Shaheen to the office in 1996; however, Shaheen was not truly the first female governor of the state. Vesta Roy served as governor of New Hampshire for a short period in 1982–1983 after the incumbent governor died while in office. Kansas elected its second female governor in 2002. The first, Joan Finney, ran as a challenger and was elected in 1990; she served during the same term as Ann Richards. The second female governor in Kansas, Kathleen Sebelius, was elected in 2002. Sebelius is the first female governor whose father also served as governor of a state (John Gilligan of Ohio served from 1971 to 1975). Besides Ella Grasso, who served from 1975 to 1980, M. Jodi Rell governed Connecticut from 2004 to 2011. Washington State can also boast about having two female governors. Dixy Lee Ray served from 1977 until 1981, and Christine Gregoire completed her second term in 2013. Finally, Arizona can claim the most female governors—four over the years. Three of the four women—Rose Mofford, Jane Hull, and Jan Brewer—assumed the office to complete the terms of their predecessors. Mofford chose not to run for reelection in 1990; however, Hull and Brewer ran as incumbents in 1998 and 2010 and won. Additionally, in 2002 the voters of Arizona elected Janet Napolitano to the governor's mansion based on her own credentials (CAWP 2013e).

Of those women who have been governor, the shortest term in office was held by Vesta Roy of New Hampshire, who served for just seven days. The longest term in office for a female governor is held by Ruth Ann Minner (DE), Linda Lingle (HI),

Jennifer Granholm (MI), and Christine Gregoire (WA). All four completed two four-year terms (CAWP 2013e).

Except for governors Ross and Ferguson during the 1920s, female governors were a rare occurrence until the mid-1970s. From 1975 to the current time, there was at least one female governor in office except for the early 1980s.[2] During the late 1980s and throughout the 1990s, the number of female governors increased incrementally so that by 2001 there were five women holding the top state executive office. In 2004 a record nine women serving simultaneously as governor was reached. That record number was matched in 2007 (CAWP 2013e).

Despite the relatively few females who have achieved the top executive leadership position of their state, the number seeking this coveted position has increased more noticeably over the years. Examining the period between 1970 and 2012, we find 1986 to be a breakout election cycle for female gubernatorial candidates, when a total of eight women ran for the office nationwide. In the sixteen years before 1986, there had been only ten female gubernatorial candidates in total, three of those election years (1970, 1972, and 1980) lacking any female candidates (CAWP 2013g).

One other point of historical significance regarding the 1986 election was that this was the first time a state (Nebraska) had two women, Republican Kay Orr and Democrat Helen Boosalis, running against each other for the governorship. The second occurrence of two competing female gubernatorial candidates took place in 2002, when Republican Linda Lingle and Democrat Mazie Hirono vied for the governorship of Hawaii. Finally, in 2010 voters had the choice between two female gubernatorial candidates in both New Mexico and Oklahoma. In New Mexico, Republican Susana Martinez ran against Democrat Diane Denish, and in Oklahoma Republican Mary Fallin competed with Democrat Jari Askins for the governor's office. In all four of these female-versus-female gubernatorial races, the Republican candidate was victorious (CAWP 2013e).

Following the trend of the 1986 election, the year 1990 demonstrated that this increase in women running for the governor's office was not a fluke; that year, there were eight female gubernatorial candidates nationwide. Looking at the election of 1994, one sees further growth in the number of female gubernatorial candidates; during that election, a total of ten women ran for the office across the country. The elections of 1998, 2002, 2006, and 2010 demonstrate that women gubernatorial candidates are becoming a more common occurrence; all four of these elections featured ten female candidates for the governor's office (CAWP 2013g).

Besides the increase in numbers of female gubernatorial candidates, the qualifications and name recognition of these candidates are contributing to their viability. For example, the 2002 cohort of female candidates included three lieutenant governors, two state treasurers, two state attorneys general, and multiple state and local executive and legislative office holders. Furthermore, since 2002, all but one of the female gubernatorial candidates had national, state, or local government experience. The only female candidate for governor without formal government credentials was businesswoman Meg Whitman, the Republican candidate for California governor in 2010. Still, Whitman had significant name recognition from her experience as former chief executive officer of eBay.

As the number of female gubernatorial candidates increases, we believe that the opportunities to elect more women to the governorship will also expand. It appears that as more women run for and win local, state, and national offices, the candidate pool of women with ample political experience to run for governor and mount viable campaigns also increases. Finally, given that four of the past six presidents came directly from the governor's house—Jimmy Carter, Ronald Reagan, Bill Clinton, and George W. Bush—the prospect of electing more women to the governorship might increase the prospect of one day electing a woman president.

## Literature about Female Gubernatorial Candidates and Governors

With the increase in the number of female gubernatorial candidates and governors, opportunities to examine the dynamics of these elections and terms in office arise. Much of the research on female gubernatorial candidates has addressed the barriers that women face when they run for governor. A significant amount of this research focuses on the media coverage of their campaigns where scholars continue to find that women are at a disadvantage when compared with their male opponents (Kahn 1996; Rausch, Rozell, & Wilson 1999; Devitt 2002; Banwart, Bystrom, & Robertson 2003; Fowler & Lawless 2009), although some argue that coverage is becoming more gender balanced (Jalalzai 2006).

In addition, the literature examines the type of voter support female gubernatorial candidates receive by analyzing preelection and exit polls (Rausch & Rausch 1997; O'Regan & Stambough 2002). These studies show that the gender, age, partisanship, and region of residence of voters have varying effects on voter support of female gubernatorial candidates. In one study on the predictive accuracy of opinion polls (Stout & Kline 2011), the authors found that voters are less supportive of female candidates in their responses to polling questions than they are when they are voting. In other words, polls underestimate the support for female candidates that might affect the competitiveness of the female candidate. To the degree that this underestimation occurs, women candidates may face additional difficulties due to the reluctance of voters and donors to support candidates who are perceived to be losing.

Furthermore, scholarship demonstrates that the novelty of being the first female gubernatorial candidate in a state's history (O'Regan & Stambough 2011) and differences in the parties' nomination of female candidates (Stambough & O'Regan 2007) can have a negative effect on the success of female candidates for governor. Additionally, the society and culture of each state may influence the likelihood of women entering and winning their respective races. States with a more progressive culture and those with a history of women winning office are more conducive to female candidates seeking high office (Windett 2011).

Besides these scholarly works, journalists have provided comparisons of female gubernatorial campaigns. Celia Morris (1992) compares the successful gubernatorial campaign of Ann Richards of Texas to the unsuccessful gubernatorial campaign of Dianne Feinstein of California during the 1990 electoral cycle. Likewise, by using the journalistic coverage of the 1986 Nebraska gubernatorial race, John Barrette (1987) provides press coverage of the historic election where Kay Orr competed against Helen Boosalis to become the first female governor of the state. Because this was a race against two female candidates, Orr was successful in her bid while Boosalis shifted her public service to leadership roles in volunteer organizations following her defeat (Davis 2008).

Due to the relatively small number of women who have served as governor, research on these successful women is limited. Most of the literature on female governors is biographical or autobiographical, focusing on the personal lives and careers of the subjects (Richards & Knobler 1989; Kunin 1994; Tolleson-Rinehart and Stanley 1994; Beard 1996; Weissman 1996; Scheer 2005; Alter 2006; Palin 2009; Roberts 2011). Although this research is somewhat limited in its scope of analysis, it still offers insights into the political development and experiences of the women.

There are studies that compare and analyze the leadership of women governors. Susan R. Madsen (2009) analyzes how ten female governors developed into leaders by examining their private and public life experiences. Further research examines the differences in notions of power in the personalities of female governors (Barth & Ferguson 2002). By comparing female and male governors, the authors conclude that women's gubernatorial personalities lead to the female governors' success as legislative leaders because women combine greater adaptability and an increased emphasis on empowerment of others than do male leaders.

We also find research on the discourse of women serving as governor. Brenda DeVore Marshall and Molly A. Mayhead (2000) offer a collection of chapters on the rhetoric of five diverse female governors demonstrating how the women used discourse strategies during their campaigns and terms in office. For example, Kaml (2000) explores how Governor Ann Richards of Texas used humor and sarcasm to thrive in a particularly masculine political environment. A further example is the finding by Mayhead and Marshall (2000) concerning how Governor Barbara Roberts of Oregon attempted to reframe the debate surrounding budgetary crises.

Finally, research is now addressing the policy priorities of female governors expanding our understanding of how women govern. Using the State of the State addresses of women who governed from 2000 until 2010, Richard Herrera and Karen Shafer (2012) determine the policy agendas of these women. The authors also examine the role of partisanship in the prioritizing of policy issues and find that Democratic women leaders are more likely to highlight health issues while Republican women leaders are more likely to emphasize social welfare issues.

## Women for Governor: Running and Winning

### Different "Years of the Woman"

Several years come to mind as watershed years for women in American politics, including the 1992 "Year of the Woman" and the vice presidential nominations of Democrat Geraldine Ferraro in 1984 and Republican Sarah Palin in 2008. Perhaps 2012 will become one of those years as women hit the 20 percent mark in the U.S Senate. For women gubernatorial candidates, however, these are not the big years. In part because most states do not hold their gubernatorial elections in presidential years, the watershed moments for women governors are almost always during the less covered midterm elections, and therefore any trends are less likely to be viewed as a national trend.

For the history of female gubernatorial campaigns, a few of these midterm years stand out as important for the future of women gubernatorial candidates. In the modern era, 1974 was the first year in which a major political party nominated a woman to be governor based on her own credentials. In fact, three women were nominated that year, with Ella Grasso of Connecticut becoming the first woman elected governor in this era. Following that year, however, the number of women nominated in a given cycle stayed relatively flat for more than a decade.

The next watershed moment was 1986 when eight women were nominated to be governor, including two in Nebraska. Only two of those eight women won, but, following 1986, the number of women nominated in a midterm gubernatorial election cycle never decreased from the 1986 record. In 1990, eight women were also nominated, and ten women were nominated in each midterm gubernatorial election cycle from 1994 to 2010. The level of consistency may indicate a plateau effect, and it will be interesting to see if it takes an additional mobilizing effort to increase beyond ten nominations in a year. It also shows that the groundbreaking year of 1986 was not an anomaly. It truly was a year that began a trend that lasted for a generation and continues to this day.

In addition to 1986, important years for the story of female gubernatorial candidates include 2002 and 2010. The 2002 election cycle was uncommon because, of the ten women running for governor, nine of them were running in open seats. Only State Treasurer Jimmie Lou Fisher of Arkansas faced an incumbent seeking reelection in her loss to Governor Mike Huckabee. In circumstances when women are nominated to run against male incumbents, many of those female candidates secure a nomination only to face long odds of beating the incumbent. The record number of women running for open seats gave rise to the expectation that women may win a higher number of these seats. In the end, four female gubernatorial candidates won that year, and four years later all four of them won reelection. Additionally, 2010 is distinct because it was a breakthrough year for Republican women, particularly ideologically conservative women gubernatorial candidates. The politics behind this watershed year are highlighted in an extended section later in this chapter.

## State Political Characteristics

In this section we examine three state characteristics. We look at the geography of women gubernatorial candidates and comment on regional differences. We then turn our attention to two unusual state characteristics: the impact of political scandals on the success of women candidates and the novelty factor of women candidates within a given state.

## Political Geography

After the 2012 elections, forty states have had at least one female candidate receive the gubernatorial nomination of a major political party. Yet ten states have not had a female candidate in the modern era.[3] The number of female gubernatorial candidates in a state's history is portrayed on the cartogram map in Figure 9.1.[4] A few patterns are visible on the map. First, there is a lack of female gubernatorial candidates in the South. In fact, approximately 23 percent of southern states[5] have never nominated

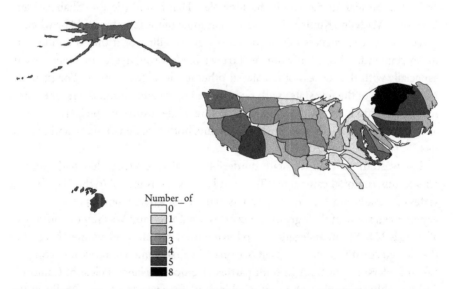

Number_of
0
1
2
3
4
5
8

*Figure 9.1* Cartogram of United States Based on Number of Female Gubernatorial Candidates

a woman for governor, and roughly 45 percent of southern states have nominated only one female gubernatorial candidate. Non-southern states, in comparison, have a much better record of nominating women for governor. Only 19 percent of these states have never nominated a female gubernatorial candidate. Furthermore, while roughly two-thirds of the southern states have nominated one or less females for governor, roughly two-thirds of the non-southern states have nominated up to three female candidates for governor.

These facts demonstrate that southern politics and political culture do not appear to be the most conducive for the rise of female politicians (Bennett & Bennett 1992; Studlar & Welch 1996). An examination of the nine southern states that have nominated either zero or only one female candidate indicates that this is not limited to the office of governor. None of these states rank in the top half of states as far as the percentage of women in the state legislatures. In addition, there is little history of women in these states being successful at other levels of statewide office or in Congress (see Chapter 16 in this volume).

The second geographic observation concerns the New England and western states, which appear to be fertile ground for such candidacies. Four or more women candidates have received a major party nomination for governor in the New England states of New Hampshire, Vermont, Rhode Island, and Connecticut. The large number of candidates in this area, however, may be a little misleading. Many of these different candidacies are multiple races by just a few individuals. For example, there have been four female gubernatorial candidacies in Rhode Island. Three of these candidacies, however, were Myrth York's unsuccessful campaigns in 1994, 1998, and 2002. Similar stories can be told for New Hampshire (Jeanne Shaheen) and Vermont (Madeline Kunin). The question in some of these states could be whether these candidacies successfully shattered the glass ceiling or if they are limited to just certain individuals. Only time will truly tell. However, the future seems bright, especially with the success of females at other levels of government. For example, Maine is one of the few states with two female U.S. senators until the recent retirement of Olympia Snowe, and New Hampshire made history in the 2012 election, after which women will hold the governorship, both U.S. Senate seats, and both of its U.S. House seats (CAWP 2013e).

For western states, each state bordering the Pacific Ocean has had multiple female gubernatorial campaigns. This trend also extends inland to the neighboring states of Nevada and Arizona. In fact, it is in the West where women politicians have experienced some of their greatest successes. California and Washington both have all-female U.S. Senate delegations. Following the 1998 election, women held all of the elected constitutional offices in Arizona. The first women to move into congressional leadership positions in both parties (Democrat Nancy Pelosi of California and Republican Jennifer Dunn of Washington) are from the West. Finally, in the 2002 elections Hawaii became only the second state to nominate two women to run against each other for governor, and these women met in a rematch of sorts in 2012.

This time Democrat Mazie Hirono beat Republican Linda Lingle for the state's U.S. Senate seat.

The obvious question is why are women candidates historically successful in the West? One answer is the reverse of the previous discussion about the South. Most of the western states have had a long history of women in lower levels of political office. Furthermore, there appears to be something culturally more welcoming of women in higher office in the West. It is often viewed as the opposite of the South in terms of traditionalism that apparently helps female candidates in the West (Burrell 1994). Furthermore, in *Madam President: Shattering the Last Glass Ceiling* (Clift & Brazaitis 2000), the authors refer to the belief that, since the West tends to be populated by people "from somewhere else," women candidates there have an extra advantage because they (1) are viewed as outsiders more than men are and (2) they do not necessarily face long-standing political and social structures to join.

In addition to these observations, there appears to be a lack of female candidacies in many states of the old industrial "rust belt" from New York to Wisconsin and neighboring Minnesota. Although it is logical for female candidates to be more prevalent in states with more progressive traditions of women in the professional workplace, women in other political offices, and in which the predominate party affiliation of female candidates is Democratic, it is somewhat surprising that traditionally "liberal" states like Minnesota, Wisconsin, and New York have never had a female gubernatorial candidate from a major party. Comparing that with the multiple candidates from more traditionalistic, agrarian states like Montana, Nebraska, and Kansas makes the point that female gubernatorial candidates are not just from populous states with a more cosmopolitan culture.

The patterns found for women winning their parties' nomination also hold for women winning the general election. Including the recent successes of southern governors Bev Purdue of North Carolina, Mary Fallin of Oklahoma, and Nikki Haley of South Carolina, non-southern states have a higher average number of winning campaigns by women. This finding, however, is mostly due to the difference in the number of candidates by region. Women can win only if they run. They run more outside of the South, and therefore they win more outside of the South. These regional trends are worth watching in the future, particularly if women start to win more party nominations and general elections in traditionally Republican areas of the South. As discussed later, this emerging trend may lead to a distinctly more ideologically conservative group of women governors than we have seen historically.

## Political Scandals

One of the important state political characteristics is a simple one: scandal. There is a long literature about media coverage and voter perception of honesty in candidates that finds women candidates to be perceived as more honest than their male counterparts (Kahn 1992). The history of women governors following male scandals dates back to when Ma Ferguson of Texas was elected governor as a surrogate for the scandal-impaired "Pa" Ferguson (National Governors Association 2011).

In more recent times, three of the women governors became governor due to scandals of their male predecessors. In Connecticut, Jodi Rell became governor as the result of the resignation of John Rowland following a financial scandal that led to his guilty plea on a corruption charge (National Governors Association 2011). Rell quickly became one of the more popular governors in the country and won election in her right in 2006 with 63 percent of the vote (CAWP 2013g).

The cases of Ma Ferguson and Rell are interesting, but the interaction between male scandals and the success of women governors is at an entirely different level in Arizona. Two of Arizona's four women governors became governor as a result of scandals. Mofford became governor in 1988 after Evan Mecham was impeached and removed from office on charges of obstruction of justice and misuse of funds. Mofford decided not to run for election and was succeeded by Fife Symington. Symington later resigned amid a scandal that led to his conviction on bank fraud charges, which were later overturned (National Governors Association 2011). Upon his resignation, Jane Hull became Arizona's second female governor. Unlike Mofford, Hull decided to run for election and received 62 percent of the vote in 1998 (CAWP 2013e). After women succeeded the last two male governors who were removed due to scandal, the voters of Arizona have entrusted the governorship to women in four straight gubernatorial elections: Hull in 1998; Janet Napolitano in 2002 and 2006; and current governor Jan Brewer in 2010. Maybe someday in the future, it will no longer be disadvantageous to be a male gubernatorial candidate in the state of Arizona!

## The Novelty of Female Candidates

The third state characteristic of interest is based on the state's history with women gubernatorial candidates. The *novelty* effect was shown to have a significant impact on the success of women gubernatorial candidates (O'Regan & Stambough 2011) and with similar findings for women congressional candidates (Ondercin & Welch 2005). In the gubernatorial study, the findings held even after taking incumbency out of the equation by examining only open-seat elections from 1980 to 2006. This study found that women candidates do worse if they are the first female gubernatorial candidate in their state's history. Although being novel is often viewed as a good thing and can bring extra media attention, often that extra attention is focused only on the historic nature of the candidacy.

It is also true that once a female candidate works through the sometimes hidden concern among party activists, donors, the media, and voters about how to react to a female candidate for a traditionally male position, the next female candidate faces an electoral environment in which all these political actors are more likely to have worked through their apprehensions with women running for governor. As the number of women running for political office has increased, this has diminished the novelty of female candidates (Smolowe & Cole 1992). We can hope as the authors suggest "that someday women candidates will simply be taken for granted" (p. 36).

# The Impact of Partisanship for Women Gubernatorial Candidates and Governors

In American politics, gender issues are generally associated with the Democratic Party. The *gender gap* refers to a consistent advantage the Democratic Party has with women voters. Democratic women have enjoyed most of the success by women over the last couple of decades. In this section, we explore partisan differences for female gubernatorial candidates historically. We then highlight the 2010 election as the first with significant success for Republican women. To provide additional detail about the new cohort of conservative women governors, we pay special attention to the 2010 election of Mary Fallin in Oklahoma.

## Party Differences Historically

Wilcox (1994) made the case that although 1992 was known as the Year of the Woman in politics it was really just the "Year of the Democratic Woman." That observation was based on the fact that, although women in general gained more political positions as a result of the 1992 elections, most of the winners were Democrats. Some early observers viewed 2002 as a potential "Year of the Woman Governor," but the same qualifier is applicable. The 2002 gubernatorial elections included *nine* Democratic women and *one* Republican woman. In more recent years there appears to be a bit more partisan balance among female gubernatorial nominees.

Figure 9.2 shows the number of female gubernatorial candidates by year and party from 1974 to 2012. The odd-numbered years contain races in so few states that it is impossible to make comparisons for those years. However, looking at both the even-numbered midterm election years (when most states have their gubernatorial elections) and the presidential election years, a possible trend becomes apparent. In the even-numbered election years since 1992, a substantially larger number of female Democrats received their party's nomination than did female Republicans, although the numbers were identical for the two parties in the last two midterm years of 2006 and 2010. That fact is not too surprising since women have become more important in the Democratic Party's coalition. The 2006 and 2010 election cycles for Republican women are encouraging signs for future growth in the nomination of Republican women, perhaps eventually becoming consistently on par with their Democratic counterparts and may represent an elite recruitment strategy to counter the image of the GOP as hostile to women.

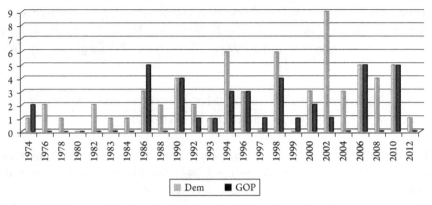

*Figure 9.2* Number of Female Gubernatorial Candidates by Party, 1974–2012

## 2010: The Year of the Conservative Republican Female Governor?

The first significant watershed moment for Republican women gubernatorial candidates may have occurred in 2010 when five women received the Republican Party nomination for governor: Jan Brewer (Arizona); Meg Whitman (California); Susana Martinez (New Mexico); Mary Fallin (Oklahoma); and Nikki Haley (South Carolina). This cohort also includes the first two women of color to be elected governor: Susana Martinez and Nikki Haley. All of these women except Meg Whitman of California were successful in their bids. However, Republicans also nominated five women for governor in 1986, five in the 1997–1998 election cycle, five in the 2006 cycle, and four women in the 1990 cycle. Although there had never been another year in which four Republican women won the governorship, as recently as 2006 three Republican women won: Sarah Palin from Alaska and incumbent governors Lingle of Hawaii and Rell of Connecticut.

The impact of 2010, however, seemed bigger and more like an identifiable new era for Republican women. It comes in the aftermath of Palin's nomination for vice president in 2008. Although her nomination did not result in a victory, it did highlight on the national scene an unapologetically conservative woman politician. Before most of the country was introduced to Palin by the John McCain presidential campaign, the most recent Republican women governors were viewed as more ideologically moderate than strongly conservative and were elected from traditionally Democratic states Hawaii (Lingle), Connecticut (Rell), and New Jersey (Christie Todd Whitman). Even Hull from Arizona, elected in 1998, was viewed as a moderate conservative governor as opposed to her earlier career as a more conservative state legislator (*National Journal* 2002).

Although there were some exceptions, the typical Republican woman elected prior to 2010 would be described as a part of the moderate wing of the Republican Party. This previous group of Republican women had to be more moderate politically if they were going to be successful in their states because those states were more liberal states. The tendency of elected Republican women being more centrist than their male counterparts is suggested by looking at the U.S. Senate. A comparison of ideological voting scores of U.S. senators from the groundbreaking election of former Senator Nancy Kassebaum of Kansas in 1978 until 2010 suggest that Republican women senators were significantly more moderate in their voting scores than their male counterparts. Using the DW-Nominate scores (Poole and Rosenthal 2007) on a scale from −1 to 1 with higher scores indicting more conservative positions, women Republicans had a mean score of 0.20 compared with a mean score of 0.35 for men Republicans during the same period.[6]

Compared with this previous era, 2010 just seems different. Of the four successful women elected governor in 2010, only Susana Martinez of New Mexico was elected in a state won by the Democratic presidential candidate in the prior presidential election. The other three women won in states where Republican candidates do not necessarily have to move to the middle to win. Although they won only 45.6 percent of the vote nationwide, Republicans McCain and Palin performance ranged from well to very well in these three states by receiving approximately 53 percent of the vote in both Arizona and South Carolina and an overwhelming 65 percent of the vote in Oklahoma. In the two decades prior to 2010, only Palin (Alaska in 2006) and Judy Martz (Montana in 2000) were elected governor in states won by the Republican presidential candidate in the previous presidential election. It is no surprise then that the 2010 class of female Republican governors skews more conservatively than previous classes because, unlike the past, Republicans were nominated and were successful in electing Republican women in predominantly Republican states. It is neither necessary nor advantageous for these governors to campaign or govern as moderates, and they can be more distinctively ideological than most other successful Republican women gubernatorial candidates.

The success of these Republican women receiving gubernatorial nominations in states likely to be won by the Republican candidate is a change from the past era, but it is too early to tell if it indicates a long-term change for the Republicans or if it is a one-time event. As time progresses, the novelty of such races will diminish, thus permitting researchers to learn more about whether differences in the barriers, opportunities, strategies, and activity of Republican women and Democratic women gubernatorial candidates are more than just the idiosyncrasies of a handful of individuals.

## Case Study: Republican Victory in All-Female Oklahoma Gubernatorial Campaign

The Oklahoma example is a great case study to highlight several unusual things about the 2010 class of Republican female governors and to delve a little deeper into this particularly conservative class of Republican women governors. Of the four Republican women elected governor in 2010, both Martinez of New Mexico and Fallin of Oklahoma won by defeating a Democratic female candidate.

Of the 2010 examples, New Mexico has a longer and more established tradition of women's success in politics than Oklahoma. Oklahoma consistently ranks among the lowest states in terms of the percentage of women in the state legislature. Women have recently received a little more success in getting elected to statewide offices, but their success at this level is still minimal. In addition, there have only been two women ever elected to the U.S. Congress from Oklahoma: current governor Fallin, who was elected to Congress in 2006; and Mary Alice Robertson, who rode President Warren Harding's coattails to election in 1920. It is safe to say that the success of women in Oklahoma politics is sporadic.

Nothing in this history of women in Oklahoma politics would have suggested that it would be one of the few states to have an all-female gubernatorial election and elect a female governor before other states that are seen as more politically female-friendly like California. However, when the contest began for nominees to replace popular but term-limited Democratic governor Brad Henry, high-profile and qualified female candidates emerged in both parties.

On the Republican side, Fallin was the favorite from the beginning. By 2010, she had held elective office for two decades: as a state legislator (1991–1995); as lieutenant governor (1995–2007); and in the U.S House of Representatives (2007–2011). Her history is one of a true trailblazing Republican woman in the state. When she was elected to the state legislature, only 8.7 percent of the entire state legislature was female, and she was one of only three Republican women in either the state senate or state house of representatives. After four years in the legislature, she was elected the first female lieutenant governor. In 2006, she was the first woman elected to Congress from Oklahoma in over eighty years. During her campaign for governor, she was opposed in the primary by State Senator Randy Brogden and easily beat him by almost twenty points; Fallin enjoyed a unified party behind her as she moved to the general election (Oklahoma Secretary of State 2010).

Her opponent in the general election was Jari Askins, who had a background in the judiciary serving as both a judge and as the first female chair of the Oklahoma Pardon and Parole Board. She was then elected to the Oklahoma state legislature and in her last term became the first woman to serve as a party caucus leader in either state legislative chamber. Following that term, she successfully ran for lieutenant governor to succeed outgoing lieutenant governor Fallin, who was running for Congress. Her path to the gubernatorial nomination in 2010 was not as smooth as her opponent's, however. During the primary she faced a well-known opponent in State Attorney General Drew Edmondson. For much of the campaign, Edmondson was perceived as the favorite until Election Day, when Askins prevailed by less than 1 percent of the total vote (Oklahoma Secretary of State 2010).

In the general election, the advantage was most definitely with Fallin. When viewed nationally, Oklahoma is a Republican state, although at times state Democrats can do well. Although term-limited Democratic governor Henry was very popular, the partisan headwinds against the Democrats in 2010 made it difficult for Askins. In addition, unlike Fallin who could run with an easily unified Republican Party, Askins had a close, contested primary and did not have the luxury of running an ideological campaign in an election cycle driven, in part, by conservative ideology. Therefore, Askins was not able to unite the Democrats as well as Fallin could unite the Republicans. According to a poll[7] (Soonerpoll.com 2010) taken in October 2010, Fallin enjoyed the support of 90 percent of self-identified Republicans, while Askins received the support of only 70 percent of self-identified Democrats. In addition, even though the same poll showed outgoing Henry with almost 70 percent approval ratings, voters were not convinced to transfer that approval to his lieutenant governor; Askins was able to secure the support of only 53 percent of those who approved of the job of the Democratic governor.

It is difficult to determine if this race is a watershed moment for women in Oklahoma politics or if this is just the culmination of the careers of two particularly successful women in Oklahoma. It is impressive and somewhat surprising that two women rose through the political ranks in each party at the same time when there were so few other women in the political pipeline within Oklahoma. It will be interesting to see if Fallin's success in Oklahoma and Haley's in South Carolina, another state with few women politicians, will begin to inspire a new generation of conservative women and reduce the barriers to women politicians within their respective states.

# Gendered Governing

How do women govern? The simple answer to the question of whether women governors govern differently than male governors is that we do not know—at least not yet. Because the number of women governors is growing with increasing variation across partisanship, geography, and ideology, we are approaching a time when the numbers will be large enough to do significant comparisons. This is not to say, however, that we know nothing about this topic. Studies have established expectations and both some comprehensive and preliminary findings using case studies, comparative case studies, and a few larger *n* studies.

## Gubernatorial Appointment Power

Few studies have looked at the actions of governors based on the sex of the governor. One of the early, more comprehensive studies looked at differences in executive appointments based on gubernatorial gender (Riccucci & Saidel 2005). Gubernatorial appointments are an important and often invisible way that governors can affect policy development and implementation in a state. The authors examined the factors that explain variations in the number of women and minorities among these appointments and found that the demographics of the state, the party of the governor, and the sex of the governor were all important in explaining the number of women in these important appointed positions. Women were more likely to appoint women. This tendency not only affects policy by creating a more diverse upper level bureaucracy but also provides new role models and career paths for young women in government.

## Power and Policy Agendas

Additional research looks at gendered differences in both the conceptualization and use of power and in the overall policy agendas of governors. Both of these areas of research employ comprehensive content analyses of State of the State addresses given by governors to determine their approach to governing and their legislative priorities. Barth and Ferguson (2002) use these speeches to investigate how governors approach coalition building. They base their expectations on an established conceptualization of more "feminine" power that produces results based on being more inclusive versus a more "masculine" power that emphasizes direct influence over others and personal prestige. They found that women governors were more likely to include appeals that are consistent with feminine power, but they also made as many masculine power references as did male governors. This indicates a more complex approach to governing as women may use a more feminine approach due to a variety of factors including socialization and traditional outsider status while effectively operating within a predominantly male political environment.

In a similar approach, additional analyses of State of the State speeches have been conducted to determine differences in policy agendas. One of the expectations that accompanied the increase in women in government was that women would bring some previously ignored issues into the public sphere. In their analysis of State of the State addresses, Herrera and Shafer (2012) found that Democratic female governors highlight health-care issues more than other governors. In addition, they found that Republican female governors focused more on social welfare policy than other governors did.

## Conclusion

The story of women governors is still evolving. We learned a lot about early trends and challenges to their election and have even begun to see changes in these patterns with the 2010 election results. We are starting to see research on the effect of women governors on policy and leadership across the United States. As the number of female gubernatorial candidates and governors increases, we will be able to learn more about the impact of these women in their state's highest political office.

## Notes

1. Two of the six are leaving office after the 2012 election. A new fifth female governor, Maggie Hassan of New Hampshire, will take office in January 2013.
2. This is not counting Roy's seven-day term.
3. For the modern era, we employ a data set from 1974 to the present, information for which was collected from CAWP and America Votes.
4. Special thanks to John Carroll of California State University, Fullerton, for his help with the cartogram.
5. For the purposes of this study, the South consists of the eleven states of the Confederacy plus Kentucky and Oklahoma.
6. DW-Nominate scores are a measure of legislator ideology using how they voted on legislation in comparison to their contemporaries in Congress. Researchers frequently use these scores.
7. Special thanks to Bill Shapard and Janeen McClure from Shapard Research for their assistance and permission to use the SoonerPoll data for this analysis.

# 10

# Representing Women's Interests in a Polarized Congress

MICHELE L. SWERS

The 113th Congress elected in the 2012 election cycle is the most diverse Congress in history. A record 20 women will serve among the 100 senators. For the first time, white men will be a minority of the House Democratic Caucus with women and racial minorities constituting the majority of the Democratic House members (Helderman 2013). Nancy Pelosi (D-CA), the first female Speaker of the House (2007–2010) and current Minority Leader, has helped lead the Democratic caucus since her election as minority whip in 2001 (Peters and Rosenthal 2010). While the contemporary Congress is more diverse than in the past, it is also highly partisan and polarized. Tracking the ideological views of members of Congress since the founding, Poole and Rosenthal (2007) note that the contemporary Congress is the most ideologically polarized since Reconstruction.

In this chapter, I explore how gender affects the policy activities of legislators in a polarized Congress. The chapter first reviews the literature on the impact of gender on the policymaking behavior of members of Congress and state legislatures. I then develop a theory of how the politics of women's rights in a polarized era shapes the policy priorities and political opportunities for women in the Democratic and Republican parties. I illustrate this theory with case studies of the confrontation over President George W. Bush's lower-court judicial nominees and the fight for the Lilly Ledbetter Fair Pay Act, the equal pay legislation that became the first piece of legislation signed by President Barack Obama. Finally, I conclude by demonstrating how the "war on women" frame in the 2012 elections reflects the new politics of women's rights, and I explore the future dynamics of gender politics within the Republican and Democratic congressional parties.

# Understanding the Policy Impact of Electing Women to Congress

Research on the policy effects of electing more women to Congress and state legislatures demonstrates that gender affects policy priorities and the nature of deliberation on issues. Gender has the greatest impact on policy activity on women's issues, variously defined. These issues generally incorporate feminist policies expanding women's rights in the public sphere such as reproductive rights and equal pay and social welfare policies that reflect women's traditional role as caregivers such as health care and education. Gender differences are most prominent in the agenda-setting phase where problems are defined and policy alternatives are proposed—as illuminated by Osborn and Kreitzer in Chapter 11. Studies of bill sponsorship and cosponsorship activity and surveys of legislators' policy priorities demonstrate that female legislators are more likely to promote social welfare and feminist initiatives (Bratton and Haynie 1999; Dodson 2006; Gerrity, Osborn, and Mendez 2007; MacDonald and O'Brien 2011; Osborn 2012; Reingold 2000; Swers 2002, 2013; Thomas 1994). Gender differences are particularly pronounced on the women's rights policies that can be directly connected to consequences for women as a group such as women's health and workplace equity.

These differences hold when other important influences on legislative activity are accounted for such as party affiliation, committee position, and constituency characteristics. For example, comparing House members who served the same districts over time Gerrity, Osborn, and Mendez (2007) and MacDonald and O'Brien (2011) found that the female representatives sponsored significantly more legislation on women's issues than the male legislators who served the same constituents. In comprehensive studies of legislative activity on women's issues from bill sponsorship to committee consideration and floor debate in both the House and Senate, Swers (2002, 2013) found that women are more aggressive advocates for legislation related to women, children, and families than are their male colleagues of the same party (Democratic men compared with Democratic women and Republican men compared with Republican women).

These gender differences persist even after accounting for constituency characteristics and important institutional factors such as committee position and freshman status. Some scholars suggest that women are broadly more prolific legislators than their male colleagues. For example, Anzia and Berry (2011) assert that because of the difficulty women face in getting elected to Congress the women who get elected are on average higher quality candidates than their male colleagues. As a result, they find that women as a group are more active legislators sponsoring and cosponsoring more bills and bringing home more federal money to their districts than their male counterparts.

The elevation of more women to legislative office also affects the nature of deliberation on issues because women are more likely to bring a distinctive perspective as women or mothers to deliberation over policy proposals. Explaining the importance of her election and expanded diversity in Congress, newly elected Wisconsin Senator Tammy Baldwin remarked, "When you're not in the room the conversation is about you. If you're in the room, the conversation is with you" (Cirilli 2012). Research demonstrates that women are more likely to advocate for women's interests in committee, to speak about women's issues on the floor, and to invoke their authority as women and mothers in committee and floor debate (Berkman and O'Connor 1993; Cramer Walsh 2002; Dodson 2006; Levy, Tien, and Aved 2002; Norton 2002; Osborn and Mendez 2010; Pearson and Dancey 2011a, 2011b; Rosenthal 1998; Shogan 2001; Swers 2002, 2013). Female legislators are more likely to view women as a distinct element of their constituency and to feel a responsibility to represent the interests of women as a group (Carroll 2002; Dodson 2006; Reingold 2000; Rosenthal 1998; Thomas 1992). There is also evidence that the inclusion of women changes the behavior of men. Examining the evolution of discourse in congressional debates over abortion, Levy, Tien, and Aved (2002) found that the way female legislators talk about abortion has influenced the substance and style of their male colleagues' floor speeches.

Looking at case studies of specific policy areas, Dodson (2006) found that female House members played pivotal roles in placing issues like domestic violence and women's health on the congressional agenda. Women lobbied their male colleagues to prioritize the Violence Against Women Act and a comprehensive women's health research bill that created an Office of Women's Health, and they helped persuade colleagues to move these bills through committee and onto the floor (see also Swers 2002). Studies of welfare reform indicate that Democratic and Republican women were instrumental in getting enhanced child support enforcement and greater childcare subsidies included in the final bill (Dodson 2006; Johnson, Duerst-Lahti, and Norton 2007; Norton 2002; Swers 2002). Moreover, women of color were uniformly opposed to the bill and joined together to offer alternative legislation and to denounce the bill on the floor as promoting racial stereotypes of welfare queens and as punitive toward women of color (Hawkesworth 2003; Johnson, Duerst-Lahti, and Norton 2007).

Moving beyond women's issues, in a study of the Senate Swers (2007, 2008, 2013) found that women bring a distinctive perspective to policy deliberations on defense policy. Female senators were more likely than their male counterparts to pursue policies that expand social welfare benefits for active duty troops and veterans. Women were more likely to engage policy debates related to the role of women in combat and other policies that uniquely affect women in the military such as sexual harassment and access to women's health services, particularly abortion. Similarly, looking at judicial nominations, Swers (2013) found that women were more likely than male senators to focus on issues of women's rights in their deliberations over judicial nominees (see also Swers and Kim 2013).

# Examining the Influence of Gender in a Partisan and Polarized Era

While the influence of gender on legislative behavior is well documented, partisanship and ideological polarization are dominant features of the contemporary Congress and state legislatures. How do gender preferences affect legislators' policy decisions in an era of extreme partisanship? In Chapter 11, Osborn and Kreitzer note that Republican and Democratic women legislators have different definitions of women's interests, which leads them to advocate markedly different policies regarding women's issues. In a study of two state legislatures, Reingold (2000) found that partisanship generally trumped gender as a predictor of legislators' priorities. Swers (2002) demonstrates the importance of majority–minority party status as a determinant of which policies a member chooses to advocate. Thus, she found that both Republican and Democratic women responded to their elevation to majority party status (Democrats in the 103rd Congress, 1993–1994; and Republicans in the 104th Congress, 1995–1996) by increasing their activism on social welfare issues. However, when Republican women achieved majority status in the 104th Congress, they reduced their advocacy of feminist issues like abortion because these issues would conflict with the Republican agenda and could alienate the party base and colleagues, harming their chance to achieve success on other priorities.

Beyond these institutional dynamics, it is clear that much of the gender differences in policy advocacy stems from activity of Democratic and moderate Republican women. However, since the 104th Congress (1995–1996), the parties have become increasingly homogeneous and polarized from each other with fewer moderates in their ranks (McCarty, Poole, and Rosenthal 2006; Poole and Rosenthal 2007). Like their male colleagues, Democratic women in the House and Senate have become more liberal over time, while polarization among Republican women has lagged that among Republican men. However, with the election of more Republican women from the South and West, the ideological positions of Republican men and women in the House converged by the 108th and 109th Congresses from 2003 to 2006 (Elder 2008; Frederick 2009, 2010). Yet in the Senate Republican women remain more moderate than their male counterparts (Frederick 2010, 2011; Swers 2013). However, two recently elected female Republican senators, Kelly Ayotte (R-NH) and Deb Fischer (R-NE), received the coveted endorsement of conservative and Tea Party icon Sarah Palin to demonstrate their conservative bona fides in contested Republican primaries (Landrigan 2010; Walton 2012).

Because the number of Republican women in Congress remains small—four in the Senate and twenty in the House for the current 113th Congress (Center for the American Woman and Politics 2013)—it is difficult to systematically analyze the policy priorities of Republican women to determine if they will advocate women's issues from a conservative and antifeminist perspective or if they will ignore these issues in favor of other policy concerns such as lowering tax rates and reducing federal regulations. However, disentangling gender differences in the policy beliefs and activities of conservative Republicans is an area ripe for future research.

Focusing on the effects of polarization on women's legislative behavior, Volden, Wiseman, and Wittmer (2013) find that in a polarized Congress women's more consensual leadership style allows them to forge greater success when they are in the minority party but harms their effectiveness as majority party legislators. Analyzing bill sponsorship activity from 1973 to 2008, the authors find that when women are in the minority they are able to keep their bills alive through later stages of the policy process. However, as a result of their more consensual style, majority party women have become less effective as Congress has become more polarized. These women are introducing more legislation, but their bills are less likely to see action than the bills of their majority party male counterparts.

## Polarization and the Politics of Women's Rights

A distinct feature of polarization is that homogeneity of issue preferences increases within the parties and the parties become increasingly distant from each other in their policy beliefs. I maintain that over time issues of women's rights have become a key element of distinction and polarization for the electoral coalitions of the Democratic and Republican parties. Social conservatives are pivotal to the base of the Republican Party, while feminist organizations are a central component of the Democratic base. As a result, it is increasingly rare to find pro-life Democratic members of Congress and pro-choice Republicans. The realignment of the parties on the abortion issue and other questions of women's rights and family values means that the reputations of the parties on women's issues have become more distinct in the minds of the voting public (Adams 1997; Sanbonmatsu 2002; Wolbrecht 2000).

At the same time, in this period of tight electoral competition when each election has the possibility to elevate a new majority party in the House and Senate, Republicans and Democrats view the mobilization of particular subgroups of women as key to electoral victory. Over the last several election cycles, Democrats wanted to increase turnout among single women, minority women, and college-educated women. Republicans targeted white, suburban mothers, a group that has been characterized as soccer moms, security moms, and Wal-Mart moms (Brownstein 2012a; Dolan, Deckman, and Swers 2011; Seelye 2012). When reaching out to voters, parties try to emphasize issues that are "owned by the party" (Petrocik 1996; Pope and Woon 2009; Sellers 2010). Thus, Republicans are viewed as more capable stewards of tax policy and national security, while Democrats are favored to handle social welfare issues like health care and education that are associated with the gender gap in public opinion. Indeed, Winter (2010) notes that voters increasingly perceive Democrats as the "feminine party" and Republicans as the "masculine party."

# A Theory of the Influence of Gender on Women's Rights Policy in a Polarized Congress

I argue that the dynamics of increased party polarization on women's rights issues and electoral competition for various subgroups of the women's vote have changed the politics of women's rights within Congress. For Democratic women, engagement of women's rights issues is almost universally positive. Democratic women can achieve action on policies that are important to them while appealing to important elements of the Democratic base that mobilize donors and voters. Advocacy for these issues in the media increases their own public profile and enhances the reputation of the party on a set of issues that the public associates with Democrats.

By contrast, for Republican women, activism on women's rights presents both benefits and pitfalls. For the dwindling ranks of moderate Republican women, activism on women's rights enhances their reputation for independence and solidifies their individual electoral coalitions. However, taking a public stand on women's rights issues such as equal pay and public funding for Planned Parenthood can alienate the Republican colleagues these women need to support their initiatives on other issues and helps the Democratic opposition by allowing them to claim proposals are bipartisan. Moreover, since the position of moderate Republican women on women's rights issues is in opposition to core elements of the Republican base, these women risk inviting a primary challenge in the next election.

For conservative women engagement of women's rights debates can provide opportunities for advancement in the caucus. Republican leaders seek out like-minded conservative women to push back against the Democratic narrative of a Republican war on women and to diversify the public face of the party. Taking on this role for the party allows conservative women to curry favor with the caucus and leadership while raising their public profile. However, women's rights issues are not core issues for the Republican Party. Therefore, engagement of women's rights can divert scarce resources of time and staff from conservative women's efforts to distinguish themselves on other more prominent Republican priorities such as advocating tax cuts and reigning in government spending. Moreover, conservative women are subject to heightened media scrutiny as women acting against the interest of women.

Finally, I maintain that the level of influence female members of Congress wield over party policy and strategy on women's rights is affected by their numerical presence within the party caucus. In her work on group dynamics in corporations, Kanter (1977) found that in male-dominated organizations, where women comprise less than 15 percent of the group, the "token women" feel pressure to conform and downplay gender differences. However, as women increase their numbers in an organization, they will feel more able to express distinctive views. Applying this theory to legislatures has yielded mixed results. Some scholars find greater activism on women's issues as women increase their presence in state legislatures and

Congress (MacDonald and O'Brien 2011; Saint-Germain 1989; Thomas 1994). However, other scholars note that business organizations are different from the political arena where legislators seek to define a policy niche and attract the media spotlight. In politics, women may be more inclined to work on women's issues when there are fewer women in the chamber (Bratton 2005; Crowley 2004). Moreover, as women increase their numbers, their presence will affect the behavior of men minimizing differences between the two groups (Bratton 2005). Finally, other scholars criticize such theories for focusing on numbers and not accounting for other factors that determine influence such as holding a party or committee leadership post that yields institutional power (Childs and Krook 2006; Dahlerup 2006; Grey 2006).

I argue that the fact that women make up a larger proportion of the Democratic than the Republican caucuses in the House and Senate combines with a Democratic Party culture that emphasizes diversity to allow women to help shape the dimensions of women's rights policy and to influence party messaging strategies on these issues. Indeed, women constituted a key part of the coalition that elevated Nancy Pelosi (D-CA) to leadership when she first ran for minority whip in 2001 (Peters and Rosenthal 2010). By contrast, the continued small numbers of women in the Republican House and Senate caucus, their diverse ideological views in the Senate, and a Republican Party culture that is less responsive to demands for increased diversity limit the ability of Republican women to leverage their numbers to gain influence over development of women's rights policy or drive party strategy. (For more on Republican leadership see Rosenthal 2008; Swers and Larson 2005).

I illustrate the new dynamics of women's rights policy in a polarized era with case studies of women's rights debates including the fight over confirmation of controversial lower-court judicial nominees during the George W. Bush Administration and the struggle to enact the Lilly Ledbetter Fair Pay Act during the Bush and Obama presidencies. The case studies are developed from analysis of media coverage of these debates, examination of the *Congressional Record* of floor debate, and interviews with Senate staffers and interest group leaders that were conducted between 2004 and 2011 as part of a larger project on gender and policymaking in the Senate (Swers 2013).[1] I then discuss the future role of Democratic and Republican women in shaping the politics of women's rights by illustrating the parts congressional women played in the war on women dynamic that shaped the 2012 election and beyond.

## Judicial Nominations and the Politics of Women's Rights

The lower federal courts play a pivotal role in determining the scope of women's rights in areas ranging from abortion to employment discrimination. Moreover, the parties compete to diversify the bench by appointing more women and minorities to the U.S. Circuit Courts of Appeals and the District Courts. President George

W. Bush made the appointment of more conservative jurists a key focus of his agenda escalating the partisan conflict over nominations. In response, Democrats took the unprecedented step of filibustering 10 appellate nominees. Reacting to Democratic obstruction, Republicans sought to deploy the "nuclear option," a plan to eliminate filibusters on judicial nominees. The crisis was averted when the Gang of 14—seven Democrats and seven Republicans—forged an agreement to preserve the filibuster while advancing some of Bush's most controversial appellate nominees (Binder and Maltzman 2009; Goldman, Schiavoni, and Slotnick 2009; Scherer 2005; Steigerwalt 2010).

Women's rights became a central feature of the confirmation wars because several of Bush's most contentious nominees had controversial records on issues from abortion to employment discrimination. For example, 5th circuit nominee Priscilla Owen, who served on the State Supreme Court of Texas, was criticized for several rulings on parental notification and access to abortion. William Pryor, 11th circuit nominee, declared in his confirmation hearing that *Roe v. Wade* is "unsupported by the text and structure of the Constitution, but it has led to a morally wrong result. It has led to the slaughter of millions of innocent unborn children" (Kaplan 2003).

In addition to the substance of women's rights, the level of diversity on the courts became a focus of the conflict when Democrats filibustered some of the president's minority and female nominees. Indeed, among the 10 appellate nominees filibustered by Democrats during the 108th Congress (2002–2003), four were women or minorities: one Hispanic male, Miguel Estrada (D.C. Circuit); Janice Rogers Brown (D.C. Circuit); an African American woman; and two white women, Priscilla Owen (5th Circuit) and Carolyn Kuhl (9th Circuit). Since the Jimmy Carter years, the parties have sought to expand the representation of women and minorities on the federal bench. Each party wants to take credit for appointing the first member of a minority group to a specific federal court or to have appointed more women and minorities than the previous president (Goldman 1997; Scherer 2005). Research on the impact of race and gender on nomination politics confirms that the parties raise the public stakes over female and minority nominees to characterize the opposition party as unfairly blocking qualified women and minorities (Bell 2002; Solowiej et al. 2005).

In their quest to move the courts in a more conservative direction and expedite the confirmation of Bush's judicial nominees, Republicans elevated the public battle over his female and minority nominees. Republicans held the most cloture votes (a parliamentary procedure for ending a debate and taking a vote) on the D.C. Circuit nomination of Miguel Estrada, a Hispanic nominee who was viewed as a possible future U.S. Supreme Court pick. They also held multiple cloture votes on Texas State Supreme Court judge Priscilla Owen (5th circuit). To highlight the unprecedented obstruction of Democrats' decision to filibuster 10 lower-court nominees, Republicans staged a 40-hour marathon debate over the use of the filibuster dubbed "Justice for Judges." They scheduled cloture votes on three female nominees—Owen,

Brown, and Kuhl—as the catalyst for the all-night debate (Binder and Maltzman 2009; Goldman et al. 2009; Steigerwalt 2010). A Republican leadership staffer who helped organize the event confirmed that the Republicans deliberately chose these women as "sympathetic figures who would embarrass the Democrats as unfair bullies in the public eye." To further elevate the unjust treatment of these women, Bush staged a Rose Lawn press conference with these three female victims of the Democratic filibuster strategy. Finally, when Republicans prepared to stage their final showdown, they chose to schedule a fifth cloture vote on Owen's nomination, as the vehicle for eliminating filibusters on judicial nominations. Owen, Brown, and Pryor were among the first nominees cleared for a vote when the Gang of 14 forged a deal on the use of the filibuster (ibid.).

Examining the involvement of women in the confirmation wars, Republican women played a very limited role in the party's efforts to paint Democrats as unfairly obstructing the confirmation of qualified women and minority nominees. Generally, party leaders and Judiciary Committee members are most engaged in confirmation politics. To date, there has never been a Republican woman on the Judiciary Committee. However, Republicans leadership and Judiciary Committee staffers reported that they wanted Republican women to take a more prominent role in the public fight over judicial nominees, and the Republican women were reluctant to engage the issue. Thus, one Republican staffer complained, "The Republican women in the Senate were MIA when it came to trying to push judges; Elizabeth Dole only went to one event. They tried to have a woman's event about opposing Kuhl, Brown, and Owen, and they had to bring women over from the House. The Republican women House members walked to the Senate steps for a press conference."

In sum, conservative women did not want to expend their political capital defending Bush's judicial nominees, preferring to focus their efforts on other issues. The moderate women were uncomfortable with the nominees' stances on women's rights and tried to avoid engaging the issue altogether. When the moderate women did object, it was behind the scenes, registering their reservations with party leaders as the leaders sought to build support for bringing individual nominees up for a vote. Thus, a Republican staffer explained that the leadership and committee staff would call meetings to respond to senators who had concerns about specific nominees and that the women spent more time studying some of the nominees with issues related to their record on women's rights before they would agree to schedule a vote. Once the votes were scheduled, the senators almost always supported the president's nominees. Thus, only moderate Lincoln Chafee (R-RI) voted against Owen; Chaffe, Susan Collins (R-ME), and Olympia Snowe (R-ME) opposed nominee Pryor, who was a strident opponent of *Roe v. Wade*.

While Republican women played a very limited role in the battle over Bush's judicial nominees, Democratic women were heavily engaged in the development of Democratic strategy over which nominees to filibuster, and they participated actively in the public battle to define the issue. Dianne Feinstein (D-CA) and Maria Cantwell (D-WA) both served on the Judiciary Committee during the showdown over the use of the filibuster. Staff reported that women outside the committee, particularly Barbara Boxer (D-CA), Debbie Stabenow (D-MI), and Hillary Rodham Clinton (D-NY), were active participants in the effort to build a public case against the nominees.

According to Democratic leadership and Judiciary Committee staff, for a nominee to be filibustered, the members of the Judiciary Committee needed to unanimously support a filibuster. The committee members would then bring the case to the full Democratic caucus. Supporting a filibuster was a hard choice for the caucus because members feared being portrayed as overly obstructionist. Moreover, conservative interest groups were running ads pressuring senators to stop obstructing the president's nominees, an attack that particularly worried Democratic senators from red states.

In this contentious atmosphere, staff reported that Democratic women played a key role in convincing the caucus to support filibusters against some of the female nominees. While the hurdles were high for initiating a filibuster on a judicial nominee, the decision to filibuster a female or minority nominee required even more discussion within the caucus. As one Democratic leadership staffer explained, "The senators would take their lead from the [Judiciary] Committee Democrats. While it was not a formal requirement, all the Democrats on the committee had to oppose a nominee for a filibuster to be considered. The standard would get higher for decisions to filibuster women and minorities. Other caucus members will listen to the women more and take their cues from them when they are deciding to filibuster a woman or minority, the women have a special role." For example, in Owen's case, a Democratic staffer maintained, "Democrats were scared to oppose Owen because she is a woman and they had already been accused of being anti-immigrant and anti-Catholic. The Democrats were scared of their own shadow at the time. Cantwell wanted to see if she could get the women to lead the charge to get the Democrats to support a filibuster of Owen. They needed someone to drive the process and get buy in. The Democratic women sent a letter to Daschle opposing her [Owen] because of her position on a range of issues like parental notification, worker's rights, and the environment. Owen had something for everyone so they did not need to focus on choice to oppose her. She was not going to be filibustered without the women stepping forward because the Democratic men did not want to be perceived as anti-women."

In addition to building support for filibustering specific female nominees, Democratic women were also active participants in party messaging efforts to shape public opinion on the issue. Female senators attended press conferences regarding specific nominees, and they were active participants in the floor debate to eliminate filibusters and in floor debates regarding specific nominees, particularly the female nominees. For example, when the Senate debated Brown's nomination, Democrats called on Boxer, Feinstein, Clinton, and Mary Landrieu (D-LA) and on two minority senators, Ken Salazar (D-CO) and Barack Obama (D-IL), to help counter the Republican picture of a sharecropper's daughter who worked her way up from humble circumstances to become a justice on the California Supreme Court (see *Congressional Record* June 6, 2005 S6075-S6094; June 7, 2005 S6129-S6146; June 8, 2004 S6176-S6207).

In sum, the showdown over Bush's judicial nominees focused public attention on jurisprudence on women's rights and expansion of diversity on the federal bench. In the effort to move nominees forward and define the debate in the public eye, Republican women played a limited role generally choosing to prioritize other issues. Individual conservative women would occasionally defend the party's position and specific nominees; however, the party leadership staff expressed disappointment that the Republican women were not more engaged. Moderate Republican women tried to avoid the debate, expressing reservations about specific nominees behind the scenes and largely voting with the party and supporting the president's nominees. By contrast, Democratic women were heavily engaged in both planning strategy over which nominees to filibuster and delivering the party message that the filibustered nominees were too extreme, particularly on issues of women's rights.

## Lilly Ledbetter, Equal Pay, and Electoral Advantage

The two-year fight over the equal pay bill, the Lilly Ledbetter Fair Pay Act, which extends the statute of limitations for filing an equal pay lawsuit regarding pay discrimination, similarly illustrates the increasingly partisan and polarized dynamic driving the politics of women's rights. For Democratic women, the debate allowed them to pursue policy changes they supported, raise their media profile, and burnish the party's image as a champion of women's rights. For Republican women, the legislation created a host of dilemmas. Support for the bill risked angering the business community, a core Republican constituency. Spearheading the opposition would help the party push back against the Democratic frame that Republicans are anti-woman and support discrimination but would also subject them to criticism and heightened media scrutiny as women acting against the interest of women.

Lilly Ledbetter spent 19 years working for the Goodyear Tire and Rubber Co. in Alabama. Just before she retired, she received an anonymous note showing that, as the lone female supervisor, she was being paid substantially less than her lowest paid male counterpart. Ledbetter sued, and the case went all the way to the Supreme Court. In their 2007 decision, the justices agreed that Ledbetter was a victim of gender discrimination. However, the majority maintained that Ledbetter could not sue because she had not filed the claim within the 180-day time frame required by

Title VII of the Civil Rights Act, regardless of whether she knew about the discrimination. Outraged by the court's decision, Justice Ruth Bader Ginsberg, then the lone woman on the court, called on Congress to correct the court's mistake (Barnes 2007a, 2007b).

Ledbetter put a human face on a cause Democrats, particularly Democratic women and their allies in the feminist community, had been pushing for years. The Democratic House majority under Pelosi's leadership quickly passed the Lilly Ledbetter Fair Pay Act in July 2007, and in July 2008 the House passed the Paycheck Fairness Act, a bill that still has not been enacted. The legislation would make it easier for women to file discrimination claims by among other things putting the burden on employers to demonstrate that pay gaps between men and women are caused by reasons other than gender. Once Obama won the presidency, the House paired the two bills and passed them both in January 2009 (DeLauro 2008, Pear 2009). In the Senate, Democrats first brought the bill to the floor on Equal Pay Day, April 22, 2008, a day that marks on average how far into the next year a woman has to work for her salary to catch up to what a man earned in the previous year (Montgomery 2008a). Despite the symbolism of the day, Democrats failed to get enough votes to invoke cloture. In 2009, with Democrats controlling the House and Senate, the bill quickly passed the Senate and was the first law Obama signed (Stolberg 2009).

Democratic women were instrumental in pushing the bill through the legislative process and keeping the public spotlight on the issue. As one male Democratic senator explained, "The party believes in it [the Lilly Ledbetter Fair Pay Act]. With no women in the caucus we would have taken up the issue but the women were more aggressive on it. They were more outraged by the Ledbetter decision and more aggressive in pushing hard for something to get done on it. It is natural for Boxer and Stabenow to care about discrimination and unfairness; they were probably treated that way themselves over the years." Thus, the personal connection the Democratic female senators felt with the issue of employment discrimination made them prioritize the legislation and devote the time and political capital necessary to move it from a political issue to legislative action.

In the Senate, during the first debate on the bill in 2008, Barbara Mikulski (D-MD), who is widely regarded as the dean of the Democratic women, organized Democratic women to wear red on Equal Pay Day and speak on the floor in favor of the bill. When the bill passed into law in 2009, Mikulski was the lead sponsor. She shepherded the bill to passage by helping to negotiate the amendments that would be considered, leading press conferences to get out the Democratic message, and serving as the bill manager during floor debate where she argued passionately for passage and rebutted Republican amendments to weaken the bill. While Mikulski was the most active Senate proponent, across the two Congresses 11 of the 13 Democratic women serving in either or both the 110th and 111th Congresses spoke during one of the floor debates held on the legislation.[2]

Similarly, in the House women were aggressive advocates for both the Lilly Ledbetter Fair Pay Act and the Paycheck Fairness Act. When the bills were first considered in the 110th Congress (2007–2008), Democratic women comprised 22 percent of the Democratic caucus. These women constituted 36 percent of the speakers in favor of the Lilly Ledbetter Fair Pay Act and 52 percent of the speakers in favor of the Paycheck Fairness Act. When the bills passed the House in the 111th Congress (2009–2010), women remained 22 percent of the Democratic caucus. Forty-eight percent of the Democratic speakers advocating the Paycheck Fairness Act and 45 percent of the Democratic members promoting the Lilly Ledbetter Fair Pay Act were women.[3] Clearly, relative to their numbers in the caucus, Democratic women played an outsized role in pressing for equal play legislation.

In addition to their personal commitment, through advocacy of equal pay legislation, Democratic women reinforced the Democratic Party's reputation with voters in a presidential election year as the party committed to advancing women's rights. The issue galvanized the Democratic base including women's groups, civil rights organizations, and labor unions. Democrats also used the issue to attract swing voters, particularly independent women (Barnes 2007b; Kellman 2008). Thus, Senate Democrats originally brought the bill to the floor on Equal Pay Day in April 2008 to sharpen the contrast between their leading presidential candidates, Clinton and Obama, and the likely Republican nominee, John McCain (R-AZ) (Hulse 2008; Kellman 2008; Montgomery 2008b).

To keep the focus on women's rights after the Senate failed to invoke cloture, Democratic women kept the issue alive for the elections by organizing press conferences, writing editorials, and promoting the issue on television news shows. They even held a joint rally with the Democratic women of the House and Senate that included Ledbetter, Pelosi, and Clinton (U.S. Senate Democratic Steering and Outreach Committee 2008).

Similarly, in the 2012 presidential election, Democrats again focused on the issue of equal pay to help Obama and Democratic congressional candidates attract women voters. Senate Democrats brought the Paycheck Fairness Act to the floor to try to force Republican presidential candidate Mitt Romney (R-MA) to take a stand against equal pay and to help Democratic Senate candidates in tough races. Thus, Elizabeth Warren, the Democratic Senate candidate in Massachusetts (now senator) used the vote to demonstrate that Republican senator Scott Brown was not a moderate and did not fully support women's rights (Kim 2012; Sargent 2012). After Republicans defeated the cloture vote, the Democratic women of the House and Senate held a joint press conference denouncing Republicans for hurting women in tough economic times (Kim 2012).

In contrast to the Democratic women, who reap both policy and political benefits from championing equal pay laws, Republican women face multiple dilemmas as they consider how to vote and how deeply to engage the issue. The Lilly Ledbetter bill and other equal pay legislation are strongly opposed by the business community because they fear that these initiatives will lead to more frivolous law-suits. Thus, for the more moderate women, equal pay legislation pits their commit-ment to women's rights against core Republican principles of reducing regulation on business. The business community vigorously lobbied against the bill (Langel 2009a). Moreover, support for the bill would also boost Democratic efforts to use the legislation against the Republican presidential and congressional candidates.

For conservative women, opposition to the legislation aligns with their ideo-logical views; however, these women also have to contend with Democratic efforts to portray them as women working against women's rights, and the media echoes that sentiment in their coverage. Indeed, after the failed cloture vote in 2008, the *Washington Post* reported that Senator Kay Bailey Hutchison (R-TX) was among those who were "clearly uncomfortable with the vote" and quoted Hutchison as saying, "I'm sure [the vote] will be spun as anti-equal pay, [but] there's definitely something I could have voted for" (Montgomery 2008b). Furthermore, Republican leaders turn to Republican women to push back against Democratic criticism by demonstrating that Republican policies are not anti-women.

Balancing these multiple goals, the Republican women in the House and Senate followed divergent paths in the fight over the Lilly Ledbetter Fair Pay Act. In the House, which has a much more conservative contingent of Republican women, all the Republican women voted against the legislation, including mod-erates like Ileana Ros-Lehtinen (R-FL) and Judy Biggert (R-IL). Among the women, only Ros-Lehtinen, along with thirteen other Republican men in 2008 and nine Republican men in 2009, supported the Paycheck Fairness Act. When the Ledbetter bill was first debated in 2007, five of the twenty Republican women in the House—Marsha Blackburn (R-TN), Biggert, Virginia Foxx (R-NC), Kay Granger (R-TX), and Michele Bachmann (R-MN)—spoke on the floor to defend the party against the claim that Republicans were condoning discrimination (See *Congressional Record* July 30, 2007 H8940-H8950; July 31, 2007 H9219-H9222). For example, Biggert proclaimed, "I know what it is like. I sat in law school class and was told by my professor that I was taking up the place of someone who belonged there, a man. As a woman who has felt discrimination, I understand her [Lilly Ledbetter's] frustration.... If this bill were an anti-discrimination bill I would be happy to vote for it and would encourage others to support it. But this bill is not about discrimination. It is about the statue of limitations..." (*Congressional Record,* July 30, 2007 H8945-H8946). Thus, Biggert and the other Republican women were trying to push back against the Democratic message that Republicans support wage discrimination. Once Obama won the presidency and it was clear the legislation would become law, the Republican women did not participate in the floor debate, leaving three Republican men to defend the party position as 31 Democrats came to the floor to laud the importance of the bill. The Republican women again all voted against the legislation (See *Congressional Record,* January 9, 2009 H113-H124).

In the Senate, where the small contingent of Republican women remains on average more moderate than their male Republican counterparts and media scrutiny is more intense than in the House, the four Republican women, including moderates Snowe and Collins, and the more conservative Lisa Murkowski (R-AK) and Hutchison all ultimately voted in favor of the legislation. However, each varied in how publicly they supported the bill and how much they tried to defend the party. Snowe was the most consistently supportive of the legislation. She was the only Republican to cosponsor the Democratic bill across the two Congresses and to speak in favor of the bill on the floor both times it was debated, emphasizing her long history of activism on the issue dating back to the Ronald Reagan years and her work in the House of Representatives (*Congressional Record*, April 24, 2008 S3395-3396; *Congressional Record*, January 22, 2009 S 769).

While Snowe strongly supported the bill and often served as the lone Republican advocate, the other women tread more carefully as they balanced their interest in women's rights and their desire to remain loyal to the Republican caucus. Thus, Collins did not cosponsor the legislation and never spoke in favor of the bill on the floor, while the most conservative of the women, Hutchison, helped develop an alternative Republican bill and advocated for it on the floor. According to Democratic and Republican staffers, Republicans knew that they needed to develop an alternative bill that business groups would support, and they needed to market it in a way that would show that Republicans are for women's rights. Therefore, the party needed a Republican woman to serve as lead sponsor and spokesperson for their bill. A Republican staffer confirmed the party's strategy, explaining:

> Republicans do want a spokesperson to put a good public face on an issue and deflect the criticism of Republicans as anti-women. [Mike] Enzi [(R-WY), the ranking member on HELP] was writing the Ledbetter alternative, but Republican leaders knew they did not want a middle-aged white guy—that won't help make their case. We needed to find a woman we can get to agree to be the leader on the Republican alternative. We went to Murkowski [who was on the HELP committee] first, but she knows she will have a race [in 2010] and she did not want to be the public voice on this. [Murkowski did cosponsor the Hutchison alternative.] She does not want to be out there in a public forum on a controversial issue. We thought about Collins. Hutchison is in leadership. She agreed, and it would help her in her governor's race. [Hutchison was planning to challenge Republican Governor Rick Perry (TX) in the primary and needed to demonstrate her strong conservative principles for primary voters]. Enzi's staff helped Hutchison's staff draft the amendment. She told the leaders that at the end of the day if the alternative fails she will vote for the Democratic bill because she and the other women do not want to be viewed as against women in the workplace.

Hutchison actively advocated for the Republican alternative on the floor. The amendment, which was supported by the Chamber of Commerce, would reinstate the six-month clock for filing a complaint after the woman knew or should have known about the discriminatory action. Thus, a woman would need to affirmatively prove that she did not know about the pay disparity before she filed the lawsuit (Langel 2009a, 2009b). On the floor, Hutchison sought to blunt Democratic criticism of the Republican position by noting, "I have certainly been a person who has known discrimination. I want everyone who believes they have a cause of action to have that right. I have also been a business owner. I know how important it is that our businesses know what their potential liabilities are ... " (*Congressional Record*, January 15, 2009 S 588-589). Ultimately, Hutchison, Collins, and Murkowski all voted in favor of the Republican alternative and then joined Snowe to pass the Democratic bill, allowing them to show their support for the Republican position and demonstrate their commitment to women's rights.

The fight over equal pay legislation demonstrates the contours of the contemporary politics of women's rights. Drawing on their personal commitment to women's rights, Democratic women worked to get equal pay legislation on the agenda, and they played a pivotal role in developing the Democratic message and selling it to the public. Because women's rights issues are central to the Democratic electoral base, championing equal pay legislation helped Democratic women reach out to voters and solidify the party's reputation as the protector of women's rights. By contrast, pay equity legislation puts Republican women in a difficult position. They must balance their ideological views and the opposition of the business community, a key Republican constituency against their own perspective on women's rights and their aversion to being portrayed as women acting against women's interests. Republican women varied in their strategic calculations over how to engage the equal pay debate, with some women in the House simply voting the party position and others vocally defending their party against Democratic efforts to paint Republicans as anti-women and supportive of wage discrimination. Meanwhile, the female Republican senators tried to both defend the party position and take a stand in favor of women's rights.

## Looking to the Future: The Politics of Women's Rights in a Polarized Era

Research on the policy impact of women in Congress has clearly established that gender affects legislators' policy priorities and the perspective they bring to the policymaking table. However, the polarization of the parties has changed the dynamics of policymaking in women's interests. The Democratic Party is increasingly perceived as dedicated to advancement of social welfare policies and women's rights, which provides more opportunities for Democratic women to legislate on these issues and raise their media and legislative profile. The increasing importance of the gender gap in a competitive electoral environment enhances the value of Democratic women as spokespersons who can mobilize women's groups and other elements of the liberal base and can turn out the women's vote. Moreover, the increasing number of women in the Democratic Party allows them to leverage their numbers and seniority into positions of power. Because women and minorities constitute key voting blocs within the party, Democrats are more responsive to calls for diversity in their leadership ranks.

In the 2012 electoral cycle, Democratic women held key leadership positions that allowed them to drive party strategy: Pelosi as House minority leader; Debbie Wasserman Schultz (D-FL) as Democratic National Committee Chair; and Patty Murray (D-WA) as chair of the Democratic Senate Campaign Committee. These three women were key proponents of the war on women frame that was a central component of the Democratic message in the 2012 elections at both the presidential and congressional level (Feder 2012; Kurtz 2012; McCarthy 2012a, 2012b).

Individually, and joining together in groups of House and Senate women, Democratic women held press conferences, wrote editorials, organized floor speeches, and went on television news shows to denounce Republican policies as a coordinated war on women. Republican efforts to cut funding for Planned Parenthood as part of a budget deal and their opposition to contraceptive coverage in Obama's health-care plan were denounced as a war on women's health with Republicans seeking to take away women's access to cancer screenings and affordable contraception (Shaheen, Boxer, and Murray 2012; McCarthy 2012b, 2012c; Sanger-Katz 2012). Democrats used their control of the Senate to bring up bills on equal pay and violence against women to further highlight the Republican war on women (Kim 2012; Weisman 2012).

Democratic women will continue to increase their policy influence in the 113th Congress. Pelosi decided to remain as Democratic leader in the House, asserting that there must be a woman among the top party leaders in the House and Senate meeting with Obama to resolve the fiscal cliff and long-term budget and entitlement issues (Rogers 2012). For the first time, Democratic women hold key leadership positions on the most prestigious committees dealing with the country's fiscal challenges: Barbara Mikulski (D-MD) chairs the Senate Appropriations Committee, Murray chairs the Senate Budget Committee, and Nita Lowey (D-NY) is the ranking member on the House Appropriations Committee (Wasson 2012; Wong 2012).

By contrast, women's issues are not central to the reputation of the Republican Party. Instead the Republican brand focuses on messages of lowering taxes, reducing regulation on business, and strengthening national security. Therefore, women cannot leverage their connection to women's interests and women voters into power and authority within the Republican caucus as easily as Democratic women can. Moreover, for the dwindling number of moderate Republican women, the focus on feminist issues like reproductive rights alienates the social conservative base of the Republican Party and puts these more moderate women in an uncomfortable position. Conservative women must decide if they want to champion the conservative view on social issues like abortion or if they prefer to focus on issues of cutting taxes and regulation on business that form the core of the Republican Party's identity. Furthermore, because the number of women in the Republican caucus remains small and the political culture of the Republican Party focuses on individualism and is not responsive to identity-based policy claims, it is more difficult for Republican women to demand more seats at the leadership table for women.

Yet Republicans do want to push back against the Democratic narrative that the Republican Party is anti-women, and they recognize that they need to attract more women and minority voters because these groups constitute a growing share of the electorate (Brownstein 2012b). Therefore, Republicans are increasingly turning to their women members, particularly the ideologically compatible conservative women in the House, to rebut the Democratic frame of a Republican war on women and to explain how Republican policies benefit women from a female perspective. As Cathy McMorris Rodgers (R-WA), the vice chair and future chair of the Republican conference, explained, "Republicans who only talk about finances are not going to attract women voters. Let's talk about healthcare choices…families, raising children and trying to find a job in a tough market. These are women's issues and Republican issues" (Ferraro 2012). Thus, conservative Republican women, many of whom were elected in the 2010 election that swept Republicans back into the majority, held press conferences and organized a colloquy on the floor describing "Why I Am a Republican Woman" to rebut Democratic claims that Republican policies are a threat to women's health and to lay out how Republican economic policies will help women (Cogan 2011; Kellman 2011; Kim 2012b). The House Republican women even formed their own "Women's Policy Committee" to showcase Republican women and to demonstrate how Republican policies improve women's lives (Cohn 2012). In the Senate, Kelly Ayotte (R-NH), who was elected in 2010, was a lead spokesperson against the contraceptive rule in Obama's health plan. Serving as the lead cosponsor on a Republican amendment to eliminate the rule, Ayotte took to the Senate floor and the news talk shows to explain that this was not a women's health issue but an issue of religious freedom because the Obama mandate forces employers to provide contraception even when it is against their religious beliefs (Ayotte 2012a, 2012b; McCormack 2012).

The experience of the 2012 election and the success of the war on women elevated the importance of increasing Republican outreach to women voters. The desire to project a more diverse public face for the Republican Party was an important factor in the decision of Republicans to elect Rodgers as their conference chair, the number four leadership position in the Republican caucus (House 2012). Republicans also chose Lynn Jenkins (R-KS) as conference vice chair and Foxx as conference secretary, thus including three Republican women in the House leadership (Raju and Sherman 2012). Clearly, Democrats and Republicans are poised to craft divergent policy positions and messages as they compete to represent women's interests and attract their votes.

## Notes

1. I interviewed 50 Senate staffers associated with 44 senators including 19 Republicans and 25 Democrats. I also interviewed one Republican and two Democratic senators. The staffers interviewed included chiefs of staff, legislative directors, legislative assistants with special responsibility for particular issues such as defense policy or health care, and campaign managers. In addition to staff, I also interviewed liberal and conservative interest group leaders who took an active role in the confirmation battles over President Bush's nominees to the Supreme Court and the lower federal courts.

2. Kirsten Gillibrand (D-NY) is not included in the count of Democratic women serving across the 110th and 111th Congresses because she was sworn in after the bill passed (CAWP 2011b). Democratic women who spoke during floor debate on the bill in the 110th Congress are Barbara Mikulski (D-MD), Patty Murray (D-WA), Claire McCaskill (D-MO), Maria Cantwell (D-WA), Hillary Rodham Clinton (D-NY), and Debbie Stabenow (D-MI). Democratic women speaking on the bill in the 111th Congress are Mikulski, Barbara Boxer (D-CA), Dianne Feinstein (D-CA), Blanche Lincoln (D-AR), Kay Hagan (D-NC), Amy Klobuchar (D-MN), and McCaskill. Among Democratic women, only Mary Landrieu (D-LA) and Jeanne Shaheen (D-NH) did not give floor speeches on the legislation. According to her office's press release, Shaheen attended a press conference to promote the bill while it was being considered on the floor. The press conference included Lilly Ledbetter, Marcia Greenberger (the president of the National Women's Law Center), Mikulski, Murray, Lincoln, Stabenow, Klobuchar, and Shaheen (http://shaheen.senate.gov/news/press/release/?i d=5312db94-d995-4560-af65-faa45b0768f9).

3. Author's analysis. See *Congressional Record,* July 30, 2007 H8940-H8950, July 31, 2007 H9219-H9222; *Congressional Record* January 9, 2009 H113-H124 for House debate on the Lilly Ledbetter Fair Pay Act. For House debate on the Paycheck Fairness Act, see *Congressional Record,* July 31, 2008 H7681-H7681-H7704; *Congressional Record,* January 9, 2009 H124-H138. I counted all members who spoke on the floor or inserted remarks and divided by the total number of speakers. I then compared the number of women as a proportion of the Democratic caucus with the proportion of Democratic women speakers on the bills. The number of women in the Democratic and Republican caucuses in the 110th and 111th Congresses was drawn from the Center for American Women and Politics Fact Sheet "Women in the U.S. Congress 2013."

# 11

# Women State Legislators: Women's Issues in Partisan Environments

TRACY OSBORN AND REBECCA KREITZER

In the 2009 session of the Iowa General Assembly, two women legislators debated a salient and complex childcare issue: whether and how in-home day-care providers should be regulated by the state. The representatives, however, promoted different solutions to the problem. The Democratic woman representative introduced one alternative to create stricter regulation of in-home providers. She argued that regulating home providers would improve the quality of day care and would ease parents' worries as well as enhance the working conditions for in-home providers by elevating their status with a license. The Republican woman representative opposed the bill, saying the cost and bother of a license would inhibit informal childcare arrangements among family members and friends, ultimately undermining low-cost quality childcare. Though both women legislators expressed a desire to represent women's best interests regarding childcare, clearly each had a distinct view of what those best interests should be.

This chapter examines the central question underlying this childcare debate in Iowa: how do partisan women in the U.S. state legislatures represent women's issues? We argue that political parties shape the ways Republican and Democratic women legislate on women's issues in two ways. First, they structure women legislators' preferences on women's issues; that is, partisan women conceive of different solutions to women's issues policy problems rooted in their party identities. Second, political party control of the legislative process helps determine whose preferences become part of the legislative agenda and, thus, have a chance to become law. Given these partisan effects, we argue that theorizing about women legislators as a whole, while useful in some ways, should also give way to work that understands how women work on women's issues through partisan channels.

As the introduction to this volume elucidates, electing women to public offices, such as the U.S. state legislatures, remains a challenge. Legislatures populated primarily by men lack the democratic legitimacy brought by the increasing inclusion of women (Phillips 1991). Additionally, women representatives contribute new, gendered perspectives to legislative debate by interjecting women's experiences and "crystallizing" previously ignored or not considered aspects of an issue (Mansbridge 1999). Even as we know women's representation in state legislatures is of utmost symbolic and substantive importance, however, we also continue to explore how generalizations about women legislators' behavior oversimplify the varied ways women legislators represent women's concerns. Women state legislators are responsible for constituents in districts; they also work within the confines of political parties that structure the election and legislative processes. Additionally, constituent and party demands on women state legislators vary across states and even chambers, from the nonpartisan Nebraska unicameral body (the only one in the nation) to the hyper-partisan New Jersey and Wisconsin Assemblies (Wright and Schaffner 2002; Wright, Osborn, and Winburn 2009).

Thus, scholars of women as legislators in the U.S. states must appreciate the interaction between gender and the legislative environment to understand how women legislators represent women's concerns. A primary factor in this interaction is clarifying whether, how, and to what extent women in different political parties represent women's issues *while also* acting as partisans. We can see the importance of this enterprise in the following example. As Norrander and Wilcox demonstrate in Chapter 16, the proportion of women elected to state legislatures varies substantially across states. Yet even in states with similar proportions of women legislators, the partisan divide between these women varies. Figure 11.1 demonstrates this trend over time for six state house chambers: Arizona, Colorado, Illinois, Indiana, Pennsylvania, and South Dakota.

State houses with similar proportions in the total number of women legislators can have very different compositions of Democratic and Republican women legislators. Beginning on the left-hand side of Figure 11.1, Pennsylvania and Indiana have similarly low trajectories in the election of women to the state house over the last thirty years. Yet the number of Republican women in Pennsylvania has increased, while the number of Democratic women in Indiana, especially since 2006, has increased relative to the number of Republican women. A similar pattern exists in South Dakota and Illinois. Though both states have between 20 and 30 percent women as of 2010, the number of Republican women in the South Dakota state house remains steady over time, while the number of Republican women sharply declines in Illinois. Finally, both the Arizona and Colorado state houses, though generally high in the proportion in the number of women over time, have substantially different numbers of partisan women. Particularly after 2002, party almost evenly divides women in the Arizona house, while women in the Colorado state house have diverged, with Democratic women constituting almost 30 percent of the

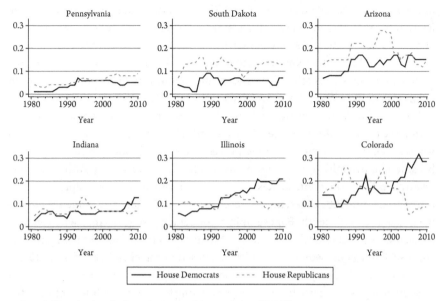

Proportion of Women Partisans in Selected State Houses

Compiled from data from the Center for American Women in Politics (CAWP)
Common scale for all state legislatures

*Figure 11.1*  Women's Representation by Party in Six States, 1980–2010

house in 2010 and Republican women less than 10 percent. Across the ninety-nine
U.S. state legislative chambers, it is much more common to have more Democratic
women legislators than Republican women legislators. Nevertheless, the balance of
women across parties in the state legislative chambers varies widely. If parties are
important to the representative process, this variation has significant implications
for the representation of women's issues in the states.

# Background: A Two-Part Puzzle of Political Parties and Women State Legislators

A central focus of much of the literature on women and state legislative representation is whether women "make a difference" as women in the legislative process
(see, e.g., Reingold 2000; Swers 2002; Thomas 1994). The reason for this focus is
twofold. First, a simultaneous focus in the literature on the pathways and barriers to
electing women to public office (Burrell 1994; Carroll 1994) begged justification of
women's election beyond the importance of physical representation and inclusion.
That is, scholars of women's representation wished to connect the physical representation of women to the substantive effects that followed from their increasing presence. Second, scholars wished to know exactly what forms such a "difference" took

and what connection this difference had to women's traditional gender roles, sex differences, and gendered power structures. Thus, scholars examined whether women legislators focused their energy on a set of "women's issues" policies (Bratton and Haynie 1999; Thomas 1994), whether women legislators accomplished the tasks of legislating differently (Kathlene 1994; Rosenthal 1995), and how women fared within masculine legislative institutions and traditional male power structures (Blair and Stanley 1991; Reingold 1996).

As the introduction in this volume discusses, one early theoretical prospect within the focus on difference revolved around critical mass, or the contention that women's influence in the legislative process would peak once women legislators became a numerically significant proportion of the legislative body. Although some research indicates that critical mass is related to improved women's representation, other studies find little difference. Among the reasons is that party influence has not been examined sufficiently. For example, some evidence suggests that, when women legislators reached critical mass, both internal diversity among women legislators and backlash against women's interests increased in the chamber (Bratton 2002). From a theoretical perspective, some scholars have indicted critical mass theory for "essentializing" state legislative women, or treating them as monolithic actors in the chamber (Bratton 2002; Childs and Krook 2006; Dovi 2004; Mansbridge 1999).

These theoretical and empirical critiques of critical mass theory offer challenges to scholars of women state legislators. The focus on numbers and representation was simultaneously important as a justification of women's presence in elective office and frustrating to the desire to understand exactly how women state legislators represent women's interests. Therefore, research on women state legislatures turned to examining pertinent differences *among* women state legislators to explain the inconsistencies in critical mass theory. Bringing political parties to the forefront of research on women in state legislatures requires being more theoretically explicit about how parties will shape the representation of women's issues.

There exist two avenues through which parties can influence representation. The first is that political parties can shape women legislators' preferences about solutions to women's issues policy problems. This avenue has been somewhat obscured in previous work because this work often emphasized which issues women legislators' *prioritized* (see, e.g., Thomas 1994). Although this prioritization might exist among women legislators of both parties, the ways they address these priorities depend on how solutions to women's issues policy problems align with political party preferences on women's issues. Evidence of this alignment is quite mixed in the literature, however. While Sanbonmatsu (2000) notes that the national political parties rarely hold distinct positions on or find electorally salient most women's issues (with the prominent exception of abortion), Wolbrecht (2000) finds that support for women's rights legislation polarized in Congress after the 1960s. Studies of women state legislators emphasize Republican women's liberalism on some women's issues, such as welfare policy (Poggione 2004), yet also demonstrate that women legislators'

preferences are closer to men's preferences in their own party than to women's preferences in the opposite party (Epstein, Niemi, and Powell 2005; Osborn 2012). If
women's issues are not aligned clearly with political parties, partisan women may
not feel compelled to articulate preferences on these issues that are in line with their
partisan beliefs. If, however, partisanship delineates clear positions on women's
issues, women legislators who identify as and run for election as partisans may then
offer these partisan alternatives on women's issues in the legislative process.

The articulation, or lack thereof, of partisan preferences on women's issues also
interacts with the second avenue of party influence: partisan legislative control.
With the exception of the nonpartisan Nebraska unicameral legislature,[1] U.S. state
legislatures organize along political party lines. The party with majority status controls much of the legislative process, such as agenda setting and committee pro-
ceedings. From recent work on women in Congress (Dodson 2006; Swers 2002),
we know that a change in majority control, at least in the U.S. House, changes the
degree to which women legislators in each party are willing to contribute certain
types of women's issues bills to the legislative agenda. Though the degree of party
strength—how cohesive the parties are internally and how distinct the parties are
from each other (Aldrich and Rohde 2001)—may vary substantially among the
states, this party control can influence women legislators' behavior. If a woman legislator is part of the minority party, she may have fewer chances to place her bills on
the agenda and have these bills succeed in the legislative process. As a member of
the minority party, however, a woman legislator may also have more opportunities
for her preferences to deviate from the party majority's agenda because punishment
for such defection may be less severe when the stakes for her party (the minority
party) are lower (Swers 2002).

## How Do Partisan Women State Legislators Represent Women?

To demonstrate the importance of understanding how political parties, by shaping
women legislators' preferences and controlling the legislative process, affect how
women represent women's issues, we examined two parts of the state legislative process across different legislative environments. First, we considered women legislators' preferences on women's issues outside of the legislative environment. That is,
we examined whether prior to entering the legislative institution women legislators
in both parties have similar preferences on certain women's issues. If they do, then
this pattern could indicate a tendency toward cooperation among women legislators, provided legislative parties are conducive to this cooperation. Second, we turn
to how women legislators' preferences emerge on the legislative agenda through bill
sponsorship under Democratic and Republican Party control. If women legislators
hold partisan preferences about women's issues, then depending on which party

controls the legislative process the entire women's issues agenda may look quite different across chambers.

## Women Legislators' Issue Preferences

We looked at women legislators' preferences using the 1998 results of the National Political Awareness Test (NPAT) administered by the nonpartisan organization Project Vote Smart. The NPAT presents state legislative candidates with a list of policy positions and asks the legislators to check the positions with which they agree. For instance, a legislator can choose whether or not they agree with the statement, "Abortion should be legal in all circumstances." The NPAT is a good measure of men and women legislators' issue opinions because the same survey is administered across states, and the survey items, though not ideal, contain several women's issues positions.

Table 11.1 gives the predicted probability that a state legislator in our sample[2] will support a selection of women's issues items.[3] We split the legislators into four ideal types: a Democratic woman; a Democratic man; a Republican woman; and a Republican man. We defined women's issues, both in this analysis and following, as issues that directly and disproportionately affect women in society (see Osborn 2012).[4] This definition includes the issues of abortion, domestic violence, sexual offenses, childcare, child custody, marriage and divorce law, women's health care, and women's rights and equality. It excludes those issues connected to women's traditional gender roles, such as education or broad health care. Our definition also encompasses both feminist and anti-feminist alternatives to these issue areas. Though we understand prior researchers' reasons for creating different or more exclusive feminist policy categories, we feel that this broad categorization best captures possible differences between partisan women.

It is clear from Table 11.1 that Democratic and Republican women have different levels of support for women's issues policies. For example, on the first abortion issue in Table 11.1, Democratic women are more than 40 percent more likely to always support abortion than Republican women. Similarly, they are almost 50 percent more likely to support using state funding for abortion. Democratic women are 65 percent more likely to support affirmative action in employment, 41 percent more likely to support funding safe-sex programs in schools, and 37 percent more likely to support funding for teen pregnancy prevention programs than Republican women. Finally, Democratic women are 40 percent more likely to support state funding for childcare programs. The only women's issue in the NPAT sample without a significant difference between women partisans is supporting state enforcement of child support, which all four legislator types support with almost equal probability.

This brief analysis of the NPAT data carries several important caveats. Chiefly, the NPAT lacks measures of other significant women's issues policies, such as women's

*Table 11.1* **Predicted Probabilities of Issue Support by Legislator Type on Selected NPAT Issues**

| NPAT Item | Democrat | Republican | Democrat | Republican |
|---|---|---|---|---|
| | Woman | Woman | Man | Man |
| Abortion should always be allowed | 0.68 | 0.24 | 0.33 | 0.06 |
| Allow state funding for abortion | 0.84 | 0.35 | 0.61 | 0.22 |
| Support affirmative action in employment | 0.91 | 0.26 | 0.71 | 0.18 |
| Support safe sex programs in schools | 0.68 | 0.27 | 0.46 | 0.12 |
| Support state money for teen pregnancy programs | 0.75 | 0.38 | 0.73 | 0.33 |
| Support using state money for childcare | 0.83 | 0.43 | 0.76 | 0.32 |
| Support state enforcing child support | 0.68 | 0.71 | 0.66 | 0.68 |

*Note*: Entries are predicted probabilities of support for the NPAT items, holding all other variables (except for party, sex, and party*sex) constant at the mean. See Osborn (2012) for analysis of additional NPAT items.

health-care policies and domestic violence and sexual violence policies. Similarly, some of the policy alternatives in the NPAT survey stipulate the use of state funds as a policy solution. Thus, it is possible that Republicans and Democrats disagree not on the substantive policy issue but on the use of government money to address the issue. Finally, the NPAT captures a brief cross section of data in many states but lacks a large enough sample for significant analysis within states. Nevertheless, the analysis demonstrates that there is substantial discord between Democratic and Republican women on women's issues policies. In fact, Democratic women and men and Republican women and men typically have more similar stances on these issues than women across parties. Therefore, it becomes somewhat difficult to expect, a priori, a tendency between Democratic and Republican women to cooperate on women's issues alternatives across party lines in the legislative body.

An interesting question following from the NPAT, then, is how these partisan preferences translate into policy *inside* the legislature. It is possible that within the legislative environment, where the majority party controls agenda setting and substantially shapes roll call voting, that these party influences exacerbate issue differences between women partisans. It may also be the case, however, that certain issues either map less clearly onto a partisan divide (such as the enforcement of child support in the Table 11.1) or unite women around gendered concerns across party lines.

## Bill Sponsorship of Women's Issues in the State Legislatures

To understand how parties influence women's representation inside the state legislatures, we turn to a two-part analysis of bill sponsorship. Bill sponsorship is an excellent measure of legislative activity. Because it is a high-visibility (to constituents and inside the chamber) and labor-intensive activity, it measures well the issue areas and policy solutions on which legislators choose to specialize. It also allows one to understand a legislator's choices beyond activities that respond to an already set agenda, such as roll call votes, which offer fewer choices to legislators (Tamerius 1995). Nevertheless, the agenda-setting process of bill sponsorship is susceptible to party influences. The majority party controls access to the agenda; it might send signals to both majority and minority parties about which types of bills are acceptable contributions to the agenda.

Our first measure of bill sponsorship is a cross section of all the legislative bills introduced to ten lower state chambers in the 1999–2000 state legislative sessions: Arkansas, California, Colorado, Georgia, Illinois, Michigan, South Dakota, Texas, Washington, and Wisconsin. Though they are not meant to be a representative sample of chambers overall, these states varied substantially on our key feature of interest—political parties. Five of the chambers, Arkansas, California, Georgia, Illinois, and Texas, were under Democratic control, and the other five, Colorado, Michigan, South Dakota, Washington, and Wisconsin, were under Republican control. This party control also varied in strength. Some of the chambers, such as Wisconsin, California, and Michigan, had stronger party government (i.e., the parties have substantial intraparty cohesion and interparty distinction; see Aldrich and Rohde 1991; Battista 2009). Other chambers, such as Arkansas, Georgia, and Illinois, had fairly large party majorities and less distinct party behavior.[5] Finally, the chambers varied in the proportion of Democratic and Republican women serving in the chamber at the time. California had the largest proportion of Democratic women (.80), while South Dakota had the smallest proportion of Democratic women (.36).

Our second measure of bill sponsorship focuses on all of the legislative bills introduced in the Washington House from 1987 to 2010. The advantage of these data is the ability to understand women legislators' attention to and preferences on women's issues bills over time. Though the Washington house is only one legislative chamber, the 1987–2010 time series offers interesting points of variation. Washington ranked among the top ten throughout the period we examine here in the number of women serving in the House chamber. The chamber consisted of roughly one-third women throughout the time series. Importantly, this one-third is composed of substantial numbers of both Democratic and Republican women; for example, in the 1995–1996 session, there were eighteen Republican women and twenty-one Democratic women out of ninety-eight legislators in the chamber. Though the number of Republican women has begun to dwindle as of late (matching a less extreme version of the trend for the Colorado house in Figure 11.1.), the Washington House still provides a substantial population of Democratic and Republican women to study. Additionally, Washington State ranked highly among the states in both the number of women legislators and the quality of women's issues policies during this time period, yielding a significant number of women's issues policies and women legislators to examine.

The Washington House is also an interesting initial case because it experienced significant majority party change from 1987 to 2010. There have been several drastic changes in party control of the Washington House during this period. From 1987 to 1994, Democrats controlled the Washington House with a commanding majority of almost two to one. In 1995, this control abruptly shifted to Republicans, who from 1995 to 1998 enjoyed a similarly commanding majority. In 1999, the House moved into a four-year period of a tie between Democrats and Republicans, each with forty-nine legislators. During this four-year period, control of the chamber (in the form of the House Speakership) resided with both parties as small changes (e.g., a legislator resignation halfway through the 1999–2000 session) and compromise yielded minimal control by either party. Finally, beginning in 2003, the Democrats regained control of the Washington House, and from 2003 to 2010 they expanded their majority control back to a nearly two-to-one ratio.

To identify women's issues bills in both data sets, we coded each bill in each session according to a coding scheme developed for the Representation in American Legislatures (RAL) Project and modified for our purposes to include several additional women's issues distinctions.[6] The larger coding scheme categorizes policies within twenty-one large categories, ranging from abortion to parks and recreation. It then contains subcategories within each large category, for a total of 235 possible content codes. For example, the larger category of health policy contains codes for physician licensing and regulation, inoculation, children's health issues, women's health issues, specific diseases, and alcohol and drug treatment.[7] To create a women's issues category, we included each code in the list in nine issue areas—abortion, women's health, domestic violence, sex offenders, equality policies, childcare, child custody, child support, and marriage and divorce/family law.[8]

Figures 11.2 and 11.3 offer overviews of the cross sectional bill sponsorship data from the 1999–2000 legislative sessions in the ten-chamber sample. In these data, we concentrate on the outcomes of agenda setting—that is, which women's issues bills, once introduced to the agenda, pass into law under different partisan majorities? Figure 11.2 shows the passage rates for different types of women's issues in Democratic-controlled (top) and Republican-controlled (bottom) legislatures. In the legislatures under Democratic control, with the exception of abortion legislation, a larger amount and a greater variety of women's issues bills become law. In Republican chambers, more abortion bills pass than in Democratic chambers, but in the other issue categories passage rates are lower (we discuss the content

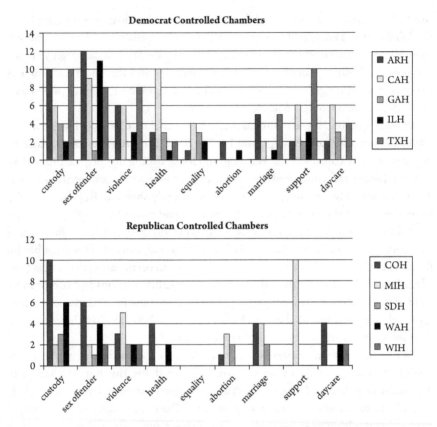

*Figure 11.2* Bill Passage by Women's Issues Topic in Ten Chambers, 1999–2000

of these bills next). This is especially true for women's health and equality and discrimination-related bills.

The patterns in Figure 11.3, which displays bill passage rates for four types of partisans (Democratic men, Democratic women, Republican men, and Republican women) in Democratic- and Republican-controlled legislatures, offer some indication of what types of women's issues bills pass. As one might expect, Democrats (both women and men) are more successful at getting their bills passed in Democratic-controlled chambers, and Republicans are more successful in Republican-controlled chambers. Republican men's success is also relatively high in Democratic chambers, particularly in Texas and Arkansas. Both of these chambers turned to Republican control not long after the 1999–2000 sessions, which might explain this pattern. Democratic women are clearly more successful in Democratic chambers; Republican women, though the least prolific of the four types in bill sponsorship, are more successful in Republican chambers. As we describe next, because these bills contain largely partisan preferences these patterns in success and

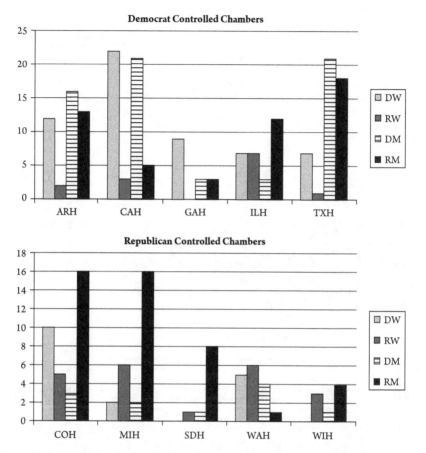

*Figure 11.3* Bill Passage by Legislator Types in Ten Chambers, 1999–2000

type of legislation have substantive implications for the types of women's issues laws each state creates.

As noted already, over the period from 1992 to 2010 the Washington House experienced substantial majority party change. These party changes coincide with changes to the women's issues agenda in the Washington State House. Figure 11.4 plots the total number of women's issues bills introduced by the four legislator types during the twelve sessions from 1987 to 2010: Republican men (diamond shape); Republican women (square shape); Democratic men (triangle shape); and Democratic women (star shape). Each part of Figure 11.5 plots bill introductions for a specific women's issue area: abortion (top); childcare (middle); and women's health (bottom). It is important to note that, again, these figures represent *all* bills introduced in each category, regardless of the ideological implications of the bill. Thus, these figures represent patterns in which groups of legislators—Republican men, Republican women, Democratic men, and Democratic women—controlled the women's issues agenda in any given session by introducing the possible policy

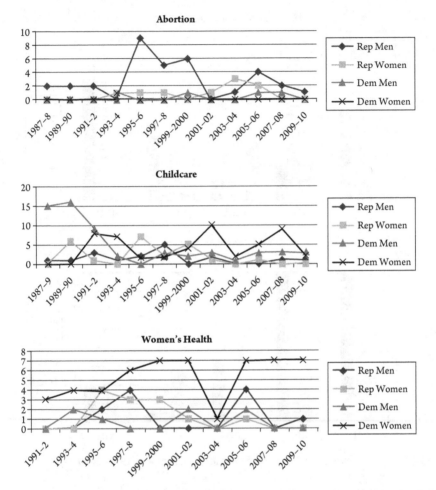

*Figure 11.4* Bill Sponsorship by Legislator Types in the Washington House, 1987–2010

alternatives. After examining these patterns, we discuss the ideological implications of the patterns in policy alternatives across each session.

The graph in the top of Figure 11.4, bill sponsorship on abortion over time, provides a clear indication that party control influences which groups of legislators contributes to the legislative agenda. Generally, Democrats (both men and women) introduce few abortion issues to the agenda, particularly when compared with the other issue areas. Republican men's introduction of abortion bills, however, peaks with their control of the legislative majority in 1995–1996 and 1997–1998. Republican men's bill introduction then falls dramatically as Democrats retake the legislature, with a second peak by Republican women and men during the early return to Democratic control of 2003–2004 and 2005–2006. This pattern is not particularly surprising given the strong division between American parties on the abortion issue since the 1980s. As Sanbonmatsu (2002) contends, abortion is the singular women's issues area in which clear delineation between Republicans and Democrats in the electorate and party platforms exists, at least up to the early 1990s when her study ends.

This pattern of Republican men and women's peaks in women's issues sponsorship during their party majorities in 1995–1996 and 1997–1998 also emerges across other issue areas. For example, on childcare issues (middle of Figure 11.4), Democratic women and men introduce more childcare bills during the 1991–1994 sessions, in which Democrats held control of the chamber. Republican introduction of childcare bills then increased when they took control of the chamber in 1995 yet lowered again in 2001–2002 just before Democrats retook control. Spikes in Democratic women's introductions of childcare bills then occur as Democrats regained large majorities. These patterns persist in other women's issues areas not pictured in Figure 11.4. Concerning child custody issues, the same spikes occur for Republican men and women and Democratic men and women when their parties control the legislature. Less dramatic but still evident patterns occur on marriage and divorce, child support, and equality and discrimination bills. Party control of the legislative process appears to coincide with spikes in women's issues bill introductions by both men and women in the majority party.

One exceptional issue with regard to this pattern is women's health bills, at the bottom of Figure 11.4. Democratic women introduced issues of women's health to the agenda regardless of party control across the twelve sessions we examine. Both women and men Republicans addressed issues of women's health to a greater degree during the sessions when they held control, although Republican men also introduced a number of women's health issues during a session of Democratic control in 2005–2006. The substance of these issues differed dramatically, as discussed next, but women Democrats maintained an interest in women's health across different partisan conditions.

Patterns of bill sponsorship also differ between women and men of each party across different kinds of women's issues. Republicans, men particularly, introduced most of the abortion legislation across this period. All four groups introduced marriage and divorce legislation (not pictured), although Democratic women were the group that addressed this area the least. Childcare issues attracted bills from both Democratic and Republican women, whereas child support and child custody bills attracted attention from all four groups. Democratic women, with the exception of the 2005–2006 session, dominated equality and discrimination and women's health bill introductions, though Republicans (both men and women) offered many alternative bills.

In sum, though previous work tends to connect women legislators, particularly Democrats, with the introduction of women's issues bills, it is clear that in the Washington State legislature men and women of both parties place women's issues on the legislative agenda. In almost all the areas of women's issues examined here, both men and women partisans are particularly inclined to do so when they hold majority control of the legislative body. Given the proportion of women to men in each party, women introduce significantly more women's issues legislation than men. However, generally, across many, though not all, of these sessions (analysis not shown) the important point affirmed by the figures is that in pure numbers women's issues proposals come from both sexes and from both sides of the aisle, dependent on short-term party forces. Consequently, the partisan origins of these proposals have an impact on the substance of the women's issues agenda under different partisan conditions.

## Agenda Content in Women's Issues Legislative Bills

Partisanship has a clear effect on the types of proposals Republicans and Democrats place on the women's issues agenda in both the 1999–2000 cross sectional data and the Washington time series. Interestingly, party influence appears more significant than the impact of a legislator's gender on the content of women's issues alternatives. Not surprisingly, one issue where stark differences exist between Democrats and Republicans is on abortion policy. All proposals introduced in both sets of data by Republicans (both women and men) limited the availability of abortion largely through administrative hurtles such as waiting periods, parental notification, and information requirements. Where Democratic men made proposals, they also typically limited abortion. Democratic women made very few abortion proposals, but where they did they were largely pro-choice proposals, such as protecting access to clinics and reaffirming access to abortion in the states.

In most of the other women's issues categories, the distinctions between partisans are not as absolute as with abortion, perhaps reflecting the entrenched status of the issue in the American party cleavage (Sanbonmatsu 2002). However, in several other issue areas clear substantive differences exist between Democratic and Republican proposals. For instance, in discrimination and equality issues Democrats (dominantly women) introduced bills to enforce Title IX (dealing with educational equity) in athletics, to create and enforce a Family and Medical Leave Act and Family and Medical Leave (FMLA) insurance (prior to the creation of the federal FMLA), and to fund women's business enterprises. Democratic men, though largely quiet on these issues, introduced similarly protective and expansive equality legislation. Republican men, however, generally proposed legislation to eliminate existing programs, such as those to fund women's business enterprises or to eliminate protections of equality, such as state requirements for gender equity in political party leadership. The only proposal by a Republican man that did not fit this trend in the Washington data was one to recognize the contributions of women in a World War II memorial. Republican women were largely quiet on equality and discrimination as well, although when they did introduce these bills they were more similar to Republican men's agendas than to those of Democratic women. For example, a woman Republican in Washington introduced a bill prohibiting retaliation against state employees who refused to take diversity training.

Bills concerning family status—childcare, child support, and child custody—similarly demonstrate differences between Republicans and Democrats on women's issues. Democratic proposals on childcare, by both men and women, tended to expand childcare opportunities, particularly through state funding, and to offer opportunities to day-care providers to bargain collectively or gain additional licensing. Alternatively, Republican women's proposals were largely concerned with licensing, but often limiting licensing requirements. Child support involved proposals on two issues: creating a child support registry and enforcing payments from it; and regulating what kinds of items could be paid for with child support. Both Democratic and Republican men concentrated on punishing those who did not pay child support in a timely manner; women were less inclined (particularly Democratic women) to focus on punishment. Cross-party cooperation ended on the matter of items paid for with child support, however. Democrats (both women and men) introduced bills to expand the items paid for by child support, such as health care and postsecondary education, while Republicans introduced legislation to limit items included in child support calculations. Finally, child custody debates also reflected party differences. Republicans were more inclined to introduce proposals expanding guardianship (e.g., allowing grandparent visitation, presuming a friendly status between parents at the beginning of a custody hearing), while Democrats tended to limit custody provisions.

Partisanship emerged on proposals regarding women's health care as well. Democratic women uniformly increased or protected access to women's health care. For example, they introduced proposals to protect breastfeeding in public places and in work environments, to protect or expand insurance coverage for contraceptives and maternity care, and to provide family planning options for low-income women. Democratic men, although to a lesser extent across sessions, introduced proposals that were substantively similar to those offered by Democratic women. Republican men's proposals, alternatively, often limited women's health-care options. For instance, Republican men introduced proposals to limit midwives' involvement to low-risk births, to fund and require abstinence education or prohibit other types of sex education, or to make drug or alcohol use by pregnant women a crime committed by the mother. Finally, for Republican women, women's health issues represent an interesting category. In some cases, Republican women's proposals for women's health looked quite similar to those of Democratic women. For example, Republican women introduced bills to provide prenatal care and breast and cervical cancer screening to low-income women. On the other hand, they also introduced bills to allow insurance carriers not to cover contraceptives and to require parental permission for sex education in schools. In all, Republican women's bills pertaining to women's health appeared more like Democratic women's bills across sessions and chambers, although there was clearly disagreement among Republican women regarding how to address women's health concerns.

Sex offender and domestic violence legislation, to some degree, follows the patterns already described. Republican attention to the issue peaks during sessions of Republican legislative control. Men of both parties clearly have more interest in sex offender legislation. Like child support legislation, the principle proposal in bills sponsored by both Democratic and Republican men is punishment. For instance, both groups introduced virtually identical bills, across sessions, to create or increase mandatory sentencing for sex offenses, to create and maintain a sex offender registry (mandated by the U.S. government in the late 1990s), to provide penalties for failing to register, and to create new sex offense crimes. Democratic and Republican men introduce an almost exclusive agenda of punishment, and the proliferation of this agenda over the Washington time series we consider is substantial. Though Republican women also introduce sex offender punishments almost exclusively, they do so to a lesser extent. Democratic women differ from all three of the other groups in that they focus on victims' rights and compensation and offender rehabilitation in addition to a much smaller number of punishment proposals. Dealing with sex offenders (and to a lesser extent domestic violence) is thus primarily the domain of male legislators.

# Conclusion

Research on women state legislators, importantly, continues to investigate the ways women legislators represent women's interests. Over time, however, this research has moved away from focusing on women as a singular group and toward understanding both intragroup distinctions among women and how the institutional contexts in which women legislators work affect representation. Political parties are key factors in both of these elements. Parties separate Democratic and Republican women legislators by helping to shape their preferences on women's issues legislation. Parties also control legislative institutions and therefore help determine which women's issues preferences appear on the legislative agenda and how likely they are to become law.

As we have demonstrated in this chapter, women state legislators have distinct, partisan preferences about many women's issues, and they introduce bills that reflect these partisan preferences to the state legislative agendas. Partisan women and men are then more or less likely to contribute their bills to the agenda and have them become law depending on whether their party holds majority control in the legislative chamber. We see these patterns using both cross sectional and over-time data on state legislative agendas.

These results suggest that women and politics researchers should pay the utmost attention to both party identification and legislative parties in examining the actions of women state legislators. These results also lead to further questions in research on women state legislators. Chief among these remaining questions is how these relationships among party identification, legislative parties, and women legislators have changed over time. Prior to and during the second wave of feminism in the 1960s and 1970s, women were just entering the state legislatures in significant numbers. We know little about whether women legislators' preferences among this earlier group of legislators differ significantly from modern women legislators. Evidence such as Schreiber's description of conservative women's interest groups in Chapter 7 and observation of women in the 2010 Tea Party Movement suggest that modern Republican women state legislators may differ radically from Democratic women legislators. Has this type of difference between women partisans always existed, or is it a by-product of party realignment and polarization over time? For women's issues, many of which emerged on legislative agendas in the 1960s and 1970s and then entered mainstream party discussion (Sanbonmatsu 2000), this is a particularly pertinent question. Differences among studies of women state legislators in the 1970s (Diamond 1977; Kirkpatrick 1974), 1980s (Thomas 1994), 1990s (Reingold 2000), and 2000s (Osborn 2012) may in fact point to our need to know more about how women legislators have changed across time.

Legislative parties also differ quite significantly across chamber and in the same chamber over different sessions. The conclusion that women "make a difference" is more common in the congressional literature (see Dodson 2006; Swers 2002; Welch 1985; see also Chapter 10 in this volume) than in the state legislative literature. This is at least partially a by-product of significant party differences among the state legislatures themselves. Some are professional and highly partisan, perhaps even more so than the U.S. House. Others function as virtually one-party chambers at various points in time (e.g., the South in the 1960s, modern Idaho, South Dakota, or Massachusetts) because of overwhelming one-party majorities. State legislatures also have significant differences in electoral rules from the national government, such as the initiative process and supermajoritarian voting requirements. Each of these additional institutional differences may compound or diminish the influence of parties on women's representation relative to Congress. To continue developing theories about how partisan women legislators represent women's issues, we should continue to use the comparative leverage of the U.S. state legislatures.

## Notes

1. Elections in Nebraska are nonpartisan, although legislators themselves generally identify with a political party. Though legislators in Nebraska express partisan preferences according to this party identification, their legislative behavior does not organize along party lines (Wright and Schaffner 2002).
2. The sample contains 1,610 legislators, or 38 percent of winning state legislative candidates in the 1998 election. The distribution of women to men and Democrats to Republicans does not differ significantly from that in the population of state legislative officeholders in 1999.
3. We create the predicted probabilities in Table 11.1 by treating each issue position as a dichotomous dependent variable. We use logistic regression and a model with three main independent variables of interest: the legislator's political party, sex, and an interaction term to capture the

additional difference between Democratic women and the rest of the sample. We also control for if the legislator is African American, the political ideology of the state from which the legislator hails, and whether the legislator comes from a Southern state.

4. Defining women's issues can be a difficult process. Other common definitions of women's issues include issues related to women's traditional roles as caregivers in the private sphere (see, e.g., Thomas 1994), the "ethic of care" that derives from this traditional separation (Thomas 1994), or social welfare issues (Swers 2002). Though we agree that these other categories of issues likely have gendered dimensions, we eliminate them from the analysis at hand to focus on the set of issues in which differences between women and men are most likely to exist.

5. We consider party strength using conditional party government measures of interparty dispersion and intraparty cohesion (see Aldrich and Rohde 1991). We measure these items using roll call votes from the Representation in America's Legislatures Project (Wright, Osborn, and Winburn 2009; Shor, Berry, and McCarty 2010).

6. More information about the Representation in American Legislatures Project can be found at http://www.indiana.edu/~ral or in Osborn (2012, chapter 3).

7. This coding scheme is roughly comparable to that used in Baumgartner and Jones's (2002) *Policy Dynamics*.

8. To code each bill, we used the online archives and official legislative journals for each state legislature. Each bill received at least one and up to two codes identifying its substantive content. For example, a bill assessing a fee for marriage licenses to pay for domestic violence treatment would receive two codes: one for marriage (901); and one for domestic violence (903). Bills received two codes only if it was warranted; the content of many bills could be accurately described using only one code. The first and second codes carried equal weight, such that the previously discussed bill would count in the tally of bills about marriage and bills about domestic violence equally. To code the bills, the authors and a variety of trained undergraduate research assistants read the content of each bill online and assigned a code. Two coders coded at least 10 percent of the bills in each session to assess intercoder reliability. The average intercoder reliability across sessions was 82 percent. In most cases of dispute, coders placed the bills in similar categories (e.g., one labeled the bill as insurance regulation (324), while the other labeled it insurance claims (1350)) or in subcategories within the same larger category (e.g., one labeled the bill as child support (904), while the other labeled it as child custody (912), as often bills regarding one also mentioned the other). In cases of dispute, the authors made all final decisions. For each session, we coded all substantive bills that originated in the regular session of the chamber; we did not code memorials, resolutions, or bills originating in the Senate or in special session.

# 12

# Entry-Level Politics? Women as Candidates and Elected Officials at the Local Level

LAURA VAN ASSENDELFT

The eligibility pool theory suggests that, as women increase their educational and occupational credentials for politics, more are likely to enter politics. A basic premise of this theory is that women's entry-level political participation expands the eligibility pool of women prepared for *and interested in* pursuing positions at the state or national levels. For example, scholars who focus on women in Congress frequently refer to women serving in local elective office as entering a "pipeline" to congressional service. These hypotheses, however, have been challenged or modified by research on political ambition and by the complexity of motivations and barriers that apply to the different types of offices and different levels of government, including studies reported in Chapter 2 of this volume (see also Deckman, 2007; Carroll and Sanbonmatsu, 2010).

Barriers to elective office faced by women at the state or national levels are often perceived as less significant at the local level (Flammang, 1984; Beck, 1991; Darcy, Welch, and Clark, 1994; Boles, 2001; Moncrieff, Squire, and Jewell, 2001; Deckman, 2007). First, there are more opportunities for women on the local level than any other level of government. The 2012 *Census of Governments* reported a total of 89,004 units of local government across the United States, including towns, counties, cities, special districts, and school districts (U.S. Census Bureau 2012). Additionally, many local races are nonpartisan, the media may be less invasive, campaigns can be less expensive, the job is often part-time, and local elected officials do not have to relocate their families. However, even at the local level women remain vastly underrepresented, and in some cases their numbers have stalled or even declined over the last decade. Women mayors, for example, led 20.8 percent of cities with populations over 30,000 in 2002 but only 17.4 percent in 2012. Of the 100 largest cities in the United States, 15 had female mayors in 2002 compared with 12 in 2012 (CAWP, 2012e). Women comprise approximately 28 percent of city councils and 40 percent of school boards (MacManus et al., 2006; National League of Cities, 2012).

Research on women as local officeholders is complicated due to the variance in size of governing bodies and by the myriad forms of government. For example, many states use nonpartisan and off-year elections for local offices. School board members can be elected or appointed. Council members may be elected at large or in districts. Mayors can be elected by the public or chosen from among city council members. Mayors may also share governing authority with a hired city manager. Some localities impose term limits. There is a directory of congressional members by state as well as statewide databases listing all of the men and women who serve in state legislatures, but there is no comparable database of locally elective officials. This makes it difficult to conduct large quantitative analyses that could produce generalizable results. Still, a wide variety of quantitative and qualitative research has suggested both interesting parallels and differences for women serving in entry-level politics.

This chapter offers a review of the literature on women in local office focused on the influence of gender on the decision to enter local politics, leadership style, and levels of political ambition to pursue higher office. These results are enriched by open-ended responses from a 2007 case study of women elected officials in rural Virginia (van Assendelft and Stottlemyer, 2009). In that study, a survey was distributed to 433 women elected officials in southwest and western Virginia.[1] The survey included questions about the elected official's background, experience, recruitment, policy influence, and goals. In the following analysis, the responses are organized by type of office to provide further insight to public service at the local level.

## Underrepresentation and the Ambition Gap

Compared with statewide and national office, local elections require less time and fewer resources. For example, the 2007 Virginia survey of local elected officials revealed that campaigning at the local level is inexpensive and minimal, and overall most respondents felt "positive" or "very positive" toward all campaign activities (van Assendelft and Stottlemyer, 2009). The majority of respondents enjoyed going door to door, meeting constituents, and attending campaign events. Although fundraising was not a favorite activity, it was also not as crucial for these elections, and in fact some did not even have to campaign. One woman explained that while she sent out a questionnaire and put out a couple of homemade yard signs, "No one else did anything for this election." Given the relative lack or burden in running for local office compared with state or national office, an interesting research question is why are more women not choosing to run for office?

In landmark studies of political ambition, Lawless and Fox (2005, 2011) reported that women who have entered the eligibility pool for political office (including membership in professions such as law, business, education, and politics) are less likely than men to consider running for office and that the gender gap in political ambition is apparent at all levels of elective office. They also found very little change in this pattern in the last decade.

Although more local-level women than men consider running for school boards (35 percent compared with 26 percent), a smaller percentage of women than men aspire to be city council members (7 percent compared with 11 percent). There was no significant difference in interest in the office of mayor or district attorney. Even when the interest in running is similar, though, women are less likely than men to decide to run. Among the factors that influence the decision to run include the fact that women were much more likely than men to consider their community's local elections as highly competitive (55 percent compared with 39 percent). Women were also less likely than men to be recruited for local office. The percentage of women versus men who reported ever being encouraged to run for office was 18 percent versus 21 percent for school board, 16 percent versus 22 percent for city council, 6 percent versus 10 percent for mayor, and 1 percent versus 2 percent for district attorney.

Women's less frequent decisions to run relative to men result from different types of socialization that can inhibit political ambition, even at the local level where opportunity costs are minimal compared with higher office. Even more puzzling, though, is that experience in elective office at the local level does not appear to whet women's appetite for higher office. While ample evidence suggests that women make a difference in bringing attention to a wider array of policy issues and in their greater emphasis on representation of constituency interests, any efficacy that might be gained rarely translates into progressive ambition. In the 2007 Virginia survey, less than one-quarter of respondents indicated interest in pursuing higher office. Three common perceptions contributed to their lack of progressive ambition: respondents considered themselves too old; felt that their family situation prevented it; or did not think they could raise enough money to run. The majority of these women serving at the local level have not entered a political pipeline toward state or national elective office.

For the most part, women who serve in local elective office are either content with serving at the local level or unwilling to risk running for higher office. Most report being very connected to their communities through civic and religious organizations, and most feel that they have high levels of efficacy and that their actions make a difference. What remains unclear is why women's experience at the local level does not increase their ambition to pursue higher office. To learn more, we review both the research of others and the Virginia survey of women who ran for local office with respect to how local-level elected women confronted identified barriers, what inspired them, what impact they felt they made, and, what, if any, future political goals they had. These findings are reported.

# Mayors

The vast majority of municipalities in the United States have the position of mayor. Municipalities vary in their selection of the mayor, however, in terms of the size and structure of the city council and whether or not there is a hired city manager. Mayors are categorized as "weak" or "strong" based on their formal powers. Strong mayors are elected directly by the public and have independent executive powers, including a veto and the authority to hire and fire city department heads. In contrast, weak mayors are selected from among city council members and serve a largely ceremonial role. Weak mayors have an equal vote on the city council, no veto power, and no independent authority to hire or fire city personnel. Both weak and strong mayor systems may also hire a city manager to carry out the daily administrative functions of the city. The council–manager structure (with or without a mayor) is used by 55 percent of municipalities (National League of Cities, 2012). In contrast, 43 percent of municipalities use a mayor–council system, which separates the legislative and executive functions.

Mayors are also restricted in their leadership capacity depending on the relationship between local governments and their state. Home rule states grant localities broad authority to govern. In contrast, a city's authority is limited to govern to the powers expressly granted by the state (Dillon's Rule). Dillon's Rule is based on an 1868 judicial ruling by Iowa Supreme Court Chief Justice John Dillon, who spelled out that local governments have powers that are only expressly granted to them, "necessarily or fairly implied" by the express powers, or powers deemed essential and indispensable to the declared purposes of local government. Mayors serving in Dillon's Rule states, therefore, do not have the same autonomy and flexibility to deal with local issues as mayors serving in home rule states.

In 2012, there were 217 women mayors in in cities with populations over 30,000. Of these, only 43, or 19.8 percent, served in larger cities with populations over 100,000. More than half (120) operate under Dillon's Rule. Only 12 women served as mayors in the top 100 cities in the United States. Only two of these mayors served in mayor–council systems with significant executive functions, and a third mayor served in a "modified" council–manager system in which the mayor has strong executive powers. The rest of the mayors served under council–manager systems of government (Table 12.1). As seen in Table 12.2, the majority of the top mayors (9) serve four-year terms, and not quite half (4) have term limits.

The pool of women mayors varies in degrees of executive power and resources. There is also wide variance among mayors in workload and compensation. In the larger cities, there are larger budgets, stronger formal powers and control (which is not necessarily correlated to the size of the city), and more executive experience, prestige, and visibility. Thus, big-city strong mayors are more likely to develop credentials needed to run for governor or congressional office.

*Table 12.1* **Women Mayors in Top 100 U.S. Cities by Local Government Structure**

| City | | Mayor | Size | Rank | Structure |
|------|------|-------|------|------|-----------|
| TX | Houston | Annise D. Parker | 2,099,451 | 5 | Mayor–council |
| TX | Fort Worth | Betsy Price | 741,206 | 17 | Council–manager |
| MD | Baltimore | Stephanie Rawlings-Blake | 620,961 | 24 | Mayor–council |
| NV | Las Vegas | Carolyn Goodman | 583,756 | 31 | Council–manager |
| CA | Fresno | Ashley Swearengin | 494,665 | 35 | Council–manager* |
| NC | Raleigh | Nancy McFarlene | 403,892 | 44 | Council–manager |
| CA | Oakland | Jean Quan | 390,724 | 48 | Council–manager |
| CA | Stockton | Ann Johnston | 291,707 | 68 | Council–manager |
| CA | Chula Vista | Cheryl Cox | 243,916 | 80 | Council–manager |
| AZ | Glendale | Elaine M. Scruggs | 226,721 | 91 | Council–manager |
| NV | North Las Vegas | Shari L. Buck | 216,961 | 96 | Council–manager |
| TX | Irving | Beth Van Duyne | 216,290 | 97 | Council–manager |

*Modified council manager system including a "strong" mayor with executive authority

*Source:* Center for American Women and Politics, "Women Mayors in U.S. Cities 2012," January, 2012. http://www.cawp.rutgers.edu/fast_facts/levels_of_office/Local-WomenMayors.php; U.S. Conference of Mayors, 2012. "Cities Online," 2012. http://www.usmayors.org/meetmayors/citieson-line.asp.

Few women currently occupy the most prestigious mayoral positions. Of the 12 women mayors in 2012 serving in the largest 100 cities in the United States, only one, Annise Parker (Houston, TX), is ranked in the top 10 (CAWP, 2012e). Using data from the 2008 Center for American Women and Politics (CAWP) Mayoral

*Table 12.2* **Women Mayors in Top 100 U.S. Cities, Terms and Term Limits**

| City | | Mayor | Term | Term Limit |
|---|---|---|---|---|
| TX | Houston | Annise D. Parker | 2 years | 3 terms |
| TX | Fort Worth | Betsy Price | 2 years | – |
| MD | Baltimore | Stephanie Rawlings-Blake | 4 years | – |
| NV | Las Vegas | Carolyn Goodman | 4 years | – |
| CA | Fresno | Ashley Swearengin | 4 years | 2 terms |
| NC | Raleigh | Nancy McFarlene | 2 years | – |
| CA | Oakland | Jean Quan | 4 years | 2 terms |
| CA | Stockton | Ann Johnston | 4 years | 2 terms |
| CA | Chula Vista | Cheryl Cox | 4 years | 2 terms |
| AZ | Glendale | Elaine M. Scruggs | 4 years | – |
| NV | North Las Vegas | Shari L. Buck | 4 years | – |

*Source*: Center for American Women and Politics, "Women Mayors in U.S. Cities 2012," January, 2012. http://www.cawp.rutgers.edu/fast_facts/levels_of_office/Local-WomenMayors.php; U.S. Conference of Mayors, 2012. "Cities Online," 2012. http://www.usmayors.org/meetmayors/citieson-line.asp.

Recruitment Study of male and female mayors, Carroll and Sanbonmatsu (2010) found that both male and female mayors were well educated and had elite socioeconomic status and prior political or community service experience. Fewer women held law degrees than men, and women were less likely to be married or have young children at home. Women, however, had slightly more prior experience in politics or community service. Not only were women mayors more likely to have held at least one elective or appointive office prior to becoming mayor, but also the women mayors were described as "joiners," equally or more actively involved than men in civic, religious, and children's or youth organizations. Thus, women clearly have strong connections to their communities that motivate their desire to serve.

Consistent with recruitment research for other offices, women mayors emphasize the importance of being asked to run for office. The encouragement to run, however, is more likely to come from a friend, coworker, or acquaintance than from political parties or even women's organizations. A plurality of women (43.3 percent) identified as "pure recruits" who would not have considered running for office without being prompted. Another 23.7 percent said that someone's suggestion in addition to their own interests influenced their initial decision to run, and a third were self-starters who decided to seek office on their own. Many of these women mayors chose to seek office despite "negative recruitment" from people who tried to discourage them from running, but the sources were more personal than political. While spouses were equally supportive of women and men, other family members (children, siblings, and parents) were less supportive of women (Carroll and Sanbonmatsu, 2010). When women and men evaluated the impact of running for and serving in office on their families, women were slightly more likely than men to consider the age of their children.

Self-confidence, or the perception that they could do the job well, also emerged as a critical decision-making factor. Carroll and Sanbonmatsu suggest that confidence was even more important to the women than men because they rated prior experience more highly and acquired more experience before running. More women than men also attended campaign workshops to gain additional training. There were no significant gender differences, however, in concern about fundraising for the campaign. Finally, compared with men, public policy issues were more likely to motivate the women to run for office than the desire to have a political career (Carroll and Sanbonmatsu, 2010).

Compared with other levels of office, media bias appears to be less prevalent in the press coverage of mayoral candidates and may even provide an advantage to female candidates by covering a wider range of issues when a woman appears on the ballot. In studying mayoral races, Atkeson and Krebs (2008) found no evidence of gender bias in coverage of the issues, traits, appearance, or electability. They conclude that party, incumbency, competitiveness, and candidate quality may explain earlier evidence of gender bias against female candidates, whereas the mayoral races were all nonpartisan, open-seat races.

Analysis of mayoral leadership styles suggests some differences based on gender (Tolleson-Rinehart, 2001). As mayors, women are rated as more collegial, hands-on, and collaborative than men. Few differences emerge in the types of issues male or female mayors prioritize. Both sexes focus on perennial municipal issues, including economic development, infrastructure, and physical safety (Tolleson-Rinehart, 2001; Weikart et al., 2006). Tolleson-Rinehart suggests that the men "looked more like 'women'" (163) in how they approached community life issues. Female mayors, however, are more likely to address these issues through teamwork that emphasizes inclusivity (Weikart et al., 2006). Women mayors were more open and flexible in discussing budgetary issues, in contrast to male mayors, who emphasized the need for budgetary controls.

The women mayors and vice mayors serving in smaller cities and towns are often overlooked in research. The 2007 Virginia survey included 16 women mayors or vice mayors serving in small rural communities. These small town leaders expressed a high degree of job satisfaction, reporting that community improvement motivated their service. One mayor liked the "satisfaction of seeing things accomplished and helping to solve problems." Another described "wanting to better the community" and "being a part of the solution." Helping to make a difference, solving problems, and helping to achieve policy were common themes that motivated the small-town mayors.

These women also believed that they brought a different perspective to the debate and that they had good communication skills. One mayor wrote, "I believed I could communicate better than the council at that time. Women are better communicators. They bring balance, they look at the whole issue, and make better decisions in a more timely process." Another commented, "I love my town very much and I just wanted to have a say so in it, and now I get to speak my peace."

The social aspects of the job are also appealing to these mayors. Meeting constituents, attending events, and helping to solve problems were all favorite aspects of the job. "I love helping people when they have a problem and usually it can be resolved without difficulty," wrote one mayor. Complaints included working with "good old boys" and "making a decision when you feel both parties are right." Another listed being "part of a system that moves so slowly." There were few complaints, however, about campaigning, public speaking, or interacting with the media.

Enjoyment of the job as mayor, however, did not correspond with desire to run for higher office. Of the mayors surveyed, the majority were over the age of 50, and a third of them had retired from other professional positions. Only two mayors, both in their 40s, expressed some interest in running for another office. One had considered it, and the other wrote that she was not sure but that if an opportunity emerged she "would consider all options."

Small-town mayors have few resources and limited power, but they provide leadership in their communities. Survey research suggests positive experiences, but not enough to interest the majority in pursuing higher office. Big-city mayors gain more credentials for higher office, and additional resources facilitate visibility and influence, including the Women's Mayor Caucus of the U.S. Council of Mayors (U.S. Conference of Mayors, 2012). However, few women have reached the ranks of the most powerful mayors.

## City and County Councils

The legislative branch of local government is composed of the city council or county board of supervisors (they may also be called alderman, selectman, freeholder, trustee, or commissioner). The size of these legislative bodies ranges from 5 to 51. They vary in structure, resources, and authority. City councils may select their own mayor or work with an independently elected mayor. Both city and county councils may hire a professional administrator. Data on city councils indicate that, for most, the job is part-time, requiring an average of 20–25 hours per week for small (populations < 70,000) and medium cities (70,000–200,000) with compensation below $20,000. Large cities with populations over 200,000 average 42 hours per week and are paid $20,000 or above. Only one in five cities holds partisan elections for council members. Women comprise approximately 28 percent of city council members (National League of Cities, 2012).

Like women mayors, women council members bring a different style of leadership to office. Beck (1991) found that women council members spend more time than men on constituency service. Antolini (1984) explains that this behavior appeared to compensate for women's exclusion from the male dominated inner circles of policymaking. Women report more time spent on preparing for meetings, taking notes, and following up with constituents. No gender differences emerged, however, in the top issue priorities of male versus female council members. Similar to mayors, both sexes on city council prioritized economic development, taxes, and quality of life (Beck 1991). Boles (1991), however, found that women brought more attention to wider range of issues, including sexual assault, domestic violence, childcare, displaced homemakers, library services, and childbirth. Boles (2001) argues that women were more likely to perceive an issue as a woman's issue and more likely to advocate for the issue.

City councils have nonpartisan reputations, attracting a diverse group of amateur politicians interested in addressing community problems. Like the office of mayor, however, the position of city council member is not a fertile breeding ground for higher office. Bledsoe and Herring (1990) found that male and female council members need different levels of political ambition to make the decision to run for higher office. Women place more emphasis on electoral vulnerability and the need to be invited to run for higher office. Men are more likely to recruit themselves, relying on resources beyond their political careers. Bledsoe and Herring conclude that men are more likely than women to have the "driving ambition for personal advancement" needed to compete in politics (221).

The literature on women serving on city councils has also focused on style of leadership. British philosopher Edmond Burke (1729-1797) distinguished between two philosophies of representation. The "delegate" acts as a messenger for his or her constituents, representing public opinion even when it violates their personal beliefs. In contrast, the "trustee" consults constituents but then relies on his or her own judgment of what is in the public interest. Beck (1991) notes that female council members put greater emphasis on the representative nature of the role than do male council members. Women are more likely to act as delegates, prioritizing accessibility and representation. In contrast, male council members are more likely to act as trustees, describing their decision-making as more analytical and that of the female council members as more emotional. Beck suggests, however, that the impact of these different leadership styles is limited, given the narrow range of issues typically addressed by city councils. She argues that both men and women tend to resist decreasing property values or increasing taxes.

Several common themes emerged from the open-ended responses of city council members in the Virginia survey. A majority of women council members emphasized improving representation as a motivating factor in their decision to run. This was expressed either as the need to add a woman's perspective to a male dominated council or the need to improve communication between city council and the school board or between city council and constituents. One city council member wrote, "I felt it was important for me to pave the way for women in my community to become involved in government." Another explained, "The members of the city council at that time did not represent *all* citizens. The council was made up of seven middle- to upper-class white males, mostly from the same area of the city." Increasing representation was not always gender related, as one city council member described, "I believe that government is 'us' not 'them,' coming together to do things collectively that don't get done individually (roads, schools, etc.). In order to ensure that government is 'us,' citizens must step up and be willing to work. I decided that I needed to 'step up.' The 2000 election was, for me, the catalyst."

Improving representation also extended to constituency service, and most of the respondents viewed their role as a delegate, or messenger, who represents all of their constituents, rather than a trustee. In describing the most important role as an elected official, one council member wrote, "To listen to the citizens and vote as they would prefer." Similarly, another wrote, "To represent the needs of constituents, not my own." A number of council members described serving in elective office as an honor. One commented, for example, "You are not as important as the people you serve. It's a privilege to help make a difference."

Another common motivating factor was the desire to bring change to a community and to solve policy problems, a sentiment often expressed by women at all levels of office. As one council member explained, "Being an elected official and running campaigns is simply a passion with me. I love solving problems for people—building schools—raising awareness, etc. making the lives of people better." Several council members were quite specific about change they wanted to effect. One wrote, "The only name on the ballot would have changed the direction of the county was taking re[garding] growth and natural resource management. Someone needed to run, and quickly. A group of citizens were desperate. All my previous activities made me as well prepared as anyone, and I was willing to try." Another explained candidly, "I was disgusted with what our then town manager was doing to the town and thought I could make a difference. Soon after I took office he started making other plans, and within a few months he took another job. Since nothing else had changed during his five-year tenure except my explanation of what I was going to be expecting from him—delivered at my first meeting—I take full and joyful credit for his departure." Others were more general in their comments, writing, for example, "I like that I can make positive changes and can stop detrimental changes," and "I like being 'in the know.' I like actually making a difference."

Analysis of the open-ended comments about likes and dislikes of the job provides insight about interest in running for higher office. The collaborative teamwork associated with serving on city councils was perceived as an advantage. One council member wrote, "I am very uncomfortable with controversy and dread being questioned by the news press for fear of misinterpretation. I am most comfortable working in the background." The social aspects of the job were also rewarding: "I really enjoy meeting the citizens. I attend many social functions and I really have fun." "Making people feel engaged in part of the process" and "the opportunity to influence outcomes" were also aspects they liked about the job.

There were very few negative reactions to serving as a city council member— some were related to politics in general, and some were related to gender. One council member wrote, "I dislike irrational, negative, selfish, narrow-minded uninformed activists." Another wrote, "What I like least is when I make a suggestion and it is ignored. However, when a 'male' makes the same suggestion it is given consideration." Likewise, another explained, "Personal attacks have been difficult. I do believe being a woman creates some degree of difficulty with what has been predominantly a 'man's' world." Put more bluntly, another wrote that she disliked the "narrow-mindedness of fellow (male) council members and a stubborn mayor."

For others, the time commitment was a barrier. "Being an elected official is very time-consuming. Your life is not your own." A number of respondents explained that the job requires a thick skin and confidence. One city council member wrote, for example, "To do this job well, you have to be willing to devote time to learning, studying, reading, discussing, THINKING, attending lots of meetings. You have to have the guts to stand up for what is right and best for your constituents—even it if is unpopular with the vocal minority. And you have to develop plenty of confidence."

The majority of respondents, however, valued their influence. One described "a feeling of pride, knowing I am doing a good job as an elected official and especially since I am only the 2nd woman to ever serve in this capacity in my city." Another wrote how she appreciates "knowing I am making a difference in my town and helping others who can't." One council member explained that " 'politics' is less important at the local level than governmental issues," arguing that problem solving at the local level is largely nonpartisan. Another explained why she felt she could make more of a difference at the local level: "I like serving as a local official because you can help people more directly." One even wrote that she had declared a candidacy for the state legislature "but withdrew feeling that local government would be more rewarding."

Nearly one in five of the city council members surveyed expressed interest in running for another elective office. Of these, a third want to run for mayor, a third are considering a run for the state legislature, and a third are open to the idea of running, but not specific about the office. Conversely, one city council member was recruited to run for the state legislature but declined, writing that her "family situation prevented her at this time." Another just got married and was planning to resign from the city council because she would be moving out of town and was not interested in pursuing another office.

In general, women city council members enjoy representing their constituents, solving problems through largely nonpartisan collaboration, and attending social events where they are likely to know many of their constituents. A common perception is that these favored aspects of local government service are less prevalent at higher levels of office. Despite gaining valuable political experience at the local level, few women city council members consider running for higher office.

## School Boards

School boards vary in selection method and in their relationship to the city or county council. Most school boards are elected, although 19 states still allow at least some appointed school boards (National Association of School Boards of Education, 2009). School boards also vary in administrative authority and budgetary independence. Members receive limited compensation (the majority are paid less than $10,000) and typically work fewer hours than city or county council members. The workload varies from an average of 25 hours per month in small to medium cities to 20 hours per week in some large cities (Hess 2002). Approximately 40 percent of school board members are female (MacManus et al., 2006).

Two theories suggest that women will have greater opportunities and success running for school board positions than other elective offices, including other local offices. First, the lower "prestige" of school board positions makes these seats less desirable and less competitive (MacManus et al., 2006). Second, women are perceived to have natural credibility in the area of education policy as mothers or childcare providers (Bers, 1978). While there are more women represented on school boards than in any other elective office, these factors appear to attract a different breed of officeholders—those who are less interested in politics and political careers and more interested in community service for policy or social reasons (Deckman, 2007).

School board members typically serve an apprenticeship in government, civic or business organizations, or education. Both male and female school board members tend to be upper middle class, well educated, white, married, and parents (approximately half have school-aged children). Female school board members are younger and twice as likely to have careers in education compared with men (Deckman, 2007).

Gender differences in leadership include the greater emphasis women place on representation of the public in their role as a school board member. In contrast, male school board members prioritize administrative oversight (Bers, 1978; Donahue, 1997). School board agendas are constrained by scarce resources and the dominant influence of school superintendents and teacher unions (Deckman, 2007; Donahue, 1997).

The office of school board does not appear to inspire progressive ambition among either women or men. Traditionally viewed as an "apolitical" office, most school board elections are nonpartisan. Deckman (2007) suggests that not only does the office of school board seem to attract women who are less interested in pursuing higher office but also the nonpartisan nature of the office does not foster the connections or provide the political experience needed to advance a political career. Few school board campaigns are competitive, incumbency rates are high, political parties are not actively recruiting from this gateway to the political pipeline, and few school board members themselves perceive their office as a steppingstone toward a political career (Deckman, 2007).

In the 2007 Virginia survey, the overwhelming motivation expressed by respondents to serve on a school board was "making a difference for children." This finding is consistent with research on other offices and levels of government; women enter politics to solve policy problems. As one school board member wrote, "I have always helped with organizations that focused on children. I thought that being a school board representative could help the children in our community." Another theme that emerged was the desire to improve representation, by increasing awareness of issues or fostering better communication. As one respondent explained, "I have found that many teachers (mostly female profession) and moms (the parent who frequently deals with school issues) find it easier to talk to a woman." Others emphasized the advantage of having careers in education. One wrote, "With 31 years of teaching experience, I felt I could bring a different perspective to the school board. I know children and teacher's frustrations and desires." Timing was also important in the decision to run for office. As one school board member explained, "I was retired from teaching but still interested in the education system. My nest was empty. The prospects looked good for my election. Running for office was a big challenge."

In describing their most important role as an elected official, the majority of school board members emphasized constituency service and having a delegate's philosophy of representation. One school board member said that the most important role is "to be available to constituents, to communicate with constituents, to do one's homework (be prepared), and to vigorously serve the best interests of *all* the people." By underlining the word all, the respondent emphasized her role as a delegate, or messenger, for constituency interests. Likewise, another wrote, "To be an objective, honest, hardworking public servant. As much as possible leave your own needs at home. Serve the public's best interest." And finally, "Listen to constituents no matter how much you may disagree with them, listen and appreciate their willingness to share their point of view."

The constituency service expected in the role as school board member, while "very fulfilling as a citizen and a taxpayer," can be time-consuming. As one school board member compared her responsibilities on school board with her law practice, "In local government, I often miss not having a research assistant or aide. The sheer volume of the work can be discouraging." After a single term, another school board member was ready to leave, writing, "I enjoyed my four years and appreciate the experience, [but]...no one told me about the LARGE time commitment that is expected. I sat on 10 different committees, which required me to travel and on average be gone three to four nights per week." She also disliked the lack of privacy that accompanied public life.

Related frustrations emerged about the nature of governmental policymaking. One school board member explained, "I enjoy the work because it has taught me patience. I have met many people and learned how all the pieces fit together, thus making me more appreciative of our government's system. That appreciation also leads to frustration as it takes so much time to accomplish even the smallest of tasks." Another explained that the "good old boy system is alive and well." At the same time, others expressed great confidence in their ability to effect change and satisfaction in making a difference. One such school board member wrote, "I like articulating clearly the reasons for my position on a policy. I like being instrumental in bringing the board to agreement."

When asked if they were interested in running for higher office, the vast majority (76 percent) said no. Only one school board member expressed immediate intention to run for a specific office—her county Board of Supervisors. The remaining school board members indicated only tentative interest in running for higher office in the future. Survey responses included "maybe city council"; "someday, maybe state legislature"; and "possibly—timing is important if the opportunity presents itself after my children are out of the house I might run for state delegate." Others were not so sure. One chose to run only for school board because the race was not partisan, writing, "I would probably not run if it were partisan."

While policy conflicts in education can spark controversy at the local level, school board members are typically less visible than city council members or mayors. School boards focus on a single policy area with limited resources and prestige. Those attracted to the position are more interested in making good public policy than gaining power or political experience. They are unlikely to be interested in running for higher office, nor are they heavily recruited to do so.

## Other Local Elective Positions

The women serving as bureaucrats in government offices provide a pool of recruits for additional local elective offices (Dometrius and Sigelman, 1997; Sanbonmatsu, 2002). Marion Palley (2001) describes these women as the "hidden players" in the policymaking process. The wide variety of elective offices beyond executives (mayors) and legislators (city council and school board members) includes sheriff, probate judge, clerk of the court, registrar, and revenue officers and various boards and commissions.

In the Virginia case study, there are five constitutional offices, and all are represented by women: sheriff, clerk of the court, Commonwealth attorney, commissioner of revenue, and treasurer. In contrast to other local elected offices, the constitutional officers expressed the lowest levels of progressive ambition. Several factors appear to depress ambition in these offices.

The constitutional officers tend to make a career in the office where they serve, first working under the elected official and then, after gaining experience, running for office themselves. Unanimously these women report that meeting people and serving the public are the best parts of their job. They love what they do and find their service to be fulfilling. As one clerk of the court reported, "I enjoy meeting the needs of the county citizens and feeling as if I have made a difference." A county commissioner of revenue wrote, "The work is very rewarding; local government work is particularly satisfying." Only two expressed interest in running for a higher office (state legislator). If the one-on-one relationships are the most appealing aspect of the job, local office (the level of government closest to the people) provides the greatest potential for constituency interaction. Progressive ambition, then, appears to be inhibited by job satisfaction.

Timing may also play a role. The surveys indicate a long apprenticeship in many cases before running for office. These women reported working 8 to 10 years and in some cases two decades or more before deciding to run or feeling they had an opportunity to run (e.g., when their boss retired). Such long lags between stepping-stones also limit political career opportunities.

Their extensive prior experience, however, translated into confidence in their initial campaign. As one commissioner of revenue explained, "I felt fully qualified, I was asked by several people to run, I was unchallenged in my position at the time, and I thought I could win." Most of the women in the survey were "insiders," gaining experience from the person they would ultimately replace. Family also played a role in the decision to run for these women. One clerk of the court explained, "An opportunity (where the political field was friendly) was available and my personal life was secure and satisfactory, so with my family's approval I ran against the incumbent."

What these elective officials enjoy least about public office is party politics, described as "the way other candidates told lies, and their negative comments," or the "dishonest people who are only in it for personal gain." Public speaking, dealing with the media, and raising campaign funds were also among their complaints. But they were overwhelmingly positive about "meeting and greeting" their constituents. As one commissioner of revenue recounted, "Even though it was the hardest thing I'd ever done, going door to door was actually enjoyable." Another described how she "received flowers, garden vegetables, a couple meals . . . " in her small town where most people already knew her. Service to these constituents was a common theme that motivated their work. As one commissioner of revenue advised, "Do not seek office for personal gain but see it as a service to your community."

In contrast to the city councils, school boards, and even mayors of small cities and towns, constitutional officers work full time with professional salaries. They have specialized credentials in their field of service. They are less motivated by social factors or single issues; instead they are more likely to pursue these offices as a career choice. More research is needed on the difference women make as leaders in these elected positions.

## Conclusions

There is a growing body of literature on local officeholders provides insight into their motivations to run and their experience once serving. First, research on local women elected officials appreciates the collaborative nature of local elected office, the opportunity to serve constituents, and the ability to influence good public policymaking. The women bring a different perspective and leadership style. Women are more likely to emphasize constituency service, and their philosophy of representation is more oriented toward the delegate than the trustee.

Like other levels of elective office, women remain less likely than men to make the decision to run—even in light of the fact that many of the barriers to running for office are less prevalent at the local level than higher levels of office. Campaigns are less expensive, the media are typically less intrusive, and the positions are often part-time. Local elected officials do not have to relocate their families to serve in public office. Yet despite these lower opportunity costs women still remain vastly underrepresented.

Recruitment does matter, however. Similar to higher levels of office, women at the local level respond positively to recruitment. The additional encouragement from a family member, friend, colleague, or political organizational representative remains a critical factor in the initial decision to run. At the local level, this type of incentive is more often provided by nonpolitical organizations, suggesting an opportunity for groups to increase their focus on local-level positions.

The women who are elected to and serve in local office also exhibit low levels of progressive ambition. Several factors contribute to this phenomenon. First, local office is more likely to attract amateur politicians who are motivated less by the desire to obtain power or to pursue a political career than by social or specific policy reasons. Second, there is a high rate of job satisfaction among elected officials at the local level. For those who find the social aspects of the job appealing, there is more interaction with constituents at the local level—the level of government closest to the people. Like other levels of elective office, another explanation is timing related to a woman's age of entry into politics. Many women serving as mayors, city council members, or school boards consider themselves to be either too old (many are retired) or too young (with children to take care of). Many of the women in local elected office also took time to gain significant experience before running for office, working in government offices for years or even decades, for example, before running for a constitutional office or waiting a long time for an "opportunity" to run.

When comparing different types of local office, city council members were more likely than school board members to express interest in seeking another elective office—either mayor or state legislative office. The position of city council has broader policy ramifications and increased visibility compared with serving on school board, experience that may increase confidence in running for higher office. The mayors of small cities and towns seemed to enjoy their jobs the most yet also had little interest in pursuing higher office. As more women mayors enter the ranks of the most prestigious big city mayors, opportunities will increase to translate experience into viable campaigns for higher office. Finally, elected constitutional officers at the local level are the least likely to pursue higher office. Their positions are viewed less as political opportunities than full-time, well-paid careers.

The key to increasing women's representation in elective office at the local level, like other levels, is increasing the number of women who are asked to run. After that, the next step is to bridge the gap between the decision to run for local office and ambition to pursue higher office. Further research is needed on the role that socialization plays and how gender influences attitudes toward political ambition at all levels of elective office.

## Notes

1. A total of 160 surveys were completed for a response rate of 37 percent. All unattributed quotes are taken from the open-ended survey responses.

# 13

# Judicial Women

SALLY J. KENNEY

Presidential, congressional, gubernatorial, and state legislative races command nearly all the attention of the media, political scientists, and citizens, even though 38 states elect judges through partisan, nonpartisan, or retention elections.[1] On election night 2012, few networks' graphics or pundits explored judicial races, even though fictional president Josiah Bartlet of the *West Wing* had starred in a YouTube video supporting Bridget Mary McCormack's successful candidacy for the Michigan Supreme Court, the most expensive judicial race ever (Stanton 2012). Few analysts reported on a campaign to oust Iowa Supreme Court Justice David Wiggins for supporting the constitutionality of gay marriage or, by Republicans, to oust three Democrats on the Florida Supreme Court (including a white woman and an African American woman)—campaigns that spent more than $28 million (Corriher 2012). Commentators celebrating women's achievements are far more likely to give attention to 20 women senators, Nancy Pelosi's speakership in 2007, or Hillary Rodham Clinton's 2008 presidential campaign (Carroll 2009) than to the appointment of Justices Sonia Sotomayor and Elena Kagan to the U.S. Supreme Court (Kenney 2010d). Political scientists and advocates for more women in politics like the media and citizenry have mostly underinvestigated the judicial branch of government.[2]

Yet courts are powerful institutions of government. American courts—state, federal, and municipal—are arenas for deciding every important public matter, and legal discourse shapes nearly all public policies. The most contentious issues of our day are decided by federal and state courts—who won an election, whether Congress can legislate on health care, whether state universities can pursue affirmative action strategies, whether states can prohibit gays from marrying, and whether women have the right to choose to have an abortion. It is difficult to think of a women and public policy issue that has not been judicialized including divorce and custody, battering and rape, equal pay and discrimination, and reproductive rights.

At times, the U.S. Senate has sparred with the president, and, based on divisions over a national bank, slavery, or civil rights, political parties have divided over who should sit on the federal courts. Since the 1980s, federal judicial appointments have become deeply contentious and many judicial districts have emergencies because the U.S. Senate has not acted on the president's nominations and left slots open (ACS 2012). And just as governors go on to run for Congress or state legislators seek federal office, the president selects some federal judges from among state court judges.

In the United States, in 2012 women made up 30 percent of all federal judgeships (Matsui 2012), only one-third of U.S. Supreme Court justices, and 27 percent of all state-level positions (NAWJ 2012). Only eight states have achieved a 33 percent threshold or more, and in eight other states women fill less than 8 percent of the positions (CWGCS 2010). Yet women make up more than half of the population and more than 45 percent of all law school graduates.[3] Contrary to popular conceptions that women are working their way up the pyramid as they ascend the legal profession, women are better represented on state Supreme Courts (32 percent) than on lower state courts (25 percent).[4]

This chapter addresses the question of why so few women serve as judges. It asks why the number of judges has stagnated and even been reversed even when women keep increasing their representation in the legal profession and why women continue to face if not a glass ceiling then a labyrinth as they move toward leadership positions in the legal profession (Eagly and Carli 2007)? It also explores whether women judge differently than men and makes the case that understanding gender as a social process—the process by which sex differences are discovered and deployed to disadvantage women—can help us understand what is happening in the federal judicial selection process and in the increasingly politicized and contested state judicial elections.

# History of Women Judges

Women have had a long road to travel before they could be judges: they first had to gain legal status as free and equal persons and citizens before they could be jurors, lawyers, and judges. Although Iowa's attorney general ruled that Belle Babb Mansfield's sex was not an obstacle to her admission to the Iowa Bar Association in 1869—the first admission of a woman to the bar in the United States (Kenney 2010a; Morello 1986; Mullenbach 2007)—most courts interpreted statutes and regulations on membership of the legal profession as excluding women. Women were not persons, nor were they sufficiently autonomous from husbands to practice law (Kerber 1998; Sachs and Wilson 1978); they had to petition their legislatures for admission state by state (Babcock 2011; Mossman 2006). Florence Allen won election to the Common Pleas Court of Ohio in 1920 and was the first woman to serve on a general jurisdiction court in the United States (Allen 1965; Berkson 1982; Cook 1980a, 1982; Kenney 2010b; Martin 1999; Organ 1998; Tuve 1984). In 1922, she won election to the Ohio Supreme Court (the first woman on any state Supreme Court), and in 1934 President Franklin D. Roosevelt appointed her to the U.S. Court of Appeals for the Sixth Circuit, where she served until 1959. She was the first woman in position for presidents to actively consider appointing to the U.S. Supreme Court, and women campaigned hard each of the 12 times a seat became open before she retired (Cook 1982; Kenney 2010b).

It would be 36 years after Allen took her seat on the Ohio Supreme Court before the next woman state Supreme Court justice, Rhoda Lewis, joined the Hawaii Supreme Court in 1959.[5] Not until 2002 would the first woman join the South Dakota Supreme Court, the last state to have its first woman justice. Four women joined their state Supreme Courts in the 1960s, twelve in the 1970s, eighteen in the 1980s, and twelve more in the 1990s. Some appointments, such as Rosalie Wahl's in Minnesota, were high drama (Kenney 2010c). Others, such as Linda Kinney Neuman's, whom Republican governor Terry Branstad appointed to the Iowa Supreme Court in 1986, generated almost no notice. California voters turned the first woman-appointed chief justice, Rose Bird, out of office in a highly contentious retention election (Kenney 2013a), and voters threw out Justice Penny White in Tennessee. Idaho and Iowa have had a woman on their state Supreme Courts but now have none. Indiana had a woman, was all male, and now has one woman member.[6] No clear norm has been established that women must serve; no clear outcry follows a court moving from integrated to all male.

## The Federal Judicial Selection Process

We do not elect federal judges, but their appointments are highly political and increasingly contentious. Appointments to the federal bench have always been party patronage positions (Goldman 1997, 9–14). As a formal matter, the president recommends candidates to the U.S. Senate, which must confirm them by a simple majority vote. Traditionally, the president has deferred to senators of his own party from the home state for district court judges, relied on them heavily for circuit court appointments, and consulted key senators as a whole on appointments to the U.S. Supreme Court. Senators from the state of the vacancy of either party, however, may in effect veto an appointment or subject committee hearings to delay by not returning their "blue slip"[7] on the nominee, although more recently not all Senate Judiciary chairs have deferred.[8] The chair of the Senate Judiciary Committee may delay or refuse to hold a hearing, and the Senate majority leader may refuse to schedule a floor vote. More recently, senators have threatened the filibuster to prevent confirmation, meaning that a nominee must have 60 votes for confirmation. Thus, senators have many ways of delaying or opposing judicial nominees while avoiding the public accountability (Burbank 2002; Hertzberg 2005; Scherer 2003; Slotnick 2002). Senators have been known to block nominees for personal grudges as well as ideological and partisan differences (Zernike 2012).

Since 1953, presidents (except George W. Bush) have called upon the American Bar Association's (ABA) Standing Committee on the Federal Judiciary to rate nominees before their public nomination as a regular part of the process (ABA 2009, 1). The ABA champions its ideal of merit rather than political loyalty (Slotnick 1988). However, feminists have criticized the gender composition of this committee and its standards (Clark 2004; Martin 1982). Brooksley Elizabeth Born was the committee's first woman member in its 25-year history, serving from 1977 to 1983 and as its chair from 1980 to 1983 (ABA 2012; Love 2006, 50; Ness and Wechsler 1979, 48). The committee favored judicial experience and large firm practice over academic work, government lawyering, or public defense and legal aid. It demanded trial experience, particularly membership in the American College of Trial Lawyers (Sloviter 2005, 858). And in President Jimmy Carter's time it automatically gave judges older than 64 years of age an unqualified rating (Goldman 1997, 261). Feminists criticized the standards and also objected to how some seemed to apply only to women and how the committee made exceptions for men.

Each president has had his own system for choosing nominees, sharing responsibilities between the attorney general (overseeing the Department of Justice with the staff to investigate large numbers of candidates) and the White House Counsel's office. While appointments to the U.S. Supreme Court have often reflected the contentious issues of the day, President Richard Nixon was the first president to make ideology rather than party loyalty or personal connections the most important criterion for selecting federal court judges (Scherer 2005). Until Carter's Administration, the Justice Department exclusively handled district and circuit court appointments, mostly by deferring to senators. Since Carter, White House staffers have actively participated in the selection of judges, and President Barack Obama is no exception.

Women have had a more difficult path to federal judicial slots than men. For example, when U.S. Supreme Court Justices Sandra Day O'Connor and Ruth Bader Ginsburg were recent law school graduates, law firms told them explicitly that they would not hire women.[9] When President Ronald Reagan nominated Justice O'Connor, critics argued she was not qualified because she had not worked for a large firm; when Bush nominated his White House Counsel Harriet Miers, who had been a managing partner for her law firm, to a seat on the U.S. Supreme Court, critics claimed she was unqualified because she had not served as a judge (Greenburg 2007; Toobin 2007). Kagan's opponents made similar arguments (Rosen 2009; Totenberg 2010).

Carter and Reagan held men and women nominees to different standards. Carter required women, but not men, to have prior judicial experience and women to have a demonstrable commitment to equal justice under law. Reagan required women, but not men, to have prosecutorial experience and party political experience (Martin 1987, 140). Debating the qualifications of one nominee at a time can often conceal the operation of a gendered double standard (Williams 2006).

## How States Select Their Judges

States vary enormously in how they select judges (AJS 2012). Some follow the federal system with governors appointing judges for life, with or without legislative confirmation. Others elect them in partisan or nonpartisan elections. Some nonpartisan election states designate on the ballot who is the incumbent. Other states have judges appointed by governors, who sometimes draw from a list made by nominating commissions—the so-called merit selection system or the Missouri Plan—and then voters periodically decide whether or not to retain those judges in office. Some states use different systems for different levels of the judiciary. It is important to understand how these different systems operate in practice. For example, Minnesota uses nonpartisan elections to select judges, so the ballot includes no party designation but does note whether the judge is an incumbent. In practice, most judges resign before the end of their term so that the governor can appoint their successor, who runs as an incumbent. This increases the likelihood that she or he will be retained. Most state judges run unopposed, and most judges are retained (Hall and Bonneau 2009). This may be because judges are often listed at the bottom of the ballot, and many voters do not vote all the way down the ticket. The aforementioned *West Wing* YouTube campaign for McCormack concentrated on getting voters to turn over the ballot to see that they had to vote for judges and were not done once they had voted a straight party ticket.

## Progress toward Women's Equality Is Slow, Erratic, and Reversible, not Inevitable

Many people assume that the number and percentage of women on state and federal courts will increase because women's graduation from law school has increased and the number and percentage of women lawyers have increased,[10] but no unmediated relationship exists between women's representation in the population, in law school classes, or as lawyers and lower court and Supreme Court justices. Presidents' appointments, too, rather than steadily increasing the number of women on federal courts, have varied widely. The first 101 justices of the U.S. Supreme Court were men. It took nearly 200 years for a president to appoint a woman. Not until 1981 did Reagan appoint O'Connor as the first woman to serve on the U.S. Supreme Court, and George W. Bush replaced her with a man. President Bill Clinton appointed the largest number of women to date over the course of his two terms (Martin

2004, 117). Following Clinton, only slightly more than 22 percent of Bush's judicial appointments were women (Diascro and Solberg 2009, 290). In his first term, 41 percent of the judges Obama nominated and the Senate has confirmed have been women, a record in percentage terms (AFJ 2012). At the state level, New York City mayor Fiorello H. La Guardia appointed the first African American woman judge, Jane Bolin, to the family court in 1939. President Lyndon Johnson appointed Constance Baker Motley, the first African American woman federal judge, to the U.S. District Court for the Southern District of New York in 1966. Fewer than 9 percent of federal judges are women of color.

What level of representation of women judges should we expect? An important part of the analysis of an employment discrimination claim is to compare the composition of the qualified labor pool with the numbers of women employers hire (Kenney 1992). If, for example, women make up 46 percent of law school graduates—and have done for approximately 25 years (ABA 2011)—but only 10 percent of the lawyers that law firms hire are women, we might suspect something about the selection procedures or criteria works to women's disadvantage. The onus is then on the employer to show the relevance of its selection criteria and that its hiring process is free of bias. The same analysis applies to women judges. If the process for choosing judges is fair and does not discriminate against women, we would expect the proportion of women judges to be close to the proportion of women lawyers with the required number of years of practice.

When political scientist Beverly Blair Cook first investigated this question, however, she found that between 1920 and 1970, states varied as to whether 1 percent or 5 percent of lawyers were women and 1 percent to 10 percent of trial court judges were women. By 1984, as the number of women lawyers grew, a wider gap emerged, leaving Cook (1984a, 574–5) to reject the "trickle-up hypothesis": that women would ascend to the bench in proportion to their numbers in the legal profession with the passage of time. Cook (1984b, 199) found a 50 percent disparity between the number of women judges and the number of women lawyers. That is, if women were 10 percent of the lawyers in a state, about 5 percent of judges would be women. Scholars continue to investigate the relationship between the proportion of women lawyers and the proportion of women judges and find little relationship between the two (Alozie 1996, 122; Bratton and Spill 2005, 130; Hurwitz and Lanier 2003, 342; Martin and Pyle 2002, 39; Reddick, Nelson, and Caufield 2009, 14). Nor does the number of women trial judges predict the number of women appellate judges (Bratton and Spill 2002, 2005, 128; Williams 2007, 1200). Thus, we cannot explain women's underrepresentation on courts simply as a result of the absence of women in the qualified labor pool, nor can we assume that the number of women judges will grow naturally or inevitably as the number of women lawyers grows. Moreover, the huge variation among states in how long it took after the admission of women to the state bar for a state to appoint its first woman to the Supreme Court (Cook 1984a, 598), the large differences among states as to when they named their first woman Supreme Court justice, the variation among states in the percentage of women judges, and the variation among presidents in appointing women suggests that something other than simply the number of women lawyers available is at work.

As early as 1978, Cook found that as a solitary token woman moved up the hierarchy she would not necessarily be replaced by another woman. Bratton and Spill's (2001, 258) research showed that President Clinton was likely to replace African American judges with other African Americans, but he replaced only one of the five women who left the bench with another woman. Bratton and Spill (2002) found it more likely that a governor would choose a woman for the state Supreme Court if the court had no women members. Their research suggests that selectors wanted at least token representation and the credit and attention for appointing a "first." But this bodes ill for women's prospect of increasing their representation on courts if selectors are less likely to pick women for positions if a woman already sits on that court—that is, if the ceiling for women is one position. The numbers of women state Supreme Court justices are increasing more slowly or have plateaued at around 30 percent. That rise, however, conceals the fact that more than 48 women justices on state Supreme Courts have been replaced by men (Kenney 2013a).

Another way to analyze women's progress, in this case, to the federal bench is to investigate presidential appointments. Roosevelt appointed the first woman to the federal bench, Allen, in 1934. And 16 years later, Harry Truman appointed a second, but Dwight Eisenhower appointed no women to the federal bench. Presidents John F. Kennedy, Nixon, and Gerald Ford appointed one each; Johnson appointed three. Carter's appointment of 40 women to the federal bench was thus a very dramatic policy change. He declared a gender-integrated and racially integrated bench to be a priority, charged his staff with implementing that policy, and as a result altered the way he chose federal judges. When Carter took office, four women served on federal courts, although women made up about 15 percent of recent law school graduates and 9.2 percent of all lawyers (Goldman 1997, 236–283; Martin 2004, 111).

An important player in the gender diversity of the bench deserves more credit for this accomplishment (Kenney 2013a). Only 32 years old, Margaret McKenna was the first woman to hold the position of deputy White House counsel. McKenna made the Carter Administration's goal of a racially and gender diverse federal bench a reality (Clark 2002, 245; McKenna, telephone interview, June 25, 2007; Wilson 1995, 6). McKenna connected Carter's commitment to merit selection and racial diversity for judges to his commitment to bringing women in to governmental positions more generally. She persuaded the newly created circuit nominating commissions, and later senators advocating for federal district court appointments, to include women on their lists of recommendations. She assumed control over the decision on judicial nominations from the Justice Department and brought the White House Counsel's office into the deliberations. The administration opposed the American Bar Association's tendency to rate all the women and minority men candidates "not qualified," destroying their chances at confirmation. McKenna succeeded because she made this issue a priority and because she was an insider working strategically with a network of women's groups on the outside.

Feminists inside the Carter Administration also formed a Washington Women's Network that grew to more than 1,200 women—women who networked with each other as well as outside groups (Clark 2002, 246; Cook 1981; Fraser 1983, 138; Martin 1987). They "publicized information about the judgeships, recruited and screened candidates, and lobbied for candidates they believed to be well qualified" (Ness and Wechsler 1979, 49). They formed specific projects to generate names and to work for their nomination—creating binders full of women, in effect. By forming broad coalitions, they ensured a wide audience for their efforts, organized troops to deploy across a broad spectrum of the women's community, and used their clout when they wrote to the White House as the Judicial Selection Project. These groups met with White House staff to press their case and plan a course of action (Goldman 1997, 253).

Such groups were also whistle-blowers who monitored the administration's performance in meeting its new policy objectives and communicated their dissatisfaction at the results to their constituencies, the media, and the White House through a series of press releases and fact sheets that highlighted their demand that the administration do more (Ness 1978). The National Women's Political Caucus, for example, released statistics in early January 1979 that 51 of the 59 recommendations from Democratic senators for the new judgeships were white males (Goldman 1997, 258). Women's groups lobbied on many fronts: they met with the administration to suggest names of panelists for the new circuit nominating commissions Carter mandated, pressured senators to appoint women to their nominating commissions, criticized recommendations of only white men, and pressed for the women who did appear on the list. They testified before the Senate Judiciary Committee about the slow pace of women's judicial appointments and pressured the committee to require nominees to refrain from membership in discriminatory clubs (Clark 2002, 247). They set up their own screening panel to decide which candidates they wanted to promote. In 1979, they formed an organization of women judges. Part of the mission of the National Association of Women Judges included advocating women's appointments at the federal, state, and local levels, as well as training women for election and selection (Clark 2002, 250). One of its first resolutions was to call for the appointment of a woman to the U.S. Supreme Court, and the group lobbied both presidential candidates. Reagan took the pledge, but Carter refused.

Feminists have not always consistently campaigned for the appointment or election of women judges, and when they have done so it has been done through projects or organizations that are separate from those seeking to increase the number of women in legislative and executive positions. And many are no longer very active. The efforts of the National Women's Political Caucus in the 1970s on behalf of women judges, for example, are now defunct at both the national and state level. Groups such as the National Association of Women Judges (NAWJ), which championed the appointment of a woman to the U.S. Supreme Court, have turned to other issues. Groups whose mission is to claim political power for women, such as EMILY's List, discussed elsewhere in this volume, do not raise money for women judicial candidates, despite the fact that many state court judges are elected officials.

However, one of the most effective and energetic groups active on the scene has been the Infinity Project.[11] The group takes its name from the sign for infinity, which is ∞. Its mission is to secure the appointment of women to the Eighth Circuit Court of Appeals, the least gender diverse of all the federal circuit courts (Kenney 2008b). Minnesota, Iowa, South Dakota, North Dakota, Nebraska, and Missouri are the seven states that make up the Eighth Circuit. Only one woman has ever served on the court, Judge Diana Murphy, out of 61 judges who have served. The group seeks to educate decision-makers about the importance of a diverse and representative judiciary, to inform and prepare women for vacancies, and to mobilize groups to advocate effectively for greater equality. Thus far, the group has successfully worked for the appointment of women to the federal district courts and for magistrate judges. Most recently, Obama has nominated Jane Kelly to serve on the Eighth Circuit from Iowa.[12]

## Women U.S. Supreme Court Clerks

Many U.S. Supreme Court justices have clerked for the Supreme Court, or judges on other prestigious courts, before they began their judicial careers. A clerkship is a marker of elite status and often a prerequisite for becoming a judge. Justices have three to four clerks per year who work for them as little law firms, helping them process the huge volume of cases petitioners would like them to hear each year. Clerks conduct legal research, draft opinions, and serve as sounding boards. Although women make up nearly half of all law school graduates, they have made up between 14 and 40 percent of U.S. Supreme Court law clerks over recent history (Cooper 2008; Kenney 2000a, 2000b). The wide variation, with a precipitous dip in 2007, suggests that more than merit is at work in the selection process and that women will not automatically increase their representation over time without public pressure. Justice William O. Douglas hired the first woman law clerk, Lucille Lomen, in 1944. Her law school professor apologized for forwarding her name but said that they had little choice since all of the men were at war. Not until 1966 would a justice choose the second woman. Current Justice Antonin Scalia has had the worst record of hiring women, and current Justice Stephen Breyer has had the best.

## Women on State Courts

A total of 38 states have had a woman chief justice. The median term for chief justice is five years. The median term for a justice is eight years. The number of seats on

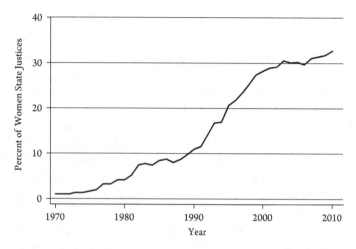

*Figure 13.1* Percent of Women State Supreme Court Justices: 1970–2010

state Supreme Courts is generally five to seven. States that have a sitting woman governor and a higher number of seats are more likely to have produced a woman state Supreme Court justice (Kenney and Windett 2013). Contrary to the pattern for legislators, southern states were more likely to have a woman state Supreme Court justice early on and have a higher probability of women justices overall.

Few obvious patterns emerge for women's progress on state courts and whatever patterns emerge vary widely over time. Of all state court judges in the United States, 27 percent are women (NAWJ 2012). Yet states vary enormously in the number of women serving: Vermont ranks first with 40 percent, and Idaho has 12 percent (NAWJ 2012). The last six states to place a woman on their state Supreme Courts were from South Dakota, New Hampshire, Wyoming, Nebraska, Alaska, and Indiana. We know that women have more difficulty being elected to legislative positions in the South as is the case in many other elected positions (see Chapter 16 in this volume) and in rural areas more generally, but little comparative data exist for state judicial elections (Reid 2004, 2010; Tokarz 1986). If political culture impedes women from legislative office in the South, it does not seem to impede women's accession to judicial office and judicial leadership: 8 of 13 chief justices of Southern state Supreme Courts were women as of 2010 (Curriden 2010).

Beverly Blair Cook (1980b, 42), the first political scientist who sought to explain why so few women served as judges, examined the large variation in the number of women serving on general jurisdiction trial courts in the 58 largest cities of the United States. She found that political culture explained some important patterns. Moralist states (states that run clean governments and believe in a collective good, such as the upper New England states, the upper Midwest, and several states in the West) had significantly higher percentages of women on appellate courts, but she could explain variation neither among states in the number of women general juris-diction trial judges nor among the cities of those states (ibid., 53). Additionally, recent studies show that political culture does not explain well the emergence of the first women Supreme Court justices, but a gender equality culture composite mea-sure does help explain the proportion of women in later decades and the emergence of the first woman chief justice (Kenney and Windett 2013).

The size of the court also matters. Cook (1980b, 54) found that women were more likely to serve on larger rather than smaller courts. She identified exactly how large a court had to be before selectors created a woman's seat: 25 judges for superior court, and 5 judges for municipal court (Cook 1984a, 581; Cook 1987, 153). Her finding was consistent with what scholars of legislative elections know about proportional representation and multimember constituencies: when voters or other selectors choose more than one city council member, legislator, or judge at a time and have many places to fill, they are more likely to present a balanced slate (see also the introduction to this volume). Choosing one at a time for a small num-ber of slots yields more homogeneity and representation from the dominant group. Thus, the U.S. Court of Appeals for the Ninth Circuit, the largest, has the highest number of women judges (although interestingly not the highest percentage of

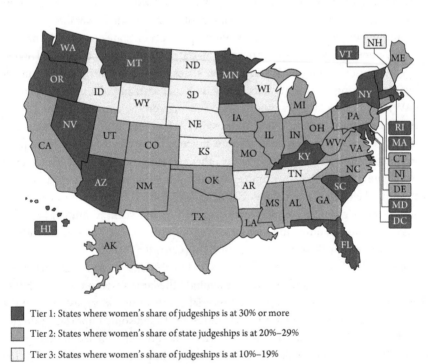

Tier 1: States where women's share of judgeships is at 30% or more

Tier 2: States where women's share of state judgeships is at 20%–29%

Tier 3: States where women's share of judgeships is at 10%–19%

*Figure 13.2*  Number of Women in State Judgeships

women judges). Another example of this size relationship is that President Clinton appointed a higher percentage of women to the larger courts than the smaller courts—he filled only 7 of the 52 small-court vacancies with women but filled 22 of the 52 large-court vacancies with them (Bratton and Spill 2001, 261). Other scholars confirm another of Cook's finding, something consistent with what legislative scholars have more recently discovered: women are more likely to represent suburban and urban rather than rural constituencies (Carbon, Houlden, and Berkson 1982, 298; Williams 1984b, 203; Alozie 1996, 118; Bratton and Spill 2002, 515; Hurwitz and Lanier 2003, 2008; Bratton and Spill 2005, 130; Williams 2007, 1198).

## Do Women Do Better under One Method of Selection?

Do women do better under merit systems or partisan or nonpartisan elections? One survey of President Carter's women appointees found that 43 percent of the women felt that they would not have been considered under the previous system rather than merit selection because they lacked the political influence and credentials (Martin 1982, 308). The adage "a judge is a lawyer who knew a senator" describes many systems of selection that place a premium on being known, arguably a requirement that may result in sex discrimination. Closer comparison of different systems by social scientists has not consistently shown that so-called merit selection systems produced more women judges—not because the requirement of being known to a senator or governor benefited more men than women but because nominating commissions can discriminate too, unless they have women members, are trained to avoid discrimination and stereotyping, and make securing a gender diverse bench a priority. For example, Githens (1995) found that the Maryland Nominating Commission employed a gender double standard on its men and women applicants. Commissioners saw women as uppity, seeking judicial positions above their station, whereas they saw men as lacking in ambition by seeking judicial appointments when they should have aspired to more lucrative partnerships in large firms (ibid.). Electoral systems, too, can discriminate against women if gatekeepers keep women from partisan endorsements, if voters discriminate, or if women have difficulty raising money.

Judges tend to declare whichever system produced them to be their preferred system for producing the highest quality bench and placing the highest number of women in judicial positions (Carbon, Houlden, and Berkson 1982). But Cook ultimately concluded that no one judicial selection system produced more women; instead, what mattered was a commitment on the part of gatekeepers to consider women and jettison discriminatory criteria. Tokarz's (1986) findings that women were more likely to serve as judges in greater Missouri under an elective system than in the two cities under merit selection was damning to the argument that women did better under merit systems. Tokarz showed how the selection system shut out women and concluded that merit systems were insufficient to guarantee women's full representation, if not indeed an impediment (ibid., 907). Subsequent analyses confirmed Tokarz's finding of no systemic effect (Alozie 1990, 1996; Brown 1998; Esterling and Andersen 1999; Martin and Pyle 2002; Hurwitz and Lanier 2003, 2008; Holmes and Emrey 2006; Reddick, Nelson, and Caufield 2009).

What little data exist for state judicial races show contradictory results. Reid (2004) examined women's electoral performance in races for North Carolina District Court between 1994 and 1998. Women raised more money for their races than men, but as she wrote, "Men received significantly more electoral bang for their campaign buck than women" (ibid., 834). Women incumbents did not enjoy the same benefits as men; women running for open seats spent much more than men to do less well. Lucas (2007) examined partisan and nonpartisan state Supreme Court elections from 1990 to 2006 and found that women won more often than men in both partisan and nonpartisan elections and that Republican women won most of all (84 percent of Republican women won compared with 60 percent of Republican men) (ibid., 15). Women incumbents, challengers, or candidates for open seats won their races more often than men. Gender was an important variable in predicting success, and incumbency did not completely trump gender. Controlling for both incumbency and partisanship, Lucas found women candidates to have won 3 percent more of the vote in their judicial races than their men counterparts. She found women to have done better in nonpartisan election states than in partisan election states, but women did better than men in both.

Reddick, Nelson, and Caufield's (2009) study classifies each state according to how each judge was selected rather than by the state's formal system. Their study did not find that the judicial selection system significantly altered the likelihood that the judge was a woman. Our most recent evidence suggests women tend to do better under appointment processes or nonpartisan election for state Supreme Courts (Kenney and Windett 2013).

In sum, method of selection does matter to whether women are likely to lead state Supreme Courts. Women do better when the members of the court choose the chief justice or the position goes to the most senior justice. They do less well when governors or voters select the chief.

## What Increases the Number of Women?

One hope for greater proportions of women judges throughout the United States was the expansion of the federal judiciary that occurred during the Carter Administration. However, Bratton and Spill (2005, 128) found that, although new seats are sometimes associated with increased diversity, no statistically significant relationship between this increase in seats and an increase in women judges. Instead, individual idiosyncratic differences may explain why a U.S. state suddenly moves up or down in the rankings. Governors such as Jerry Brown in California

(Cook 1984b, 208) or Rudy Perpich in Minnesota catapulted their states forward. Torres-Spelliscy, Chase, and Greenman's (2008) study of 10 state nominating commissions in the United States found that some nominating commissioners saw themselves as headhunters who made it a priority to recruit a diverse candidate pool, and some saw themselves as background checkers who passively waited for candidates to apply. This study recommended encouraging commissioners to actively recruit diverse candidates, to train commissioners on implicit bias, appoint diversity compliance officers or ombudspersons, and to make diversity of commissioners and judges an explicit statutory goal (ibid.).

Canada has served as a beacon of relative success and a clear example of how the headhunter model can produce dramatic results. At the federal level, the proportion of federally appointed women judges in the country grew from just over 3 percent in 1980 to 26 percent by June 2003. For provincially appointed judges, the province of Ontario led the way. A judicial appointments advisory committee (JAAC) made representativeness and gender balance explicit goals (JAAC 2007, 10, 21), advertised, and wrote to every woman lawyer with 10 years' experience asking her to apply. Out of the first 75 appointments to the Ontario provincial court made on the basis of the JAAC process, 37 were women and 38 were men. When the committee began its work, only 10 (4 percent) of the provincially appointed judges were women (Russell 1990, 10). Scotland and South Africa also tried to increase the representativeness of their judiciaries, with more limited success (Mackay 2005, 3; Paterson 2006, 31).

This effort demonstrated that it clearly helps to eliminate requirements that can indirectly discriminate against women, such as being politically well connected, being known to senior judges, being young, or having served as a partner in a large firm. If nominating commissions choose judges, it helps to have women attorney members to encourage commissioners to actively recruit rather than to merely vet, to train about implicit bias, and to make diversity an explicit goal and a benchmark for which commissioners are held accountable. The evidence from Ontario shows that a gender representative bench is achievable. Yet gains can too easily be reversed. Women's groups need to continue to demand progress. A representative judiciary will not come about of its own accord.

## Judicial Selection Processes as Gendered

Using sex as a variable in quantitative analyses of state judicial races shows that women candidates as a group are as likely to succeed as men, even if, as Reid (2010) shows, their campaign dollars do not seem to go as far when they are challenged, nor do they enjoy the same advantages of incumbency that men do. An important lesson at the state level is that if women candidates faced with aggressive challenges fight back hard, such as Justice Rosalie Wahl in Minnesota in 1978, Justice Dana Fabe in Alaska in 2010, Justice Alice Robie Resnick in Ohio in 2000, Chief Justice

Shirley Abrahamson in Wisconsin in 2009, and Chief Justices Barbara Pariente and Peggy Quince in Florida in 2012, they can prevail. Those who hope to appeal to judicial independence and stay above the campaign fray when challenged, such as Rose Bird in California in 1986, Penny White in Tennessee in 1996, Marsha Ternus in Iowa in 2010, lose. At the federal level, groups such as the Alliance for Justice and People for the American Way have demonstrated that Obama's women and minority men have waited longer for a hearing and are more likely to never get a vote or be voted down than white men nominees. Judicial candidates from nondominant groups are more likely to have their qualifications questioned or to be framed as too political.

Understanding how the processes are gendered—that is, how gendered differences are created to work to women's disadvantage—requires a combination of qualitative and quantitative analyses, little of which has been done for state judicial races. Those who watched the judicial confirmation hearings of U.S. Supreme Court Justices Sotomayor and Kagan saw a number of blatant gender double standards in operation[13]—processes familiar to those who study legislative and presidential campaigns. Both nominees were criticized for their weight (while men Supreme Court nominees and justices have not routinely been svelte)[14] and were interrogated about their sexuality. Kagan was criticized for the way she sat with legs apart (Clark-Flory 2010), and Sotomayor was critiqued for being too aggressive in her questioning of attorneys at oral arguments. Additionally, Sotomayor was vilified for a comment that was a feature of her speeches over the years: "I would hope that a wise Latina woman with the richness of her experiences would, more often than not, reach a better conclusion." She was accused by senators and others of lacking in judicial temperament and being partial, biased, and emotional (Greenhouse 2010). Yet senators had not objected to those remarks during Sotomayor's confirmation to the U.S. Court of Appeals for the 2nd Circuit.

This gendered double standard began with Bird, the first woman on the California Supreme Court and its first female chief justice. She had served for 10 years, but in the November 1986 state election she also became the only chief justice in California history to be removed from office by the voters. Explaining Bird's demise merely as a result of the antipathy agribusiness had for her after her stint as secretary of agriculture or as a result of her opposition to the death penalty, as the media recounted, fails to fully account for the hostility of her colleagues and the legal profession, and her electoral vulnerability. Only by adding gender and perhaps backlash to the equation can we understand what happened (Medsger 1983). This kind of double standard continues unabated in state judicial races and in the federal judicial selection process.

A gender analysis thus sees gender as constructed in a specific social context and abandons an all-or-nothing approach. To make the gender aspects of judicial selection visible, next I identify a series of six separate phenomena and argue that they constitute a backlash against women judges (Kenney 2013a). These are based on the perceptions of women trailblazers who have spoken out about the gender bias they experienced, including the judicial selection process itself, both the nomination and confirmation processes. First, women have their competence and objectivity more frequently and brazenly called into question than do men. Women judges have suffered unprecedented personal attacks from lawyers, other judges, and the press and many of the first women selected to serve on courts faced hostility from some or all of their colleagues. Second, they have had charges of judicial misconduct leveled against them when men in similar circumstances have not. Third, women judges have faced tougher confirmation battles than their men counterparts, voters have removed women from office in states where judges are routinely retained, and women judges have faced challengers where judges have always run unopposed. Fourth, evidence suggests litigants more frequently file motions to recuse against women judges, and lawyers interrupt women judges more often than men. Fifth, women elected state judges enjoy fewer electoral benefits from incumbency, and it takes more campaign dollars to generate fewer votes than for men. Sixth, women have broken through barriers and become the first woman appointed or elected to courts that have then reverted to being all male when they leave. I analyze these phenomena together and call the pattern that emerges backlash.

An undercurrent of hostility toward women judges shows no sign of abating (Omatsu 1997; Backhouse 2003; Hunter 2006, 282); rather, it may be fed by women's success. Women judges continue to experience heightened attention: their colleagues and the media dispute their qualifications and show open hostility to them. Women judges' colleagues simply "hold them in contempt for being women" (Hunter 2006, 295). The assumption is that men are the natural occupants of such positions, that women obtain them through political maneuvering and not merit, and that enough women have been appointed.

## Do Women Judge Differently than Men?

Scholars have hypothesized that, based on disparate life experiences, women judges are more likely to be concerned with children and better at juvenile justice, to be pro-plaintiff in sex discrimination cases, to be pro-choice in abortion cases, to be pro-woman in divorce cases, to employ communitarian reasoning, and to be more inclined to seek mediate solutions. Approximately three dozen studies have investigated whether or not women judges' decisions are different from men's decisions. The results have been mixed, with about one-third of studies showing that gender does make a difference, one-third providing mixed results, and another third showing no patterns. The differences across these studies seem to be what areas of law and what level of the judicial system has been under investigation. For example, Boyd, Epstein, and Martin (2010) find that gender effects are strong in sex discrimination in employment cases that have been handed down by the U.S. appellate courts. These authors found that the probability of a judge deciding in favor of the plaintiff (the party alleging the discrimination) increased when a woman judge was on the panel (see also Martin and Pyle 2005; Peresie 2005; Kenney 2008a, 2013a).

How then should we think about gender differences in judging in ways that are theoretically sophisticated and empirically true? Scholars who study women judges across legal systems and jurisdictions have been grappling with this problem for 30 years (Mezey 2000; Palmer 2001a, 2001b; Schultz and Shaw 2003; Kenney 2008a, 2013a). Besides the dangers of overgeneralization that can lead to claims of a false dichotomy, such research may find that gender is the explanation for differences when biological sex may mask other determinants such as party, ideology, or even experience as a prosecutor versus experience as a public defender (or experience in law enforcement versus social work for immigration judges). And we must account for the effects of intersectional identities such as race, ethnicity, sexual orientation, disability status, and more.[15] Identity categories work in many intersecting ways that may not be true for all members of the group. Not all black women think alike, but black women lawyers who went to law school in the 1970s were likely to have had many common experiences. Scholars go beyond seeing sex as a category to conceptualize gender as a social process if we are to fully understand the effects of being female on judges' behavior.

## Are Courts Political and Representative Institutions?

Many of those who champion the cause of a gender diverse judiciary, such as former Supreme Court Justice Sandra Day O'Connor, the American Judicature Society, and Justice at Stake, also advocate for judicial independence and merit selection (Kenney 2013a). They define law as a system of rules and principles governed by decision-making processes vastly different from legislatures and bureaucracies. U.S. Supreme Court Chief Justice John Roberts characterizes judges as impartial umpires. Some political scientists, on the other hand, see courts as simply another set of political actors who hide their policy preferences behind legal doctrine. I argue that law and legal decision-making are inherently political; judicial doctrine constrains even if it does not simply determine legal outcomes. Operating in the arena of principle is different from the arena of power and interest. While applying narrow litmus tests to judges is problematic, mostly because we cannot foresee the issues that will divide us in the future, huge differences separate potential judges on constitutional philosophy and the role of courts in a constitutional democracy and federal system. As a feminist scholar, I am less interested in selecting someone who simply scored the highest on law school exams but want someone who also understands how gender structures life chances. I also want someone with the humility to change his or her mind rather than always approach issues ideologically. Unfortunately, the politics of judicial selection are almost always conducted using rhetoric that eschews politics. This conundrum plagues campaigns to create a gender diverse bench, since most advocates have to try to expose the politics and cronyism of reigning judicial selection regimes while contending that their motivations are not political; they believe in merit selection, but they also want more women.

## Making the Case for Women Judges

The best case for a gender-diverse bench is one that advocates for democracy and legitimacy, recognizes the symbolic role of judges, calls for simple nondiscrimination, and draws analogies between the sex of judges and geographic representation (Kenney 2013a). And arguments based on an understanding of gender as a social process are better than those based on sex differences. Gender continues to be an important concept in understanding the third branch of government in the United States, and we can learn much by asking questions about women judges.

### Notes

1. American Bar Association. "Fact Sheet on Judicial Selection Methods in the United States." http://www.americanbar.org/content/dam/aba/migrated/leadership/fact_sheet.auth-checkdam.pdf (accessed January 21, 2013).
2. The work of more than 120 scholars in the Collaborative Research Network on Gender and Judging of the Law and Society Association shows the rich possibilities of a gender analysis. See http://genderandjudging.com (accessed November 16, 2012) for a list of scholars working in this area and a blog on recent developments. Also see the March–July 2008 issue of *International Journal of the Legal Profession* 15(1–2) as well as the Critical Perspectives Section on Gender and Judging of the September 2010 issue of *Politics & Gender*. Ulrike Schultz and Gisela Shaw have edited the papers from the 2009 Oñati conference that Hart will publish in 2013.
3. Debra Cassens Weiss. 2011. "Have Women's Law School Numbers Peaked? NAWL Report Suggests the Pipeline May be Shrinking." *ABA Journal*. November 10. http://www.abajournal.com/news/article/have_womens_law_school_numbers_peaked_nawl_report_suggests_the_pipeline_is_/ (accessed January 21, 2013).
4. National Association of Women Judges. 2012. "2012 Representation of United States State Court Women Judges." http://www.nawj.org/us_state_court_statistics_2012.asp (accessed January 21, 2013).
5. In August 2010, an all-male Senate Committee rejected the Governor's nomination of Katherine Leonard to be the state's first woman chief justice of the Hawaiian Supreme Court ostensibly because she lacked judicial experience (Lauer 2010).
6. In July 2010, the Indiana Judicial Nominating Commission sent three names to the governor for the next vacancy, including one woman (Associated Press 2010). Of the 34 applications, 19 were from women.
7. Once the president makes a nomination, the chair of the Senate Judiciary Committee sends out blue slips to the two senators from the nominee's home state. If either senator returns the slip with the mark "objection," traditionally no hearing on the nomination is scheduled. If both senators return the slip marked "no objection," the subcommittee and then full committee proceed to hearings. Senators who object to a choice may simply fail to return the blue slip altogether, delaying the process without having to take responsibility for opposing the nomination.
8. 1979. Senate Judiciary Committee chair Edward Kennedy shared Carter's commitment to a diverse and representative bench and relaxed the policy, announcing that failure to return

a blue slip would no longer automatically stall a hearing on a nominee, making it easier for Carter's nominees to be confirmed (Slotnick 1979; Goldman 1997, 12; Pacelle 1997, 155).

9. Not until 1984, 20 years after Congress passed the Civil Rights Act of 1964 outlawing sex discrimination in employment, did the Supreme Court declare that the act covered law firms in *Hishon v. King & Spalding,* 467 U.S. 69 (1984).

10. Nearly 32 percent. Bureau of Labor Statistics. 2012. "Household Data. Annual Averages." http://www.bls.gov/cps/cpsaat11.pdf (accessed January 21, 2013).

11. See the Infinity project. http://www.theinfinityproject.org/ (accessed November 16, 2012).

12. White House. 2013. "President Obama Nominates Two to Serve on US Court of Appeals." Office of the Press Secretary. January 31. http://www.whitehouse.gov/the-press-office/2013/01/31/president-obama-nominates-two-serve-us-court-appeals (accessed March 20, 2013).

13. Stephanie Francis Ward. 2011. "Female Judicial Candidates are Held to Different Standards, Sotomayor Tells Students." *ABA Journal.* March 8. http://www.abajournal.com/news/article/female_judicial_candidates_are_held_to_different_standards_sotomayor_tells_/ (accessed August 4, 2011).

14. Paul Campos. 2009. "Fat Judges Need not Apply." *Daily Beast.* May 4. http://www.thedaily-beast.com/articles/2009/05/04/fat-judges-need-not-apply.html (accessed August 4, 2011); Megan Carpentier. 2009. "Women Too Stupid to Stay Thin Are not Smart Enough for the Supreme Court." *Jezebel.* May 5. http://jezebel.com/5241128/women-too (accessed August 4, 2011).

15. See the special 2007 issue of *Politics & Gender* 2(3) on intersectionality.

# 14

# Indelible Effects: The Impact of Women of Color in the U.S. Congress

LISA GARCIÁ BEDOLLA, KATHERINE TATE, AND JANELLE WONG

**Indelible**: 1a: that cannot be removed, washed away, or erased, b: making marks that cannot easily be removed <an *indelible* pencil>, 2a: Lasting <*indelible* memories> b: Unforgettable, memorable <an *indelible* performance>.

—Merriam-Webster Online

As the numbers of women and racial minorities winning seats to the U.S. Congress have increased, scholars have begun to explore the impact of gender, race, and ethnicity on the legislative products and representational styles of elected officials. From the founding of this nation, the normative claim has been that the social background of legislators was irrelevant to the task of political representation, as their role was to faithfully execute the will of the people. Although some scholars still contend that elected officials have and can represent fairly citizens across the boundaries of social class, gender, race, ethnicity, and sexuality, the vast majority of empirical evidence accumulated reveals that female and Black legislators are the most consistent advocates of the dominant interests of women and Blacks (Canon 1999; Carroll 2001; Lublin 1997; Swers 1998; Tate 2003; Thomas 1994; Thomas and Welch 1991; Whitby 1998). The empirical investigation of how elected officials represent the American people supports the claim that social backgrounds matter and have a profound influence on public policies and legislative priorities.

In addition, the symbol of a socially diverse elected government has political consequences well beyond the realm of public policy. Diversity in legislatures can affect citizens profoundly. Research demonstrates that Blacks felt better represented in Washington when their legislator was Black, even accounting for their representative's political party (Tate 2003). Blacks were more likely to recognize and contact their representatives when that representative was Black (Gay 2002; Tate 2003). Yet the effect of descriptive representation (sharing demographic and other characteristics with those who are represented) in the U.S. Congress is mixed. Blacks descriptively represented in Congress are not more likely to vote in national elections than those not represented by Blacks (Gay 2001; Tate 2003). However, Latinos are more likely to vote in districts where minorities represent a voting majority than Latinos living in districts where Whites are majority (Barreto, Segura, and Woods 2004).

Women also express more interest in politics in congressional districts that have women elected officials or women running for office (Burns, Schlozman, and Verba 2001). Nevertheless, Lawless (2004a) found no evidence that increases in the elections of women to the U.S. Congress have increased levels of trust, efficacy, competency, or political engagement of women. She suggests that the presence of women in government may still increase support for feminism and heighten feelings of gender consciousness, however.

In all, diversity can transform political environments, change attitudes, and make citizens feel better represented in government when they are represented from someone of their own racial or social group. In this chapter, we explore the history of women of color in the U.S. Congress, their backgrounds and career trajectories, the levels of representation compared with White women and men of color, experiences of differential treatment, and the question of what influence women of color legislators have had in the American political system. Since the path-breaking publication of *A Portrait of Marginality* by Marianne Githens and Jewel Prestage in 1977, researchers have found that women of color are increasing their rates of officeholding faster than White women (Hardy-Fanta et al. 2007). Some of this new work has focused on women of color in state legislatures (Barrett 1995, 2001; Bratton and Haynie 1999; Bratton, Haynie, and Reingold 2006a, 2006b; Fraga et al. 2006, 2008; Orey et al. 2006; Smooth 2001a, 2001b), while other work has focused on minority female legislators working in the U.S. Congress (Fenno 2003; Garciá Bedolla 2005; Hawkesworth 2003; Swain 1993; Tate 2003, 2013). Because of their minority status, Blacks, Asian Americans, and Latinas bring into their elective office significantly different experiences from their White female and minority male counterparts. The effects of these experiences, while difficult to measure, are in fact indelible and cannot be erased from the face of American politics.

## The First Women of Color in Congress

As discussed in the introduction to this volume, the entrance of women of color to the U.S. House and U.S. Senate came well after that of their male and White female counterparts.[1] The first woman of color to be elected was U.S. House Representative Patsy Takemoto Mink (D-HI) in 1964. Her election came nearly fifty years after the first White woman was elected. The second Asian American female legislator would not be sent to Congress until Patricia Fukuda Saiki (R-HI) was elected in 1986. Shirley Chisholm made history in 1968 by becoming the first Black woman to be elected to the U.S. House of Representatives—nearly 100 years after the first Black man was elected. In 1989, Ileana Ros-Lehtinen, a Cuban American from Florida, became the first Latina elected to Congress. She is from the state that elected the first Latino to Congress in 1822 (Martin 1999: 195).[2] Barbara Charline Jordan (D-TX) was another trailblazer. Elected in 1972, she and Andrew Young of Georgia were the first Blacks from the South elected to Congress since Reconstruction. In 1992, Carol Moseley Braun became the first African American female to be elected to the U.S. Senate and that chamber's first Black Democrat. She narrowly lost her reelection bid in 1998. Nearly a decade and a half would pass before another woman of color (Mazie Hirono) would be elected to the U.S. Senate in 2012.

Shirley Chisholm also made history in 1972 when she became the first African American woman to have her name placed in nomination for president by a major political party (Martin 1999: 122). She ran for president to take advantage of the new groups that were gaining power within the Democratic Party's rank-and-file and the "new politics"—not only Blacks but also feminists and the young (Chisholm 1973; Gill 1997). Well before Jesse Jackson seized on the same initiative to empower Black Democrats through his 1984 and 1988 presidential bids, Chisholm hoped that her candidacy would cement the party's wavering stance against the Vietnam War (Chisholm was staunchly opposed to it) and as a party working for the oppressed and weak. Although Chisholm was a founding member of the Congressional Black Caucus (CBC) and a charter member of the National Organization for Women (NOW), neither group endorsed her. A few more progressive CBC members, such as Representative Ron Dellums of California, supported her bid. Most others CBC members were downright hostile to her and her candidacy.

Chisholm's lack of support among other Black members of Congress shows the politics of political endorsements and interactions among members. Although Chisholm and her supporters felt that sexism got in the way of her earning support from her male Black colleagues on the Hill, more was going on. After all, Jackson failed to receive endorsements from Black lawmakers in his 1984 bid for the Democratic Party's presidential nomination. Like Jackson, many of her CBC colleagues felt that the one-term congresswoman from New York had not yet paid her dues. Her confrontational and steamroller working style had also alienated them. The fact that women were mobilizing and organizing politically for gender equality was criticized by Black civil rights leaders as untimely. If anything, Black male leaders felt that Chisholm's candidacy, rather than providing a forum for Black interests that had been suppressed and slighted within the party, was itself divisive to the Black political cause.

Although Chisholm's leadership bids caused division and were met with opposition, it opened the door to the presidential bid of former U.S. Senator Carol Moseley

Braun in 2004. African American leaders did not oppose her bid for the Democratic Party's presidential nomination. Moseley Braun withdrew just days before the Iowa caucuses; however, her candidacy was not marked as controversial by Black elected officials (Tate 2011).

Many of the Latinas currently serving in Congress have made history either with their election or through their committee service and appointments while in office.

The first Mexican American woman, Democrat Lucille Roybal-Allard, was elected in 1992 to the U.S. Congress to represent the 33rd Congressional District of California. During the 105th Congress (1997–1998), Roybal-Allard was the first woman and first Latina to be elected to serve as chair of the California Democratic Congressional delegation. During the 106th Congress (1999–2000), she served as the first female chair of the Congressional Hispanic Caucus. Roybal-Allard is also the first Latina to serve on the powerful Appropriations Committee—the committee that controls congressional spending.

Linda Sánchez (D-CA) is the first Latina to serve on the influential Judiciary Committee and the Ways and Means Committee. A former union organizer, she also cofounded the House Labor and Working Families Caucus.

Among the some of the Latinos in the 113th Congress, serving is a family affair. The Sánchez family made history in 2002 by becoming the first family to send two sisters to the U.S. House of Representatives. Loretta Sánchez's (D-CA) sister, Linda Sánchez, was elected to fill an open seat in 2000. Michelle Lujan Grisham (D-NM) was elected to Congress in 2012. Her cousin, Ben R. Luján, has been representing New Mexico's 3rd Congressional District since 2008.

Elected in 2010, Jaime Herrera Beutler is one of the youngest women serving in the 113th Congress and was the first Latino, male or female, to represent Washington state in Congress.

## The Backgrounds of Black Women in Congress

Of the ninety-seven women serving in the 113th Congress, thirteen are African American. In addition, two African American nonvoting delegates serve in Congress, representing the District of Columbia and the U.S. Virgin Islands. The occupations of Black women elected to Congress diverge from that of most House members. In fact, Black women legislators come from less privileged backgrounds even in comparison with Black men. Although some of the Black women have been attorneys, a significant number started out like Chisholm as teachers or as college administrators. The educational backgrounds of Black females elected to Congress are consistent with that of their Black male counterparts, except that some lacked college diplomas. With the exception of former Representative Oscar De Priest (R-IL), who served from 1929 to 1935 and was the first Black elected to Congress from outside the southern states and the first in the twentieth century, all other Black members of Congress of the twentieth century had degrees.

The somewhat lower ranking of Black women legislators on education may be the legacy of a number of things. Although only former Representative Cardiss Collins (D-IL), the longest serving Black women in the U.S. Congress, belonged to the generation of Americans who experienced the Second World War, the G.I. Bill from that war gave men, such as Representative Louis Stokes (D-OH), unprecedented educational opportunities from which the vast majority of women were excluded.

Perhaps the single most striking difference between Black women members and all other members of the House relates to their marital status. Within the U.S. adult population, there are significant differences across race and gender on the social dimension of marital status. According to the Census Bureau's 2011 American Community Survey, among those fifteen years and older, 26 percent of Black women were married and living with their spouse. This is in contrast to 33 percent of Black men, 50 percent of White women, and 53 percent of White men. However, in the U.S. House of Representatives, in the 103rd and 104th Congresses, only one-third of the Black women elected were married when they entered Congress (Tate 2003). Of the married women-of-color legislators, spouses seem to play important roles in their wives' careers. For example, Shirley Chisholm's husband facilitated her entrance into New York politics and into the House of Representatives. Her biographer writes that the "unassuming Conrad [Chisholm] was a powerful force behind the soon-to-be dynamic politician" (Gill 1997: 21).

Child-raising responsibilities often have also been identified as a principal reason that so few women choose to run for elective office, as outlined in Chapter 2 in this volume. However, only three Black females elected to the House, including Chisholm, had no children, and a number of the Black females entered into the U.S. House of Representatives with children under eighteen years of age. Many women of color legislators have been single mothers, which is very different from other groups of women legislators. Since the U.S. Census finds that over half of all Black women are single parents, this fact heightens the descriptive representational role of Black women representatives. Former Representative Cynthia McKinney, Democrat from Georgia (the youngest Black female legislator), is one example. Another is former Representative Carrie Meek (D-FL), whose divorce left her responsible for three children. Former Representative Barbara-Rose Collins (D-MI) had been separated from her husband after about ten years of marriage when she became his widow. They had two children whom she worked full-time to support. Representative Corrine Brown (D-FL) never married and raised a daughter alone (see Gill 1997; Tate 2003). And even some of the successfully married Black congresswomen experienced life as single moms. Representative Maxine Waters (D-CA) was a single mom but had remarried by the time she entered Congress.

# The Backgrounds of Latina Representatives

Among the thirty-one Latino representatives[3] in the 113th Congress (2011–2013), only nine are women. There are twenty-eight Latino representatives in the House of Representatives and three Latino senators. Thus, Latinos make up 7 percent of the U.S. Congress but constitute almost 17 percent of the U.S. population. In contrast to African Americans and Asian Americans, no Latina has ever served in the U.S. Senate. Of the nine Latinas in the 113th Congress, seven are Democrats and two are Republicans. Of the nine Latinas currently serving, five served in their state legislatures before their election to Congress.[4] Term limits in the state of California seem to be promoting the election of Latinas to Congress: five of the nine Latina representatives are from that state, and three of those ran for Congress after serving their maximum of six years in the state legislature.[5] This supports Fraga et al.'s (2006) finding that state traditions and institutional design affect the patterns of Latina representation in public office.

In terms of their marital status, all of the Latina representatives were married when they entered Congress. (Loretta Sánchez has divorced and remarried since she began serving.) Nationally, about 63 percent of Latino households are married-couple households, 30 percent have never married, and 9 percent are divorced. So Latina members of Congress are more likely to be married than Latinas nationally. They are also much more likely to be married than African American representatives. None of the Latina congresswomen is a single mother, and five of the nine have children. Three of the Latinas who have children—Ros-Lehtinen, Roybal-Allard, and Grace Napolitano (D-CA)—entered politics later in their lives than those without children. Their collective experiences suggest that child-rearing affected the trajectory of their political careers.

In terms of their educational levels, the Latino congressional delegation as a whole, and Latinas especially, is much more educated than Latinos nationally, 14 percent of whom have an undergraduate degree. Interestingly, the Latina representatives are slightly more educated than their male counterparts—86 percent hold bachelor's degrees compared with 84 percent of the men. In addition, 57 percent of Latina members hold a master's degree or higher compared with only 44 percent of the men.

There are gender differences in terms of the professions that led Latina women to elected office. Although nine of the twenty-seven Latino male House members hold a J.D., only one of the Latina representatives does. The remainder holds master's degrees in public or business administration or in particular academic disciplines. Latinas are less likely than Latino men or African American women to have worked in the educational field prior to entering public office. These trajectories are important because they often influence the types of policies these representatives pursue in office.

As an example, Ros-Lehtinen began her career as an educator and founded a private elementary school in South Florida, which led her to emphasize school reform as a congresswoman. Similarly, her experience as a Cuban political exile led to her interest in foreign affairs, particularly in terms of issues relating to U.S.–Cuba relations. In the 112th Congress she chaired the House Committee on Foreign Affairs.

Similarly, Nydia Velázquez (D-NY), the first Puerto Rican woman elected to the U.S. Congress, has emphasized economic development and opportunity during her congressional career. Growing up in the small town of Yabucoa, Puerto Rico, she became concerned about the economic opportunities available to disadvantaged communities. Now representing parts of Brooklyn, Queens, and the Lower East Side of Manhattan, she continues to work for economic empowerment, becoming the first Latina to chair the House Small Business Committee.

# The Backgrounds of Asian American Women Elected to the U.S. Congress

Beginning in 2005, a dramatic change in the descriptive representation of Asian American women in Congress took place. Representative Doris Matsui (D-CA) succeeded her husband in a special election to fill his seat after his death in 2005. Four years later, Judy Chu (D-CA), first elected to a local school board in 1985, was elected to Congress. In 2006 and 2010, Mazie Hirono (D-HI) and Colleen Hanabusa (D-HI) won their respective elections to the House of Representatives. Both are Japanese Americans. Until Matsui's election, only two Asian American women had ever served in the U.S. Congress: Mink and Saiki, both in the House of Representatives. In 2012, Mazie Hirono won a successful bid to represent Hawaii in the Senate, becoming the first Asian American female senator in U.S. history. With the election of Grace Meng (D-NY), Tammy Duckworth (D-IL), and Tulsi Gabbard (D-HI) in 2012, a total of nine Asian American women have served in the House. Of these, seven were elected in 2005 or later.

Mink's groundbreaking election as the first woman of color to serve in the House of Representatives marked just one of a series of firsts she established for Asian American women in the public sphere. In 1953, Mink became the first Asian American woman to practice law in Hawaii. In 1956, three years prior to Hawaii's becoming the nation's fiftieth state, she was the first Asian American woman to be elected to the Hawaiian Territorial House.

Mink was the victim of racial and gender discrimination, and these experiences likely influenced her policy priorities. After Pearl Harbor was bombed, her father was detained and questioned for no other reason than his Japanese background. The dorms at the University of Nebraska, where she completed her B.A., were racially segregated. Even after she passed the state bar in 1953, she could not find work as an attorney. Prospective employers expressed concern that she had a child and would not be able to work long hours. Early in her career, Mink emerged as a fighter for gender equality, civil rights, environmental protection, education, labor rights, and other social justice issues. She ran as a presidential candidate in the Oregon primary in 1972 on an anti-Vietnam war platform and, from 1978 to 1981, she served as the national president for the liberal group Americans for Democratic Action. Her willingness to support liberal policies earned Mink the nickname "Patsy Pink" among her conservative critics. During her second stint in the House (1990–2000), Mink opposed Republican cuts in social programs, worked to obtain funding for the poor, supported labor, and backed President Bill Clinton's universal health-care plan. Mink died in 2002 at the age of seventy-four, just days after winning the primary election for her congressional seat.

At first glance, Patricia ("Pat") Fakuda Saiki does not appear to have very much in common with Mink. While the former was a strong liberal Democrat, Saiki served as a Republican and is one of Hawaii's most well-known and popular GOP figures. Saiki served just two terms in the House (1987–1991) compared with veteran Mink, who served for twenty-four years. Despite their differences, there are also striking similarities between the two women. Both were elected from Hawaii, a state notable for its long history of sending Asian Americans to Congress and the only state with a majority Asian American population. After Hawaii became a state in 1959, the island population sent Chinese American Republican Hiram Fong to the Senate and Japanese American Daniel Inouye to the House of Representatives. Mink and Saiki were born in Hawaii and attended the University of Hawaii. In addition, Saiki, like Mink, was Japanese American. Further, both entered public office fairly early in their careers. Mink obtained her University of Chicago Law School degree in 1951 and practiced law from 1953 until her election to the Hawaiian Territorial Legislature three years later. Saiki was a teacher and businesswoman from her graduation in 1952 until her election to the Hawaiian State House in 1968. Both women were married when they ran for office. Like Mink, Saiki served in political office while balancing family obligations. She is the mother of five children.

Because there have been relatively few Asian Americans elected to Congress as a whole, it is difficult to make generalizations when comparing Asian American females with their Asian American male counterparts. However, there are some relevant distinctions worth noting. Although only one female Asian American has been elected to the Senate, and only in recent times (2012), two Asian American male senators served for decades (Daniel Inouye and Daniel Akaka, both Democrats from Hawaii). In all, six Asian American men have been elected to the Senate since 1959. Inouye and Akaka both served in the House of Representatives before their Senate runs. By 2012, more than fifteen Asian American men—including Indian American Dalip Singh Saund, the first Asian American Congressman, who began his term in 1957—had served in the House.

Historically, the male Asian American members of Congress have been more ethnically diverse than the female members. Men of Chinese, Japanese, South Asian, Korean, Filipino, Vietnamese, and Native Hawaiian–Chinese backgrounds have been elected to Congress. In contrast, all of the Asian American women elected to Congress have been of Japanese and Chinese national origin, with the exception of Samoan American Gabbard, elected in 2012. Duckworth, elected that same year, is of Chinese origin, born in Thailand. Asian American men are more diverse in terms of partisanship as well. Although most of the Asian American men elected to Congress have been Democrats, a large proportion have been Republicans. Three of the six Asian American men who have served in the Senate and about a third of the eighteen Asian American men who have served in the House have been Republicans. Regardless of sex, Asian American Republicans tenure in Congress tends to be much shorter than that of Asian American Democrats. With the exception of Saiki, all Asian American women in Congress have been Democrats and have represented states and districts with strong Democratic voting histories. While Asian American women have launched successful bids from just a handful of states, particularly California and Hawaii, Asian American men have run for federal office from these states as well as in Florida, Oregon, Tennessee, New Jersey, Pennsylvania, and Washington. Asian American men have represented Oregon, Louisiana, and Ohio—states where less than 5 percent of the population is Asian American. Nonetheless, most Asian American men and women have represented California and Hawaii.

Notably, it was not until 2005 that an Asian American woman was elected to Congress from outside Hawaii. This is relevant, because in terms of their backgrounds Asian American congresspersons from Hawaii are distinct from those from the mainland (Lien 2001). The demographic context of mainland elections is very different from that of Hawaii, which is the only Asian American majority state in the nation. With the exception of Representative Mike Honda (D-CA), who represents a district that is just over 50 percent Asian American and Pacific Islander in northern California, all of the members elected from the mainland represent congressional districts that are majority White or multiracial. Matsui represents a congressional district in northern California. When her husband was first elected in 1971, the district was predominantly White, but when she ran for office in 2006 the district was closer to 50 percent non-Hispanic White and about 15 percent Black, 15 percent Asian American, and 20 percent Latino. Chu was elected to a district that was equally diverse. She won a special election in 2009 to represent California's 27th Congressional District, which was just over 62 percent Latino, nearly 20 percent Asian American, and 15 percent non-Hispanic White.

Matsui followed the well-worn path of forty-five women elected to the House and Senate before her who directly succeeded their late husbands into office. Her initial entrance into public life in the 1960s and 1970s began with the Lawyers' Wives of Sacramento County club in Sacramento, California, an organization that did volunteer activities as well as hosted other social functions. However, by the 1990s Matsui had established a political career. She was an early supporter of Clinton when he launched his first presidential campaign. After he was elected, he selected Matsui as one of eight people to serve on his transition team. Later, she served as a deputy assistant to the president in the Office of Public Liaison.[6]

The number of Asian American candidates for federal office has been rising fast in recent years. In 2008, there were eight Asian Americans running for congressional office. Four years later, there were thirty bids by Asian Americans for congressional office. APAICS reports that twenty-eight of these candidates ran in the 2012 primaries and eight women advanced to the general election (seven House races and one Senate race). In 2013, a record seven Asian American women served in the 113th Congress.

The number of Asian American women in Congress has been relatively few— but we do see some fairly consistent career trajectory trends. Except for Matsui, Gabbard, and Duckworth, all of the Asian American women who have been elected to Congress have had law degrees or worked in the field of education. In addition, Matsui and Duckworth are the only Asian American elected to Congress who did not spend some time in their state's legislature. Chu, for example, was first elected to her local school board in 1985. She served as a member of the City Council of Monterey Park from 1988 to 2001 and as mayor of Monterey Park three terms during that period. She served for three terms as a State of California assembly member. Before her election to the House of Representatives in 2009, she was a member of the California State Board of Equalization, the state's elected tax commission. Though Duckworth did not serve in her state's legislature, she was well-known prior to her 2012 bid because she is a wounded veteran of the Iraq war who lost both her legs and suffered damage in one arm. From 2006 to 2009, she was director of the Illinois Department of Veterans Affairs and later held a high-level position in the U.S. Department of Veterans Affairs. Duckworth lost a close congressional race that received wide attention in 2006.

## The "Overrepresentation" of Minority Female Legislators in Congress?

In general, women of color make up a larger proportion of representatives of their respective racial groups than White women. In the 113th Congress, fourteen of the Black lawmakers are female, representing 33 percent of all elected Black lawmakers.[7] Latinas make up 27 percent of the Latino delegation. Similarly, Asian American women make up more than half (53 percent) of Asian American lawmakers in the 113th Congress. In contrast, only 18 percent of all U.S. congressional representatives are female. The growth in the number of female Black, Latina, and Asian legislators is a relatively recent phenomenon. Are Black, Latina, Asian women electorally advantaged relative to White women?

With regard to Black women, while a substantial literature has emerged attempting to make explicit the factors associated with the high failure rates of Black men and White women in winning statewide, prestigious seats, little has been written about Black women's political chances in this arena (Darcy and Hadley, 1988; Hardy-Fanta et al. 2007; Tate 1997). State-level research on Latina elected officials suggests that they are elected at higher rates than their male counterparts, but no study to date has looked at their experiences across states (Cruz Takash 1997; Hardy-Fanta 2000; Montoya, Hardy-Fanta, and García 2000).

As illuminated in this volume, female candidates generally have a tough time winning elective office because of the electoral advantages political incumbents— often males—enjoy (Darcy, Welch, and Clark 1994). African American and racial minorities are additionally disadvantaged because of racial and ethnic bias that manifests in the voting booth (Reeves 1997). Despite these difficulties, minority women candidates may still have special advantages over their White female and minority male counterparts. First, limited evidence suggests that Black females are more inclined to run for political office than are White women. In contrast to White women, Black women have a much longer tradition of simultaneously working and raising families. Thus, sex-role expectations may have a less dampening effect on Black women's political ambitions.

Research has found that Black women tend to have higher levels of political ambition than do White women (Darcy and Hadley 1988). Black women delegates at a Democratic Party state convention, for example, were more likely than White women delegates to express a desire to hold higher party positions and elected positions. This may be due to African American women's historical experience of participation and activism in the civil rights movement. Researchers have also suggested that resources extant within the African American community help African American women with political ambitions to overcome individual disadvantages such as low earning power and single-parent status. Two such resources are strong religious orientation and family background (Perkins 1986).

Because African Americans constitute a powerful voting bloc, Black women candidates can seek support from a more ready-built coalition (Tate 1997). Black women may also be better able to mobilize women voters as a whole across racial barriers. Notwithstanding, the "women's vote" in contrast to the "Black vote" has historically been far more elusive because women, for a variety of reasons, are less likely than Blacks to vote as a bloc. Nevertheless, the single most important fact that explains the higher percentage of Black women serving in the U.S. Congress is the opportunities the Voting Rights Act created in providing new majority-Black districts from which to run. With rare exception, almost all the Black women who have been elected to the U.S. House of Representatives have been elected in new majority-Black districts. The largest surge in the numbers of women occurred in 1992 when thirteen new Black lawmakers were added to the House, all because of new Black districts that had been created. Among the thirteen new Black lawmakers, five were women.

The first group of Black women to win elective office won in open-seat races, Maxine Waters (D-CA), Barbara-Rose Collins (D-MI), and Eleanor Holmes Norton (D-DC), won in open-seat contests, having prudently waited for the retirement of the Black congressmen whom they succeeded. Diane Edith Watson (D-CA) won her seat to the 107th Congress in a special election in 2001 in a race overflowing with Democrats; thus, it was no easy feat. Her victory was made harder by the fact that Congresswoman Maxine Waters endorsed the bid of one of her Democratic rivals. A seasoned campaigner and politician, having been the first Black woman elected to California's state senate in 1978 until the effects of term limits kicked in, Watson earned even more congressional endorsements than her rivals, including one from the chair of the Congressional Black Caucus. Thus, a mixture of strong ambition, open seats and new districts explain why Black women are "overrepresented" in Congress.

In terms of Latina overrepresentation in Congress, few scholars have looked systematically at Latina officeholding, so we know little about the reasons that this is the case (Sierra and Sosa-Riddell 1994). We do know that this pattern seems to hold true for Latina representation across all levels of government. According to the National Association of Latino Elected and Appointed Officials (NALEO), in 2004 Latinas made up 29 percent of the Latino congressional delegation and 28 percent of Latino state legislators (NALEO 2004: vii). Nationally, women made up 13.8 percent of Congress and 22.5 percent of state legislators at that time (CAWP 2004). Most Latina officeholders are concentrated at the school board and county levels of government, making up 38 percent and 35 percent of Latino elected officials, respectively. Latina officeholding has also increased dramatically since 1990, particularly at the state and congressional levels. Since 1990, Latina representation in Congress has increased from one to seven and Latina representation in state offices has increased from sixteen to sixty-one. Latina officeholding grew more modestly at the county (37 percent), municipal (55 percent), and school board (41 percent) levels, but at all levels of government their increases far outpaced increases in Latino representation overall (Fraga and Navarro 2004: 4).

This suggests that Latinas are increasingly successful at winning elective office, despite the socioeconomic and structural barriers they may face as women and as people of color. The few studies that have examined Latina elected officials support this contention. In her study of Latina elected officials in Massachusetts, Hardy-Fanta (2000) found that between 1968 and 1994 56 percent of Latinas won their election campaigns, compared with only 15 percent of Latino men. Montoya, Hardy-Fanta, and Garciá (2000) argue that most of these women draw their early support from Latina organizations. In her survey of Latina elected officials in California, Cruz Takash (1997) has similar findings, although she found that the organizational membership was not always necessarily Latina focused. Of her respondents, 43 percent had participated in non-Latina women's organizations and 40 percent in Latino organizations, but only 26.3 percent had been part of a Latina organization prior to winning public office (424).

In terms of their path to office, 64 percent of Latinas had never held public office previously, but over two-thirds of those reported having been politically active at the local level through campaign work (68 percent), in community activism (61 percent), or as board members of local organizations (70 percent) (Cruz Takash 1997: 423). In addition, 55.8 percent had received awards recognizing their community service (424). So these women clearly were very politically active on the local level prior to their elections, and this likely facilitated their electoral success.

Like African American women, structural factors, particularly the availability of open seats, have also contributed to Latinas being elected to serve in Congress. Four of the women—Ros-Lehtinen, Napolitano, Roybal-Allard, and Linda Sanchez—were elected to open seats. Roybal-Allard and Sanchez were elected to represent new districts that were created after the redistricting that followed the 1990 and 2000 censuses, respectively. Ros-Lehtinen succeeded an incumbent congressman who died in office, and Napolitano took the seat of a legislator who retired. Only three of the seven Latinas holding office in the 108th Congress won in competitive races where they defeated an incumbent. Term limits in the state of California has helped promote the election of Latinas to Congress; five of the seven are from that state, and three of those chose to run for Congress after serving their maximum of six years in the legislature.

Finally, all the Latina members of Congress represent majority–minority districts, suggesting that the protections of the Voting Rights Act support Latina representation much as they do the representation of African American women. The story is different here, though in that Latino population growth will ensure the continual creation of new "Latino" seats into the foreseeable future, assuming that the 1965 Voting Rights Act will be extended in 2007 and that the courts will enforce it as states draw new lines for 2012. Past Latina electoral success suggests that it is reasonable to assume that many of those new seats will be won and held by Latina women.

Asian Americans are underrepresented in Congress, and this is especially true of Asian American women. Lack of descriptive representation for Asian Americans in Congress can be attributed to several factors. First, because they represent racially diverse places, most Asian American candidates must work to build multiracial coalitions to win elections. Second, like Latinos, Asian Americans as a group tend to exhibit lower rates of registration and voting than the general public. One reason for this is that as part of a predominantly immigrant population many lack citizenship and are therefore ineligible to vote. Third, Asian Americans are an extremely diverse group in terms characteristics like national origin, religion, language background, nativity, citizenship status, education, and income. The group as a whole leans Democrat; however, a significant portion is Republican, and the majority consists of those not committed to a political party. This political, demographic, and socioeconomic diversity makes organizing Asian Americans as a cohesive voting bloc a major difficulty for any Asian American candidate.

The seven Asian American women who have served in Congress were elected in places that have served as popular for Asian American settlement, even if they have not been majority Asian American congressional districts. The vast majority of these women have won open seats or were elected in special elections. The surest road to Congress for Asian American female candidates has been to serve in local and state level prior to making a bid for federal office.

Despite these challenges, the future holds some promise for Asian American women who might choose to seek congressional office. Asian American women are beginning to move up the political ladder and exhibit the potential to attain higher political office. In 2002, Minnesota State Senator Mee Moua of the Minnesota Democratic-Farm Labor party became the first Hmong American elected to a state legislature in the United States, and there were four Asian American women in the 2011–2012 California Legislature.

## Differential Treatment of Women of Color

Scholars have found that women of color legislators are treated differently from others in a variety of ways. Through in-depth interviews conducted with minority women serving in the 103rd and 104th Congresses (1993–1997), Hawkesworth (2003) found that they had experienced both demeaning exchanges with their colleagues as well as invisibility—experiences that they sought to correct and overcome. For example, racial conservative Senator Jesse Helms (R-NC) once whistled "Dixie" in an elevator he shared with Carol Moseley Braun (D-IL), the first Black woman ever elected the U.S. Senate.

Hawkesworth (2003) also found that women of color legislators have been marginalized as actors in the legislative process. For example, although women of color legislators possess formal authority and powers that, in theory, place them equally alongside their male and White female counterparts, in practice, through subtle and at times blatant tactics, they are silenced and ignored. This is similar to Tate's (2003: 74–76) finding that Black House members in the 104th Congresses were less likely than others to serve on prestigious committees, even controlling for differences in seniority. Whereas 39 percent of White Democrats held party leadership positions, only 27 percent of Blacks did.[8] In addition, while a large plurality of White Democratic legislators (39 percent) served on prestigious committees, including Rules, Appropriations, Budget, and Ways and Means, only 18 percent of Black Democrats served on such committees. Even when taking into account the somewhat lower rates of seniority for Black Democrats than others, for Blacks elected prior to the 103rd Congress only 29 percent held seats on prestigious committees, while 43 percent of White Democrats did. For Blacks elected to the 103rd and 104th Congresses during the mid-1990s, only 6 percent of Blacks held seats on prestigious committees, while 21 percent of newly elected White Democrats served on prestigious committee.

The finding that significantly fewer committees on which Blacks serve are as prestigious as those served of their White counterparts in the House is difficult to explain. There is no evidence that Black members are less ambitious than their White counterparts. Take, for example, the case of Carrie Meek (D-FL), who was elected in 1992. Shortly after winning her primary, she traveled to Washington to meet with House Democratic Party leaders to indicate her interest in serving on the House Appropriations Committee, one the most powerful in Congress. Her campaign for this particular committee assignment was effective, and the Democratic Party leadership granted Meek her request (Deering and Smith 1997).

New York Democratic representative Chisholm tells the story that she was originally assigned to the Agriculture Committee, but after protesting that there were "no trees in Brooklyn" she was reassigned to the Veterans Affairs Committee (Singh 1998, 79–80). The Democratic Caucus also refused the requests of other Black members to serve on the prestigious Budget Committee in the 1980s (Tate 2003: 78). So it is clear that there is history of discrimination by party leaders in the assignments allocated to Blacks and that only extraordinary efforts have pieced those barriers.

The realities of their marginalization, despite the equal stature and pay they share with their colleagues, lead Hawkesworth (2003) to question the effectiveness of this small group of women of color as legislators. One indicator of how they are valued comes from the 104th Congress. During that session, a number of women of color representatives denounced Republicans' characterizations of welfare recipients in the debate over welfare reform that was eventually enacted during the Clinton Administration. These voices promoting an alternative bill were ignored. For example, as a member of the Senate's powerful Finance Committee, Moseley Braun tried, unsuccessfully, to amend the welfare reform bill (ibid.). In the end, all of the women of color, including Republican Ros-Lehtinen, voted against welfare reform, but to not effect; the legislation was enacted.

This historical experience, in addition to Tate's and Hawksworth's work, suggests that important structural obstacles remain in Congress, obstacles that make it difficult for women of color to be as effective as possible in exercising their responsibilities as legislators. All these issues must be taken into consideration when examining their roles as representatives and as legislators.

## Defining and Measuring Impact

The number of women of color in Congress remains small. The 113th Congress (2013–2015), includes twenty-nine women of color out of 435 House members.[9] Thus, measuring their collective impact is methodologically problematic. Hawkesworth (2003) contends that the mere presence of women of color in the U.S. Congress is transforming the institution as they battle stereotypes of minority women and shape the public policy debate on issues pertaining to women and minority groups. In this way, one can theorize that there is an indelible effect that cannot be washed away, even in circumstances when no female of color is represented. These effects can take a variety of forms. For example, Moseley Braun's legacy includes her service on the Senate Finance Committee, and she was the first Black and female Democrat to serve on a committee that not only writes tax policy laws but also legislates on issues of Social Security, welfare, and Medicare. In 1993, she successfully blocked the Senate's renewal of a design patent sponsored by Helms for the United Daughters of the Confederacy, which used the Confederate flag in its emblem.

Yvonne Brathwaite Burke (D-CA) was the first female chair of the CBC and was also the first member of Congress to have a child while serving. Burke's decision to have a child while serving as a U.S. Representative would garner additional public attention because she was forty. As biographer LaVerne McCain Gill (1997: 63) writes, "The reality was that in the 1970s, forty-year-old women were not having babies and large numbers, and certainly not congresswomen. Conventional wisdom and taboos dictated that women avoid middle-aged pregnancies." Burke served only three terms, leaving, in part, to "raise her daughter" (65).

Barrett's (1995) analysis of the political priorities of Black female state legislators found that Black women were no different from their Black male counterparts in terms of having a pro-Black legislative agenda. Black female lawmakers were much like their White female counterparts in having a pro-women's policy agenda as well. However, unlike any other social group serving in thirty-three state governments, Black women shared a strongly unified consensus on which policies should be priorities. This is equally true of the Black women serving the U.S. Congress. While not enough scholarship has been devoted to analyzing gender differences in the legislative priorities of Black men and women in the U.S. House, Tate's (2003) scholarship reveals that Black women House legislators have been notably very active in initiating bills. Although the average number of bills sponsored was seven for Black Democrats, Maxine Waters (D-CA) sponsored twenty-six pieces of legislation. Eleanor Holmes Norton (D-DC) and the House veteran Cardiss Collins (D-IL) sponsored thirty-one and thirty-eight bills, respectively. Among those, Collins initiated legislation that imposed tougher safety standards on toy manufacturers that became law.

Like these African American women, Asian American Mink's presence in Congress also had an effect on the institution, and her experience as a woman of color no doubt affected her policy priorities. Mink's co-authorship of Title IX, which prohibits gender discrimination at any educational institution receiving federal funds, is one of her greatest legislative accomplishments. Title IX passed in 1972 and not only changed the face of college athletics but also opened opportunities for women to pursue degrees in male-dominated disciplines and institutionalize antisexual harassment policies.

Since there are so few Latinas in Congress, and most of them have been serving for less than ten years, it is difficult to determine their institutional and policy impacts. From a leadership standpoint, Roybal-Allard was the first Latina to chair the Hispanic Caucus, and Hilda Solís (D-CA) was the first Latina assistant whip for the Democratic Party (she later served as secretary of labor for the United States, the first Latina to serve in the U.S. Cabinet). From a policy standpoint, studies of House members with over 5 percent Latinos in their districts have found that representatives vote along the lines of Latino interests (as defined by the Southwest Voter Research Institute) 80 percent or more of the time and that Latino representatives have distinctive voting patterns (Kerr and Miller 1997). Looking at the Latina representatives' committee assignments and legislative priorities, most of which focus on education, workers' rights, the environment, economic development, and immigrant rights, their policy approach does not seem to differ markedly from Latino men. The main difference is the emphasis they place on women's issues. All of the Latina representatives are members of the Women's Caucus, and most list questions of women's health and domestic violence as among their top priorities; this is not true of the Latino representatives. So it is likely that the presence of Latina members provides support for policy issues of importance to all Latinos and promotes a greater focus on the concerns of women of color, particularly of those who are living in poverty.

Women of color legislators have also left important, albeit subtle, symbolic legacies. Along with Mikulski, Moseley Braun wore pants on the Senate floor, breaking a long-standing tradition dictating that female Senators wear only dresses or skirts. Two other legislative women of color, Cynthia McKinney (D-GA) and Carolyn Cheeks Kilpatrick (D-MI), wore braided, African-styled hair in the U.S. House even though African braids remain controversial in the workplace and are generally unacceptable in corporate America as well as the military. Black professional women normally have their hair straightened because natural Black hairstyles invite public disapproval. These two women's preference for braids, while clearly personal, has strong political implications.

# Conclusion

Although women of color are more represented within their respective racial group than White women, African Americans, Latinos, and Asian Americans remain significantly underrepresented within the United States Congress. Given the fact that most of these female representatives of color were elected as a result of majority–minority districts, it is unlikely that underrepresentation will decrease significantly in the near term.

However, there is some cause for optimism. African American women, Asian American women, and Latinas have been quite successful at getting elected. Their growing presence bodes well for the future presence of these women as representatives at the national level. Women of color who have served and are serving in the U.S. Congress have had important effects on the institution itself and on its policy direction, particularly within the Democratic Party. Regardless of what happens in the future, those effects cannot be erased. Their legacy will ensure that the issues of women and communities of color will remain an integral part of America's legislative agenda.

### Notes

1. No Latina or Asian American woman has ever been elected to the U.S. Senate.
2. This representative was Romualdo Pacheco, who was selected as the nonvoting delegate to Congress for the territory of Florida.
3. The Congressional Research Service includes the three members of Portuguese ancestry who are part of the Congressional Hispanic Caucus in their list of Latino representatives). Since *Latino* is used to denote individuals whose origins rest in the Spanish-speaking countries of Latin America, we do not include them in our calculation here. Our number does include the nonvoting representative from Puerto Rico, Pedro Pierluisi.
4. Nydia Velázquez served on the New York City Council prior to her election to Congress but not the New York state legislature. Similarly, Michelle Lujan Grisham (D-NM) was elected Bernalillo County Commissioner and headed the New Mexico Department of Health prior to her election to Congress but did not serve in the New Mexico state legislature.
5. The other California Latina politician who was elected to Congress thanks to term limits was Hilda Solís. When she left to become U.S. Secretary of Labor, Congresswoman Solís was replaced by Democrat Judy Chu.
6. *Washington Post.* "Who Runs Gov: Doris Matsui." *Washington Post Politics.* http://www.washingtonpost.com/politics/doris-matsui-d-calif/gIQAK2naKP_topic.html (accessed March 20, 2013).
7. This calculation does not include the recently appointed Black U.S. Senators.
8. These figures were calculated from the 252 House representatives whose districts randomly fell into the forty-eight-state national sample of Blacks she conducted in 1996, including the District of Columbia's nonvoting delegate to the House, and not all 435 House members.
9. See the Center for American Women and Politics Fact Sheet (http://www.cawp.rutgers.edu).

# 15

# Lesbian Candidates and Officeholders

DONALD P. HAIDER-MARKEL AND CHELSIE LYNN MOORE BRIGHT

## Introduction

In 1998, Tammy Baldwin became the first woman elected to Congress from Wisconsin. It was a notable accomplishment during an election season that featured many accomplishments for women in elective office. But even more notable was that Baldwin was openly lesbian and had consistently run for office (earlier in the state legislature) being open about her sexual orientation. Her 1998 victory meant that she was the first openly lesbian or gay nonincumbent elected to Congress. Then, in 2012, Baldwin made history again by becoming the first female senator elected from Wisconsin and the first nonincumbent gay or lesbian elected to the U.S. Senate.

Although Baldwin's political career has been historically significant, it is also emblematic of a dramatic increase in the number of lesbian, gay, bisexual, and transgender (LGBT) candidates and elected officials since the 1990s. Nearly every election cycle since 1992 has seen greater numbers of LGBT candidates running for local, state, and national office under major party labels. Although much of the action has been at the local and state level (Button, Wald, and Rienzo 1999; Haider-Markel 2010; Haider-Markel, Joslyn, and Kniss 2000; Rayside 1998; Smith and Haider-Markel 2002), the numbers have increased significantly in state legislative and congressional races (Haider-Markel 2010).

In this chapter, we explore lesbian candidates and officeholders in the context of LGBT candidates and officeholders overall by making use of case studies and empirical data concerning (1) elections and campaigns, (2) public attitudes about LGBT candidates and officeholders, and (3) lesbian officeholders and political representation.[1] Our analysis suggests that lesbians are increasingly running for office and being elected, although a significant portion of the population is opposed to lesbian (and gay) candidates, this portion of the public is unlikely to support Democrats (which is how most lesbians identify), and the result is that lesbians electoral chances are not lowered when they are open about their sexual orientation and that lesbian officeholders do represent the interests of the LGBT community in the policy process even if this representation is sometimes indirect.

## Elections and Lesbian Candidates for Office

Although several gay or lesbian candidates had run before her, Kathy Kozachenko became the first openly lesbian or gay person elected to public office in the United States when she was elected to the Ann Arbor, Michigan, city council in April 1974. Later that year, Elaine Noble became the first openly gay or lesbian candidate elected to a state legislature (the Massachusetts House) and State Senator Allan Spear (D-MN) came out as the first openly gay incumbent state legislator in December.

Since these early milestones the number of openly gay and lesbian candidates and officeholders has continued to rise. In 2012, there were over 40 lesbians serving in state and national elected offices across the country (see Figure 15.1). Although gay men make up a greater percentage (62 percent) of openly LGBT elected officials in state and national offices, LGBT woman continue to make historical strides.[2] The gender balance of female LGBT officeholders is especially impressive when compared with state legislatures (76 percent male) and Congress (82 percent male) overall.[3]

At the local level, the gains have been impressive as well. Most of those elected for local office have served on city councils or commissions, but some have served in executive positions. For example, openly lesbian Annise Parker was elected as

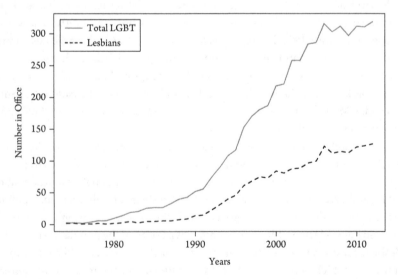

*Figure 15.1*   LGBT Elected Officials in the U.S., Local, State, and National Offices

the mayor of Houston, Texas, in 2009. Prior to that, she served on the Houston city council and as city controller. Both her city council and controller positions were citywide, which gave her a solid foundation for her mayoral run. In 2011, Parker defeated all challengers and was elected to a second term as mayor. As the mayor of Houston, Parker has the largest constituency of any LGBT official in the country at over 2,100,000, and it is also notable that Houston is the fourth largest city in the country.[4]

Although most openly LGBT candidates that run for office are gay or lesbian, the 2012 election cycle saw a significant increase in bisexual candidates, which also tend to be female. In addition to the election of the first bisexual to Congress, Kyrsten Sinema (D-AZ), State Senator Angie Buhl (D-SD) was reelected (her first victory was in 2011), Oregon secretary of state Kate Brown (D) was reelected and had previously served in the state legislature, and State Representative JoCasta Zamarripa (D-WI) of Milwaukee was reelected after serving one term; she was also the first Latina to be elected to the Wisconsin state legislature in 2010.

There are few LGBT candidates who run as Republicans and even fewer lesbian candidates at all levels of government in the United States. Indeed, at the state and national level, there have only been nine Republican LGBT officials, and all of these were gay men. At the local level, partisan affiliation can be a bit more uncertain because many Midwestern and Western states have nonpartisan elections at the local level. And some particular cases can confuse the issue; for example, Houston Mayor Annise Parker identifies as a Democrat, but she was endorsed in her 1997 city council bid by the Log Cabin Republicans, a gay Republican political action committee (PAC). That few LGBT candidates run as Republicans is not that surprising considering that LGBT voters overwhelmingly, but not exclusively, identify as Democrat or support Democratic candidates.[5] Additionally, although the Tea Party Movement had a dramatic influence on elections in 2010 and 2012, that influence was generally limited to primary races between Republicans and therefore had no significant influence on lesbian or female bisexual candidates.

## Predicting Attitudes about Gay and Lesbian Candidates

Although it is clear that lesbian candidates have had remarkable success in achieving public office over the past 25 years, it also seems that, given the long-term discrimination faced by women, lesbian candidates for office would be fighting an uphill battle. As such, it seems prudent to consider who might oppose LGBT candidates overall and lesbian candidates in particular (see, e.g., Doan and Haider-Markel 2010).

Most of the early research examining candidate sexual orientation on preferences was conducted through experiments in which respondents evaluated fictional candidates (see Golebiowska 2001; Golebiowska and Thomsen 1999; Herrick and Thomas 1999). These studies suggested that hypothetical LGBT candidates receive lower evaluations than their heterosexual counterparts and that these candidates would be less likely to receive votes. Interestingly, the lack of support was most apparent for gay male candidates who fit a gay male stereotype and somewhat less true for lesbian candidates (Golebiowska 2001).

But in perhaps the most careful study in the line of experimental studies, Herrick and Thomas (1999) created hypothetical elections where respondents were asked more directly to state their voting preferences and their perceptions of candidates. Controlling for a variety of other factors, including gender and ideology, they found that a candidate's sexual orientation does have a slight influence on voting preference and on perceptions of a candidate's electoral viability (ability to win the election), but the effect was small. In addition, lesbians were not viewed any more negatively than gay men, suggesting that lesbians do not face double discrimination on the bias of sexual orientation and gender. A similar study suggests that although lesbian and gay candidates might face stereotyping stereotyping does not necessarily translate in to less support. Tadlock and Gordon's (2003) experimental research on college students suggests that candidates who are labeled as openly lesbian or gay in hypothetical news accounts are stereotyped, but gay and lesbian candidates were not less likely to be supported and might even be preferred over heterosexual candidates with the same qualities.

We can also examine data from several polls of American adults. If we examine national polls between 1994 and 2004 regarding support for hypothetical homosexual candidates for public office we find that at least 25 percent of respondents were opposed to supporting an openly homosexual candidate for elective office (Haider-Markel 2010, 40–41). Interestingly, the gender of a homosexual candidate seems to matter little to Americans. A November 2003 poll of national adults conducted by Scripps suggests that 27 percent of respondents would oppose a gay congressional candidate, while 28 percent would oppose a lesbian congressional candidate.[6]

We can also assess public support for homosexual candidates for specific offices with data using a 2008 Zogby poll (of American adults). A similar pattern emerges with at least 25 percent of respondents opposing a gay or lesbian person for a variety of national offices, from the president to vice president to a cabinet appointee to the U.S. Senate. Although levels of opposition vary across specific offices, there does appear to be a core of opponents that is unlikely to support a gay or lesbian candidate regardless of office or whether the candidates share the voters' views.[7] Opposition to a gay or lesbian presidential candidate is considerably higher in a 2012 Gallup poll at 30 percent than it is for a woman (5 percent) or African American (4 percent). Indeed, opposition was only higher toward a Muslim (40 percent) or atheist (43 percent) (Jones 2012).

To examine support for lesbian candidates specifically, we can look to one early statewide race in 1994 and one recent race in 2012. In 1994, Democratic candidate for New York Attorney General, Karen Burstein, publicly stated that she was a lesbian; Burstein's won her party's nomination, but she lost in the general election. In one poll, less than 40 percent of respondents had heard anything about a gay candidate, and of those who had heard less than half could identify Karen Burstein as the lesbian candidate. Of this small (174) group of respondents, 18 percent indicated that Burstein's sexual orientation would make it less likely that they would vote for her (Haider-Markel 2010, 48–49). In 2012, openly lesbian Tammy Baldwin ran for the U.S. Senate from Wisconsin after having served in the House since 1999. According to an August 2012 poll of likely Wisconsin voters that focused on the race, 60 percent indicated that they would support a gay or lesbian candidate for public office, while 25 percent said they would oppose a gay candidate and 15 percent were unsure; support increased to 80 percent among respondents who identified as Democrats.[8] Although conducted years apart in different states, both polls at least suggested that opposition to the lesbian candidates was 25 percent or less and likely included individuals who would not have supported the Democratic candidate regardless of sexual orientation.

This leads us to ask: who is more likely to oppose a lesbian (or gay) candidate for office? We suspect that support or opposition to lesbian (or gay) candidates can be predicted by factors that also predict affect toward homosexuals and support for gay civil rights (Doan and Haider-Markel 2010; Haider-Markel 2010). Analysis of attitudes toward gays and lesbians, gay civil rights, and same-sex marriage reveals that women, the educated, Democrats, liberals, youth, and nonreligious infrequent churchgoers tend to be more supportive (Brewer 2003a, 2003b; Egan and Sherrill 2005; Haider-Markel and Joslyn 2008; Herek 2002). To test what individual characteristics predict support for gay or lesbian candidates, we estimated statistical models predicting opposition to gay and lesbian candidates and attitudes about candidate attributes; these models included the following characteristics of survey respondents: living in the South (where relevant); gender; being born again; Protestant religion; church attendance; education; race; ideology; partisanship; age; and city size for place of residence.

Our analysis of survey data from the 1994 New York race suggests that liberals, Democrats, whites, the educated, youth, and women were more likely to indicate they would vote for a gay or lesbian candidate. Likewise, analysis of the poll conducted for the 2012 Wisconsin Senate race indicate that liberals, Democrats, Independents, whites, youth, and women were more likely to say that they would vote for a gay or lesbian candidate.[9] Although most voters are willing to support a lesbian candidate, there is a distinctive profile to those who are not. On average white, males, those with less education, those who are conservative, Republicans, those who are religious, and those who live in rural areas are less likely to support a lesbian candidate. In short, a lesbian candidate for office would be advised to avoid running in areas where the median voter is closer to this profile.

Next, we turn to national polls that ask about gay and lesbian candidates as well as those that distinguish between lesbian and gay candidates. Making use of the basic statistical model explained earlier, we examined individual-level responses from a 2006 Zogby International Polling survey of American adults. The first relevant question is:

> Let me read you the opinions of two people. One person says that a gay candidate does not share our values and would focus too much on gay issues. Another says sexual orientation is not important to the job as long as the candidate has a strong record getting things done for everyone in the community. Do you 1) Strongly agree that a lesbian candidate does not share values (16.1 percent), 2) Somewhat agree that a lesbian candidate does not share values (8.2), 3) Somewhat agree that sexual orientation is not important (21 percent), or 4) Strongly agree that sexual orientation is not important (46.5 percent) (8.2 percent indicated neither or refused).

The second question is similar, but here respondents were asked about a gay candidate:

> Let me read you the opinions of two people. One person says that a gay candidate does not share our values and would focus too much on gay issues. Another says sexual orientation is not important to the job as long as the candidate has a strong record getting things done for everyone in the community. Do you 1) Strongly agree that a gay candidate does not share values (13.2 percent), 2) Somewhat agree that a gay candidate does not share values (8.6 percent), 3) Somewhat agree that sexual orientation is not important (24.7 percent), or 4) Strongly agree that sexual orientation is not important (47.4) (6.0 percent indicated neither or refused).

Our statistical analysis predicting responses to these questions indicates that the models do a reasonable job of predicting attitudes about a gay or lesbian candidate. Women, the more educated, Democrats, and non-born-again individuals were more likely to indicate that a candidate's sexual orientation does not matter. Older respondents, Republicans, males, and those who are born again were more likely to indicate that gay and lesbian candidates do not share their values. These findings are consistent with previous research on gay and lesbian candidates (Doan and Haider-Markel 2010; Haider-Markel 2010).

Our results also suggest that there is not a distinct difference in the way voters view lesbian versus gay candidates, but lesbian candidates might be somewhat less likely to receive support from men and the better educated than are gay male candidates. However, we also explore how individuals compare the attributes of lesbian candidates versus gay candidates.

In a 2003 Scripps poll, respondents were asked a number of questions regarding the personal attributes of gay and lesbian candidates. They were also asked how competent they thought gay and lesbian candidates would be dealing with specific issues. The distribution of responses to these questions is displayed in Table 15.1. In terms of the honesty, morality, and strength of gay and lesbian candidates for Congress, the great majority of respondents indicate there would be no difference compared to the typical congressional candidate. However, at least 9 percent suggested that gay and lesbian candidates would be at least somewhat less honest; 17 percent indicated that gay and lesbian candidates would be at least somewhat less moral, and 13 percent suggested that lesbian and gay candidates would be at least somewhat less strong than the typical candidate for Congress. In terms of negative attributes, such as being less strong, respondents ranked gay and lesbian candidates nearly the same but did attribute slightly more negative characteristics to gay male candidates.

The lower half of Table 15.1 displays attitudes concerning the competency of gay and lesbian candidates on education, military, and tax issues. Across all three issues, at least 76 percent of respondents believed gay and lesbian candidates would be at least as competent as the typical candidate for Congress. About 5 percent of respondents thought gay and lesbian candidates would be more competent, while at least 8 percent thought gay and lesbian candidates would be less competent than the typical congressional candidate. There are some small differences between gay and lesbian candidates: gay male candidates were seen as less competent on education and military issues than were lesbians.

And although we do not display multivariate analysis of the attribute and competence questions here, the results presented in Doan and Haider-Markel (2010) allow us to make a few inferences. First, women are less likely to attribute negative traits to lesbian candidates but differ little from men in attributing negative traits to gay male candidates. Second, conservatives, on average, hold significant negative attitudes toward the traits of gay candidates but not toward lesbian candidate traits, accounting for the same factors we considered in our earlier models. Third, if we examine the predictors of honesty, morality, and strength, there is no appreciable statistical difference between male and female respondents' opinions about gay male candidates, but there is a significant gender difference when it comes to the traits of lesbian candidates. In short, women are less likely than men to stereotype lesbian political candidates with negative characteristics. Stereotypes about lesbians may mediate the effects of gender stereotypes in evaluations of lesbian candidates, but only among female respondents. When it comes to gay male candidates, female respondents are just as likely as male respondents to attribute negative characteristics to them.

In addition, Doan and Haider-Markel (2010) suggest that female respondents evaluated lesbian candidates more favorably. Women were less likely than men to say lesbian candidates were less competent on education, but there was no gender difference in respondents' evaluation of gay male competency regarding the issue of education. Evaluations of competency on the military indicate that men were more

*Table 15.1* **Attitudes Concerning Gay and Lesbian Congressional Candidates**

*Think about how honest the typical candidate for Congress is. By comparison, how honest would a _____ candidate likely be?*

| Gay Male | | Lesbian Woman | |
|---|---|---|---|
| Much more honest | 4% | Much more honest | 3% |
| Somewhat more honest | 7% | Somewhat more honest | 5% |
| No difference | 81% | No difference | 82% |
| Somewhat less honest | 5% | Somewhat less honest | 5% |
| Much less honest | 4% | Much less honest | 5% |

*What about moral? How moral would a _____ candidate be compared to the typical candidate for Congress?*

| Gay Male | | Lesbian Woman | |
|---|---|---|---|
| Much more moral | 2% | Much more moral | 3% |
| Somewhat more moral | 6% | Somewhat more moral | 4% |
| No difference | 73% | No difference | 76% |
| Somewhat less moral, | 9% | Somewhat less moral, | 9% |
| Much less moral | 10% | Much less moral | 8% |

*What about strong? How strong would a _____ candidate be compared to the typical candidate for Congress?*

| Gay Male | | Lesbian Woman | |
|---|---|---|---|
| Much more strong | 3% | Much more strong | 3% |
| Somewhat more strong | 5% | Somewhat more strong | 4% |
| No difference | 73% | No difference | 80% |
| Somewhat less strong | 11% | Somewhat less strong | 7% |
| Much less strong | 8% | Much less strong | 6% |

*Think about how competent the typical candidate for Congress is on the following issues. By comparison, how competent would a _____ candidate likely be on education?*

| Gay Male | | Lesbian Woman | |
|---|---|---|---|
| Much more competent | 4% | Much more competent | 4% |
| Somewhat more competent | 4% | Somewhat more competent | 2% |
| No difference | 83% | No difference | 86% |
| Somewhat less competent | 5% | Somewhat less competent | 3% |
| Much less competent | 4% | Much less competent | 5% |

*Table 15.1* (**Continued**)

| *What about military issues? How competent would a _____ candidate be compared to the typical candidate for Congress?* | | | |
|---|---|---|---|
| *Gay Male* | | *Lesbian Woman* | |
| Much more competent | 3% | Much more competent | 2% |
| Somewhat more competent | 2% | Somewhat more competent | 3% |
| No difference | 76% | No difference | 80% |
| Somewhat less competent | 10% | Somewhat less competent | 8% |
| Much less competent | 9% | Much less competent | 7% |
| *What about on taxes? How competent would a _____ candidate be compared to the typical candidate for Congress?* | | | |
| *Gay Male* | | *Lesbian Woman* | |
| Much more competent | 1% | Much more competent | 2% |
| Somewhat more competent | 3% | Somewhat more competent | 2% |
| No difference | 88% | No difference | 88% |
| Somewhat less competent | 4% | Somewhat less competent | 4% |
| Much less competent | 4% | Much less competent | 4% |

*Notes:* Compiled by the authors based on Doan and Haider-Markel (2010); data are from a Scripps Survey Research Center, Ohio University, October 20 to November 4 national survey of approximately 950 adults.

likely to believe that both gay and lesbian candidates would be less competent. On taxes, women were less likely than men to indicate that a gay or lesbian candidate would be less competent. These findings suggest that lesbian candidates may benefit on an issue such as education, which is an issue where women are stereotypically viewed as stronger (Dolan 2005). In addition, lesbians, who are often stereotyped as being masculine, might be seen as more competent on military issues than gay men, who are often stereotyped as more effeminate (Golebiowska 2001), especially by female respondents.

In summary, although adult respondents do not make many distinctions between gay and lesbian candidates, it appears that women are more likely to attribute positive traits to lesbian versus gay male candidates, even though women are more likely to attribute positive attributes to both gays and lesbians relative to men.

Additionally, lesbians fair better on issues such as the military among both men and women, perhaps in part because of stereotyping about gay male femininity versus lesbian femininity.

Finally, we explore support for gay and lesbian candidates across different types of offices.[10] Employing a Zogby 2008 poll of American adults we construct a statistical model to predict the likelihood of a respondent supporting a gay (man or woman) presidential candidate,[11] vice presidential candidate, senate candidate, or a presidential appointee.[12]

There is little substantive difference between a respondents support for a gay candidate running for the office of the president, vice president, or senate. The likelihood of supporting a gay presidential and vice presidential candidate is shaped by gender, race, education, partisanship, religiosity and being born again. In sum, female, white, more educated, Democrats, less religious, and non-born-again respondents were more likely to support gay and lesbian candidates for national offices.

These analyses clearly indicate that gender, education, partisanship, and religion strongly shape the likelihood of supporting a lesbian or gay candidate for a variety of offices. Place or residence and race are inconsistent predictors of support, all other factors considered. Additionally, lesbian candidates fair no better or worse than gay candidates and may even have some advantage on attributes that could help in elections.

What should be clear is that, although about 25 percent of adults appear to be unlikely to support a lesbian or gay candidate, this group has clearly identifiable characteristics, especially in terms of party (Republican) and religion (highly religious and born-again Christians). As such, these adults are most likely supporters of Republican candidates. When this information is combined with the fact that few lesbian or gay candidates run as Republicans and instead run as Democrats, we can begin to see that candidate sexual orientation may not play a significant negative role in campaigns.

## Voices of Candidates

To better understand how lesbian candidates fare in elections, we can also turn to the candidates. Anecdotal evidence suggests that lesbian candidates for a variety of offices sometimes face opponents that attempt to make their sexual orientation an issue in the campaign or face outside groups that raise the specter of "the lesbian/gay" candidate who will only bring "their agenda" to office (Button, Wald, and Rienzo 1999; Haider-Markel 2010; Smith and Haider-Markel 2002). Before she was elected mayor of Houston, Parker noted that being open about her sexual orientation may have helped her win by providing considerable free media attention to her candidacy. However, she says, "There aren't many city issues that are gay issues. City government is concerned with potholes and sewers and such, not social and sexual matters" (Freyer 1999).

In perhaps the most systematic survey of LGBT candidates, Haider-Markel (2010, Chapter 2) surveyed and interviewed openly LGBT candidates for state legislative offices who ran in primary and/or general elections across all states where there were such candidates (30) during the 2003–2004 elections.[13] In the 2003 to 2004 cycle, there were 95 LGBT candidates running for state legislative offices. In 24 (25 percent) of these races candidates were running for the upper legislative chamber, typically called the state senate. Most candidates (73) ran as Democrats or for the Democratic nomination, but 17 of the candidates ran for the Republican nomination or ran on the Republican ticket (all of the Republicans were men) and 5 candidates ran on the Green Party ticket. In total, 22 percent of the candidates lost in the primary election, withdrew, or failed to file enough signatures to obtain a spot on the general election ballot.[14]

Most respondents to the survey ran in districts that favored Democrats, and all of the lesbian candidates did so. Interviews with candidates helped to confirm that this pattern was not an accident. Most lesbian candidates tend to run as Democrats and select districts where they believe their sexual orientation will be less of an issue. Many candidates had prior political experience in the district, through activism, a staff position, or holding lower-level elective offices, so they were familiar with the ideological and partisan orientations of the district.

Most candidates reported that they were recruited at least partially by others to run, including incumbent legislators, party activists, interest groups, and party leaders. For most of the candidates, the decision to run was based somewhat on a seat coming open through retirement, term limits, or the pursuit of a higher office by an incumbent.

Many candidates suggested that the LGBT community was very supportive, and they had participated in community events during the campaign. One respondent even indicated that 50 percent of her volunteers were from the LGBT community and more than 50 percent of her contributions were from the LGBT community. Other candidates indicated that they had the support of the LGBT community, but either did not attend events or the community's support was less than vocal.

Very few candidates indicated there was any active opposition by religious conservatives against them, and only about half of these candidates described substantial efforts by religious conservatives to defeat them. For example, one lesbian candidate described the formation of a new group whose sole purpose was to oppose her candidacy; their efforts were not effective, and she won the race. Most of these opposition campaigns were led by local chapters of the Christian Coalition, the Eagle Forum, and Right to Life groups and may have mobilized to oppose any Democratic candidate.

Nearly all lesbian candidates indicated that the media did not print or air more than a few reports on their race. However, a few candidates did report a considerable amount of coverage and, in most of these cases, the coverage tended to focus on the fact that one or more candidates in the race were openly gay or lesbian. Virtually all of the candidates reported that coverage was fair and accurate. In one case, a candidate indicated her sexual orientation was highlighted by the national news media, but she noted that the attention may have helped her campaign rather than hurt.

Lesbian candidates mostly indicated they had no problems raising money, and nearly all candidates received at least some money from PACs as well as small individual donations. Some candidates received bundled contributions from the Victory Fund, a national group that is focused on electing LGBT candidates to office. Lesbian candidates tended to receive contributions from labor, environmental, and pro-choice organizations, but some also received contributions from a variety of business and development organizations. The view that raising money is easy as a lesbian candidate was especially prevalent among incumbents, with challengers being less likely to espouse such a view, but they by no means viewed fundraising as a substantial hurdle. This may have been because on average most lesbian state legislative candidates had held previous public office.

Candidates were asked to list the four central issues in their campaign. Most lesbian candidates listed education or support for public schools. About half of candidates listed environmental issues—about the same percentage listed health-care issues. Only a few listed equality or civil rights issues as being central to their campaigns.

Although some lesbian candidates indicated that the issue of gay and lesbian civil rights was important in their campaigns, very few actively campaigned on the issue, and for some candidates the issue became important either because opponents raised the issue or external events, such as ballot measures to ban same-sex marriage, forced the issue into the spotlight.

In terms of the campaign tone, spending levels, and tactics of their opponents during the primary election, about half of candidates either had no primary or were unopposed in the primary, which is a little higher than normal for state legislative elections (Hamm and Moncrief 2008). In other races, the primary is the key race simply because the district is heavily partisan, often Democratic, in one direction. Only a few respondents described the primary race as fairly nasty in terms of attacks, and a small number of candidates even faced opponents who were also gay or lesbian. One candidate even indicated that her opponent said she "wasn't gay enough." Only a few indicated that their opponents tried to make an issue of their sexual orientation, and in none of these cases did the issue play a role in the outcome, at least from the perspective of the candidates.

Candidates were also asked directly if sexual orientation played any role in the general election campaign. Many indicated that sexual orientation played no role in the campaign, but a fair number did say that sexual orientation played a small, negative role in the campaign. In most of these cases, sexual orientation became important because opponents raised the issue of same-sex marriage. In other cases, a same-sex marriage ban was being considered by the state, and the issue was brought into media coverage of the campaign; in only a few races did respondents indicate the issue became significant in a negative manner. One respondent said, "My opponent made it a central part of her campaign—it backfired on her. I had Republicans donating to my campaign to defeat her." In another race, the respondent said that the state Republican Party had funded telephone push polls that scared voters to believe they might elect a lesbian who could become a legislative leader in their state. At the same time, many incumbent lesbian legislators indicated that the issue had been significant in past campaigns but no longer was an issue. But even for incumbent legislators, the role played by sexual orientation in past elections was not a deciding factor in the election outcome. And no candidate indicated that she had ever lost a race because of her sexual orientation.

Several candidates even suggested that being a lesbian was an asset. One respondent said that her candidacy rallied political progressives and the LGBT community in her district, and this may have made opponents afraid of attacking her sexual orientation. Two candidates said that being openly lesbian gave them a volunteer network and staff that they would not have had otherwise. Both indicated that the volunteers were important in their election victories. And one incumbent indicated that although the issue had been important for her in past campaigns, at this point being an openly lesbian legislator seems to help her maintain her seat.

In summary, the results of the surveys and interviews reported in Haider-Markel (2010) suggest a number of interesting findings. First, LGBT candidates and lesbian candidates in particular do tend to be somewhat more politically experienced than the average state legislative candidate (Hamm and Moncrief 2008). If they obtain a legislative seat, like most incumbents, they are reelected. Second, based on candidate comments and other evidence concerning where candidates run, it seems as though lesbian candidates are quite selective in choosing when and where and how to run. Indeed, all lesbian candidates in this cycle ran as Democrats in a left-leaning district. These candidates appear to be quite aware that their district is likely to be accepting of an LGBT candidate, whereas many other districts may not be. Combined with the political experience of most, the average Democratic LGBT candidate may be more successful than the average Democrat running for state office (also see Haider-Markel 2010, Chapter 3).

Haider-Markel (2010) also makes it clear that sexual orientation is not a deciding factor in most, if any, races. In the few races where lesbian candidates faced a mobilized campaign by religious conservatives or a candidate who tried to make sexual orientation a focus of the campaign, candidates did not suggest that these efforts did or could have defeated them. In fact, some candidates indicated that they had managed to capitalize on being lesbian to win their elections by attracting contributors and volunteers. This is not to say that sexual orientation does not matter for state legislative candidates, only that given that it could be a factor, as indicated by the polling data presented earlier, potential lesbian candidates are strategic in choosing when and where and how they run. These strategic maneuvers tend to downplay or eliminate the possible negative role that sexual orientation could play in a state legislative campaign. This pattern is consistent for gay men, lesbians, and bisexual candidates.

Additionally, systematic analyses of election results across 10 states from 1992 to 2006 (Haider-Markel 2010, Chapter 3) reveals that gay and lesbian state legislative candidates' electoral success is not hindered by being open about their sexual orientation, either in terms of the likelihood of victory or their share of the vote. And although Democratic female candidates were slightly more likely to be elected than their male peers (and all of the lesbian candidates were Democrats), being a gay versus lesbian Democratic candidate had no significant influence on the likelihood of being elected or on the candidate's percentage of the vote. In short, lesbian state legislative candidates were not less likely to be elected, and some of the models suggest that they had a relative advantage compared with their Democratic heterosexual counterparts.

## Lesbian Officeholders and Representation

Of course, all groups hope to achieve a seat at the table to ensure that their interests are represented in the policy process. Existing research does suggest that the interests of the LGBT community can be represented by heterosexual as well as LGBT elected officials (Haider-Markel 2007, 2010; Haider-Markel, Joslyn, and Kniss 2000), but many would argue that lesbians, as gay and female, have a special urgency to ensure that their voice is heard in the policy process. Indeed, in 2006, openly lesbian Arizona State Senator Paula Aboud (D) argued:

> ...It is impossible to not relate to hate crimes issues, GLBT issues. It's impossible to not relate to it from sexual orientation. While its legislation that somebody out there needs, it's also legislation that I need, that I want. In the same way that a small business person will stand up and say this is how it affects small business, I'm going to be able to stand up and say this is how it's going to affect me and my life...I will speak up to that which affects me. (Haider-Markel 2010, 84)

However, simply electing a member of your group does not guarantee substantive representation of the groups' interests in the policy process. Substantive representation can occur because elected representatives that identify with a group are introducing and championing proposals that benefit the group, but their substantive representation might occur through other means as well. For example, simply having representatives of a group in a policymaking body may influence other deci-sion-makers' attitudes about the group and subsequent support for policy proposals related to the group (Bratton 2002; Hawkesworth 2003; Rayside 1998). In a role model capacity, elected representatives of a group could also influence public percep-tions of the group, and public and legislator preferences concerning policies related to the group (Barrett 1995; Hawkesworth 2003; Smith and Haider-Markel 2002).

So are these lesbian officeholders having an impact on LGBT-related policy once elected? The anecdotal evidence suggests yes. For example, in 2006, Utah repre-sentative Jackie Biskupski and representative Christine Johnson helped to ensure that a bill that would have banned domestic partner benefits did not move out of committee and assisted in blocking the worst anti-LGBT portions of another bill on student clubs in public schools. Montana's only openly LGBT legislator, State Senator Christine Kaufmann (D-Helena), sponsored bills in 2005 and 2007 to include sexual orientation in the state's antidiscrimination statutes. The measures were supported by the governor but failed to pass both chambers (Haider-Markel 2010, 88). And Colorado state senator Jennifer Veiga (D-Denver) annually spon-sored legislation to ban sexual orientation discrimination in the 2000s, and a ver-sion of her bill banning sexual orientation discrimination in employment eventually passed in 2007 while a measure to expand discrimination protection to housing and public accommodations was codified in 2008 (Haider-Markel 2010, 88).

It is also true that lesbian legislators do not always pursue direct efforts at pol-icy representation, such as sponsoring legislation or lobbying other legislators to defeat an anti-LGBT bill. In Alabama, for example, Representative Patricia Todd (D-Jefferson) participated in a 2008 "stealth campaign" to pass bills on hate crimes and reducing bullying of LGBT students. When the House came to considering the hate crime measure, Todd says that supporters did not go to the floor to discuss the measure. Instead, the bill's sponsor, Representative Alvin Holmes, had quietly asked proponents not to discuss the bill on the floor to avoid mobilizing conservative opponents. The strategy was effective, and the bill passed 46 to 44 (Haider-Markel 2010, 88).

Although brief examples indicate that lesbian officeholders often attempt to represent the interests of the LGBT community once elected, the institutional and political context in which they operate may limit or prohibit their opportunities for representing the interest of the LGBT community. To get a sense of the role of context we turn to two states to provide detailed examples of lesbian officeholders in the remainder of this section.

In California, the first LGBT legislator in the state, Assembly Member Sheila Kuehl (D), played an important role in increasing the number the number of pro-gay bills introduced in the legislature. Kuehl's first significant battle on pro-LGBT leg-islation came in 1997 when she introduced a bill that would have banned discrim-ination bias based on sexual orientation in school employment, curriculum, and the treatment of students on campus. Republicans had the majority and defeated a similar bill by Kuehl in 1996. By 1997, Democrats were in control of the chamber, and Republicans coordinated their efforts with conservative religious groups, such as the Traditional Values Coalition. Kuehl was able to steer the bill through the Assembly Education Committee before it failed on the Assembly floor (36–40). In 1999 Kuehl also sponsored one of the first of its kind antibullying bills that provided protection for LGBT students in K–12 schools. The measure was opposed by the Traditional Values Coalition, which provided the governor's office with 20,000 signatures against the measure. Nevertheless, Kuehl's influence in the now Democrat controlled chamber and helped ensure eventual passage (Haider-Markel 2010, 91).

Openly lesbian Assembly Member Carol Migden was elected to the California Assembly in a May 1996 special election. She assisted Kuehl in her 1996 and 1997 legislative efforts to pass pro-LGBT legislation, including a 1999 bill to cement anti-discrimination laws in employment and housing and establishing a state domestic partner registry. When Kuehl ran for and was elected to a seat in the state senate in 2000, two additional open lesbians, Jackie Goldberg and Christine Kehoe, were elected to seats in the State Assembly. During the 2000 primary election, California voters adopted an initiative banning same-sex marriage. The event led LGBT legislators to pursue a statutory change that would allow civil unions for same-sex partners, and in 2001 LGBT legislators, led by Migden, spearheaded the adoption new benefits to domestic partners (Haider-Markel 2010, 91–92).

By 2007 LGBT legislators were dominating the debate over LGBT issues in the legislature. Of the 14 pro-LGBT related bills in 2007, 8 were sponsored by LGBT legislators. These included Migden's bill to protect LGBT youth in the criminal justice system, Kuehl's proposal to protect LGBT students in public schools and ban curriculum that discriminates against LGBT people, Migden's measure to allow California registered domestic partners to file joint tax returns, Kehoe's bill to reverse discriminatory tax increases for domestic partners, and Kehoe's resolution urging the Congress and the president to repeal the federal "Don't Ask, Don't Tell" policy. Of the 14 measures, 11 became state policy.

Lesbian legislators in California have also held important posts in the legislature and some have built strong alliances with the governor's office. Migden served as chairwoman of the powerful Assembly Appropriations Committee and was annually named as "one of the hardest-working and most influential legislators by California Journal" (Warren 2001). Kuehl built strong relationships with the governor and quickly won the trust of Senate leader John Burton (ibid.). Assembly Member Kehoe held assistant speaker pro tempore, which meant that she was often able to run Assembly floor sessions. The three become known as the "Lavender Caucus," and their influence was spread across a range of issues, including energy and crime, not simply LGBT-related legislation (ibid.).

Moving to the East Coast, Massachusetts is clearly viewed as a liberal enclave in a fairly liberal region of the country. Female representation in the legislature is high, at around 25 percent, but ethnic minority groups are not well represented.

Notably, in November 2003, Massachusetts became the first state in the country to allow, and not rescind, same-sex marriage when the Supreme Judicial Court ruled (*Goodridge v. Department of Public Health*) that the state could not legally deny marriage licenses to same-sex couples and gave the legislature 180 days to change state statutes.[15] The *Goodridge* decision drove much of the LGBT-related legislation from 2004 to 2007.

As noted earlier, Massachusetts was home to the first openly LGBT person directly elected to a state legislature in the country. Elaine Noble, a community activist from Boston, ran as an open lesbian in 1974 and won. In a 2007 interview she described the campaign and taking a seat in the state legislature:

> I was emotionally and physically exhausted...There were people all over the Country calling and asking if I would come and speak. They'd say 'Well, you have a responsibility to a bigger constituency.' I was pulled a thousand different ways.... [In the legislature] it really got harder in terms of the threats and being a target that was readily available to people. One day, I was walking to the State House and there was a guy, 85 years old, and he walked up and said, 'Representative Noble.' And I reached up to shake his hand and he spit on me. And then I turned around and he started doing his diatribe. I walked all the way home and showered and changed my clothes. So even walking to work or riding my bike to work was not terribly safe. (Nichols 2007)

Noble did little to advocate for the LGBT in terms of formal legislative activity in part because she became overwhelmed with the position. In fact, her stress over the position, and perhaps the murder of Harvey Milk (San Francisco Board of Supervisors), led her to retire her seat after two terms (Nichols 2007).[16]

The next lesbian was not elected to state office until 1998; Elizabeth Malia (D-11) was first elected to the State House in a special March 1998 election after her boss, the incumbent legislator, resigned for another position. Malia was consistently reelected to her seat through the 2008 election. She led a legislative fight to obtain domestic partner benefits in 2001 but is probably best known for her work on children's, health, and crime issues. In 2007 and 2008, Malia was on the forefront of an effort to pass the MassHealth Equality bill, a measure that requires equal treatment of same-sex and opposite-sex married couples in the administration of the MassHealth insurance program. Aided by the mobilization of the LGBT community on same-sex marriage in 2005 and 2006, Malia was able to move the bill forward in 2008, having failed in 2007. One observer suggested that several factors contributed to the successful adoption of the bill, one being "...Liz Malia making it her number one commitment..." (Haider-Markel 2010, 96). Malia argued that the success on the MassHealth measure, as well as the repeal of a law banning marriages of nonresidents, was because of the visible profile of LGBT legislators. She said, "I think we've humanized [the issue in] the legislature in the past few years, and with us being LGBT folks a lot of the mythology has been lost and buried in the same way it has in society at large and in Massachusetts" (Haider-Markel 2010, 96).

In a dramatic moment, State Senator Cheryl Jacques (D) came out as a lesbian in June 2000. She had first been elected in 1992, and she continued to be reelected after coming out. She has been credited with the inclusion of sexual orientation in the state hate crime law in 1996, but at the time she was not open about her sexual orientation. In 2001, she ran openly as lesbian for the U.S. House in the 9th District, but her bid failed. From 2000 to 2003, she sponsored or cosponsored a number of bills addressing the needs of LGBT youth and as well as persons with HIV/AIDS. Jacques has been a key advocate for gay rights in the legislature and in 2003 was the sponsor of the first bill ever introduced in the state to legalize same-sex marriage; she also used her position on the Joint Committee on the Judiciary to oppose attempts to ban same-sex marriage. In fact, in April 2003 she made a personal appeal to her colleagues on the committee, arguing, "We serve side by side. Many of you are friends of mine. Explain to me how in any way my partner Jenn and our two little boys Tommy and Timmy threaten your family" (Haider-Markel 2010, 96). The ban did not pass. She served through 2003 when she left to head the Human Rights Campaign, the largest national LGBT group in the country.

Additionally, lesbian Sarah K. Peake (D-4) served in Massachusetts after first running for the legislature in 2004 in large part because the incumbent refused to support the *Goodridge* decision, but her bid against an incumbent was unsuccessful. When the incumbent stepped down in 2006, Peake was able to defeat opponents in the primary and general election in what is a traditionally Republican district. Peake focused on affordable housing, veterans' affairs, and home rule designations for local government. Peake was able to vote against the constitutional amendment banning same-sex marriage in 2007 and vote for repeal of the law banning nonresident marriages in 2008. During her 2008 race, voters were more concerned with the economy than LGBT issues, but she did accuse her opponent of trying to make an issue of her sexual orientation during the contest (Haider-Markel 2010, 98–99).

One of the most recent freshman lesbian state officeholders in Massachusetts is Kate Hogan. Hogan ran for the 3rd House District when the incumbent stepped down in 2008. She received the endorsement of the former incumbent and was able to overcome her Republican opponent in a fairly conservative district. When Hogan took office in 2009, the central LGBT issues in the legislature were the passage of a bill to add gender identity and expression to the state's nondiscrimination and hate crimes laws (similar measures had died in the 2007–2008 session) and to ensure that LGBT and HIV/AIDS programs did not receive cuts. She did not sponsor the transgender bill, and the HIV/AIDS programs were reduces, as many programs were across the states in the 2009 session (Haider-Markel 2010, 99).

# Conclusion

In this chapter, we examined lesbian candidates and officeholders in the context of LGBT candidates and officeholders overall. We explored (1) elections and campaigns, (2) public attitudes about lesbian and gay candidates and officeholders, and (3) lesbian officeholders and political representation in the policymaking process.

Our analyses allow us to draw several important conclusions. First, lesbians (and female bisexuals) are increasingly running for office and being elected, although a significant portion of the population is opposed to lesbian (and gay) candidates. Still, this portion of the public is unlikely to support Democrats (which is how most lesbians identify), and the result is that lesbians' electoral chances are not lowered when they are open about their sexual orientation.

Second, evidence from candidate interviews indicates that sexual orientation does not play a significant role in determining the outcome of primary or general elections when there is a lesbian candidate. Although some lesbian candidates reported attempts by an opponent or an outside group to use sexual orientation in a negative manner, none indicated that these efforts affected their electoral chances. Indeed, lesbian candidates were more likely to indicate that their sexual orientation worked to their benefit in the race by bringing in additional campaign funds and volunteer workers that were part of or sympathetic with the LGBT community. We do not wish to suggest that sexual orientation is a not factor in elections; instead, we infer that the evidence indicates that most lesbian candidates are able to avoid negative electoral consequences of their sexual orientation by being strategic about where and when they run for office and by being honest with voters about who they are without being single issue candidates.

Third, the evidence from case studies of lesbian descriptive representation suggests that lesbian officeholders effectively represent the interests of the LGBT community in the policy process, even if that representation does not always occur directly through sponsorship of legislation or being the most vocal advocate of policies that benefit the LGBT community. Likewise, on policy that the LGBT community opposes, we see significant evidence that lesbian officeholders play important roles in delaying and sometimes blocking these policy measures.

Finally, lesbian candidates and officeholders behave in manner similar to other politicians—they are strategic as candidates and in office, they advocate for their communities, but they are also advocates for the overall consistencies that they represent. In short, the imperatives of election and reelection focus the attention of lesbian candidates and officeholders in much the same way they do for any candidate or incumbent. Nevertheless, female LGBT candidates do appear to be cognizant of the role they play beyond that of the traditional challenger or incumbent; they tend to believe their role is that of politician, policymaker, but also role model and educator. Given the example provided by so many lesbian officeholders, we expect the number of lesbian candidates and officeholders will continue to grow.

## Notes

1. In this chapter we focus on elective office. We do note, however, that the number of appointed lesbians at the national and state level has increased dramatically as well. At the national level, President Bill Clinton was the first to appoint more than one or two LGBT officials (Smith and Haider-Markel 2002), and that trend was reinvigorated under President Barack Obama, who has appointed many openly lesbian officials, including Nitza Quinones Alejandro for U.S. District Court for the Eastern District of Pennsylvania in 2012. If approved by the Senate, Alejandro would be the first ever out lesbian Latina to serve as a federal judge.

2. There have been several female bisexual and transgender candidates and officeholders as well.

3. Based on 2012 data from the Center for Women in Politics: http://www.cawp.rutgers.edu/fast_facts/elections/election2012.php

4. When Baldwin is sworn in as senator in January 2013, she will have the largest constituency of any gay or lesbian official.

5. In 2012, 76 percent of lesbian, gay, and bisexual voters supported Obama (Cohen 2012; see also Egan 2012).

6. See Doan and Haider-Markel (2010) for more detailed analysis of the Scripps poll.

7. Discussion based on topline data from an unpublished Zogby America Nationwide Poll of Likely Voters between August 14, 2008, and August 16, 2008; topline is available from the lead author.

8. Discussion based on an internal campaign poll conducted by Public Policy Polling of 1,308 Likely Wisconsin Voters between August 16, 2012, and August 19, 2012.

9. Public Policy Polling graciously made the individual-level data available to us for this analysis.

10. The level of support for a gay or female presidential candidate has increased significantly over time. In 1978, 1983, 1999, and 2007, Gallup asked the following: If your party nominated a generally well-qualified person for president who happened to be a homosexual, would you vote for that person?" In 1978 only 26 percent of respondents said yes, in 1983 29 percent said yes, but by 1999 59 percent said they would vote for a homosexual candidate for president (Jones 2007). The 2012 survey (which used the term gay or lesbian rather than homosexual) saw the level of support increase to 68 percent (Jones 2012).

11. We also conducted a similar analysis of a May 25–30, 2011, Pew Research Center poll asking about voting for a gay or lesbian presidential candidate; the analysis does not differ significantly from the results presented here.

12. Similar to the previous analyses, in the statistical model we included variables to account for gender, age, city size for place of residence, race, education, partisanship, and religiosity.

13. Most of the analysis in this section relies on Haider-Markel (2010, chapter 2) and additional analysis of the data collected for that chapter.

14. Of the candidates that had reliable contact information, 38 provided completed the survey questionnaire. Although the response rate was 44 percent, the respondents were generally representative of the population of candidates.

15. The Hawaii Supreme Court had taken a similar step in 1993, but that decision was reversed through a constitutional amendment.

16. No other LGBT official served at the state level until 1993. In 1992 Althea Garrison (R-5) became the first transgendered person to be elected to a state legislature and appears to have been the first LGBT Republican elected to a state legislature. However, Garrison was not entirely open about being transgender and appears to have been outed in a Boston Globe article. Garrison did not have a notable term in the legislature and lost her seat to a Democrat in 1994 (Smith and Haider-Markel 2002).

# 16

# Trends in the Geography of Women in the U.S. State Legislatures

BARBARA NORRANDER AND CLYDE WILCOX

Between 1979 and 1993, the number of women in the 50 U.S. state legislatures doubled. The starting point was a low of 10 percent of legislative seats held by women; 14 years later, women occupied 20.5 percent of state legislative positions. Over the next two decades, women earned college degrees, started new businesses, and moved up the corporate ladder, though they continued to make less money and held fewer top corporate positions than men. Still, given a variety of improvements in the educational and professional status of women, it would not have been unreasonable to have expected that the number of women in state legislatures to continue to expand. After all, women are half of the U.S. population, and to reach parity with men they should hold half of the legislative posts. Yet the number of women in state legislatures did not double over the next two decades. In fact, by 2012 women had gained only 3.2 percentage points and occupied only 23.7 percent of the total seats across the 50 state legislatures.

Why the growth in female legislators has slowed is a perplexing question. Not only are women making advances in the economic sphere, but many of the barriers that prevented women from winning elections in earlier decades have lessened as well. Although as discussed in the introduction to this volume women running for office in earlier decades were less able to raise campaign funds than male candidates, by the 1990s female candidates were as successful as similarly situated men in raising funds (Burrell 1994). And although voters continue to hold stereotypes about women that may advantage, disadvantage, or have no effect on the success of female candidates depending on the major concerns in each election cycle (Dolan 2004b: 61–67; see also Chapter 3 in this volume), they no longer systematically discriminate against female candidates. Additionally, although not yet equal, in the past two decades media coverage of female candidates has improved in terms of the amount of coverage and the attention given to candidates' issue positions (Smith 1997). To be sure, instances of fundraising, voter, and media bias endure. Yet the overall playing field for female candidates has improved over the past two decades, while the number of female state legislators has increased only marginally.

This chapter investigates two main questions. First, we look at the trends in female state legislators across the 50 states. We note particular states where the growth in female legislatures has been the slowest in recent decades and even a few where the numbers have declined. Then we identify key factors that explain the changing number of female legislators across the 50 states over the past two decades. One additional avenue of inquiry explores the geography of women holding state legislative seats in 2011. We identify explanations for the variations in female representatives across the states and whether these factors hold equally for women who are Democrats or Republicans or occupy seats in the upper or lower houses of the state legislatures.

## The Slowing of Growth in Female State Legislators

The plateauing of women in state legislatures after the early 1990s is demonstrated in Figure 16.1. The trend line in the figure rises steadily until 1993, at which point the rate of increase slows for the remaining years. In every two-year election cycle between 1979 and 1993, women gained on average 1.38 percentage points more legislative posts. After 1993, the gain averaged a mere 0.38 percentage points per election year.[1] Figure 16.1 also demonstrates a drop in the percent of seats held by women after the 2010 elections. To date, the national average for the percentage of female state legislators has not broken the 25 percent barrier.

The rate of change in female state legislators, however, was not the same across all 50 states. Table 16.1 presents the percentage of female state legislators for all 50 states in 1981, 1993, and 2011 and lists the amount of change during the two time periods of 1981 to 1993 and 1993 to 2011. States are ordered by the percentage of female legislators in 1993, the pivot point in the national trend. Thus, Kentucky had the fewest female legislators in 1993, at only 4 percent. This was a decline since 1981, but more typical of the states in the lower third for 1993 was slow growth in female legislators in the previous decade. As revealed by the numbers at the bottom of the table, states that fell in the lowest third for percentage of female legislatures in 1993 (Kentucky through West Virginia) on average had only 12 percent of their legislative seats held by women in that year. These states previously saw only a slow growth of female legislators, averaging an increase of only 5 percentage points over 1981, when women in these states held an average of 7 percent of the legislative seats. Thus, a low starting point and slow growth during the earlier time period characterize the states in the bottom third of the country.

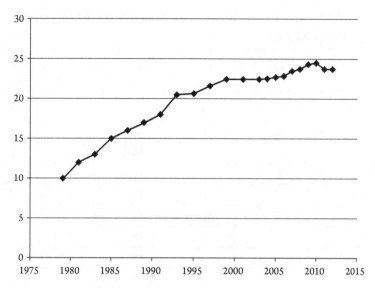

*Figure 16.1*  Percentage of State Legislative Seats Held by Women: 1979 to 2012
*Source:* "Women in Elective Office 2012," Center for American Women and Politics (CAWP), Eagleton
Institute of Politics, Rutgers University.

Many of the states in the lower third were southern or border states (including Kentucky, Alabama, Louisiana, and Oklahoma) or mid-Atlantic States (Pennsylvania and New Jersey). One explanation for this may be that southern women were slower than northern women in exercising their right to vote and had a lower level of participation continuing into the early 1970s (Cassel 1979). As such, a smaller number of female elected officials followed. On the other hand, the mid-Atlantic states often had traditional party organizations that were less open to recruiting female candidates (Sanbonmatsu 2002). This combination of more traditional patterns for participation and less open political parties kept the number of female legislators low in the states in these two regions up to the 1990s. But the numbers of female legislators continued to grow at a quicker pace in the subsequent two decades. Still, these states continued to have a lower percentage of female legislators in 2011 than the rest of the nation.

In contrast, states in the top third of the nation for female state legislative representation in 1993 (Hawaii through Washington) also had distinctive geographic patterns. Eight were western states that granted women the right to vote prior to the 19th Amendment, which granted the vote to all women in the United States. These western states also generally had weaker and more open political party structures, allowing for other avenues of political recruitment. Five of these states are characterized by a moralistic political culture (Wisconsin, Minnesota, Maine, Vermont, and Colorado) that encourages high levels of participation and is associated with more female legislators (Hill 1981; Norrander and Wilcox 1998). Other states in

*Table 16.1:* **Changes in Percent of State Legislatures Seats Held by Woman: 1981, 1993, and 2011**

| State | 1981 | 1993 | 2011 | Change 1981–1993 | Change 1993–2011 |
|---|---|---|---|---|---|
| Kentucky | 7 | 4 | 19 | −3 | 14 |
| Alabama | 4 | 5 | 14 | 1 | 9 |
| Louisiana | 1 | 8 | 16 | 6 | 8 |
| Oklahoma | 8 | 9 | 13 | 1 | 3 |
| Arkansas | 4 | 10 | 22 | 6 | 13 |
| Pennsylvania | 5 | 10 | 17 | 5 | 8 |
| Mississippi | 1 | 11 | 15 | 10 | 4 |
| Tennessee | 5 | 12 | 18 | 8 | 6 |
| Virginia | 6 | 12 | 19 | 6 | 7 |
| New Jersey | 7 | 13 | 28 | 6 | 16 |
| South Carolina | 6 | 13 | 9 | 6 | −4 |
| Utah | 8 | 13 | 17 | 6 | 4 |
| Delaware | 15 | 15 | 26 | 0 | 11 |
| Iowa | 12 | 15 | 21 | 3 | 7 |
| Texas | 7 | 16 | 21 | 9 | 5 |
| North Dakota | 12 | 16 | 15 | 4 | −1 |
| West Virginia | 12 | 16 | 18 | 4 | 1 |
| New York | 9 | 17 | 21 | 8 | 5 |
| Georgia | 7 | 17 | 24 | 10 | 6 |
| Florida | 11 | 18 | 26 | 7 | 8 |
| North Carolina | 13 | 18 | 22 | 5 | 4 |
| Missouri | 11 | 19 | 24 | 8 | 5 |
| Indiana | 8 | 19 | 21 | 11 | 2 |
| New Mexico | 6 | 20 | 27 | 13 | 7 |
| Montana | 11 | 20 | 24 | 9 | 4 |
| South Dakota | 10 | 20 | 20 | 10 | 0 |
| Michigan | 11 | 20 | 21 | 9 | 1 |
| Nebraska | 10 | 20 | 22 | 10 | 2 |
| Ohio | 8 | 21 | 23 | 14 | 2 |

| State | 1981 | 1993 | 2011 | Change 1981–1993 | Change 1993–2011 |
|-------|------|------|------|------------------|------------------|
| Alaska | 10 | 22 | 23 | 12 | 2 |
| Massachusetts | 10 | 23 | 25 | 14 | 2 |
| Illinois | 14 | 23 | 31 | 10 | 8 |
| California | 10 | 23 | 28 | 13 | 5 |
| Hawaii | 18 | 24 | 34 | 5 | 11 |
| Maryland | 15 | 24 | 31 | 9 | 7 |
| Wyoming | 18 | 24 | 14 | 6 | −10 |
| Rhode Island | 10 | 25 | 26 | 15 | 1 |
| Connecticut | 24 | 25 | 30 | 2 | 5 |
| Nevada | 12 | 27 | 29 | 15 | 2 |
| Wisconsin | 15 | 27 | 26 | 12 | −2 |
| Minnesota | 12 | 27 | 31 | 15 | 4 |
| Oregon | 22 | 28 | 28 | 6 | 0 |
| Kansas | 13 | 29 | 27 | 16 | −2 |
| Idaho | 10 | 30 | 28 | 21 | −3 |
| Maine | 23 | 32 | 29 | 9 | −3 |
| New Hampshire | 29 | 33 | 25 | 4 | −9 |
| Vermont | 22 | 34 | 38 | 12 | 4 |
| Colorado | 23 | 35 | 41 | 12 | 6 |
| Arizona | 19 | 36 | 34 | 17 | −1 |
| Washington | 24 | 39 | 32 | 16 | −7 |
| Bottom Third | 7 | 12 | 18 | 5 | 7 |
| Middle Third | 10 | 20 | 24 | 10 | 4 |
| Top Third | 18 | 29 | 30 | 11 | 0 |

*Source*: Center for American Women and Politics (CAWP), Eagleton Institute of Politics, Rutgers University, "Women in State Legislatures" Fact Sheets for 1981, 1993 and 2011.

this group are from New England, another traditional stronghold for female legislators in part because their legislatures are very large and have low pay and fewer staffers. These states were early leaders for female state legislative participation, and they had a strong growth rate of 11 percentage points between 1981 and 1993. Yet after 1993 this growth stopped, and in eight of these states the number of female state legislators fell.

The state of Washington, which for a number of years led the nation in female state legislators, had 7 percentage points fewer female legislators in 2011 than in 1993. Comments from female legislators and activists in Washington suggest that the reasons for this trend include lack of effective recruitment of female candidates, the low salary for state legislators making it difficult to support a family, and disproportionate family pressures on women, especially in the area of childcare (Rosenthal 2012). In addition, Kim Abel of the Washington League of Women Voters suggested that the increasing incivility of politics today is unattractive to potential female candidates. In Wisconsin, where the number of female state legislators fell by 2 percentage points, female activists and legislators mentioned similar concerns about family issues and perceptions that politics is a man's field (Forster 2009). In both states, opinions were expressed about the importance of increasing recruitment efforts aimed at female candidates.

In general, states with early gains in female state legislators found growth stalled by the late 1990s. In contrast, states with fewer female legislators in the 1980s experienced modest growth in both subsequent periods but still did not catch up to the level of female representatives in the top tier of states. States in the middle of the pack in 1993 had a high growth rate in the 1980s but continued at a more moderate rate in the post-1993 era. In general, the faster the growth rate of female state legislators in the 1980s, the slower the growth rate in the late 1990s and into the twenty-first century. By the 2010s, state legislatures with the most female members had the benchmark of one-third of these seats held by women within reach, but this goal remained elusive when growth rates stalled. States in the middle rank approached the 25 percent mark, and if a moderate growth rate continues it may lead them to surpass this range and match the numbers of women in the top tier of states. The final third of states had yet to reach the milepost of one in five (20 percent) state legislative seats being held by women, but a continuing growth rate could improve on these figures.

To uncover reasons for the slower growth in numbers of female state legislators after 1993, we look at a variety of politically relevant factors that changed during this time period, some of which may increase the proportions of women legislatures and some of which may decrease them. One of the obstacles to broader descriptive representation in all levels of political office in the United States is that most incumbents are men. In most electoral settings, incumbents easily win reelection, and this slows the amount of turnover in legislative bodies. Disgruntlement with the performance of government institutions in the late twentieth century led to the term-limit movement to force turnover in government posts. By the start of the twenty-first century, 15 states had instituted term limits for their state legislatures. Many scholars speculated that term limits would open up new seats for which women could compete on an even par (Reed and Schansberg 1995; Thompson and Moncrief 1993). Yet term limits could also push out women already holding seats in state legislatures. Lawless and Fox (2005; see also Chapter 2 of this volume) demonstrate that many qualified women do not think of themselves as political candidates. Thus, term limits could have a negative effect on the number of female state legislators if female incumbents cast out by term limits are not replaced by a new crop of female representatives.

Multimember districts (multiple representatives elected from one geographic unit) have been consistently demonstrated to be associated with higher numbers of female state legislators (Arceneaux 2001; Carroll 1994; Hogan 2001; King 2002; Matland and Brown 1992). Darcy, Welch, and Clark (1994) argue that parties and voters in multimember districts use this opportunity to seek representational balance by sex. Today, most U.S. state legislative districts are single-member districts. Only one person is elected from each geographically determined electoral district. During the first half of the twentieth century, half to three-quarters of the state legislatures employed multimember districts (Niemi, Hill, and Grofman 1985). The number of multimember districts began to decline in the mid-twentieth century: the number of multimember districts continued to decline in the 1990s, dropping from 13 to 10 states in 2013 (Kurtz 2012; National Conference of State Legislatures 1999).

The strength of the Republican Party in state legislatures has also grown over the past two decades. In 1993, Republicans controlled 41 percent of the legislative seats across 49 state legislatures (Nebraska has a nonpartisan unicameral legislature). In 2011, the Republican Party held 53 percent of the state legislative seats.[2] Of course, the rate of change was not the same across all states. In 11 states, Republicans lost seats, with the largest decline in New Jersey. The largest growth in Republican legislators is found in the southern states, where the Republican realignment unfolded slowly from presidential elections (in the 1960s–1970s) to congressional seats (in the 1990s) and finally to the state legislative level. Even as late as 1993, Republicans held a third or less of the seats in the state legislatures of Alabama, Georgia, Louisiana, Mississippi, North Carolina, and Oklahoma. By 2011, Republicans held the majority of seats in these southern legislatures. The Republican Party made gains in other parts of the country as well, such as the Midwest and the Rocky Mountain states. This growth in Republican Party strength may matter for the numbers of female state legislators because, in recent decades, more women have been elected from the Democratic Party.

As was demonstrated in Table 16.1, the growth in female legislators between 1993 and 2011 was most pronounced in southern states that have a traditional political culture. Elazar (1984) classifies the political traditions in the U.S. states as traditionalistic, individualistic, and moralistic.[3] Moralistic political cultures, found in many of the northern states, emphasize participation and in the past have been the most accepting of female candidates. Individualistic political cultures characterize many of the mid-Atlantic and Midwestern states. These states view politics in terms of personal gains, are dominated by social and economic elites, and feature traditional political party organizations that were reluctant to endorse female candidates. However, the traditional political culture appears to be changing and becoming more accepting of female candidates. In fact, Louisiana, North Carolina, Oklahoma, and South Carolina have all elected female governors in the past decade.

A final factor to consider in explaining changes in the number of female state legislators is the changing role of women in society. As more women gain economic and educational resources, the number of women available to run for elective office could increase. A basic indicator of these changing resources for women is the increase in the number of women earning college degrees.[4] In the 1990s, 17.6 percent of women had earned a college degree, which was double the number holding such degrees in 1970, when the proportion was 8.1 percent. The number of women earning college degrees continued to grow, and in 2007–2009 27.2 percent of women versus 28.4 percent of men possessed a bachelor's degree.

To access the influence of these five factors on the slow rate of change in the number of female state legislators between 1993 and 2011, a statistical technique, ordinary least squares regression equation, was used.[5] The model to assess the percentage of upper- and lower-state legislative seats held by women includes 47 of the 50 states. Alaska and Hawaii are excluded because they lack a reliable measure of political culture, and Nebraska is excluded because it has a nonpartisan, unicameral legislature. In addition to the previously introduced factors, a variable measuring the percentage of state legislative seats held by women in 1993 is included in the model. Table 16.2 presents the results of the regression model.

The results in Table 16.2 indicate that the most important explanation for the slow rate of growth for female state legislators between 1993 and 2011 was the change in the political party composition of the legislatures. As signified by the size of the standardized coefficient for this variable, the changing strength of the Republican Party is most strongly related to the changing number of female legislators. In states where the Republican Party gained the most seats, the number of total legislative seats held by women decreased. Since more women have been elected as Democrats in recent decades, when the fortunes of the Democratic Party decline in particular states the growth in the number of female legislators declines as well.

In contrast, the standardized coefficient for the traditional political culture variable indicates a moderate influence on the changing patterns of female representation. Despite a growth of Republican Party strengths in these traditional political culture states, female candidates are becoming more successful. Thus, women can make gains as Republican candidates, but recruitment efforts must be made across both parties to sustain a continued growth in female state legislators across all 50 states.

The final two factors in the model had moderate influences on increasing the number of female state legislators across the nation over the past two decades. States that imposed term limits on their legislators saw a faster growth in female members. States where women increased their educational attainment also had larger increases in the number of female legislators.

*Table 16.2* **Explaining Changes in Percentage of Females in Combined Upper and Lower Houses of State Legislatures, 1993–2011**

| Variable | Unstandardized Coefficient | Standard Error | Level of Statistical Significance | Standardized Coefficient |
|---|---|---|---|---|
| Female legislators in 1993 | .53 | .08 | .00 | .67 |
| Term limits | 2.67 | 1.23 | .04 | .19 |
| Dropped multimember districts | 1.75 | 2.20 | .43 | .06 |
| Change in percent Republican legislators | −.18 | .05 | .00 | −.40 |
| Traditional political culture | 4.34 | 2.00 | .04 | .26 |
| Change in female college graduates | .82 | .37 | .03 | .22 |
| Constant | 5.52 | 3.99 | .17 | |
| $R^2$ | .75 | | .00 | |

*Notes:* $N = 47$. The statistical procedure is ordinary least squares (OLS) regression. Missing states are Alaska and Hawaii, which do not have political culture scores, and Nebraska, which has a nonpartisan legislature.

## Continuing Patterns of Cross-State Variation in Female State Legislators: Considering Party and Legislative Chamber

Most previous research on women in state legislatures examined patterns of representation by combining members from the lower and upper houses, just as we did in the preceding analysis of changing rates of representation. Yet the lower house is often a first step for those with political ambition, with progression to the upper house as a subsequent career move. This could be true especially in term-limit states, where an individual term limited out of the lower chamber may run for a seat in the upper chamber. The chambers houses of state legislatures also are typically smaller, perhaps making races for these elective seats more difficult to win. Historically, women have been more prevalent in the lower houses of state legislatures. For example, in 1981, women held twice as many seats in lower chambers (13.5 percent compared with 7.3 percent of the upper chambers), and in 1993 there was a difference of 4 percentage points (21.6 percent in the lower and 17.5 in the upper chambers). Today, however, the differences are not as sizeable. In 2011, women occupied 24.5 percent of the lower chamber seats and 22.3 percent of upper chamber seats. Still, any differences in factors that explain the level of female representatives in the upper versus lower chambers of the state legislatures may be important nuances to our understanding of where women win elective office.

Earlier research on women in state legislatures also tended to ignore party, clumping together Democratic, Republican, and nonpartisan women into one group. Research by Sanbonmatsu (2002), however, revealed that different models are necessary to understand the election of Democratic versus Republican women. She found that most of the variables used to explain the election of women to state legislatures fit for Democratic women but proved less able to explain the success of Republican women. Thus, a full explanation of the geographic variations in women elected to state legislatures needs to consider both political party and legislative chambers.

Here we present evidence explaining the percent of legislative seats held by women in four groups: Democratic women in lower chambers; Republican women in lower chambers; Democratic women in upper chambers; and Republican women in upper chambers. The largest contingent of female state legislators is Democratic women in the lower chambers: they occupied, on average, 14.9 percent of the lower chamber seats in 2011. The fewest Democratic women were found in North Dakota (3.2 percent), a heavily Republican state, while the highest numbers were present in Vermont, at 28.7 percent. Democratic women controlled almost as many of the upper chamber seats, with an average of 14.3 percent. Three states had no female Democrats in their upper chamber (South Carolina, Wyoming, and West Virginia), with Colorado leading the way with 40 percent of the seats in its upper chamber being held by women. Republican women were slightly more prevalent in the lower chambers, averaging 9.5 percent of the seats. Interestingly, the highest and lowest numbers were found in two adjacent states: the highest percentage of lower chamber seats held by Republican women was in Arizona, at 21.7 percent of the seats, while the lowest numbers were in Nevada, at 2.4 percent. (Nevada has a high percentage of Democratic women in it lower chamber, at 26.2 percent.) On average, Republican women occupied 8 percent of the seats in the upper chambers of state legislatures, with the highest proportions occurring in Arizona and Kansas (20 percent). Four states had no Republican women in their upper chambers: South Carolina, Alabama, Massachusetts, and Hawaii.

We begin our explanation of women's representation among the four groups of state legislators by using variables from our previous model on trends, this time using their values for 2011: term limits; multimember districts; traditional and moralistic political cultures; and female college graduates. Then we added to this list as follows: to represent the political orientations of each state, we used a measure of the partisanship and ideology of voters. These measures are based on the pooled 2004 and 2008 general election exit polls and were recoded so that higher values indicate Republican or conservative leanings.[6] We also used a measure of state legislative professionalism because previous research indicates that women are less likely to be elected to state legislatures that are categorized as more professional, where the legislature meets for longer periods of time, legislative pay is higher, and legislators have more staff to assist them (Rule 1981; Squire 1992, 2007). Because female candidates may perceive that fundraising will be more difficult, we added a measure of the average dollars spent by winning candidates in 2008 (Evilsizer 2010) and whether a state assisted with fundraising by providing a system of public financing (Quist 2010). To retest Sanbonmatsu's (2002) findings about the negative effects of traditional party structures on the election of female representatives, we used a classification of party structures (Mayhew 1986). Finally, to consider the possibility that Republican women have been recruited through the Christian Right movement, we used a measure of the influence of the Christian Right on the states' Republican parties (Conger 2010).

Table 16.3 presents results of the four models using ordinary least squares regression statistical methods. The first value in each cell is the unstandardized regression coefficients, which can be compared across all four models to judge the comparative influence of each variable on the proportions of women present. The second value in each cell is the level of statistical significance for the regression coefficient. These significance levels are repeated in the use of asterisks attached to the unstandardized coefficients to indicate levels of statistical significance. The third value in each cell, listed within the brackets, is the standardized coefficient. These standardized coefficients can be used within a single equation to judge which variables have the most influence on the proportion of women in state legislatures.

The results indicate that five of the variables had insignificant effects in all four models, so we dropped them from the analysis (state voter ideology, moralistic political culture, average dollar spent to win elections, traditional party structure, and role of Christian Right in state Republican parties). This left us with seven variables in our models that show differences in explanations across parties and across the two chambers.

First, the $R^2$ values for the two Democratic models indicate that about half of the cross-state variation in the election of Democratic women can be explained by the independent variables included in the models. Then the individual effects of each variables show first that more continuity in these models exists within party rather than by legislative chamber. Thus, for the election of Democratic women to either the upper or lower chambers of state legislatures, higher percentages were found in states with more highly educated female populations. Thus, the pool of

*Table 16.3* **Explaining Percentage of Seats Held by Democratic and Republican Women in the Lower and Upper Houses of the State Legislatures in 2011**

| Variable | Democratic WomenLower House | Democratic WomenUpper House | Republican WomenLower House | Republican WomenUpper House |
|---|---|---|---|---|
| Term limits | .40 | 4.51** | 1.54 | .60 |
| | (.80) | (.03) | (.13) | (.71) |
| | [.03] | [.26] | [.18] | [.05] |
| Multimember districts | −1.27 | −1.07 | 3.36*** | 3.33* |
| | (.46) | (.63) | (.00) | (.07) |
| | [−.09] | [−.06] | [.35] | [.26] |
| Public partisanship | −22.14*** | −9.11 | 17.08*** | 14.08** |
| | (.00) | (.24) | (.00) | (.03) |
| | [−.49] | [−.15] | [.57] | [.35] |
| Traditional political culture | −3.04 | 1.50 | −.53 | −3.78* |
| | (.13) | (.56) | (.68) | (.07) |
| | [−.20] | [.07] | [−.05] | [−.28] |
| Women college graduates | .41** | 1.19*** | .06 | −.32* |
| | (.03) | (.00) | (.60) | (.09) |
| | [.32] | [.71] | [.07] | [−.28] |
| Professional legislature | .02 | −.02 | −.05 | −.12** |
| | (.67) | (.80) | (.16) | (.05) |
| | [.06] | [−.03] | [−.19] | [−.32] |
| Public funding | 1.11 | −1.15 | 4.28*** | 3.37 |
| | (.67) | (.73) | (.01) | (.21) |
| | [.05] | [−.04] | [.29] | [.17] |
| Constant | 3.92 | −18.49*** | 7.94** | 19.43*** |
| | (.48) | (.01) | (.03) | (.00) |
| $R^2$ | .52*** | .55*** | .55*** | .36*** |
| | (.00) | (.00) | (.00) | (.01) |

*Notes:* $N = 47$. The statistical procedure is ordinary least squares (OLS) regression. The first value in each cell is the unstandardized coefficient. The second value, within parentheses, is the level of statistical significance. The third value, inside the brackets, is the standardized regression coefficients. Missing states are Alaska and Hawaii, which do not have political culture scores, and Nebraska, which has a nonpartisan legislature.

* $p \leq .10$; ** $p \leq .05$; *** $p \leq .01$.

potential female candidates matters for the election of Democratic women. This is not true for Republican women, however. In fact, the variable had a negative coefficient for Republican women serving in the upper house model. Thus, the recruitment of Republican women is not well explained by these models, as the pool of potential candidates is insignificant or in the wrong direction, and the influence of the Christian Right in the Republican Party was insignificant.

The models also show that Democratic women are most likely to be elected to lower chambers of state legislatures from more heavily Democratic states. For movement into the upper chambers, it is term limits that seem to drive the election of Democratic women. Perhaps Democratic women from the lower chambers move on to the upper houses as their terms in the lower house expire. This could, however, have unfortunate longer-term consequences if more women are not first elected to the lower houses in these term-limit states.

The pathway to election for Republican women is more varied. The election of Republican women to both the lower and upper chambers is enhanced by the presence of multimember districts. In addition, as to be expected, Republican women are elected from more heavily Republican states. Public financing of candidates appears to be solely beneficial to Republican women running for the lower chambers of the state legislatures. Meanwhile, the movement of Republican women into state senates is hampered by the traditional political culture of many southern states and by professional state legislatures. Our variables are least able to explain the cross-state variation in female Republicans in the upper houses, as the $R^2$ is.36, meaning that the model explains only about one-third of the variation in women in state legislatures.

In sum, separating the analysis of the cross-state variations in women in state legislatures into four subgroups lends some additional information to our understanding of electoral processes leading to the election of women to these important government posts. Like Sanbonmatsu (2002), we found that party matters. On the Democratic side, the pool of potential female candidates, as measured by their educational status, is significant. Multimember districts only enhance the electoral prospects of Republican women. And only the measure of public partisanship has cross-party influence, though it was not significant for Democratic women in the upper chambers. In addition, explanatory factors do vary across the lower and upper houses of the state legislature. Term limits facilitate the election of Democratic women to the upper but not the lower chambers of the state legislatures. The movement of Republican women into the upper chambers appears to be the most difficult, as the presence of either a traditional political culture or a professional legislature diminishes the number of women serving in these legislative bodies.

# Conclusions

State legislatures are important in shaping public policies that affect our daily lives. They are the primary venues for setting educational, criminal justice, tax, morality policies, and many others in the United States. State legislatures also determine how joint federal and state programs will be implemented, setting benefits and eligibility requirements for such programs as welfare (e.g., Temporary Assistance for Needy Families), unemployment compensation, and Medicaid, which provides medical insurance to needy citizens. Women in state legislatures have an important role in shaping these policies. Indeed, studies have shown that female members influence the policymaking outcomes and decision-making processes of state legislatures as outlined in the introduction to this volume (Berkman and O'Connor 1993; Epstein, Niemi, and Powell 2005; Medoff 2002; Norrander and Wilcox 1999; Thomas 1994).

Beyond their policy activities, the presence of women in state legislatures matters for the political aspirations of a state's citizens and political candidates. More female representatives enhance the descriptive representation of the state legislatures, such that the membership of these legislative bodies more closely matches the characteristics and backgrounds of the general population. Greater descriptive representation enhances the legitimacy of these state legislatures (Mansbridge 1999). In addition, when more women hold elective offices in a state, the political participation of women in the state increases (Burns, Schlozman, and Verba 2001). State legislatures also can be an important component of a woman's political career. For some women, serving in the state legislature is their career goal because they want to influence the important policies determined at the state level. For other women, the state legislature may be part of a career path that will lead them to statewide or national offices, possibly including the presidency and vice presidency of the United States. For all these reasons, processes that enhance or limit women's access to posts in the state legislatures matter.

Our research contributes to the understanding of the election of women to state legislative seats by noting both national trends and current factors associated with the cross-state variations in the numbers of female legislators. The slowing of the growth in the number of female state legislators in the past two decades underscores the importance of continuing recruitment efforts to encourage more women to run for public office. These recruitment efforts need to be in place for states with histories of fewer female representations to allow these states to continue their growth trends and possibly to catch up to the other states. Recruitment efforts, however, also must be present for states with a history of higher levels of female representatives. As the breakdown of the trend patterns revealed, it is in these states where the growth in female representatives has stalled or in some cases has been reversed. Recruitment efforts also need to occur across both parties. State legislatures are filled by Democrats and Republicans, and the fates of these two parties ebb and flow across time. For a continued, and growing, presence of women in state legislatures, women must be successful candidates across both parties.

## Notes

1. These values are based on ordinary least squares (OLS) regression equations modeling percent of state legislative seats held by women by year and doubling the regression coefficients by two to represent the two-year election cycle. The equation for the 1979–1993 period is $Y = -1362.01 + .69$ (year), with an $R^2$ value of .98, while the equation for the 1993–2012 period is $Y = -361.28 + .19$ (year), with an $R^2$ value of .88. All values are statistically significant at the .01 level.
2. The number of state legislative seats held by Republicans came from the *Statistical Abstract of the United States* from 1981, 1992, and 2012.
3. States are coded for political culture in three separate variables. For each variable, a scale gives the level of presence of a particular political culture. For example, for the moralistic political culture variable, states that are fully classified as moralistic are scored as 1, those that have a mixed political culture where the moralistic component is dominant are scored as .6, mixed political cultures with the moralistic component as secondary are coded as .3, and states with no aspect of a moralistic political culture are scored as 0.
4. Women with a college degree in the states came from U.S. Census Bureau. "A Half-Century of Learning: Historical Census Statistics on Educational Attainment in the United States, 1940 to 2000: Detailed Tables." http://www.census.gov/hhes/socdemo/education/data/census/half-century/tables.html, (accessed March 5, 2013); Digest of Education Statistics. 2011. "Table 13." http://nces.ed.gov/programs/digest/d11/tables/dt11_013.asp (accessed March 5, 2013).
5. The dependent variable is the percentage of upper and lower chamber state legislative seats held by women in each state.
6. The exit polls provide for three answers for ideology (liberal, moderate, conservative) and three categories for partisanship (Democrat, Independent, Republican). For more information on methodology used see Norrander and Manzano (2010).

# 17

# Women in Elective Office
# Worldwide: Barriers and Opportunities

PIPPA NORRIS AND MONA LENA KROOK

In the early twenty-first century, the goal of achieving gender equality in worldwide politics continues to remain elusive. Today women cast voting ballots in equal, or even greater, numbers than men (Coffe and Bolzendahl 2010; Inglehart and Norris 2003). Yet women continue to lag behind men as party members and campaign activists; as candidates running for legislative office; as elected members and leaders of local councils, regional assemblies, national parliaments, and the European Parliament; as members of the judiciary and top civil service; and in the highest positions as cabinet ministers and heads of government and state. For example, the 2012 American elections saw a modest improvement in the proportion of women elected to the House of Representatives (17.7%) and the U.S. Senate (20%), but this still left the House of Representatives below the world average, ranking eighty-second worldwide. In late 2012, women were one in five parliamentarians worldwide (IPU 2012). This situation persists despite the fact that equal rights for women, including rights to citizenship and suffrage, are guaranteed in the constitutions of all modern democracies (Towns 2010). The world's governments have explicitly committed themselves to eliminating sex discrimination and achieving gender equality in public office as part of the U.N. Millennium Development Goals, the global development targets that were agreed by the United Nations to be achieved by 2015. When women are the majority of the electorate and few of the elected leaders, the disparity between theory and practice raises fundamental problems of social justice. It also has negative effects on future generations, as ongoing imbalances in equal opportunities can affect the prospects for social and economic development in the longer term.

Beyond these principled reasons, evidence also suggests that incorporating women provides tangible benefits for political parties and legislatures. On one hand, women are the majority of voters in every country, since women tend to live longer than men. In many countries, women are also more likely than men to turn out to vote—with the result that women can deliver the margin of victory for successful parties and candidates. Thus, parties cannot afford to ignore female voters. Growing numbers of parties around the world have recognized this and have found that nominating more female candidates can be one way to attract women's votes, such as in the United Kingdom, Belgium, and Germany (Davidson-Schmich 2006; Kittilson 2006).

Once elected, women can strengthen parties in important ways (Freedman 2002; Lovenduski and Norris 1993). Female members of parliament (MP), for example, have been found to be more loyal to the party in their legislative work, straying less than men in voting along party lines, for example, in countries as diverse as Turkey and the United Kingdom (Ayata and Tütüncü 2008; Cowley and Childs 2003). This facilitates coordination by the party in terms of policy outcomes. In the United States, the United Kingdom, and France, women have also been found to be more effective than men in their legislative work, attending more sessions, proposing more bills, and meeting more often with their constituents (Anzia and Berry 2011; Chaney 2006). These activities can heighten public trust in parliament, an effect bolstered by the tendency of voters to view women as more honest and less corrupt.

Thus, political parties across the world have important reasons—both normative and pragmatic—for promoting greater gender equality in politics. Many cases help to identify what practical strategies work most effectively to expand opportunities for women's empowerment in the political sphere. Recognizing the central role of political parties in this process, we can focus in particular on gender equality strategies that might be undertaken by political parties to enhance women's political representation.

To consider these issues, this chapter outlines the reasons that gender equality is widely recognized as an important challenge and summarizes the situation worldwide, including global trends. We then consider four sets of factors that serve as the core barriers facing women in elected office. In each case, we outline initiatives that may be pursued to overcome these barriers and thereby expand equal opportunities.

Understood as a sequential model, we can identify several stages for potential interventions to empower women in politics, highlighting the role of constitutional rights, electoral systems and party laws, legal quotas, internal party rules and procedures, capacity development initiatives, and gender-sensitive rules and procedures in parliament that could facilitate women's inclusion into political office (see Figure 17.1). The most effective type of intervention depends on the specific opportunity structure within each context.

Most policy attention has focused on what political parties can do to strengthen gender equality in public office—the middle steps in this process—through expanding the capacity of women to run for office and reforming internal rules and procedures governing candidate selection. This focus recognizes that, while

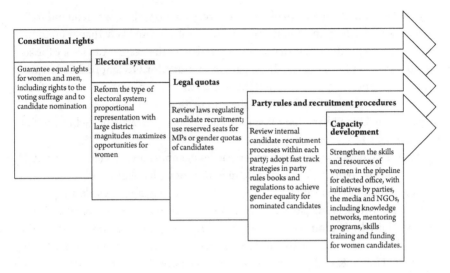

*Figure 17.1* Six-Step Action Plan

independents do run for office, political parties play a central role in nominating the majority of elected officials. In addition, political parties function as one of the main mechanisms linking citizens and the state in any society. This suggests that working with political parties may be the most effective way to empower women politically.

A new global norm has emerged endorsing electoral gender quotas—for example, reserved seats and legal quotas—as a means for strengthening gender equality in politics (Dahlerup 2006; Krook 2009; Towns 2010). Yet many countries are reluctant to pass such measures, for example, due to their association with now discredited Communist regimes in Central and Eastern Europe or liberal cultural traditions, as in the United States (LaFont 2001). However, even if conditions are unfavorable for legal quotas, individual parties can still take effective actions to expand equal opportunities in the internal rules and procedures used when nominating candidates for elected office (Lovenduski and Norris 1993; Kittilson 2006).

Other actors can also complement the role of political parties when strengthening gender equality in elected office. These include electoral management bodies, equal opportunity agencies and ministries, legislative bodies, and the news media and civic society organizations.

The *opportunity structure* facing candidates for elected office is set by constitutional rights, regime institutions, and legal frameworks. These include types of regimes (e.g., democratic or electoral autocracies) and levels of democratization, structures of electoral contests and electoral systems (e.g., single-member plurality or party list), laws regulating candidate nomination and party ballot access, the existence of reserved seats and legal candidate quotas, the nature of party competition, rules concerning campaign funding, and constitutional requirements of gender equality.

The *demands of gatekeepers* arise when parties select candidates from among the pool of eligible nominees. This includes the criteria, rules, and procedures used for choosing candidates by party leaders, party members, voters, and nonpartisan officials.

The *supply of candidates* concerns those willing to pursue a political career. The focus here is on the attitudes and motivations, experiences shaping perceived qualifications, and capacities and resources of and men in the pipeline to becoming nominated.

Last, *civil society* can take actions to promote gender equality in political office. These strategies include media campaigns, fundraising initiatives, capacity development strategies, knowledge networks, and gender audit monitoring.

The conclusion summarizes the core findings and the implications for women's representation in the United States.

## The Challenge of Gender Equality in Elected Office

The proportion of seats held by women in national parliaments is a common yardstick used to judge broader progress toward gender equality in public life—as well as political empowerment more generally.

The Universal Declaration of Human Rights, adopted in 1948, enshrines "the equal rights of men and women," including the right to participate in government.[1] These commitments were further amplified in the 1979 United Nations (UN) Convention on the Elimination of All Forms of Discrimination against Women (CEDAW), endorsed by 189 UN member states, although not the United States.[2] The 1995 UN Beijing Platform of Action went further by legitimizing the use of positive action, pledging member states to "take measures to ensure women's equal access to and full participation in power structures and decision-making."[3]

Five years later, the world's governments at the 2000 Millennium Declaration resolved "to promote gender equality and the empowerment of women as effective ways to combat poverty, hunger and disease and to stimulate development that is truly sustainable." This indicator has been adopted to monitor how far the world's government will have achieved the 2015 targets set by the Millennium Development Goals. UN Security Council Resolution 1325, also passed in 2000, reaffirms the importance of women's "equal participation and full involvement in all efforts for the maintenance and promotion of peace and security." As signatories to these various international conventions, *governments have committed themselves to achieving equal rights for women and men, including in decision-making positions.*

Beyond human rights, a common expectation is that female politicians will do politics differently than men—primarily in terms of promoting "women's issues" in the policymaking process. Although women in politics contribute to legislation in all areas, including those conventionally defined as "women's issues," substantial evidence suggests that the inclusion of women's voices—especially when addressing complex challenges—broadens the range of diverse experiences, interests, and expertise brought into parliamentary debates (Mansbridge 1999; Phillips 1995). Electing women from different backgrounds and political parties can further enhance these positive effects by allowing women's diverse viewpoints to be heard in discussions over public policy.

A considerable body of research does show that women in politics also *bring vital attention to issues that disproportionately affect women* (Childs 2004; Swers 2002; Thomas 1994). There remain many major challenges in achieving gender equality in education and the labor market; in social policies, health care, and reproductive rights; as well as in the home and care of dependents (Van Der Lippe and Fodor 1998). Women also have particularly serious problems arising from domestic violence, sexual harassment, sex trafficking, and economic restructuring, for example in post-Communist states (Avdeyeva 2007; Hardy, Kozek, and Stenning 2008; Johnson 2007). If women are absent from—or constitute only a small minority of—elected assemblies, important issues such as these are not likely to be prioritized or addressed, with negative implications for the broader society.

## Global Trends

In late 2012, women were 20.3 percent of parliamentarians worldwide.[4] Gender equality has certainly advanced according to this benchmark: women held only 11.3 percent of seats in the single or lower chamber of national parliaments in 1995. Yet the rate of incremental progress for women has often been slow, and states have experienced significant retreats as well as advances (Matland and Montgomery 2003; Saxonberg 2000). Worldwide, only two dozen countries have achieved the 30 percent target for women in decision-making positions set by the 1995 Beijing Platform. A few exceptional parliaments have approached equality, nearly all in the Nordic region, but several others continue to include no female representatives at all, including in the Middle East/North Africa and the Pacific. Women are even rarer in climbing the slippery rungs to the top decision-making posts as elected ministers and heads of state or government: today there are only 7 women presidents and 10 women prime ministers (Jalalzai 2004, 2008).

## Explanations and Remedies

What accounts for the remarkable cross-national contrasts in gender inequalities in elected office? What is to be done? There are various stages for potential reform, including the structure of opportunities set by constitutional rights, electoral systems and party laws, and legal quotas. No single one-size-fits-all solution is suitable for all national contexts. Instead, the most effective strategies for achieving gender equality in elected and appointed office depend on specific social, cultural, institutional, and political conditions.

## Constitutions

Many attempts to explain these patterns have focused on political institutions. There is robust evidence indicating that formal institutions matter. At the same time, these "rules of the game" are also open to effective policy interventions and reform. Constitutions have traditionally been considered relatively fixed and determined by technocratic elites, such as constitutional lawyers. Modern perspectives regard constitutions as more dynamic and flexible, engaging multiple actors in deliberative debates.

Constitutional designs determine the basic institutional arrangements in any regime, such as the provision of presidential, prime ministerial, or mixed executives—or the adoption of federal versus unitary state structures. These can have indirect effects that affect men and women differently (Irving 2008). Through these arrangements, biases can be built into core political institutions in ways that serve to empower some groups over others.

More fundamentally, however, constitutions can include provisions that directly affect women's civil rights, including rights to vote and to hold public office irrespective of sex. They may also influence women's daily lives by establishing laws preventing discrimination against women, such as those related to the family and children, property and inheritance, citizenship qualifications, and equality in marriage. As the new Egyptian constitution reveals, there are also many other aspects where women's rights remain restricted to those compatible with the "rules" of Islamic jurisprudence.

Reflecting the Universal Declaration of Human Rights, nearly all states now grant women full citizenship on equal terms to men, with the right to stand for elected office and to cast a ballot. Nevertheless, there remain some glaring exceptions, notable Saudi Arabia, and some reforms have occurred relatively recently: women attained the full voting franchise on the same basis as men only in 1971 in Switzerland, in 1976 in Portugal, and in 1994 in Kazakhstan and Moldova.

Going well beyond provisions establishing equal civil rights for women and men as citizens, a dozen states worldwide have now enshrined gender quotas for the lower or upper houses of parliament into national constitutions or Basic Laws. The remarkable effect of these provisions can be illustrated by the positive action clauses in the Afghan constitution, which were implemented in the new electoral law passed in 2005. This requires that the parliament set aside seats for at least 68 women of 249 members (27 percent) in the lower house of parliament (the Wolesi Jirga). Despite a highly traditional culture in attitudes toward girls and women and an atmosphere of violence and intimidation during the recent elections to the Wolesi Jirga in 2005 and 2010, many female candidates ran for office and many were also successfully elected. Hence, in 2010, women constituted 28 percent of the lower house (Norris 2007).

## Electoral Systems

*Electoral systems* as a concept concern multiple aspects of electoral law. The most basic features involve the *ballot structure*, determining how voters can express their choices; the *electoral threshold*, or the minimum votes needed by a party to secure representation; the *electoral formula*, determining how votes are counted to allocate seats; and the *district magnitude*, referring to the number of seats per district.

Electoral systems are categorized in this study into three primary families—majoritarian, combined, and proportional—each with many subsidiary types.[5]

The idea that electoral systems per se matter for women's political representation has been confirmed by a long series of studies since the mid-1980s, finding that more women are usually elected to parliament under party list proportional representation (PR) systems than under majoritarian electoral systems. This pattern has been established in research comparing both established democracies and also confirmed in a broader range of developing societies worldwide (Kenworthy and Malami 1999; Lijphart 1994; Matland 1998; Norris 1985; Reynolds 1999; Rule 1987, 1988; Siaroff 2000). The proportion of women elected under mixed or combined systems usually falls somewhere between pure majoritarian and PR systems, with women elected disproportionately from the party list ballot (Moser 2001). Within PR electoral systems, district magnitude has commonly been regarded as a particularly important factor, with more women usually elected from larger rather than smaller multimember constituencies.

The main reason usually put forward to explain the greater success of women under PR is that in this system each party presents the public with its collective list of candidates for each multimember district. As such, parties have an *electoral incentive* to maximize their collective appeal in party lists by including candidates drawn from all major social cleavages in the electorate. Multimember districts encourage collective party accountability for the complete list of candidates. Where parties have to nominate a slate of candidates for a multimember district, the exclusion of any major social sector, including women, could signal discrimination and could therefore risk an electoral penalty at the ballot box.

By contrast, in first-past-the-post systems parliamentary candidates are selected to run within each single-member district. Where the selection process is in the hands of the local constituency party, this creates minimal incentive for each particular constituency to pick a ticket that is "balanced" at the district or national level. Local party members in Britain often want a representative who they think will maximize their chances of winning in that constituency, irrespective of the broader consequences for the party or parliament (Norris and Lovenduski 1995). A common default strategy, designed to minimize electoral risks, is to select a candidate reflecting the characteristics and qualifications of previous MPs—usually male—even though research has shown that this may not be the optimal election strategy, with female candidates often winning at similar or greater rates than men (Black and Erickson 2003; Brians 2005; Mily and Schosberg 2000; Murray 2008).

Electoral systems also shape *patterns of incumbency turnover* and affect how many "winnable seats" may be available to a political party in any given election. One major barrier to the entry of new candidates in established democracies is that elected officials are often returned over successive contests due to the advantages of greater familiarity and name recognition, higher levels of media attention, as well as access to the financial and organizational resources that accompany legislative office (Schwindt-Bayer 2005; Somit et al. 1994). A comparison of elections to national parliaments in 25 established democracies from 1979 to 1994 found that on average about two-thirds of all incumbents were returned from one general election to the next, including 66 percent in PR systems and 70 percent in majoritarian elections (Matland and Studlar 2004).

A key challenge facing women is thus not only being nominated but also in being placed in a seat or position that will result in election. In PR systems, this requires being ranked near the top of the party list of candidates, whereas in majoritarian systems it entails nomination in a district that is considered a "safe seat" for the party. While electoral volatility in many multiparty newer democracies has reduced the incumbency advantage, women do not appear to have benefited, largely due to the need to be nominated to a winnable slot.

An example of the effectiveness of these two factors combined can be seen in Britain, where the massive turnover in MPs following the Labour Party's landslide victory in 1997, coupled with the use of positive action placing women in target seats, doubled the number of women in the U.K. House of Commons overnight. As incumbents, Labour women MPs were then reelected in the 2001 British general election, despite the fact that by then the original positive action strategy had been discontinued. Evidence from the United States suggests that term limits on their own are insufficient: whereas from 1998 to 2000 female challengers were more successful in states where term limitations expanded the opportunities for open seats, the effect was reversed in California, where many women were incumbents (Carroll and Jenkins 2001; Caress 1999).

Finally, electoral systems shape the prospects for *using positive action* in candidate selection, with the proportional logic of PR facilitating the application of legal and party gender quotas. Positive action has been applied in majoritarian electoral systems as well, as shown by the French or British cases, but it can be harder to implement within single-member districts than within party lists (Murray 2004). For all these reasons, PR systems are likely to be more "women-friendly" than majoritarian electoral systems. These qualities are also present in the party list ballot in "combined" or "mixed" electoral systems. Hence, in Germany, Hungary, and New Zealand women have usually proved more successful in gaining office via party lists rather than through single-member districts.

## Legal Quotas and Reserved Seats

Recognition of the importance—but also the limits—of electoral systems in shaping patterns of female representation has led to efforts around the world to revise existing laws to incorporate gender quota regulations. Electoral quotas have become an increasingly popular solution to the problem of women's underrepresentation, appearing in more than 100 countries worldwide (Krook 2009). These policies take three main forms: *reserved seats; legal quotas* applying to all parties; and *party quotas* specified in internal party rules and procedures.

Reserved seats are found in Africa, Asia, and the Middle East. They involve setting aside parliamentary seats for women that men are not eligible to contest. Early policies reserved between 1 and 10 percent of seats for women, but more recent measures have entailed much larger provisions of 30 percent (Krook 2009). Reserved seats can be implemented through either appointment or competitive election, with the latter providing better prospects for members who have an independent base beyond party leaders.

Legal quotas appear primarily in Latin America, Africa, and the Middle East but have become increasingly popular in Western Europe and to a lesser extent in Central and Eastern Europe. They are usually enacted through reforms to electoral laws requiring that all parties nominate a certain percentage of female candidates. Legal quotas have also been adopted in established democracies like Belgium, France, Portugal, and Spain—and most recently Ireland, where a quota law was approved by the Senate in March 2012 and is now under consideration in the lower house (Dáil). A growing number of post-Communist states have also begun to adopt legal provisions, including Albania, Armenia, Kyrgyzstan, Poland, and Uzbekistan, primarily within the last five years. Some of the most effective legal quotas have been introduced in countries emerging from conflict, namely, the Balkan states of Bosnia and Herzegovina, Macedonia, and Serbia.

Variations in the design and implementation of legal quotas mean that the numerical effects of these policies have been mixed. Hence, gains have been relatively modest in some countries, like Armenia, France, and Romania, and far more dramatic in others, including in Belgium, Kyrgyzstan, and Macedonia. These differences stem from a number of factors including the *design of quota policies*, in terms of their wording, requirements, and sanctions for noncompliance as well as in their *perceived legitimacy* (Dahlerup and Freidenvall 2008; Krook 2009).

Quotas have generally been found to be more effective when they are clearly worded with little room for interpretation, establish strict placement mandates to ensure women appear high on party lists, and impose stiff sanctions—including ineligibility of lists—if parties do not comply. The evidence suggests that in general, legal quotas are most successful in establishing gender equality in elected office when:

(1) These laws require a relatively *high proportion* of female candidates to be nominated by political parties;

(2) These laws have *placement mandates* (also known as "double quotas") that regulate the alternative rank order of women and men candidates on party lists ("zipping");

(3) These laws include *penalties for noncompliance* that strictly bind the behavior of political parties through financial sanctions or the rejection of nomination lists which do not comply with the law or, alternatively, that create positive incentives for parties to nominate more women; and,

(4) *Compliance is monitored* by independent bodies, including electoral commissions, the courts, nongovernmental organizations (NGOs), and women groups, using legal and political means if necessary, to ensure that parties implement these policies to their fullest degree.

# Candidate Selection Procedures

Candidate selection procedures have been described by scholars as a "secret garden" or a "black box," as they are typically considered to be a very private matter taking place within political parties, and thereby requiring substantial country- and party-specific expertise on the part of outsiders (Field and Siavelis 2008; Gallagher and Marsh 1988; Hazan and Rahat 2010). Academic research identifies two dimensions—centralization and institutionalization—seen as vital to understanding the internal party selection processes that determine who is nominated to stand for election in a given party.

*Centralization* refers to the degree of control by the party leadership of the nomination process. Other relevant actors may include local branches or regional party bodies, which may be authorized—or vie—to override the central office when making decisions regarding candidate selection. Determining the key location of power in these multistage processes is far from straightforward.

At one extreme, democratic procedures may allow all citizens or all party members to select party nominees, typically through primary elections or caucuses, as used in the United States. Nonparty officials may also be important at the district level, including local nonparty-affiliated organizations, district oligarchies, financial supporters, or the news media, all of which may endorse some potential candidates over others.

More commonly in many European parties there is a multistage internal selection process engaging local party members and party officials, regional party assemblies or conventions, and the central party office and leadership. At the other extreme, elitist decision-making in some parties means that just a few, such as the party leader, the central party office, or the parliamentary party, determine party nominees.

*Institutionalization* captures the extent to which formal rules matter or whether informal norms and tacit procedures operate to determine the outcome (Hazan 2002; Norris 1997). Candidate selection can be described as "institutionalized" when formal rules and procedures are well-established, transparent, and clear, typically embodied in written party rulebooks and constitutions. It is not considered institutionalized when the process is governed primarily by informal norms and tacit conventions.

This distinction is important because where formal rules are meaningful; it is possible to target reform of these rules to ensure that selectors take gender equality into account in their decision-making processes. In contrast, if the selection process is more informal, the impact of formal rule changes is likely to be more symbolic and aspirational rather than substantive and binding.

Devising concrete strategies is further complicated by the nature of the electoral system, which imposes a particular ballot structure that may require bargaining among groups within the parties when composing their slates of candidates. This task is also difficult in light of the fact that even political parties within the same country have developed different rules or may alter their selection strategies from election to election. Candidate selection procedures across many newer democracies reflect the fluidity of party systems in these states, in which many parliamentary parties have central offices but relatively weak organizational structures. This situation suggests that changing internal party rules to strengthen opportunities for women, while valuable, may not be translated into practice.

## Voluntary Party Quotas

Demystifying the secret garden of candidate selection is a key first step for thinking about how to promote greater gender equality in elected office. A major reason that legal quotas have such disparate effects across countries—and across political parties in the same state—is that candidate selection processes are different to penetrate and "manage" from the outside. From this perspective, party-level quotas may serve as a more effective intervention into existing dynamics precisely because they are oriented toward changing party practices and traditional criteria of candidate selection—and are undertaken at the initiative of the party itself, whose officials do have intimate knowledge of the candidate selection process (Krook 2009).

In international research on gender quotas, party quotas are defined as measures adopted voluntarily by political parties, usually through reforms to party constitutions, statutes, and rulebooks, to pledge that the party will nominate a certain proportion of women among its candidates to political office. These measures were first adopted in the early 1970s by a few socialist and social democratic parties in Western Europe. Over the course of the 1980s and 1990s, however, they spread to all regions of the world and now appear in parties on the left, right, and center of the political spectrum—such that they are today the most common type of quota reform worldwide. Party quotas typically involve a commitment to nominating between 25 and 50 percent female candidates. The phrasing of this requirement varies to some extent. Some policies identify women as the group to be promoted by the quota, as in Argentina, South Africa, and Spain. Others set out a more gender-neutral formulation, establishing a minimum or maximum representation of "either sex," as in Italy and several Nordic countries. The gender-neutral formulation has been especially effective in precluding the possibility of legal challenges on the grounds of sex discrimination, as it transforms both men and women into beneficiaries of the policy. Party quotas govern the composition of party lists in countries with PR electoral systems, which is the case in much of the world, and are directed at collections of single-member districts in countries with majoritarian electoral arrangements, such as the United Kingdom.

Party quotas have been particularly effective in Sweden, where women have mobilized inside and outside the political parties since the 1920s to ensure the selection of female candidates. Over time, they gradually increased the proportion each party considered for women to be adequately represented, from one woman per list to now equal numbers of women and men. In the 1990s, more informal goals, targets, and recommendations in many parties gave way to more formal quota policies. While gains have been made possible through the use of a PR electoral system, party strategies have been of paramount importance. Today, almost all Swedish parties embrace the principle of alternation (or zippering), meaning that they alternate between male and female names on party lists to ensure that women form not only 50 percent of candidates but also close to 50 percent of those elected. The result is that the country ranks second in the world in terms of women's representation, with women occupying 45 percent of all seats in parliament.

Party quotas tend to have a greater impact on the numbers of women elected when:

(1) *Many parties*, especially several *larger parties*, adopt these policies;
(2) The quotas adopted call for a relatively *high proportion* of women to be nominated as party candidates;

(3)  The quotas are framed in ways that link them to well-understood and widely accepted *cultural practices and traditions*; and,

(4)  Parties are institutionalized with organizational structures, and formal nomination procedures so that *rules are enforced* by internal party bodies. Where party nomination procedures are more informally determined—for example, in clientelistic parties where the top party leadership personally handpicks a shortlist of loyal supporters as candidates—few enforcement mechanisms will be able to guarantee the inclusion of women.

## Capacity and Training Initiatives

Political parties can also take steps to enhance the supply of women willing to run for office by sponsoring activities to stimulate women's interest and capacities in the political sphere. In countries where it may be difficult to introduce quotas, whether legal or party based, capacity development initiatives are vital to efforts to bring more women into politics. They are also essential in countries where quotas are in force, as together these two strategies offer a more holistic approach to addressing problems of both "supply" and "demand."

Many women possess the experience and qualifications needed to hold political office but due to gender discrimination do not always have access to the same information as men in terms of learning how to launch a political career. For this reason, programs focused on developing this knowledge form a crucial part of any campaign to enhance women's political representation. Capacity development initiatives, which may be run by political parties or by bipartisan civil society groups, seek to provide women with training who are currently running—or in the future may decide to run—for political office.

One example is that women inside the Norwegian Labour Party designed a program known as Women Can Do It, which arranges candidate training opportunities in more than 25 countries worldwide. Funded by Norwegian People's Aid, the topics covered in the program range from democracy and women's participation to communication; argumentation, speeches, and debate; handling the media; negotiations; networking; advocacy training; and violence against women. Seeking to facilitate women's participation in public affairs, the program offers training in particular skills but also views the program as a chance for women to meet and form networks (Wistrand 1981).

## Recruitment Initiatives

Capacity-building initiatives received by far the most attention in the interviews. A related issue is the need to identify and encourage women to run more generally—women who might subsequently be the focus of training programs. There is little comparative data on the existence of such programs initiated by political parties per se—although a number of recruitment initiatives have been launched by civil society organizations. One example, however, can be seen in Sweden in the 1970s prior to the adoption of formal quota policies. To combat the claim that no qualified women could be found, the women's sections inside the major political parties assembled databases containing the names and curriculum vitae of potential female candidates, which could be presented to party officials as they sought to find women to put on their electoral lists. Such a task need not be allocated to the party's women's section, although they may have more contacts with women inside and outside the party. A list of this type could also be initiated by the central leadership as a means of demonstrating the party's commitment to finding good female candidates.

## Women's Sections

Related to this last suggestion, another way that political parties could enhance women's participation is through establishing and strengthening women's organizations within the party itself. Around the world, women's sections have traditionally played a role in recruiting female party members and in performing important tasks for the party, including electoral canvassing. Theoretically, these organizations can bring together all of the women who are members of a particular party—although in practice they have traditionally involved a smaller proportion of women.

Civil society initiatives can both inspire and supplement political party strategies to promote gender equality in the political realm. This work can be especially effective in raising broader awareness on the need for more women in politics—stimulating both the "supply" of women interested in pursuing elected office as well as the "demand" for female candidates on the part of elites and voters. Like party-based initiatives, these strategies can be pursued even in the absence of gender quotas, although multipronged strategies—engaging laws, political parties, and civil society groups together—are more likely to support progress toward gender equality than single actors and activities alone.

## Media Campaigns

Beliefs that women should not run for political office are informed and reinforced by gender stereotypes, which associate men with the public sphere of politics and women with the private sphere of the home. Changing these stereotypes can increase the number of women considering a political career and can alter how voters—and political parties—view female candidates. A strategy for combating such stereotypes is through media campaigns aimed at changing how citizens think about gender and politics.

An example is a media campaign funded by a multipartisan parliamentary committee in Iceland between 1997 and 2002. It aimed to increase the proportion of women in politics through humorous advertisements, alongside training courses, education networks, public meetings, and mentoring programs. The advertisements sought to challenge stereotypes at the top levels of government to frame gender balance as an issue affecting both women and men. In one poster a female MP is shown shaving, while in another the male foreign minister is holding a pair of pantyhose, with the captions reading, "Half the nation is not reflected democratically in the parliament," and, "Some experiences are beyond our reach," respectively.

## Recruitment and Training Initiatives

A second prong in promoting equal opportunities entails recruitment initiatives to identify and encourage women to run for office, whether in the immediate or distant future. In contrast to media campaigns that address all four audiences identified by respondents in the five pilot countries, programs of this type primarily target women—especially those who might be persuaded to come forward as candidates. The common thread of these projects is to convince women to consider a political career—and, more broadly, to promote a shift in women's mentalities over the long term.

Recruitment and training initiatives organized by civil society organizations are particularly well developed in the United States, where the use of a majoritarian electoral system, combined with hostility to gender quotas, makes it difficult to achieve dramatic increases in women's political representation, at least overnight. There are a variety of groups dedicated to this goal, including NEW Leadership, that attempts to expand political knowledge and participation among female university students through programs serving educational institutions in 25 states; Emerge, which provides a seven-month program for Democratic women who want to run for elected office, working in nine states; and Political Parity, a nonpartisan initiative to double the number of women at the highest levels of government by 2022 through advocacy and research activities.

## Fundraising Initiatives

Once women have been recruited to run for political office, other programs can be implemented to enhance their chances of electoral success. To this end, a growing number of civil society organizations have developed fundraising initiatives to encourage female candidates and ensure that they have the resources necessary for waging successful campaigns. A focus on removing the financial obstacles to elected office takes on special importance in countries where public funding is not available for candidates' campaigns.

Perhaps the most well-known among these initiatives is the U.S.-based EMILY's List, discussed throughout this volume, a group that recruits and trains women but, more uniquely, publicizes their names to solicit campaign contributions from supporters across the country. Similar fundraising groups have been established in other countries, including in Australia, the United Kingdom, and Italy.

## Knowledge Networks

Extending this theme, the Internet has also become a useful tool for information sharing through the creation of knowledge networks, primarily across national borders, to exchange ideas on effective ways to raise public awareness, to identify prospective female candidates, and to assist women in running successful campaigns. This work complements the information available on websites like the Global Database of Quotas for Women, which assembles data on the existence and design of electoral quotas in countries around the world.

At the global level, a group of transnational NGOs have come together to facilitate the exchange of information on how to empower women in politics through the International Knowledge Network of Women in Politics, or iKNOWPolitics, a website funded by the United Nations Development Programme, the UN Development Fund for Women, the National Democratic Institute for International Affairs, the Inter-Parliamentary Union, and the International Institute for Democracy and Electoral Assistance. The project is described as an "online workspace" designed to serve the needs of elected officials, candidates, political party leaders and members, researchers, students, and other practitioners interested in advancing women in politics.

## Gender Audit Monitoring

A related strategy, albeit one that could operate at a variety of different levels, is gender audit monitoring, which could track and publicize the composition of candidate seats and elected and appointed bodies. Publicizing a list of the worst performing political parties in terms of women's participation, for example, can damage the party's reputation and ultimately its electoral success. In the run-up to the 2010 U.K. parliamentary elections, for example, the significantly lower percentage of female MPs in the Liberal Democrat party compared with in the Labour and Conservative parties was extensively discussed in the media and was the subject of much negative attention. This brought the issue of women's representation further onto the popular agenda and meant that parties were forced to discuss and justify their own records.

In Sweden, an internal process has been used to assess the gender sensitivity of parliament (Engström 2009). The results of a survey revealed that female members faced several challenges in parliament: they usually struggled to reach high positions within the parliament; they viewed themselves and their work as being invisible; they were often subject to ridicule and belittling; and they often did not have access to full information about parliamentary work.

The research resulted in a document with "15 Proposals for Gender Equality in Parliament." A gender equality plan is adopted for each parliamentary session, which requires reporting and follow-up, falling under the responsibility of the Secretary General of Parliament. Some of the reforms that Sweden has implemented to make parliament more family-friendly included the provision of subsidized childcare facilities, the possibility of taking parental leave without resigning, and a standardization of rules regarding working hours and sick days to bring them closer to the rules guiding the rest of the workforce.

Rethinking parliamentary rules and procedures can potentially go a long way in reshaping both the supply of and demand for female candidates, if elected assemblies are pushed to consider how their operating procedures may—directly or indirectly—lead both women and party leaders to believe that women's traditional roles cannot be reconciled with a political career.

## Conclusions and Discussion

There are many reasons that gender equality in political office matters. Based on the Millennium Development Goals alone, governments have committed themselves to achieving equal rights for women and men, including in decision-making positions. There is also a growing consensus among international actors that gender equality is not only the "right" thing to do but also the "smart" thing to do. The World Bank (2012), for example, argues that promoting gender equality is "smart economics" because it "can enhance productivity, improve development outcomes for the next generation, and make institutions more representative."

Research suggests that the same is true for gender equality in politics. In particular, a national or regional list of candidates that reflects a cross section of society can help to maximize the potential electoral appeal of political parties to all groups in the electorate. By contrast, parties that clearly exclude certain sectors of the population in their list of candidates—whether on the basis of sex, region, class and status, religion, age, race, or ethnicity—risk failing to appeal to these sectors on the basis of identity politics (Lovenduski and Norris 1993; Kittilson 2006).

Nevertheless, progress toward this goal has been slow and erratic. In many countries there has been an expansion in the proportion of women in elected office in recent decades, but the process of democratizations has also generated processes of "two steps forward, one step back," where parties have abandoned positive action strategies for women in the attempt to "modernize" and "liberalize" without simultaneously implementing other types of action to ensure gender equality in elected office. Elsewhere, many of the newer democracies have managed to advance faster than some of the established democracies, including the United States. The use constitutional amendments, electoral reforms, and candidate gender quotas all seem too radical for the United States to even debate seriously on the policy agenda, let alone pass and implement. Many factors inhibit the sort of structural reforms taken by other countries, including the individualistic American culture, the "tyranny of structurelessness" of the U.S. primary selection process, the weakness and decentralization of party recruitment, the strength of incumbency due to partisan gerrymandering, campaigns awash with money, and extreme constitutional rigidity. Nevertheless, many other softer interventions in the "demand" and "supply" factors could be adopted to improve the representation of women in Congress, where America could learn lessons from successful interventions used elsewhere around the globe.

## Notes

1. United Nations. *The Universal Declaration of Human Rights.* Article 2. http://www.un.org/en/documents/udhr/ (accessed March 20, 2013). "Everyone is entitled to all the rights and freedoms set forth in this Declaration, without distinction of any kind, such as race, colour, sex, language, religion, political or other opinion, national or social origin, property, birth or other status."
2. United Nations. "Convention on the Elimination of all forms of Discrimination Against Women." Article 7. http://www.un.org/womenwatch/daw/cedaw/text/econvention.htm#-article7 (accessed March 20, 2013).
3. United Nations. 1995. "The United Nations Fourth World Conference on Women, Beijing, China. Platform Strategic Objective G1." September. http://www.un.org/womenwatch/daw/beijing/platform/decision.htm (accessed March 20, 2013).
4. Inter-Parliamentary Union. 2013. "Women in National Parliaments." February 1. http://www.ipu.org/wmn-e/world.htm (accessed March 20, 2013).
5. *Majoritarian* formula include first-past-the-post, second ballot, the block vote, single non-transferable vote, and alternative voting systems; *mixed* (or *combined*) systems incorporate both majoritarian and proportional formula in elections to the same body; while *proportional formula* include party lists as well as the single transferable vote systems.

# REFERENCES

Arceneaux, Kevin. 2001. "The 'Gender Gap' in State Legislative Representation: New Data to Tackle an Old Question." *Political Research Quarterly* 54: 143–160.

Adams, Brian E., and Ronnee Schreiber. 2011. "Gender, Campaign Finance, and Electoral Success in Municipal Elections." *Journal of Urban Affairs* 33(1): 83–97.

Adams, Greg D. 1997. "Abortion: Evidence of an Issue Evolution." *American Journal of Political Science* 41: 718–737.

Adams, Kimberly S. 2007. "Different Faces, Different Priorities: Agenda-Setting Behavior in the Mississippi, Maryland, and Georgia State Legislatures." *Nebula* 4: 58–95.

Aldrich, John, and David Rohde. 2001. "The Logic of Conditional Party Government: Revisiting the Electoral Connection." In *Congress Reconsidered*, eds. Lawrence C. Dodd and Bruce I. Oppenheimer. Washington, DC: Congressional Quarterly, 269–292.

Alexander, Deborah, and Kristi Andersen. 1993. "Gender as a Factor in the Attribution of Leadership Traits." *Political Research Quarterly* 46(3): 527–545.

Allen, Florence Ellinwood. 1965. *To Do Justly*. Cleveland, OH: Western Reserve University Press.

Alliance for Justice (AFJ). 2012. "Judicial Selection Snapshot." *Alliance for Justice.* http://www.afj. org/judicial-selection/judicial-selection-snapshot.pdf (accessed July 23, 2013).

Alozie, Nicholas O. 1990. "Distribution of Women and Minority Judges: The Effects of Judicial Selection Methods." *Social Science Quarterly* 71(2): 315–325.

——. 1996. "Selection Methods and the Recruitment of Women to State Courts of Last Resort." *Social Science Quarterly* 77(1): 110–126.

Alter, Judy. 2006. *Miriam "Ma" Ferguson: First Woman Governor of Texas*. Abilene, TX: State House Press.

American Bar Association (ABA). 2009. *Standing Committee on the Federal Judiciary: What It Is and How It Works*. http://www.abanet.org/scfedjud/federal_judiciary09.pdf (accessed November 2, 2012).

——. 2011. "First Year and Total J.D. Enrollment by Gender, 1947–2011." http://www.americanbar. org/content/dam/aba/administrative/legal_education_and_admissions_to_the_bar/statistics/jd_enrollment_1yr_total_gender.authcheckdam.pdf (accessed November 15, 2012).

——. 2012. "Standing Committee on the Federal Judiciary, 2011–2012." http://www.americanbar.org/groups/committees/federal_judiciary/about_us/members.html (accessed May 28, 2012).

American Constitution Society (ACS). 2012. "Federal Judicial Vacancies." http://judicialnominations.org/ (accessed November 14, 2012).

American Judicature Society (AJS). 2012. "Judicial Selection in the States." http://www.judicialselection.com/ (accessed November 14, 2012).

Angyal, Chloe. 2013. "Nancy Pelosi: We Need More Women in Politics." *Salon.com*. March 12. http://www.salon.com/2013/03/12/nancy_pelosi_we_need_to_make_our_own_environment_partner/ (accessed July 23, 2013).

Antolini, Denise. 1984. "Women in Local Government: An Overview." In *Political Women: Current Roles in State and Local Government*, ed. Janet A. Flammang. Beverly Hills, CA: SAGE, 23–40.

Anzia, Sarah F., and Christopher R. Berry. 2011. "The Jackie (and Jill) Robinson Effect: Why Do Congresswomen Outperform Congressmen?" *American Journal of Political Science* 55: 478–493.

Arnold, Douglas R. 2004. *Congress, the Press, and Political Accountability*. Princeton, NJ: Princeton University Press.

Arnold, Laura W., and Barbara M. King. 2002. "Women, Committees, and Institutional Change in the Senate." In *Women Transforming Congress*, ed. Cindy Simon Rosenthal. Norman: University of Oklahoma Press, 284–315.

Associated Press. 2007. "Hillary Clinton Drops Maiden Name 'Rodham' from 2008 White House Campaign." *Fox News*. April 30. http://www.foxnews.com/story/0,2933,269263,00.html#ixzz2DH2Ui7V0 (accessed July 23, 2013).

Atkeson, Lonna Rae. 2003. "Not All Cues Are Created Equal: The Conditional Impact of Female Candidates on Political Engagement." *Journal of Politics* 65(4): 1040–1061.

Atkeson, Lonna Rae, and Nancy Carrillo. 2007. "More Is Better: The Influence of Collective Female Descriptive Representation on External Efficacy." *Politics & Gender* 3(1): 79–101.

Atkeson, Lonna Rae, and Timothy B. Krebs. 2008. "Press Coverage of Mayoral Candidates: The Role of Gender in News Reporting and Campaign Issue Speech." *Political Research Quarterly* 61 (March): 239–252.

Avdeyeva, O. 2007. "When Do States Comply with International Treaties? Policies on Violence against Women in Post-Communist Countries." *International Studies Quarterly* 51(4): 877–900.

Ayata, Ayse Günes, and Fatma Tütüncü. 2008. "Critical Acts without a Critical Mass: The Substantive Representation of Women in the Turkish Parliament." *Parliamentary Affairs* 61(3): 461–475.

Ayotte, Kelly. 2012a. "Ayotte: Health Care Mandate Is Affront to Religious Freedom." February 7. http://www.ayotte.senate.gov/?p=video&id=423 (accessed July 23, 2013).

——. 2012b. "Ayotte: We Must Respect Conscience Rights for All Religions." February 8. http://www.ayotte.senate.gov/?p=video&id=426 (accessed July 23, 2013).

Babcock, Barbara. 2011. *Woman Lawyer: The Trials of Clara Foltz*. Stanford, CA: Stanford University Press.

Backhouse, Constance. 2003. "The Chilly Climate for Women Judges: Reflections on the Backlash from the *Ewanchuk* Case." *Canadian Journal of Women and the Law* 15(1): 167–179.

Baker, Beth. 2012. "Fighting the War on Women." *Ms.*, Spring/Summer, 27–31.

Banwart, Mary Christine, Dianne G. Bystrom, and Terry Robertson. 2003. "From the Primary to the General Election." *American Behavioral Scientist* 46(5): 658–676.

Barbara Lee Family Foundation. 2012. "Pitch Perfect: Winning Strategies for Women Candidates." *Barbara Lee Family Foundation*. http://www.barbaraleefoundation.org/our-research/topics/pitch-perfect-winning-strategies-for-women-candidates (accessed July 23, 2013).

Barnello, Michelle A., and Kathleen A. Bratton. 2007. "Bridging the Gender Gap in Bill Sponsorship." *Legislative Studies Quarterly* 32(3): 449–474.

Barnes, Robert. 2007a. "Over Ginsburg's Dissent, Court Limits Bias Suits." *Washington Post*, May 30. http://www.washingtonpost.com/wp-dyn/content/article/2007/05/29/AR2007052900740.html (accessed July 26, 2013).

——. 2007b. "Exhibit A in Painting Court as Too Far Right." *Washington Post*, September 5.

Barone, Michael, and Richard E. Cohen. 2007. *The Almanac of American Politics*. Washington, DC: National Journal Group.

Barr, Andy. 2009. "Hillary Clinton: I'd Have Hired Barack Obama." *Politico*. October 14. http://www.politico.com/newa/stories/1009/28278.html (accessed July 23, 2013).

Barrett, Edith J. 1995. "The Policy Priorities of African American Women in State Legislatures." *Legislative Studies Quarterly* 20(2): 223–247.

———. 1997. "Gender and Race in the State House: The Legislative Experience." *Social Science Journal* 34(2): 131–144.

———. 2001. "Black Women in State Legislatures: The Relationship of Race and Gender to the Legislative Experience." In *The Impact of Women in Public Office*, ed. Susan J. Carroll. Bloomington: Indiana University Press, 185–204.

Barreto, Matt A., Gary M. Segura, and Nathan D. Woods. 2004. "The Mobilizing Effect of Majority-Minority Districts on Latino Turnout." *American Political Science Review* 98(1): 65–75.

Barrette, John. 1987. *Prairie Politics, Kay Orr vs. Helen Boosalis: The Historic 1986 Gubernatorial Race*. Lincoln, NE: Media Publishing & Marketing, Inc.

Barth, Jay, and Margaret R. Ferguson. 2002. "Gender & Gubernatorial Personality." *Women & Politics* 24(1): 63–82.

Battista, James. 2009. "Why Information? Choosing Committee Informativeness in U.S. State Legislatures." *Legislative Studies Quarterly*: 34(3): 375–397.

BBC News Online. 2011. "Hillary Clinton Declares 'Gay Rights are Human Rights.'" December 7. http://www.bbc.co.uk/news/world-us-canada-16062937 (accessed on July 23, 2013).

Beard, Patricia. 1996. *Growing up Republican Christie Whitman: The Politics of Character*. New York: Harper Collins Publishers.

Beck, Susan Abrams. 1991. "Rethinking Municipal Governance: Gender Distinctions on Local Councils." In *Gender and Policymaking: Studies of Women in Office*, ed. D. L. Dodson. New Brunswick, NJ: Center for American Women and Politics, 103–113.

Berkman, Michael B., and Robert E. O'Connor. 1993. "Do Women Legislators Matter? Female Legislators and State Abortion Policy." In *Understanding the New Politics of Abortion*, ed. Malcolm Goggin. Newbury Park, CA: SAGE.

Bedolla, Lisa Garciá, Katherine Tate, and Janelle Wong. 2005. "Indelible Effects: The Impact of Women of Color in the U.S. Congress." In *Women and Elective Office: Past, Present, and Future*, eds. Sue Thomas and Clyde Wilcox. New York: Oxford University Press, 152–175.

Bell, Lauren Cohen. 2002. "Senatorial Discourtesy: The Senate's Use of Delay to Shape the Federal Judiciary." *Political Research Quarterly* 55: 589–607.

Bennett, Stephen Earl, and Linda L. M. Bennett. 1992. "From Traditional to Modern Conceptions of Gender Equality in Politics: Gradual Change and Lingering Doubts." *Western Political Quarterly* 45(1): 93–110.

Berkman, Michael B., and Robert E. O'Connor. 1993. "Do Women Legislators Matter? Female Legislators and State Abortion Policy." *American Politics Quarterly* 21: 102–124.

Berkson, Larry. 1982. "Women on the Bench: A Brief History." *Judicature* 65(6): 286–293.

Bernstein, Carl. 2007. *A Woman in Charge: The Life of Hillary Clinton*. New York: Alfred A. Knopf.

Berry, Deborah Barfield. 2011. "Black Women Proud of Electoral Gains but See Long Road Ahead." *Shreveport Times*. February 25. http://www.shreveporttimes.com/article/20110226/NEWS/110225016/Black-women-proud-electoral-gains-see-long-roadahead?odyssey=mod%7Cnewswell%7Ctext%7CFRONTPAGE%7Cs (accessed July 23, 2013).

———. 2012. "Roby and Sewell: Friendship Crosses Party Lines in D.C." *Montgomery Advertiser*. February 11. http://www.montgomeryadvertiser.com/article/20120211/NEWS02/202110338/Roby-Sewell-Friendship-crosses-party-lines-D-C-?odyssey=tab%7Ctopnews%,Ctext%7CFrontpage (accessed July 23, 2013).

Bers, Trudy Saffron. 1978. "Local Political Elites: Men and Women on Boards of Educations." *Western Political Quarterly* 31 (September): 381–391.

Bickers, Kenneth N., Diana Evans, Robert M. Stein, and Robert D. Wrinkle. 2007. "The Electoral Effect of Credit Claiming for Pork Barrel Projects in Congress." Presented at the Workshop on Elections and Distribution, Oct. 26–27, Yale University, New Haven, CT.

Binder, Sarah A., and Forrest Maltzman. 2009. *Advice and Dissent: The Struggle to Shape the Federal Judiciary*. Washington, DC: Brookings Institution.

Bishin, Benjamin G., Daniel Stevens, and Christian Wilson. 2006. "Character Counts? Honesty and Fairness in Election 2000." *Public Opinion Quarterly* 7: 235–248.

Black, Alida M. 2001. "The Modern First Lady and Public Policy: From Edith Wilson through Hillary Rodham Clinton." *Organization of American Historians Magazine of History* 15(3): 15–20.

Black, Jerome H., and Lynda Erickson. 2003. "Women Candidates and Voter Bias: Do Women Politicians Need To Be Better?" *Electoral Studies* 22(1): 81–100.

Blair, Diane D., and Jeanie R. Stanley. 1991a. "Personal Relationships and Legislative Power: Male and Female Perceptions." *Legislative Studies Quarterly* 16(4): 495–507.

———. 1991b. "Gender Differences in Legislative Effectiveness: The Impact of the Legislative Environment." In *Gender and Policymaking: Studies of Women in Office*, ed. Debra L. Dodson. New Brunswick, NJ: Center for the American Woman and Politics, 115–130.

Blakely, Shelby. 2011. "Citizen Journalist, Tea Party Patriots." Interview. May 31.

Bledsoe, Timothy, and Mary Herring. 1990. "Victims of Circumstances: Women in Pursuit of Political Office." *American Political Science Review* 84 (March): 213–223.

Bligh, Michelle C., Jeffrey C. Kohles, and James R. Meindl. 2004. "Charisma under Crisis: Presidential Leadership, Rhetoric and Media Responses before and after September 11 Terrorist Attacks." *Leadership Quarterly* 15(2): 211–239.

Bligh, Michelle C., Jennifer Merolla, Jean Reith Schroedel, and Randall Gonzalez. 2010. "Finding Her Voice: Hillary Clinton's Rhetoric in the 2008 Presidential Campaign." *Women's Studies: An Interdisciplinary Journal* 39(8): 823–850.

Boles, Janet. 1991. "Advancing Women's Agendas within Local Legislatures: The Role of Female Elected Officials." In *Gender and Policymaking: Studies of Women in Office*, ed. D. L. Dodson. New Brunswick, NJ: Center for American Women and Politics, 39–49.

———. 2001. "Local Elected Women and Policy-Making: Movement Delegates or Feminist Trustees?" In *The Impact of Women in Public Office*, ed. Susan J. Carroll. Bloomington: Indiana University Press, 68–86.

Bos, Angela L. 2011. "Out of Control: Delegates' Information Sources and Perceptions of Female Candidates." *Political Communication* 28(1): 87–109.

Boulard, Garry. 1999. "Women as Leaders: Vive la Différence." *State Legislatures Magazine*. http://www.ncsl.org/programs/pubs/599womn.htm (accessed February 12, 2009).

Boxer, Barbara. 1994. *Politics and the New Revolution of Women in America*. Washington, DC: National Press Books.

Boyd, Christina L., Lee Epstein, and Andrew D. Martin. 2010. "Untangling the Causal Effects of Sex on Judging." *American Journal of Political Science* 54(2): 389–411.

Bratton, Kathleen A. 2002. "The Effect of Legislative Diversity on Agenda Setting: Evidence from Six State Legislatures." *American Politics Review* 30(2): 115–142.

———. 2005. "Critical Mass Theory Revisited: The Behavior and Success of Token Women in State Legislatures." *Politics and Gender* 1: 97–125.

Bratton, Kathleen A., and Kerry L. Haynie. 1999. "Agenda-Setting and Legislative Success in State Legislatures: The Effects of Gender and Race." *Journal of Politics* 61: 658–679.

Bratton, Kathleen A., Kerry L. Haynie, and Beth Reingold. 2006a. "Agenda Setting and African American Women in State Legislatures." In *Intersectionality and Politics: Recent Research on Gender, Race, and Political Representation in the United States*, ed. Carol Hardy-Fanta. New York: Haworth Press, 71–96.

———. 2006b. "Agenda Setting and African American Women in State Legislatures." *Women, Politics, and Public Policy* 28(Summer/Fall): 71–96.

Bratton, Kathleen A., and Rorie L. Spill. 2001. "Clinton and the Diversification of the Federal Judiciary." *Judicature* 84(5): 256–261.

———. 2002. "Existing Diversity and Judicial Selection: The Role of the Appointment Method in Establishing Gender Diversity in State Supreme Courts." *Social Science Quarterly* 83(2): 504–518.

———. 2005. "Diversifying the Federal Bench: Presidential Patterns." *Justice System Journal* 26(2): 119–133.

Brewer, Paul R. 2003a. "The Shifting Foundations of Public Opinion about Gay Rights." *Journal of Politics* 65(4): 1208–1220.

———. 2003b. "Values, Political Knowledge, and Public Opinion about Gay Rights." *Public Opinion Quarterly* 67(2): 173–201.

———. 2008. *Value War: Public Opinion and the Politics of Gay Rights.* Lanham, MD: Rowman & Littlefield.

Brians, Craig Leonard. 2005. "Women for Women? Gender and Party Bias in Voting for Female Candidates." *American Politics Research* 33: 357–375.

Brooks, Deborah Jordan. 2011. "Testing the Double Standard for Candidate Emotionality: Voter Reactions to the Tears and Anger of Male and Female Politicians." *Journal of Politics* 73: 597–615.

Brown, Clyde, Neil Heighberger, and Peter Shocket. 1993. "Gender-Based Differences in Perceptions of Male and Female City Council Candidates." *Women and Politics* 13: 1–17.

Brown, Gary. 1998. "Characteristics of Elected versus Merit-Selected New York City Judges, 1992–97." Report. New York: Fund for Modern Courts.

Brownstein, Ronald. 2012a. "Why Obama Is Leading in Swing States." *National Journal*, October 1. http://www.nationaljournal.com/2012-presidential-campaign/why-obama-is-leading-in-swing-states-20121001 (accessed July 23, 2013).

———. 2012b. "The American Electorate Has Changed, and There's No Turning Back." *National Journal*, November 8. http://www.nationaljournal.com/magazine/the-american-electorate-has-changed-and-there-s-no-turning-back-20121108 (accessed July 23, 2013).

Bullock, Charles, Susan MacManus, F. E. Atkins, L. J. Hoffman, and A. Newmark. 1999. "Winning in My Own Backyard: County Government, School Board Positions Steadily More Attractive to Women Candidates." In *Women in Politics: Outsiders or Insiders?*, 3rd ed., ed. L. D. Whitaker. Upper Saddle River, NJ: Prentice Hall, 121–137.

Burbank, Stephen B. 2002. "Politics, Privilege, and Power: The Senate's Role in the Appointment of Federal Judges." *Judicature* 86(1): 24–27.

Burns, Lisa M. 2008. *First Ladies and the Fourth Estate: Press Framing of Presidential Wives.* DeKalb: Northeastern Illinois Press.

Burns, Nancy, Kay Lehman Schlozman, and Sidney Verba. 2001. *The Private Roots of Public Action.* Cambridge, MA: Harvard University Press.

Burrell, Barbara C. 1994/1996. *A Woman's Place Is in the House: Campaigning for Congress in the Feminist Era.* Ann Arbor: University of Michigan.

———. 1997. "The Office of the First Lady and Public Policymaking." In *The Other Elites: Women, Politics, and Power in the Executive Branch*, eds. MaryAnne Borrelli and Janet M. Martin. Boulder, CO: Lynne Rienner Publishers, 169–188.

———. 1998. "Campaign Finance: Women's Experience in the Modern Era." In *Women and Elective Office: Past, Present, and Future*, eds. Sue Thomas and Clyde Wilcox. New York: Oxford University Press, 26–37.

Button, James W., Kenneth D. Wald, and Barbara A. Rienzo. 1999. "The Election of Openly Gay Public Officials in American Communities." *Urban Affairs Review* 35(2): 188–209.

Bystrom, Dianne G., and Lynda Lee Kaid. 2002. "Are Women Candidates Transforming Campaign Communication? A Comparison of Advertising Videostyles in the 1990s." In *Women Transforming Congress*, ed. Cindy Simon Rosenthal. Norman: University of Oklahoma Press, 146–169.

Bystrom, Dianne G., Mary Christine Banwart, Lynda Lee Kaid, and Terry A. Robertson. 2004. *Gender and Candidate Communication.* New York: Routledge.

Caiazza, Amy. 2004. "Does Women's Representation in Elected Office Lead to Women- Friendly Policy? Analysis of State Level Data." *Women and Politics* 26(1): 35–70.

Calabresi, Massimo. 2011. "Hillary Clinton and the Rise of Smart Power." *Time*, November 7. http://www.time.com/time/magazine/article/0,9171,2097973,00.html (accessed July 26, 2013).

Campbell, Angus, Philip Converse, Warren Miller, and Donald Stokes. 1960. *The American Voter.* Ann Arbor: University of Michigan Press.

Canon, David T. 1999. *Race, Redistricting, and Representation: The Unintended Consequences of Black Majority Districts.* Chicago: University of Chicago Press.

Cantor, Dorothy W., and Toni Bernay, with Jean Stoess. 1992. *Women in Power: The Secrets of Leadership.* Boston: Houghton Mifflin.

*Caperton v. AT Massey Coal Co., Inc.,* 129 S. Ct. 2252—Supreme Court (2009).

Carbon, Susan, Pauline Houlden, and Larry Berkson. 1982. "Women on the State Bench: Their Characteristics and Attitudes about Judicial Selection." *Judicature* 65(6): 294–305.

Caress, A. N. 1999. "The Influence of Term Limits on the Electoral Success of Women." *Women and Politics* 20(3): 45–63.

Carey, John M., Richard G. Niemi, and Lynda Powell. 1998. "Are Women State Legislators Different?" In *Women and Elective Office: Past, Present, and Future,* eds. Sue Thomas and Clyde Wilcox. New York: Oxford University Press, 87–102.

Carrero, Jacquellena. 2013. "HOPE Inspires Women to Lead in Politics and Beyond." *NBC Latino.* March 30. http://nbclatino.com/2013/03/30/hope-inspires-women-to-lead-in-politics-and-beyond/ (accessed July 23, 2013).

Carroll, Susan J. 1989. "The Personal Is Political: The Intersection of Private Lives and Public Roles among Women and Men in Elective and Appointive Office." *Women & Politics* 9: 51–67.

——. 1993. "The Political Careers of Women Elected Officials: An Assessment and Research Agenda." In *Ambition and Beyond: Career Path of American Politicians,* eds. Shirley Williams and Edward L. Lascher Jr. Berkeley, CA: Institute of Governmental Studies Press, 197–230.

——. 1994. *Women as Candidates in American Politics,* 2nd ed. Bloomington: Indiana University Press.

Carroll, Susan J. 2001. "Representing Women: Women State Legislators as Agents of Policy-Related Change." In The Impact of Women in Public Office, Susan J. Carroll, Ed. Bloomington and Indianapolis: Indiana University Press, pp. 3-21.

——. 2002. "Representing Women: Congresswomen's Perception of Their Representational Roles." In *Women Transforming Congress,* ed. Cindy Simon Rosenthal. Norman: University of Oklahoma Press, 50–68.

——. 2003. "Have Women State Legislators in the United States Become More Conservative?: A Comparison of State Legislators in 2001 and 1988." *Atlantis* 27(2): 128–139.

——. 2004. "Committee Assignments in State Legislatures: A Missing Link in Understanding Gender Differences in Policy Related Impact." Presented at the Annual Meeting of the Western Political Science Association, Portland, OR, March 11–13.

——. 2006. *The Impact of Women in Congress.* New York: Oxford University Press.

——. 2008. "Committee Assignments: Discrimination or Choice?" In *Legislative Women: Getting Elected, Getting Ahead,* ed. Beth Reingold. Boulder, CO: Lynne Rienner Publishers, 135–156.

——. 2009. "Reflections on Gender and Hillary Clinton's Presidential Campaign: The Good, the Bad, and the Misogynic." *Politics and Gender* 5(1): 1–20.

Carroll, Susan J., Debra L. Dodson, and Ruth B. Mandel. 1991. *The Impact of Women in Public Office: An Overview.* New Brunswick, NJ: Eagleton Institute of Politics' Center for American Women and Politics.

Carroll, Susan J., and K. Jenkins. 2001. "Unrealized Opportunity? Term Limits and the Representation of Women in State Legislatures." *Women and Politics* 23(4): 1–30.

——. 2005. "Increasing Diversity or More of the Same? Terms Limits and the Representation of Women, Minorities, and Minority Women in State Legislatures." *National Political Science Review* 10: 71–84.

Carroll, Susan J., and Kira Sanbonmatsu. 2010. "Entering the Mayor's Office: Women's Decisions to Run for Municipal Office." Presented at the annual meeting of the Midwest Political Science Association, Chicago, IL, April 22–25.

——. 2013. "Entering the Mayor's Office: Women's Decisions to Run for Municipal Elections." In *Women & Executive Office: Pathways and Performance,* ed. Melody Rose. Boulder, CO: Lynne Rienner Publishers, 115–136.

Carroll, Susan J., and Ronnee Schreiber. 1997. "Media Coverage of Women in the 103rd Congress." In *Women, Media, and Politics,* ed. Pippa Norris. New York: Oxford University Press, 131–148.

Carsey, Thomas M., Robert A. Jackson, Melissa Stewart, and James P. Nelson. 2011. "Strategic Candidates, Campaign Dynamics, and Campaign Advertising in Gubernatorial Races." *State Politics and Policy Quarterly* 11(3): 269–298.

Carver, Joan S. 1979. "Women in Florida." *Journal of Politics* 41: 941–955.

Cassel, Carol A. 1979. "Change in Electoral Participation in the South." *Journal of Politics* 41: 907–917.

Caul-Kittilson, Miki. 2001. "Political Parties and the Adoption of Candidate Gender Quotas: A Cross-National Analysis." *Journal of Politics* 63(3): 1214–1429.

Center for Media and Public Affairs. 2008. "Study Finds Obama's Media Momentum Slows." March 3. http://www.cmpa.com/Studies/Election08/election%20news%203_3_08.htm (accessed July 23, 2013).

Center for the American Woman and Politics (CAWP). 2001. *Women State Legislators: Past, Present, and Future*. New Brunswick, NJ: Eagleton Institute of Politics, Rutgers University.

——. 2004. *Fact Sheet: Women in Elective Office 2004*. Rutgers, NJ: Eagleton Institute of Politics, Rutgers University.

——. 2012a. *Fact Sheet. Number of Women Officeholders: 1975 State Summaries*. New Brunswick, NJ: Eagleton Institute of Politics, Rutgers University. http://www.cawp.rutgers.edu/fast_facts/level_of_office/documents/stleg75.pdf.

——. 2012b. *Fact Sheet: Women Candidates for Congress 1974–2012: Party and Seat Summary for Major Party Nominees*. New Brunswick, NJ: Eagleton Institute of Politics, Rutgers University.

——. 2012c. *Women in State Legislatures 2012*. New Brunswick, NJ: Eagleton Institute of Politics, Rutgers University.

——. 2012d. *Women in the U.S. Congress 2012*. New Brunswick, NJ: Eagleton Institute of Politics, Rutgers University.

——. 2012e. *Women Mayors in U.S. Cities 2012*. New Brunswick, NJ: Eagleton Institute of Politics, Rutgers University.

——. 2012f. *Women Surpass House, Senate Candidate Records as Final November Slates Are Set*. New Brunswick, NJ: Eagleton Institute of Politics, Rutgers University. http://www.cawp.rutgers.edu/press_room/news/documents/PressRelease_09-13-12.pdf (accessed March 20, 2013).

——. 2012g. *Women In State Legislative Elections: 1992–2012*. New Brunswick, NJ: Eagleton Institute of Politics, Rutgers University. http://www.cawp.rutgers.edu/fast_facts/elections/documents/canwinleg_histst.pdf (accessed March 20, 2013).

——. 2013a. *Fact Sheet: Women in the U.S. Congress 2013*. New Brunswick, NJ: Eagleton Institute of Politics, Rutgers University. http://www.cawp.rutgers.edu/fast_facts/levels_of_office/documents/elective.pdf (accessed March 20, 2013).

——. 2013b. *Women in Congress: Leadership Roles and Committee Chairs*. New Brunswick, NJ: Eagleton Institute of Politics, Rutgers University. http://www.cawp.rutgers.edu/fast_facts/levels_of_office/documents/conglead.pdf (accessed March 20, 2013).

——. 2013c. *2013 Fact Sheets on Women in State Legislatures*. New Brunswick, NJ: Eagleton Institute of Politics, Rutgers University. http://www.cawp.rutgers.edu/fast_facts/levels_of_office/StateLeg-CurrentFacts.php (March 20, 2013).

——. 2013d. *2012 Women Mayors (cities over 30,000)*. New Brunswick, NJ: Eagleton Institute of Politics, Rutgers University. http://www.cawp.rutgers.edu/fast_facts/levels_of_office/Local-WomenMayors.php (March 20, 2013).

——. 2013e. *2013 Fact Sheets on Women in Statewide Elected Executive Office*. New Brunswick, NJ: Eagleton Institute of Politics, Rutgers University. http://www.cawp.rutgers.edu/fast_facts/levels_of_office/Statewide-CurrentFacts.php (March 20, 2013).

——. 2013f. *Firsts for Women in U.S. Politics*. New Brunswick, NJ: Eagleton Institute of Politics, Rutgers University. http://www.cawp.rutgers.edu/fast_facts/resources/Firsts.php (March 20, 2013).

——. 2013g. Center for the American Woman and Politics. *Fact Sheet: Women Candidates for Governor: 1970–2012*. New Brunsick, NJ: Eagleton Institute of Politics, Rutgers University. http://www.cawp.rutgers.edu/fast_facts/elections/documents/canwingov_histlst.pdf.

Center for Women in Government & Civil Society (CWGCS). 2010. "Women in Federal and State-level Judgeships." Rockefeller College of Public Affairs & Policy, University at Albany, State University of New York, Spring.

Chaney, Paul. 2006. "Critical Mass, Deliberation and the Substantive Representation of Women: Evidence from the UK's Devolution Programme." *Political Studies* 54(4): 691–714.

Childs, Sarah. 2004. *New Labour's Women MPs: Women Representing Women.* London: Routledge.

Childs, Sarah, and Mona Lena Krook. 2006. "Should Feminists Give Up on Critical Mass? A Contingent Yes." *Politics & Gender* 2: 522–530

Chisholm, Shirley. 1973. *The Good Fight.* New York, Harper & Row.

Cirilli, Kevin. 2012. "Tammy Baldwin: It's More Than Being Gay." *Politico.* 7 November. *Citizens United v. Federal Election Commission,* 558 U.S. 310 (2010).

Clark, Janet. 1994. "Getting There: Women in Political Office." In *Different Roles, Different Voice,* eds. M. Githens, P. Norris and J. Lovenduski. New York: Harper-Collins, 63–76.

Clark, Jennifer Hayes and Veronica Caro. 2013. "Multimember Districts and the Substantive Representation of Women: An Analysis of Legislative Cosponsorship Networks." *Politics & Gender.* (9):1–30.

Clark, Mary L. 2002. "Changing the Face of the Law: How Women's Advocacy Groups Put Women on the Federal Judicial Appointments Agenda." *Yale Journal of Law and Feminism* 14(2): 243.

———. 2004. "One Man's Token Is Another Woman's Breakthrough? The Appointment of the First Women Federal Judges." *Villanova Law Review* 49(3): 487–549.

Clark-Flory, Tracy. 2010. "Elena Kagan, Cross Your Legs!" *Salon.* May 24. http://www.salon.com/2010/05/24/kagan_clothing_givhan/ (November 15, 2011).

Clement, Scott, and John C. Green. 2011. "The Tea Party, Religion and Social Issues." http://pewresearch.org/pubs/1903/tea-party-movement-religion-social-issues-conservative-christian (accessed July 23, 2013).

Clift, Eleanor, and Tom Brazaitis. 2000. *Madam President: Shattering the Last Glass Ceiling.* New York: Scribner Press.

CNN Political Ticker. 2008. "McCain Praises Palin as 'Role Model' and 'Reformer.'" October 15. http://politicalticker.blogs.cnn.com/2008/10/15/mccain-praises-palin-as-role-model-and-reformer/ (accessed 23 July, 2013).

Coffe, Hilde, and Catherine Bolzendahl. 2010. "Same game, different rules? Gender differences in political participation." *Sex Roles* 62(5-6): 318–333.

Cogan, Marin. 2011. "GOP Freshman Women Make Their Mark." *Politico.* June 20.

Cohen, Cathy J. 2002. "A Portrait of Continuing Marginality: The Study of Women of Color in American Politics." In *Women and American Politics: New Questions, New Directions,* ed. Susan J. Carroll. New York: Oxford University Press, 190–214.

Cohen, Micah. 2012. "Gay Vote Proved a Boon for Obama," *The New York Times.* November 15. http://www.nytimes.com/2012/11/16/us/politics/gay-vote-seen-as-crucial-in-obamas-victory.html?_r=0 (accessed July 26, 2013).

Cohn, Alicia M. 2012. "House GOP Launches Women's Policy Panel in New Video." *The Hill* May 22. http://thehill.com/blogs/blog-briefing-room/news/228845-house-republicans-launch-womens-policy-committee-with-new-video-introducing-gop-women-in-congress (accessed July 26, 2013).

Collins, Jr., P. M., Manning, K. L. and Carp, R. A. 2010. "Gender, Critical Mass, and Judicial Decision Making." *Law & Policy* 32: 260–281. doi: 10.1111/j.1467-9930.2010.00317.x

Conger, Jay. 1991. "Inspiring Others: The Language of Leadership." *Academy of Management Executive* 5 (February): 31–45.

Conger, Kimberly H. 2010. "A Matter of Context: Christian Right Influence in U.S. State Republican Politics." *State Politics and Policy Quarterly* 10: 248–269.

Conover, Johnson Pamela, and Stanley Feldman. 1989. "Candidate Perception in an Ambiguous World: Campaigns, Cues, and Inference Processes." *American Journal of Political Science* 33(4): 912–940.

Conway, M. Margaret, David W. Ahern and Gertrude A. Steuernagel. 2004. *Women and Political Participation: Cultural Change in the Political Arena.* 2nd ed. Washington, DC: Congressional Quarterly, Inc.

Costantini, Edmond. 1990. "Political Women and Political Ambition: Closing the Gender Gap." *American Journal of Political Science* 34: 741–770.

Cook, Beverly Blair. 1978. "Women Judges: The End of Tokenism." In *Women in the Courts*, eds. Winifred L. Hepperle and Laura Crites. Williamsburg: National Center for State Courts, 84–105.

———. 1980a. "Florence Allen." In *Notable American Women: The Modern Period—A Biographical Dictionary*, eds. Barbara Sicherman and Carol Hurd Green. Cambridge: Harvard University Press, 10–13.

———. 1980b. "Political Culture and Selection of Women Judges in Trial Courts." In *Women in Local Politics*, eds. Debra W. Stewart. Metuchen, NJ: Scarecrow Press, 42–60.

———. 1981. "The First Woman Candidate for Supreme Court—Florence Allen." In *Supreme Court Historical Society Yearbook.* Washington, D.C.: Supreme Court Historical Society, 19–35.

———. 1982. "Women as Supreme Court Candidates: From Florence Allen to Sandra O'Connor." *Judicature* 65(6): 314–326.

———. 1984a. "Women Judges: A Preface to Their History." *Golden Gate University Law Review* 14(3): 573–610.

———. 1984b. "Women on the State Bench: Correlates of Access." In *Political Women: Current Roles in State and Local Government*, ed. Janet A. Flammang. Beverly Hills: SAGE, 191–218.

———. 1987. "Women Judges in the Opportunity Structure." In *Women, the Courts, and Equality*, eds. Laura L. Crites and Winifred L. Hepperle. Newbury Park, CA: SAGE, 143–174.

Cook, Elizabeth. 1998. "Voter Reaction to Women Candidates." in *Women and Elective Office: Past, Present, and Future*, ed. Sue Thomas and Clyde Wilcox. New York: Oxford University Press, 56–72.

———. 1994. "Voter Responses to Women Senate Candidates." In *The Year of the Woman: Myths and Realities*, eds. Elizabeth Adell Cook, Sue Thomas, and Clyde Wilcox. Boulder, CO: Westview Press, 217–236.

Cook Political Report. 2006. Washington, DC: Cook Political Report.

Cook, Timothy. 1989. *Making Laws and Making News: Media Strategies in the U.S. House of Representatives.* Washington, DC: Brookings Institution.

Cooper, Cynthia L. 2008. "Women Supreme Court Clerks Striving for 'Commonplace.'" *Perspectives: The Quarterly Magazine of the American Bar Association Commission on Women in the Profession* 17(1): 18–19, 22.

Cooper, Johnathon J. 2012. "Oregon Will Have 1st Lesbian Legislative Leader." *Seattle Post Intelligencer*, November 15.

Cordova. Alyssa. 2011. Interview. Lecture director, Clare Boothe Luce Policy Institute. March 6.

Corriher, Billy. 2012. "Money Undermines Judges' Impartiality." *USA Today.* November 12. http://www.usatoday.com/story/opinion/2012/11/12/supreme-court-judici al-elections-campaign-finance/1697941/ (accessed November 14, 2012).

Cottle, Michelle. 2008. "What Went Wrong." *New Republic.* May 16. www.tnr.com/politics/story. html?id=f7a4a380-c4a4-4f84-b653-f252e8569915 (accessed July 23, 2013).

Cowley, Philip, and Sarah Childs. 2003. "To Spineless to Rebel? New Labour's Women MPs." *British Journal of Political Science* 33(3): 345–365.

Cox, Elizabeth M. 1994. "The Three Who Came First." *State Legislatures* 20: 12–19.

Cramer Walsh, Katherine. 2002. "Resonating to Be Heard: Gendered Debate on the Floor of the House." In *Women Transforming Congress*, ed. Cindy Simon Rosenthal. Norman: University of Oklahoma Press, 370–396.

Crowley, Jocelyn Elise. 2004. "When Tokens Matter." *Legislative Studies Quarterly* 29: 109–136.

Cruz Takash, Paula. 1997. "Breaking Barriers to Representation: Chicana/Latina Elected Officials in California." In *Women Transforming Politics: An Alternative Reader*, eds. Cathy J. Cohen, Kathleen B. Jones, and Joan C. Tronto. New York: New York University Press, 412–434.

Curriden, Mark. 2010. "Tipping the Scales: In the South, Women Have Made Huge Strides in the State Judiciaries." *ABA Journal*. July 1. http://www.abajournal.com/magazine/article/tipping_the_scales (accessed September 7, 2010).

Cutler, Frederick. 2002. "The Simplest Short-Cut of All: Voter-Candidate Socio-Demographic Similarity and Electoral Choice." *Journal of Politics* 64(2): 466–490.

Dabelko, Kirsten L., and Paul S. Herrnson. 1997. "Women's and Men's Campaigns for the U.S. House of Representatives." *Political Research Quarterly* 50(1): 121–135.

Dahlerup, Drude. 2006. "The Story of the Theory of Critical Mass." *Politics and Gender* 2: 511–522.

Dahlerup, Drude and Freidenvall, L., eds. 2008. *Electoral Gender Quota Systems and Their Implementation in Europe*. Report. Committee on Women's Rights and Gender Equality, European Parliament, Strasbourg, France.

Dannenfelser, Marjorie. 2011. Interview. President, Susan B. Anthony List. March 28.

Darcy, Robert. 1996. "Women in the State Legislative Power Structure: Committee Chairs." *Social Science Quarterly* 77: 888–898.

Darcy, Robert, and Charles D. Hadley. 1988. "Black Women in Politics: The Puzzle of Success." *Social Science Quarterly* 69: 629–645.

Darcy, Robert, Charles D. Hadley, and Jason F. Kirksey. 1993. "Election Systems and the Representation of Black Women in American State Legislatures." *Women and Politics* 13: 73–89.

Darcy, Robert, Susan Welch, and Janet Clark. 1994. *Women, Elections & Representation*, 2nd ed. Lincoln: University of Nebraska Press.

Davidson, Roger H., Walter J. Oleszek and Frances E. Lee. 2011. *Congress and Its Members*, 13th ed. Washington, DC: CQ Press.

Davidson-Schmich, Louise K. 2006. "Implementation of Political Party Gender Quotas: Evidence from the German Lander, 1990–2000." *Party Politics* 12(2): 211–232.

Davis, Beth Boosalis. 2008. *Mayor Helen Boosalis: My Mother's Life in Politics*. Lincoln: University of Nebraska Press.

Deckman, Melissa. 2007. "Gender Differences in the Decision to Run for School Board." *American Politics Research* 35(4): 541–563.

——. 2011. "Mama Grizzlies and the Midterms: Women and the Tea Party." Presented at the Annual Meeting of the American Political Science Association, Seattle. http://ssrn.com/abstract=1916693 or http://dx.doi.org/10.2139/ssrn.1916693 (accessed July 23, 2013).

Deen, Rebecca E., and Thomas H. Little. 1999. "Getting to the Top: Factors Influencing the Selection of Women to Positions of Leadership in State Legislatures." *State and Local Government Review* 31(2): 123–134.

Deering, Christopher J., and Steven S. Smith. 1997. *Committees in Congress*, 3rd ed. Washington, DC: CQ Press.

DeLauro, Rosa. 2008. "The Paycheck Fairness Act: A Victory in Closing the Wage Gap." *Huffington Post*, August 21. http://www.huffingtonpost.com/rep-rosa-delauro/the-paycheck-fairness-act_b_120469.html (accessed July 26, 2013).

Devitt, James. 2002. "Framing Gender on the Campaign Trail: Female Gubernatorial Candidates and the Press." *Journalism & Mass Communication Quarterly* 79(2): 445–463.

Diamond, Irene. 1977. *Sex Roles in the State House*. New Haven, CT: Yale University Press.

Diascro, Jennifer Segal, and Rorie Spill Solberg. 2009. "George W. Bush's Legacy on the Federal Bench: Policy in the Face of Diversity." *Judicature* 92(6): 289–301.

Dittmar, K. 2013. "What's the Hold-Up? Women's Delayed Entry into Political Office." *Footnotes*. Center for American Women and Politics. January 8. http://cawp.rutgers.edu/footnotes/whats-the-hold-up-womens-delayed-entry-into-political-office (accessed March 23, 2013).

Doan, Alesha E., and Donald P. Haider-Markel. 2010. "The Role of Intersectional Stereotypes on Evaluations of Political Candidates." *Politics & Gender* 6(1): 63–91.

Dodson, Debra L. 1997. "Change and Continuity in the Relationship between Private Responsibilities and Public Officeholding: The More Things Change, the More They Stay the Same." *Policy Studies Journal* 25: 569–584.

————. 1998. "Representing Women's Interests in the U.S. House of Representatives." In *Women and Elective Office*, eds. Sue Thomas and Clyde Wilcox. New York: Oxford University Press, 130–149.

————. 2001. "Acting for Women: Is What Legislators Say, What They Do?" In *The Impact of Women in Public Office*, ed. Susan J. Carroll. Bloomington: University of Indiana Press, 225–242.

————. 2006. *The Impact of Women in Congress.* New York: Oxford University Press.

Dodson, Debra, and Susan J. Carroll. 1991. *Reshaping the Agenda: Women in State Legislatures.* New Brunswick, NJ: Eagleton Institute of Politics' Center for American Women and Politics.

Dolan, Julie, and Jonathan Kropf. 2004. "Credit Claiming from the U.S. House: Gendered Communications Styles?" *Harvard International Journal of Press/Politics* 9(1): 41–59.

Dolan, Julie, Melissa Deckman, and Michele L. Swers. 2007. *Women and Politics: Paths to Power and Political Influence.* Upper Saddle River, NJ: Pearson: Prentice Hall.

————. 2011. *Women and Politics: Paths to Power and Political Influence*, 2nd ed. New York: Longman.

Dolan, Kathleen. 1997. "Gender Differences in Support for Women Candidates: Is There a Glass Ceiling in American Politics?" *Women and Politics* 17: 27–41.

————. 1998. "Voting for Women in the 'Year of the Woman.'" *American Journal of Political Science* 42: 272–293.

————. 2004a. "The Impact of Candidate Sex on Evaluations of Candidates for the U.S. House of Representatives." *Social Science Quarterly* 85(1): 206–217.

————. 2004b. *Voting for Women: How the Public Evaluates Women Candidates.* Boulder, CO: Westview Press.

————. 2005. "Do Women Candidates Play to Gender Stereotypes? Do Men Candidates Play to Women? Candidate Sex and Issue Priorities on Campaign Websites." *Political Research Quarterly* 58(1): 31–44.

————. 2006. "Symbolic Mobilization? The Impact of Candidate Sex in American Elections." *American Politics Research* 34(6): 687–704.

————. 2010. "The Impact of Gender Stereotyped Evaluations on Support for Women Candidates." *Political Behavior* 32: 69–88.

Dolan, Kathleen, and Lynne E. Ford. 1995. "Women in the State Legislatures: Feminist Identity and Legislative Behavior." *American Politics Quarterly* 23: 96–108.

————. 1997. "Change and Continuity among Women State Legislators: Evidence from Three Decades." *Political Research Quarterly* 50: 137–151.

————. 1998. "Are All Women State Legislators Alike?" In *Women and Elective Office: Past, Present, and Future*, eds. Sue Thomas and Clyde Wilcox. New York: Oxford University Press, 73–86.

Dolan, Kathleen, and Kira Sanbonmatsu. 2009. "Gender Stereotypes and Attitudes toward Gender Balance in Government." *American Politics Research* 37: 409–428.

Dometrius, Nelson C., and Lee Sigelman. 1997. "Organizational Regeneration Reconsidered: Women in State and Local Government, 1980–90." *American Journal of Political Science* 41: 333–338.

Donahue, Jesse. 1997. "It Doesn't Matter: Some Cautionary Findings about Sex and Representation from School Committee Conversations." *Policy Studies Journal* 25(4): 630–647.

Dovi, Suzanne. 2002. "Preferable Descriptive Representatives: Will Just Any Black, Woman, or Latino Do?" *American Political Science Review* 96(4): 729–743.

————. 2007. "Theorizing Women's Representation in the United States." *Politics & Gender* 3(3): 297–320.

Druckman, James N. 2004. "Priming the Vote: Campaign Effects in a U.S. Senate Election." *Political Psychology* 25(4): 577–594.

Duerst-Lahti, Georgia. 1997. "Reconceiving Theories of Power: Consequences of Masculinism in the Executive Branch." In *The Other Elites: Women, Politics, and Power in the Executive Branch*, eds. MaryAnee Borrelli and Janet M. Martin. Boulder, CO: Lynne Rienner Publishers, Inc, 11–32.

————. 1998. "The Bottleneck, Women as Candidates." In *Women and Elective Office*, eds. Sue Thomas and Clyde Wilcox. New York: Oxford University Press, 15–25.

——. 2002. "Governing Institutions, Ideologies and Gender: Toward the Possibility of Equal Political Representation." *Sex Roles: A Journal of Research* 47: 371–388.

——. 2004. "Masculinity on the Campaign Trail." In *Rethinking Madam President: Are We Ready for a Woman in the White House?* eds. Lori Cox Han and Caroline Heldman. Boulder, CO: Lynne Rienner Publishers, 87–112.

——. 2005. "Institutional Gendering: Theoretical Insights into the Environment of Women Officeholders." In *Women and Elective Office: Past, Present and Future*, eds. Sue Thomas and Clyde Wilcox. New York: Oxford University Press, 244–263.

——. 2006. "Presidential Elections: Gendered Space and the Case of 2004." In *Gender and Elections: Shaping the Future of American Politics*, eds. Susan Carroll and Richard Fox. New York: Cambridge University Press, 12–42.

Duerst-Lahti, Georgia, and Cathy Marie Johnson. 1992. "Management Styles, Stereotypes, and Advantages." In *Women and Men of the States: Public Administrators at the State Level*, ed. M. E. Guy. Armonk: M.E. Sharpe, 67–120.

Duerst-Lahti, Georgia, and Rita Mae Kelly, eds. 1995. *Gender Power, Leadership, and Governance*. Ann Arbor: University of Michigan Press.

Duke, Lois Lovelace, ed. 1996. *Women In Politics: Outsiders or Insiders?* 2nd ed. Upper Saddle River, NJ: Pearson.

Eagly, Alice H. 1987. *Sex Differences in Social Behavior: A Social Role Interpretation*. Hillsdale, NJ: Erlbaum.

——. 1997. "Sex Differences in Social Behavior: Comparing Social Role Theory and Evolutionary Psychology." *American Psychologist* 52(12): 1380–1383.

Eagly, Alice H., and Linda L. Carli. 2007. *Through the Labyrinth: The Truth about How Women Become Leaders*. Boston, MA: Harvard Business School Press.

Eagly, Alice H., Wendy Wood, and Amanda B. Diekman. 2000. "Social Role Theory of Sex Differences and Similarities: A Current Appraisal." In *The Developmental Social Psychology of Gender*, eds. Thomas Eckes and Hanns Martin Trautner. Mahwah, NJ: Erlbaum, 123–174.

*Economist*. 2011. "Congress with a Woman's Touch." July 5. http://www.economist.com/blogs/democracyinamerica/2011/07/women-politics (accessed July 23, 2013).

Egan, Patrick J. 2012. "Group Cohesion without Group Mobilization: The Case of Lesbians, Gays, and Bisexuals." *British Journal of Political Science* 42(3): 597–616.

Elazar, Daniel J. 1984. *American Federalism: A View from the States*, 3rd ed. New York: Harper & Row.

Elder, Laurel. 2008. "Whither Republican Women: The Growing Partisan Gap among Women in Congress." *Forum* 6(1), April. doi: 10.2202/1540-8884.1204.——. 2012. "The Partisan Gap among Women State Legislators." *Journal of Women, Politics & Policy* 33(1): 65–85.

Elder, Laurel, and Steven Greene. 2012. "The Politics of Parenthood: Parenthood Effects on Issue Attitudes and Candidate Evaluation in 2008." *American Politics Research* 40(3): 419–449.

Emrich, Cynthia, Holly H. Brower, Jack Feldman, and Howard Garland. 2001. "Images in Words: Presidential Rhetoric, Charisma and Greatness." *Administrative Science Quarterly* 46(3): 527–557.

Engström, H. 2009. "Gender Sensitive Parliaments: The Swedish Experience." In *Is Parliament Open to Women?* Geneva: Inter-Parliamentary Union. http://www.ipu.org/pdf/publications/gsp11ex-e.pdf (accessed July 23, 2013).

Epstein, Michael, Richard G. Niemi, and Lynda W. Powell. 2005. "Do Women and Men State Legislators Differ?" In *Women and Elective Office: Past, Present, and Future*, 2nd ed., eds. Sue Thomas and Clyde Wilcox. New York: Oxford University Press, 94–109.

Erbring, Lutz, Edie N. Goldenberg, and Arthur H. Miller. 1980. "Front-Page News and Real-World Cues: A New Look at Agenda Setting by the Media." *American Journal of Political Science* 24(1): 16–49.

Esterling, Kevin M., and Seth S. Andersen. 1999. "Diversity and the Judicial Merit Selection Process: A Statistical Report." In *Research on Judicial Selection 1999*. Chicago: American Judicature Society, 1–39. http://www.judicialselection.com/uploads/documents/Diversity_and_the_Judicial_Merit_Se_9C4863118945B.pdf (accessed July 23, 2013).

Eulau, Heinz, and Paul Karps. 1977. "The Puzzle of Representation: Specifying Components of Responsiveness." *Legislative Studies Quarterly* 2(3): 233–255.

Evilsizer, Tyler. 2010. "Competitiveness in 2007–2008 State Legislative Races." *FollowTheMoney. org*, National Institute on Money in State Politics. http://www.followthemoney.org/press/ReportView.phtml?r=424&ext=9 (accessed December 29, 2010).

Falk, Erika. 2008. *Women for President: Media Bias in Eight Campaigns*. Urbana: University of Illinois Press.

———. 2010. *Women for President: Media Bias in Nine Campaigns*. Urbana: University of Illinois Press.

Falk, Erika, and Kate Kenski. 2006. "Issue Saliency and Gender Stereotypes: Support for Women as Presidents in Times of War and Terrorism." *Social Science Quarterly* 87(1): 1–18.

Feder, J. Lester. 2012. "Murray Hits GOP on Women's Health." *Politico*, February 17. http://www.politico.com/news/stories/0212/73027.html (accessed July 23, 2013).

Feldman, Linda. 2010. "Tuesday Primaries: Year of the Republican Woman Dawning?" *Christian Science Monitor*. June 7. http://www.csmonitor.com/USA/Politics/2010/0607/Tuesday-primaries-Year-of-the-Republican-woman-dawning (accessed July 23, 2013).

Fenno, Richard F., Jr. 1978. *Home Style: House Members in Their Districts*. Boston, MA: Little, Brown.

———. 1996. *Senators on the Campaign Trail: The Politics of Representation*. Norman: University of Oklahoma Press.

———. 1998. "Introduction." In *Explorations in the Evolution of Congress*, ed. H. Douglas Price. Berkeley, CA: IGS Press, 1–9.

———. 2003. *Going Home: Black Representatives and Their Constituents*. Chicago: University of Chicago Press.

Ferraro, Thomas. 2012. "Top Republican Woman in Congress Becomes a Force." *Reuters*, May 18.

Fiber, Pamela, and Richard L. Fox. 2005. "A Tougher Road for Women? Assessing the Role of Gender in Congressional Elections." In *Gender and American Politics: Women, Men, and the Political Process*, 2nd ed., eds. Sue Tolleson-Rinehart and Jyl J. Josephson. Armonk, NY: M.E. Sharp, 64–80.

Field, Bonnie N., and Peter M. Siavelis. 2008. "Candidate Selection Procedures in Transitional Polities." *Party Politics* 14(5): 620–639.

Fiorina, Morris P., and Paul E. Peterson. 2002. *The New American Democracy*, 2nd ed. New York: Longman.

Fiske, Susan T., Jun Xu, Amy J. C. Cuddy, and Peter Glick. 1999. "(Dis)respecting versus (Dis)liking: Status and Interdependence Predict Ambivalent Stereotypes of Competence and Warmth." *Journal of Social Issues* 55(3): 473–491.

Flammang, Janet A. 1984. "Filling the Party Vacuum: Women at the Grassroots Level in Local Politics." In *Political Women: Current Roles in State and Local Government*, ed. Janet A. Flammang. Beverly Hills, CA: SAGE, 87–113.

———. 1985. "Female Officials in the Feminist Capital: The Case of Santa Clara County." *Western Political Quarterly* 38: 94–118.

Flatow, Nicole. 2012. "California Federal Court Home to First All-Female Bench." *ThinkProgress*. November 27. http://thinkprogress.org/justice/2012/11/27/1237551/california-federal-court-home-to-first-all-female-bench/ (accessed July 23, 2013).

Flyvberg, Bent. 2011. "Five Misunderstandings about Case Study Research." *Qualitative Inquiry* 12(2): 219–245.

Forster, Stacy. 2009. "Number of Women in State Legislature Declining." *Milwaukee Journal Sentinel*. January 10. http://www.jsonline.com/news/statepolitics/37396194.html (accessed March 4, 2013).

Fortini, Amanda. 2008. "The Feminist Reawakening: Hillary Clinton and the Fourth Wave." *New York Magazine*. April 14. http://nymag.com/news/features/46011/ (accessed December 20, 2009).

Foss, Sonja K. 1979. "Equal Rights Amendment Controversy: Two Worlds in Conflict." *Quarterly Journal of Speech* 65: 275–288.

Fowler, Linda L., and Jennifer L. Lawless. 2009. "Looking for Sex in All the Wrong Places: Press Coverage and the Electoral Fortunes of Gubernatorial Candidates." *Perspectives on Politics* 7(3): 519–537.

Fowler, Linda L., and Jennifer L. Lawless. 2009. "Looking for Sex in all the Wrong Places: Press Coverage and the Electoral Fortunes of Gubernatorial Candidates." *Perspectives on Politics* 7(3): 519–536.

Fox, Richard Logan. 1997. *Gender Dynamics in Congressional Elections.* Thousand Oaks, CA: SAGE.

——. 2000. "Gender and Congressional Elections." In *Gender and American Politics: Women, Men and the Political Process,* eds. Sue Tolleson-Rinehart and Jyl J. Josephson. Armonk, NY: M.E. Sharpe, 227–256.

——. 2010. "Congressional Elections: Women's Candidacies and the Road to Gender Parity." In *Gender and Elections,* 2nd ed., eds. S. Carroll and R. Fox. New York: Cambridge University Press, 187–209.

Fox, Richard Logan, and Jennifer L. Lawless. 2010. "If Only They'd Ask: Gender, Recruitment, and Political Ambition." *Journal of Politics* 72(2): 310–336.

——. 2011. "Gendered Perceptions and Political Candidacies: A Central Barrier to Women's Equality in Electoral Politics." *American Journal of Political Science* 55(1): 59–73.

Fox, Richard Logan, Jennifer L. Lawless, and Courtney Feeley. 2001. "Gender and the Decision to Run for Office." *Legislative Studies Quarterly* 26(3): 411–435.

Fox, Richard Logan and Zoe Oxley. 2003. "Gender Stereotyping in State Executive Elections: Candidate Selection and Success." *Journal of Politics* 65(3): 833–850.

Fox, Richard Logan, Jennifer L. Lawless, and Robert Schuhmann. 1999. "Gender and Local Government: A Comparison of Women and Men City Managers." *Public Administration Review* 59(3): 231–242.

Fraga, Luis Ricardo, Linda Lopez, Valerie Martinez-Ebers, and Ricardo Ramirez. 2006. "Gender and Ethnicity: Patterns of Electoral Success and Legislative Advocacy among Latina and Latino Officials in Four States." In *Intersectionality and Politics: Recent Research on Gender, Race, and Political Representation in the United States,* ed. Carol Hardy-Fanta. New York: Haworth Press, 121–146.

Fraga, Luis Ricardo, Valerie Martinez-Ebers, Linda Lopez, and Ricardo Ramirez. 2008. "Representing Gender and Ethnicity: Strategic Intersectionality." In *Legislative Women: Getting Elected, Getting Ahead,* ed. Beth Reingold. Boulder, CO: Lynne Reiner Publishers, 157–174.

Fraga, Luis Ricardo, and Sharon Navarro. 2004. "Latinas in Latino Politics." Presented at the Latino Politics: The State of the Discipline conference, College Station, TX.

Frandina, Michael Mahoney. 2009. "A Man's Right to Choose His Surname in Marriage: A Proposal." *Duke Journal of Gender, Law and Policy* 16(1): 155–158.

Fraser, Arvonne. 1983. "Insiders and Outsiders: Women in the Political Arena." In *Women in Washington: Advocates for Public Policy,* ed. Irene Tinker. Beverly Hills, CA: SAGE, 120–139.

Frederick, Brian. 2009. "Are Female House Members Still More Liberal in a Polarized Era? The Conditional Nature of the Relationship between Descriptive and Substantive Representation." *Congress and the Presidency* 36: 181–202.

——. 2010. "Gender and Patterns of Roll-Call Voting in the Senate." *Congress and the Presidency* 37: 103–124.

——. 2011. "Gender Turnover and Roll Call Voting in the US Senate." *Journal of Women, Politics & Policy* 32: 193–210.

Freedman, Jo. 2002. *A Room at a Time: How Women Entered Party Politics.* Lanham, MD: Rowman & Littlefield.

Freyer, Felice J. 1999. "Officials Say Being Openly Gay Isn't a Detriment." *Providence Journal-Bulletin,* November 21. http://www.glapn.org/sodomylaws/usa/rhode_island/rinews19.htm (accessed July 23, 2013).

Fridkin, Kim L., Jill Carle, and Gina S. Woodall. 2011. "The Vice-Presidency as the New Glass Ceiling: An Examination of Sarah Palin's Media Coverage." In *Women and the Executive Branch,* ed. Melody Rose. Boulder, CO: Lynne Rienner Publishers, 33–52.

Fridkin, Kim L., and Patrick J. Kenney. 2009. "The Role of Gender Stereotypes in U.S. Senate Campaigns." *Politics and Gender* 5(3): 301–324.

Fridkin, Kim L., Patrick J. Kenney, and Gina Serignese Woodall. 2009. "Bad for Men, Better for Women: The Impact of Stereotypes During Negative Campaigns." *Political Behavior* 31(1): 53–77.

Fridkin, Kim L., and Gina Woodall. 2005. "Different Portraits, Different Leaders? Gender Differences in US Senators' Presentation of Self." In *Women and Elective Office: Past, Present, and Future*, 2nd ed., ed. Sue Thomas and Clyde Wilcox. New York: Oxford University Press, 81–93.

Friedman, Sally, A. 1996. "Committee Assignments of Women and Blacks in Congress—1964–1990." *Legislative Studies Quarterly* 21: 73–81.

Fulton, Sarah A., Cherie D. Maestas, L. Sandy Maisel, and Walter J. Stone. 2006. "The Sense of a Woman: Gender, Ambition and the Decision to Run for Congress." *Political Research Quarterly* 59(2): 235–248.

Gaffney, Amber M., and Danielle L. Blaylock. 2010. "Hillary Clinton's Race: Did She Match the Presidential Prototype?" *Advancing Women in Leadership* 30(6): 1–15.

Gallagher, Michael, and Michael Marsh, eds. 1988. *Candidate Selection in Comparative Perspective: The Secret Garden of Politics*. London: SAGE.

García Bedolla, Lisa. 2005. "Latinas in the U.S. Congress, 1989–2002." In *Latinas in the United States: An Historical Encyclopedia*, eds. Virginia Sánchez-Korrol and Vicki Ruiz. Bloomington: University of Indiana Press, 375–377.

Gay, Claudine. 2001. "The Effect of Black Congressional Representation on Political Participation." *American Political Science Review* 95: 589–602.

———. 2002. "Spirals of Trust? The Effect of Descriptive Representation on the Relationship between Citizens and Their Government." *American Journal of Political Science* 46(4): 717–732.

Gerrity, Jessica C., Tracy Osborn, and Jeanette Morehouse Mendez. 2007. "Women and Representation: A Different View of the District." *Politics & Gender* 3: 179–200.

Gershon, Sarah Allen. 2009. "Gendered Appeals Online: A Study of Female Representatives' Websites." Presented at the annual meeting of the American Political Science Association, Toronto.

———. 2013. "When Race, Gender, and the Media Intersect: Campaign News Coverage of Minority Congresswomen." *Politics & Gender* 33: 105–125.

Gerth, Jeff, and Don Van Natta Jr. 2007. *Her Way: The Hopes and Ambitions of Hillary Rodham Clinton*. New York: Little, Brown and Company.

Gertzog, Irwin N. 1995. *Congressional Women: Their Recruitment, Integration, and Behavior*, 2nd ed. Westport, CT: Praeger.

———. 2002. "Women's Changing Pathways to the U.S. House of Representatives: Widows, Elites, and Strategic Politicians." In *Women Transforming Congress*, ed. Cindy Simon Rosenthal. Norman: University of Oklahoma Press, 95–118.

Gierzynski, Anthony, and Paulette Burdreck. 1995. "Women's Legislative Caucus and Leadership Campaign Committees." *Women & Politics* 15: 37–54.

Gill, LaVerne McCain. 1997. *African American Women in Congress: Forming and Transforming History*. New Brunswick, NJ: Rutgers University Press.

Githens, Marianne. 1977. "Spectators, Agitators or Lawmakers: Women in State Legislatures." In *A Portrait of Marginality: The Political Behavior of the American Women*, eds. Marianne Githens and Jewel Prestage. New York: McKay, 196–209.

———. 1995. "Getting Appointed to the State Court: The Gender Dimension." *Women & Politics* 15(4): 1–24.

Githens, Marianne, and Jewel L. Prestage. 1977. *A Portrait of Marginality: The Political Behavior of the American Woman*. New York: Longman.

Goldman, Sheldon. 1997. *Picking Federal Judges: Lower Court Selection From Roosevelt Through Reagan*. New Haven, CT: Yale University Press.

Goldman, Sheldon, Sara Schiavoni, and Elliot Slotnick. 2009. "W. Bush's Judicial Legacy: Mission Accomplished." *Judicature* 92: 258–288.

Golebiowska, E. A. 2001. "Group Stereotypes and Political Evaluation." *American Politics Research* 29: 535–565.

———. 2002. "Political Implications of Group Stereotypes: Campaign Experiences of Openly Gay Political Candidates." *Journal of Applied Social Psychology* 32: 590–607.

Golebiowska, E. A., and Thomsen, C. J. 1999. "Group Stereotypes of Individuals: The Case of Gay and Lesbian Political Candidates." In *Gays and Lesbians in The Democratic Process: Public Policy, Public Opinion and Political Representation*, eds. E. D. B. Riggle and B. Tadlock. New York: Columbia University Press, 192–219.

Goren, Paul. 2007. "Character Weakness, Partisan Bias, and Presidential Evaluations: Modifications and Extensions." *Political Behavior* 29: 305–325.

Green, Joshua. 2008. "Inside the Clinton Shake-Up." *Atlantic Monthly*. February. http://www.the-atlantic.com/doc/200802u/patti-solis-doyle (accessed July 23, 2013).

———. 2010. "Trait Voting in U.S. Senate Elections." *American Politics Research* 38(6): 1102–1129.

Greenburg, Jan Crawford. 2007. *Supreme Conflict: The Inside Story of the Struggle for Control of the United States Supreme Court*. New York: Penguin.

Greenhouse, Carol J. 2010. "Judgment and the Justice: An Ethnographic Reading of the Sotomayor Confirmation Hearings." *Law, Culture and the Humanities*. November 25. http://lch.sagepub.com/content/early/2010/11/12/1743872110374916 (accessed November 23, 2011).

Grey, Sandra. 2006. "Numbers and Beyond: The Relevance of Critical Mass in Gender Research." *Politics & Gender* 2: 492–502.

Graber, Doris A. 2009. *Mass Media and American Politics*, 8th ed. Washington, DC: CQ Press.

Greenlee, Jill. 2010. "Soccer Moms, Hockey Moms and the Question of 'Transformative' Motherhood." *Politics & Gender* 6: 405–431.

Griffin, John D., Brian Newman, and Christina Wolbrecht. 2012. "A Gender Gap in Policy Representation in the US Congress?" *Legislative Studies Quarterly* 37(1): 35–66.

Grimmer, Justin. 2010. "A Bayesian Hierarchical Topic Model for Political Texts: Measuring Expressed Agendas in Senate Press Releases." *Political Analysis* 18(1): 1–35.

Haider-Markel, Donald P. 2001. "Shopping for Favorable Venues in the States: Institutional Influences on Legislative Outcomes of Same-Sex Marriage Bills." *American Review of Politics* 22: 27–54.

———. 2007. "Representation and Backlash: The Positive and Negative Influence of Descriptive Representation." *Legislative Studies Quarterly* 32(1): 107–134.

———. 2010. *Out and Running: Gay and Lesbian Candidates, Elections, and Policy Representation*. Washington, DC: Georgetown University Press.

Haider-Markel, Donald P., and Mark R. Joslyn. 2008. "Understanding Beliefs about the Origins of Homosexuality and Subsequent Support for Gay Rights: An Empirical Test of Attribution Theory." *Public Opinion Quarterly* 72(2): 291–310.

Haider-Markel, Donald P., Mark R. Joslyn, and Chad J. Kniss. 2000. "Minority Group Interests and Political Representation: Gay Elected Officials in the Policy Process." *Journal of Politics* 62(2): 568–577.

Hall, Melinda Gann, and Chris Bonneau. 2009. *In Defense of Judicial Elections*. New York: Routledge.

Hamm, Keith E., and Gary F. Moncrief. 2008. "Legislative Politics in the States." In *Politics in the American States*, 9th ed., eds.Virginia Gray and Russell L. Hanson. Washington, DC: CQ Press, 154–191.

Hansen, Susan B. 1993. "Differences in Public Policies Toward Abortion: Electoral and Policy Context." In *Understanding the New Politics of Abortion*, ed. Malcolm L. Goggin. Newbury Park, CA: SAGE, 222–248.

Hardisty, Jean. 1999. *Mobilizing Resentment*. Boston, MA: Beacon Press.

Hardy, J., W. Kozek, and A. Stenning. 2008. "In the Front Line: Women, Work and New Spaces of Labour Politics in Poland." *Gender Place and Culture* 15(2): 99–116.

Hardy-Fanta, Carol. 2000. "A Latino Gender Gap? Evidence from the 1996 Election." *Milenio* 2. Notre Dame, IN: Inter-University Program for Latino Research.

Hardy-Fanta, Carol, Pei-te Lien, Dianne M. Pinderhughes, and Christine Marie Sierra. 2007. "Gender, Race, and Descriptive Representation in the United States: Findings from the Gender and Multicultural Leadership Project." *Journal of Women, Politics & Policy* 28(3–4): 7–41.

Harris, John F., and Beth Frisking. 2008. "Clinton Aides: Palin Treatment Sexist." *Politico*. December 8. http://www.politico.com/news/stories/0908/13129.html. Accessed 7/23/13

Hart, Roderick P. 2001. "Redeveloping DICTION: Theoretical Considerations." In *Theory, Method, and Practice of Computer Content Analysis*, ed. Mark D. West. New York: Ablex.

——. 1984. *Verbal Style and the Presidency: A Computer-Based Analysis*. Orlando: Academic Press.

Hawkesworth, Mary. 2003. "Congressional Enactments of Race-Gender: Toward a Theory of Raced-Gendered Institutions." *American Political Science Review* 97: 529–550.

Hayes, Danny. 2011. "When Gender and Party Collide: Stereotyping in Candidate Trait Attribution." *Politics & Gender* 7: 133–165.

Hazan, Reuven. 2002. "Candidate Selection." In *Comparing Democracies 2: New Challenges in the Study of Elections and Voting*, eds. L. LeDuc, P. Norris, and R. G. Niemi. London: SAGE, 108–126.

Hazan, Reuven Y., and Gideon Rahat. 2010. *Democracy within Parties: Candidate Selection Methods and Their Political Consequences*. New York: Oxford University Press.

Healy, Patrick. 2007a. "In Elderly Women, Clinton Sees an Electoral Edge." *New York Times*. November 27. http://www.nytimes.com/2007/11/27/us/politics/27ladies.html. Accessed 7/23/13

——. 2007b. "The Resume Factor: Those 2 Terms as First Lady." *New York Times*, December 26. http://www.nytimes.com/2007/12/26/us/politics/26clinton.html?pagewanted=all (accessed July 26, 2013).

Healy, Patrick, and Jeff Zeleny. 2008. "Obama Extends Streak to 10, Makes Inroads among Women." *New York Times*. February 20. http://www.nytimes.com/2008/02/20/us/politics/20cnd-campaign.html?_r=2&nl=pol&emc=pol&oref=slogin&oref=slogin (accessed July 23, 2013).

Helderman, Rosalind. 2013. "The 113th Congress Is the Most Diverse in History." *Washington Post*, January 3. http://www.washingtonpost.com/politics/113th-congress-has-more-women-minorities-than-ever/2013/01/03/7d1aaf30-55e5-11e2-8b9e-dd8773594efc_story.html (accessed July 26, 2013).

Heldman, Caroline, Susan J. Carroll, and Stephanie Olson. 2005. "She Brought Only a Skirt: Print Media Coverage of Elizabeth Dole's Bid for the Presidential Nomination." *Political Communication* 22(3): 315–335.

Heldman, Caroline, Sarah Oliver, and Meredith Conroy. 2009. "From Ferraro to Palin: Sexism in Media Coverage of Vice Presidential Candidates." Presented at the Annual Meetings of the American Political Science, Toronto.

Herek, Gregory M. 2002. "Gender Gaps in Public Opinion about Lesbians and Gay Men." *Public Opinion Quarterly* 66(1): 40–66.

Herrera, Richard, and Karen Shafer. 2012. "Women in the Governor's Mansion: How Party and Gender Affect Policy." In *Women and Executive Office: Pathways and Performance*, ed. Melody Rose. Boulder, CO: Lynne Rienner Publishers, 91–114.

Herrick, Rebekah. 1996. "Is There a Gender Gap in the Value of Campaign Resources?" *American Politics Quarterly* 24(1): 68–80.

Herrick, Rebekah, Jeanette Mendez, Sue Thomas, and Amanda Wilkerson. 2012. "Gender and Perceptions of Candidate Competency." *Journal of Women, Politics and Policy* 33: 126–150.

Herrick, Rebekah, and Sue Thomas. 1999. "The Effects of Sexual Orientation on Citizen Perceptions of Candidate Viability." In *Gays and Lesbians in the Democratic Process*, eds. Ellen D. B. Riggle and Barry Tadlock. New York: Columbia University Press, 170–191.

Herrnson, Paul S. 2004. *Congressional Elections: Campaigning at Home and in Washington*, 4th ed. Washington, DC: CQ Press.

Herrnson, Paul S., and Jennifer C. Lucas. 2006. "The Fairer Sex? Gender and Negative Campaigning in U.S. Elections." *American Politics Research* 34(1): 69–94.

Herrnson, Paul S., J. Celeste Lay, and Atiya Kai Stokes. 2003. "Women Running 'as Women': Candidate Gender, Campaign Issues, and Voter Targeting Strategies." *Journal of Politics* 65(1): 244–255.

Hertzberg, Hendrik. 2005. "Filibluster." *New Yorker*, June 13. http://www.newyorker.com/archive/2005/06/13/050613ta_talk_hertzberg (accessed July 26, 2013).

Hess, Frederick M. 2002. *School Boards at the Dawn of the 21st Century*. Alexandria, VA: American School Boards Association.

Hill, David B. 1981. "Political Culture and Female Political Representation." *Journal of Politics* 43: 159–168.

Hirschfelder, Arlene, and Paulette F. Molin. 2012. *The Extraordinary Book of Native American Lists*. New York: Scarecrow Press.

*Hishon v. King & Spalding*, 467 U.S. 69 (1984).

Hogan, Robert. 2001. "The Influence of State and District Conditions on the Representation of Women in U.S. State Legislatures." *American Political Research* 29(1): 4–24.

——. 2008. "Sex and the Statehouse: The Effects of Gender on Legislative Roll Call Voting." *Social Sciences Quarterly* 89(4): 955–968.

Hogg, Michael A., Sarah C. Hains, and I. Mason. 1998. "Identification Leadership in Small Groups: Salience, Frame of Reference, and Leaders Stereotypicality Effects on Leader Evaluations." *Journal of Personality and Social Psychology* 75(5): 1248–1263.

Holman, Mirya R., Jennifer L. Merolla, and Elizabeth J. Zechmeister. 2011. "Sex, Stereotypes, and Security: A Study of the Effects of Terrorist Threat on Assessments of Female Leadership." *Journal of Women, Politics, & Policy* 32(3): 173–192.

Holmes, Lisa M., and Jolly A. Emrey. 2006. "Court Diversification: Staffing the State Courts of Last Resort through Interim Appointments." *Justice System Journal* 27(1): 1–13.

House, Billy. 2012. "Win for McMorris Rodgers Seen as Needed Change." *National Journal*, November 14. http://www.nationaljournal.com/member/daily/win-for-mcmorris-rodgers-seen-as-needed-change-20121114 (accessed July 26, 2013).

House, Robert J., William D. Spangler, and James Woycke. 1991. "Personality and Charisma in the U.S. Presidency: A Psychological Theory of Leader Effectiveness." *Administrative Science Quarterly* 36(3): 364–396.

Huddy, Leonie, and Nayda Terkildsen. 1993a. "The Consequences of Gender Stereotypes for Women Candidates at Different Levels and Types of Office." *Political Research Quarterly* 46(3): 503–525.

——. 1993b. "Gender Stereotypes and the Perception of Male and Female Candidates." *American Journal of Political Science* 27(1): 119–147.

Huddy, Leonie, and Teresa Capelos. 2002. "Gender Stereotyping and Candidate Evaluation: Good News and Bad News for Women Politicians." In *The Social Psychology of Politics*, ed. Victor Ottati, et al. New York: Kluwer Academic Press, 29–54.

*Huffington Post*. 2012. "Susan Allen, Minnesota Democrat, Becomes First Native American Lesbian to Serve on a State Legislature." January 11. http://www.huffingtonpost.com/2012/01/11/susan-allen-minneapolis-democrat-native-american-lesbian_n_1199647.html (accessed July 23, 2013).

Hulse, Carl. 2008. "Republican Senators Block Pay Discrimination Measure." *New York Times*, April 24. http://www.nytimes.com/2008/04/24/washington/24cong.html (accessed July 26, 2013).

Hunter, Rosemary. 2006. "The High Price of Success: The Backlash against Women Judges in Australia." In *Calling for Change: Women, Law, and the Legal Profession*, eds. Elizabeth Sheehy and Sheila McIntyre. Ottawa, ON: University of Ottawa Press, 282–301.

Hurwitz, Mark S., and Drew Noble Lanier. 2003. "Explaining Judicial Diversity: The Differential Ability of Women and Minorities to Attain Seats on State Supreme and Appellate Courts." *State Politics and Policy Quarterly* 3(4): 329–352.

——. 2008. "Diversity in State and Federal Appellate Courts: Change and Continuity across 20 Years." *Justice System Journal* 29(1): 47–70.

Inglehart, Ronald, and Pippa Norris. 2003. *Rising Tide: Gender Equality and Cultural Change.* New York: Cambridge University Press.

International IDEA. *Women in Politics: Beyond Numbers.* Stockholm: International IDEA.

Inter-Parliamentary Union (IPU). 2012. "Women in National Parliaments: Situation as of Late 2012." http://www.ipu.org/wmn-e/world.htm (accessed July 23, 2013).

———. 2013. "Women in National Parliaments as of 1st February 2013." http://www.ipu.org/wmn-e/classif.htm (accessed July 23, 2013).

Irving, Helen. 2008. *Gender and the Constitution.* New York: Cambridge University Press.

Iyengar, Shanto, and Donald Kinder. 1987. *News That Matters.* Chicago: University of Chicago Press.

Iyengar, Shanto, Nicholas A. Valentino, Stephen Ansolabehere, and Adam F. Simon. 1997. "Running as a Woman: Gender Stereotyping in Women's Campaigns." In *Women, Media, and Politics,* ed. Pippa Norris. New York: Oxford University Press, 77–98.

Jackson, Brooks. 2008. "Giving Hillary Credit for SCHIP." *FactCheck.org.* March 18. http://www.factcheck.org/2008/03/giving-hillary-credit-for-schip/ (accessed July 23, 2013).

Jacobson, Gary. 2009. *The Politics of Congressional Elections.* New York: Addison-Wesley Educational Publishers, Inc.

Jaffe, Ina. 2008. "Clinton Exits Race, Vows to Fully Support Obama." *National Public Radio.* June 7. http://www.npr.org/templates/story/story.php?storyId=91282297 (accessed July 23, 2013).

Jalalzai, Farida. 2004. "Women Political Leaders: Past and Present." *Women and Politics* 26(3–4): 85–108

———. 2006. "Women Candidates and the Media: 1992–2000 Elections." *Politics & Policy* 34(3): 606–633.

———. 2008. "Women Rule: Shattering the Executive Glass Ceiling." *Politics & Gender* 4(2): 205–231.

Jamieson, Kathleen Hall. 1995. *Beyond the Double Bind: Women and Leadership.* New York: Oxford University Press.

Jensen, Jennifer M., and Wendy L. Martinek. 2009. "The Effects of Race and Gender on the Judicial Ambitions of State Trial Court Judges." *Political Research Quarterly* 62(2): 379–392.

Jewell, Malcom E., and Marcia Lynn Whicker. 1994. *Legislative Leadership in the American States.* Ann Arbor: University of Michigan Press.

Johnson, Cathy Marie, Georgia Duerst-Lahti, and Noelle H. Norton. 2007. *Creating Gender: The Sexual Politics of Welfare Policy.* Boulder, CO: Lynne Rienner.

Johnson, J. E. 2007. "Domestic Violence Politics in Post-Soviet States." *Social Politics* 14(3): 380–405.

Johnson, Marilyn, and Susan J. Carroll, with Kathy Stanwyck and Lynn Korenblit. 1978. *Profile of Women Holding Office II.* New Brunswick, NJ: Center for the American Woman and Politics.

Jones, Jeffrey M. 2007. "Some Americans Reluctant to Vote for Mormon, 72-Year-Old Presidential Candidates." *Gallup Poll News Service.* February 20. http://www.gallup.com/poll/26611/some-americans-reluctant-vote-mormon-72yearold-presidential-candidates.aspx (accessed July 23, 2013).

———. 2012. "Atheists, Muslims See Most Bias as Presidential Candidates." *Gallup Poll News Service.* June 21.

Judicial Appointments Advisory Committee (JAAC). 2007. *2006 Annual Report.* http://www.ontariocourts.on.ca/jaac/en/annualreport/2006.pdf (accessed November 28, 2011).

Kahn, Kim Fridkin. 1992. "Does Being Male Help? An Investigation of the Effects of Candidate Gender and Campaign Coverage on Evaluations of U.S. Senate Candidates." *Journal of Politics* 54: 497–517.

———. 1993. "Gender Differences in Campaign Messages: The Political Advertisements of Men and Women Candidates for U.S. Senate." *Political Research Quarterly* 46(3): 481–502.

———. 1994. "Does Gender Make a Difference? An Experimental Examination of Sex Stereotypes and Press Patterns in Statewide Campaigns." *American Journal of Political Science* 38(1): 162–195.

———. 1996. *The Political Consequences of Being a Woman: How Stereotypes Influence the Conduct and Consequences of Political Campaigns.* New York: Columbia University Press.

Kahn, Kim. F., and Ann Gordon. 1997. "How Women Campaign for the U.S. Senate: Substance and Strategy." In *Women, Media, and Politics*, ed. P. Norris. Oxford: Oxford University Press, 59–76.

Kahn, Kim F., and Patrick J. Kenney. 1999. *The Spectacle of U.S. Senate Campaigns*. Princeton, NJ: Princeton University Press.

Kalantry, Sital. 2012. "Women in Robes." *Americas Quarterly*. Summer. http://ssrn.com/abstract=2130174 (accessed July 23, 2013).

Kaml, Shannon Skarphol. 2000. "The Fusion of Populist and Feminine Styles in the Rhetoric of Ann Richards." In *Navigating Boundaries: The Rhetoric of Women Governors*, eds. B. Devore Marshall and M. A. Mayhead. Westport, CT: Praeger Publishers.

Kanter, Rosabeth Moss. 1977. "Some Effects of Proportions on Group Life: Skewed Sex Ratios and Responses to Token Women." *American Journal of Sociology* 82: 965–990.

Kaplan, Jonathan. 2003. "Hatch Charges Bias over Ala. Nominee." *The Hill*, June 18.

Kathlene, Lyn. 1994. "Power and Influence in State Legislatures: The Interaction of Gender and Position in Committee Hearing Debates." *American Political Science Review* 88(3): 560–576.

———. 1995. "Alternative Views of Crime: Legislative Policymaking in Gendered Terms." *Journal of Politics* 57(3): 696–723.

———. 1998. "In a Different Voice: Women and the Policy Process." *Women and Elective Office: Past, Present, and Future*, eds. Sue Thomas and Clyde Wilcox. New York: Oxford University Press, 188–202.

———. 2005. "In a Different Voice: Women and the Policy Process." In *Women and Elective Office: Past, Present, and Future*, 2nd ed., eds. Sue Thomas and Clyde Wilcox. New York: Oxford University Press, 213–229.

Kathlene, Lyn, Susan E. Clarke, and Barbara A. Fox. 1991. "Ways Women Politicians Are Making A Difference." In *Reshaping the Agenda: Women in State Legislatures*, eds. D. Dodson and S. Carroll. Brunswick, NJ: Eagleton Institute of Politics' Center for American Women and Politics, 31–38.

Kaufmann, Karen M., and John R. Petrocik. 1999. "The Changing Politics of American Men: Understanding the Sources of the Gender Gap." *American Journal of Political Science* 43: 864–887.

Kellman, Laurie. 2008. "Republicans Kill Pay Disparity Bill." *Associated Press Online*. April 23.

———. 2011. "Republican Women Defend Party Against 'Anti-Women' Charge." *Huffington Post*. June 22. http://www.huffingtonpost.com/2011/06/22/republican-women-defend-p_n_881967.html (accessed July 23, 2013).

Kelly, Michael. 1993. "Again, It's Hillary Rodham Clinton. Got That?" *New York Times*. February 14. http://www.nytimes.com/1993/02/14/us/again-it's-hillary-rodham-clinton-got-that.html (accessed July 23, 2013).

Kennedy, John Fitzgerald. 1961. "Remarks to a U.N. Delegation of Women." Charlottesville, VA: Miller Center. http://millercenter.org/president/speeches/detail/5954 (accessed July 23, 2013).

Kenney, Sally J. 1992. *For Whose Protection? Reproductive Hazards and Exclusionary Policies in the United States and Britain*. Ann Arbor: University of Michigan Press.

———. 1996. "Field Essay: New Research on Gendered Political Institutions." *Political Research Quarterly* 49: 445–466.

———. 2000a. "Beyond Principals and Agents: Seeing Courts as Organizations by Comparing *Référendaires* at the European Court of Justice and Law Clerks at the U.S. Supreme Court." *Comparative Political Studies* 33(5): 593–625.

———. 2000b. "Puppeteers or Agents? What Lazarus's *Closed Chambers* Adds to Our Understanding of Law Clerks." *Law & Social Inquiry* 25(1): 185–226.

———. 2008a. "Thinking about Gender and Judging." *International Journal of the Legal Profession* 15(1–2): 87–110.

———. 2008b. "Infinity Project seeks to increase gender diversity of the Eighth Circuit Court of Appeals." *Judicature* 92(3): 1–2.

——. 2010a. "Julia C. Addington from Stacyville, Iowa: First Woman Elected to Public Office in the United States? The World?" *Women/Politics, Newsletter of the American Political Science Association's Women and Politics Research Section* 21(1): 12.

——. 2010b. "It Would Be Stupendous for Us Girls: Campaigning for Women Judges without Waving." In *Breaking the Wave: Women, Their Organizations, and Feminism, 1945–1985*, eds. Kathleen A. Laughlin and Jacqueline Castledine. New York: Routledge, 209–228.

——. 2010c. "Mobilizing Emotions to Elect Women: The Symbolic Meaning of Minnesota's First Woman Supreme Court Justice." *Mobilization* 15(2): 135–158.

——. 2010d. "Critical Perspectives on Gender and Judging," *Politics & Gender* 6(3): 433–495.

——. 2013a. *Gender and Justice: Why Women in the Judiciary Really Matter.* New York: Routledge.

——. 2013b. "Which Judicial Selection Systems Generate the Most Women Judges? Lessons from the United States." In *Gender and Judging*, eds. Ulrike Schultz and Gisela Shaw. Oxford: Har, 461–480.

Kenney, Sally J., and Jason Windett. 2013. "Diffusion of Innovation or State Political Culture: Explaining the First Women State Supreme Court Justices." Unpublished manuscript.

——. 1998. *No Constitutional Right to Be Ladies: Women and the Obligations of Citizenship.* New York: Hill and Wang.

Kenworthy, L., and M. Malami. 1999. "Gender Inequality in Political Representation: A Worldwide Comparative Analysis." *Social Forces* 78(1): 235–269.

Kerber, Linda K. *No Constitutional Right to Be Ladies: Women and the Obligations of Citizenship.* New York: Hill & Wang, 1998.

Kerr, Brinck, and Will Miller. 1997. "Latino Representation: It's Direct and Indirect." *American Journal of Political Science* 41: 1066–1071.

Kiely, Kathy. 2008. "Two Clintons: One Too Many?" *USA Today*. January 23. http://usatoday30. usatoday.com/news/politics/election2008/2008-01-22-billclinton_N.htm (accessed July 23, 2013).

Kim, Seung Min. 2012a. "Paycheck Fairness Act Fails to Advance in Senate." *Politico*. June 5.

——. 2012b. "GOP Lawmakers Rebutting 'War on Women.'" *Politico*. June 4.

Kinder, Donald R. 1986. "Presidential Character Revisited." In *Political Cognition: The 19th Annual Carnegie Symposium on Cognition*, eds. Richard R. Lau and David O. Sears. Hillsdale, NJ: Lawrence Erlbaum, 233–255.

Kinder, Donald R., Mark D. Peters, Robert P. Abelson, and Susan T. Fiske. 1980. "Presidential Prototypes." *Political Behavior* 2(4): 315–337.

King, David, and Richard Matland. 2003. "Sex and the Grand Old Party: An Experimental Investigation of the Effect of Candidate Sex on Support for a Republican Candidate." *American Politics Research* 31: 595–612.

——. 1999. "Partisanship and the Impact of Candidate Gender in Congressional Elections: Results of an Experiment." Presented at the Women Transforming Congress Conference, Norman, OK.

King, James D. 2002. "Single-Member Districts and the Representation of Women in American State Legislatures: The Effect of Electoral System Change." *State Politics and Policy Quarterly* 2: 161–175.

Kirkpatrick, Jeanne J. 1974. *Political Woman.* New York: Basic Books.

Kittilson, Miki Caul. 2006. *Challenging Parties, Changing Parliaments: Women and Elected Office in Contemporary Western Europe.* Columbus: Ohio State University Press.

Klapper, Bradley, and Matthew Lee. 2012. "Jet-Setting Hillary Clinton Breaks Travel Record." *National Public Radio*. July 17. http://www.npr.org/templates/story/story.php/storyId=156889852 (accessed July 23, 2013).

Klatch, Rebecca. 1987. *Women of the New Right.* Philadelphia: Temple University Press.

Koch, Jeffrey W. 1999. "Candidate Gender and Assessments of Senate Candidates." *Social Science Quarterly* 80: 84–96.

——. 2000. "Do Citizens Apply Gender Stereotypes to Infer Candidates' Ideological Orientations?" *Journal of Politics* 62: 414–429.

——. 2002. "Gender Stereotypes and Citizens' Impressions of House Candidates' Ideological Orientations." *American Journal of Political Science* 46(2): 453–462.

Kornblut, Anne E. 2010. *Notes from the Cracked Ceiling: Hillary Clinton, Sarah Palin, and What It Will Take for a Woman to Win.* New York: Crown.

Krippendorff, Klaus. 1980. *Content Analysis: An Introduction to Its Methodology.* Newbury Park, CA: SAGE.

Kristof, Nicholas D. 2008. "When Women Rule." *New York Times.* February 10. http://www.nytimes.com/2008/02/10/opinion/10kristof.html (accessed July 23, 2013).

Krook, Mona Lena. 2009. *Quotas for Women in Politics: Gender and Candidate Selection Reform Worldwide.* New York: Oxford University Press.

Kuhn, David Paul. 2008. "Hillary Clinton's 5 Mistakes." *Politico.com.* June 7. http://www.politico.com/news/stories/0608/10911.html (accessed July 23, 2013).

Kunin, Madeleine M. 1994. *Living a Political Life.* New York: Alfred A Knopf, Inc.

Kurtz, Karl. 2012. "Changes in Legislatures Using Multimember Districts after Redistricting." *The Thicket at State Legislatures.* Posted September 11. http://ncsl.typepad.com/the_thicket/2012/09/a-slight-decline-in-legislatures-using-multimember-districts-after-redistricting.html (accessed March 4, 2013).

La Corte, Rachel. 2007. "State's Gay Lawmakers Won't Stop until Same-Sex Marriage Is Reality." *Daily World.* January 12.

——. 2008. "State's Gay Caucus Is 2nd-Largest in U.S." *Seattle Times,* January 24.

LaFont, Suzanne. 2001. "One Step Forward, Two Steps Back: Women in the Post-Communist States." *Communist and Post-Communist Studies* 34(2): 203–220.

LaFranchi, Howard. 2010. "Hillary Clinton's Vision for Foreign Policy on a Tight Budget." *Christian Science Monitor,* December 5. http://www.csmonitor.com/USA/Foreign-Policy/2010/1215/Hillary-Clinton-s-vision-for-foreign-policy-on-a-tight-budget (accessed July 26, 2013).

LaHaye, Beverly, and Janice Shaw Crouse. 2001. *A Different Kind of Strength.* Eugene, OR: Harvest House Publishers.

Lammers, Joris, Ernestine H. Gordijn, and Sabine Otten. 2009. "Iron Ladies, Men of Steel: The Effects of Gender Stereotyping on the Perception of Male and Female Candidates Are Moderated by Prototypicality." *European Journal of Social Psychology* 39(2): 86–195.

Langel, Stephen. 2009a. "Securing Cloture Not a Certainty for Ledbetter Bill." *CongressNow.* January 14.

——. 2009b. "After Easy Cloture Vote, Senators Look Ahead to Debate over Ledbetter Bill, Alternative." *CongressNow.* January 15.

Landrigan, Kevin. 2010. "Palin Endorses, Ayotte, Hits Rivals in Senate Race." *Telegraph.* July 20. http://www.nashuatelegraph.com/news/statenewengland/800277-227/palin-endorses-ayotte-hits-rivals-in-senate.html (accessed July 26, 2013).

Lauer, Nancy. 2010. "Hawaii Passes on Chance at Female Chief Justice." *Women's eNews.* August 20. http://womensenews.org/story/in-the-courts/100819/hawaii-passes-chance-female-chief-justice (September 6, 2010).

Law, Steve. 2007. "Oregon Senate OKs Bill Granting Domestic Partnerships for Same-Sex Couples." *Statesman Journal,* May 2.

Lawless, Jennifer L. 2004a. "Politics of Presence: Women in the House and Symbolic Representation." *Political Research Quarterly* 57(1): 81–99.

——. 2004b. "Women, War, and Winning Elections: Gender Stereotyping in the Post-September 11th Era." *Political Research Quarterly* 57: 479–490.

——. 2009. "Sexism and Gender Bias in Election 2008: A More Complex Path for Women in Politics." *Politics & Gender* 5: 70–80.

——. 2012. *Becoming a Candidate: Political Ambition and the Decision to Run for Office.* New York: Cambridge University Press.

Lawless, Jennifer L., and Richard L. Fox. 2005. *It Takes A Candidate: Why Women Don't Run for Office.* New York: Cambridge University Press.

———. 2010. *It Still Takes a Candidate: Why Women Don't Run for Office*. New York: Cambridge University Press.

———. 2012. "Men Rule: The Continued Under-Representation of Women in U.S. Politics." Washington, DC: Women & Politics Institute.

———. 2013. *Girls Just Wanna Not Run: The Gender Gap in Young Americans' Political Ambition*. Washington, DC: Women and Politics Institute, American University.

Lawless, Jennifer L., Richard L. Fox, and Kathryn Pearson. 2008. "The Primary Reason for Women's Under-Representation: Re-Evaluating the Conventional Wisdom." *Journal of Politics* 70(1): 67–82.

Lawless, Jennifer L., Richard L. Fox, and Sean M. Theriault. 2005. "Will She Stay or Will She Go? Career Ceilings and Women's Retirement from the U.S. Congress." *Legislative Studies Quarterly* 30(4): 581–596.

Lawrence, Regina G., and Melody Rose. 2009. *Hillary Clinton's Run for the White House: Media, Gender Strategy, and Campaign Politics*. Boulder, CO: Lynne Rienner Publishers.

———. 2011. "Bringing Out the Hook: Exit Talk in Media Coverage of Hillary Clinton and Past Presidential Campaigns." *Political Research Quarterly* 64(4): 870–883.

Leader, Shelah Gilbert. 1977. "The Policy Impact of Elected Women Officials." In *The Impact of the Electoral Process*, eds. Louis Maisel and Joseph Cooper. Beverly Hills, CA: SAGE, 265–284.

Leeper, Mark S. 1991. "The Impact of Prejudice on Female Candidates: An Experimental Look at Voter Inference." *American Politics Quarterly* 19(2): 248–261.

Legal Momentum. 2012. "Addressing Gender Bias in the Courts." *Legal Momentum: The Women's Legal Defense and Education Fund*. http://www.legalmomentum.org/our-work/njep/njep-task-forces.html (accessed November 16, 2012).

Lemmon, Gayle Tzemach. 2011. "The Hillary Doctrine." *Newsweek*, March 6.

Leubsdorf, Ben. 2012. "Analysis: Men Rule Local Politics: Women Often Reluctant to Run for Elected Office." *Concord Monitor*. March 11. http://www.concordmonitor.com/article/316460/analysis-men-rule-local-politics (accessed July 23, 2013).

Levy, Dena, Charles Tien, and Rachelle Aved. 2002. "Do Differences Matter? Women Members of Congress and the Hyde Amendment." *Women & Politics* 23: 105–127.

Lewis, Carolyn. 1999. "Are Women for Women? Feminist and Traditional Values in the Female Electorate." *Women and Politics* 20:1–28.

Lewis, Deborah Shaw, and Charmaine Crouse Yoest. 1996. *Mother in the Middle*. Grand Rapids, MI: Zondervan Publishing House.

Lewis, Gregory B. 2003. "Black–White Differences in Attitudes toward Homosexuality and Gay Rights." *Public Opinion Quarterly* 67(1): 59–78.

Libby, Sara. 2012. "The Cracked Pipeline: How Redistricting Targeted Women Lawmakers in Statehouses around the Country." *TPM*. May 24. http://2012.talkingpointsmemo.com/2012/05/that-democrats-became-roadkill-during.php?m=1 (accessed July 23, 2013).

Lien, Pei-te. 2001. *The Making of Asian America through Political Participation*. Philadelphia: Temple University Press.

Lien, Pei-te, Carol Hardy-Fanta, Dianne M. Pinderhughes, and Christine Marie Sierra. 2008. "Expanding Categorization at the Intersection of Race and Gender: 'Women of Color' as a Political Category for African American, Latina, Asian American, and American Indian Women." Presented at the Annual Meeting of the American Political Science Association, Boston, MA.

Lien, Pei-te, and Katie E. O. Swain. 2013. "Local Executive Leaders: At the Intersection of Race and Gender." In *Women & Executive Office: Pathways and Performance*, ed. Melody Rose. Boulder, CO: Lynne Rienner Publishers, 137–158.

Lijphart, Arend. 1994. *Electoral Systems and Party Systems*. Oxford: Oxford University Press.

Lilie, Joyce R., Roger Handberg Jr., and Wanda Lowrey. 1982. "Women State Legislators and the ERA: Dimensions of Support and Opposition." *Women & Politics* 2: 23–38.

Lipinski, Daniel. 2001. "The Effect of Messages Communicated by Members of Congress: The Impact of Publicizing Votes." *Legislative Studies Quarterly* 26(1): 81–100.

Lipinski, Daniel, and Gregory Neddenriep. 2004. "Using 'New' Media to Get 'Old' Media Coverage: How Members of Congress Utilize Their Web Sites to Court Journalists." *Harvard International Journal of Press/Politics* 9(1): 7–21.

Lord, Robert G., Douglas J. Brown, and Jennifer L. Harvey. 2001. "System Constraints on Leadership Perceptions, Behavior and Influence: An Example of Connectionist Level Processes." In *Blackwell Handbook of Social Psychology: Group Processes*, eds. Michael. A. Hogg and Scott Tindale. Oxford: Blackwell Publishers, 283–310.

Lord, Robert G., Christy L. de Vader, and George M. Alliger. 1986. "A Meta-Analysis of the Relation between Personality Traits and Leadership Perceptions: An Application of Validity Generalization Procedures." *Journal of Applied Psychology* 71(3): 402–410.

Lord, Robert G., and Karen Maher. 1991. *Leadership and Information Processing*. New York: Routledge.

Love, Barbara J., ed. 2006. *Feminists Who Changed America, 1963–75*. Champaign: University of Illinois Press.

Lovenduski, Joni, and Pippa Norris, eds. 1993. *Gender and Party Politics*. London: SAGE.

Lublin, David. 1997. *The Paradox of Representation: Racial Gerrymandering and Minority Interests in Congress*. Princeton, NJ: Princeton University Press.

Lucas, Jennifer. 2007. "Is Justice Blind? Gender and Voting in Judicial Elections." Presented at Midwest Political Science Association annual meeting, April 15–19, Chicago.

Luis, Cindy. 2002. "Female Athletes Have Mink to Thank." *Starbulletin.com*. September 29. http://starbulletin.com/columnist/column.php?id=1251&col_id=37 (accessed August 10, 2004).

MacDonald, Jason A., and Erin E. O'Brien. 2011. "Quasi-Experimental Design, Constituency, and Advancing Women's Interests: Reexamining the Influence of Gender on Substantive Representation." *Political Research Quarterly* 64: 472–486.

Mackay, Fiona. 2005. "Gender and Diversity Review: Critical Reflections on Judicial Appointments in Scotland." Report for the Judicial Appointments Board for Scotland and Scottish Executive Justice Department.

MacManus, Susan A., Charles S. Bullock III, Karen Padgett, and Brittany Penberthy. 2006. "Women Winning at the Local Level: Are County and School Board Positions Becoming More Desirable and Plugging the Pipeline to Higher Office?" In *Women and Elections: Outsiders or Insiders*, ed. Lois Duke Whitaker. Upper Saddle River, NJ: Prentice Hall, 117–136.

Madsen, Susan R. 2009. *Developing Leadership: Learning from the Experiences of Women Governors*. Lanham, MD: University Press of America.

Main, Eleanor C., Gerard S. Gryski, and Beth Schapiro. 1984. "Different Perspectives: Southern State Legislators' Attitudes about Women in Politics." *Social Science Journal* 21: 21–28.

Malbin, Michael J., Norman J. Ornstein, and Thomas E. Mann. 2008. *Vital Statistics on Congress 2008*. Washington, DC: Brookings Institution.

Mandel, Ruth B. 1981. *In the Running: The New Woman Candidate*. New Haven, CT: Ticknor & Fields.

Manin, Bernhard, Adam Przeworski, and Susan C. Stokes. 1999. "Introduction." In *Democracy, Accountability, and Representation*, eds. Adam Przeworski, Susan C. Stokes, and Bernhard Manin. Cambridge: Cambridge University Press, 1–26.

Mansbridge, Jane. 1986. *Why We Lost the ERA*. Chicago: University of Chicago Press.

———. 1999. "Should Blacks Represent Blacks and Women Represent Women? A Contingent 'Yes.'" *Journal of Politics* 61(3): 628–657.

Marcus, Ruth. 2011. "Are Women in Politics Making Two Steps Forward, One Step Back?" *Washington Post*. April 5. http://www.washingtonpost.com/opinions/are-wo men-in-politics-making-two-steps-forward-one-step-back/2011/04/05/AFmQ7PlC_story. html?hpid=z5 (accessed July 23, 2013).

Mariani, Mack D. 2008. "A Gendered Pipeline? The Advancement of State Legislators to Congress in Five States." *Politics & Gender* 3(3): 285–308.

Markus, Gregory. B. 1982. "Political Attitudes during an Election Year: A Report on the 1980 NES Panel Study." *American Political Science Review* 76(3): 538–560.

Marshall, Brenda Devore, and Molly A. Mayhead, eds. 2000. *Navigating Boundaries: The Rhetoric of Women Governors.* Westport, CT: Praeger Publishers.

Marshall, Judi. 1993. "Organizational Communication from a Feminist Perspective." In *Communication Yearbook,* ed. Stanley Deetz. Vol. 16. Newbury Park, CA: SAGE, 122–141.

Marshall, Susan E. 1997. *Splintered Sisterhood.* Madison: University of Wisconsin Press.

Martin, Elaine. 1982. "Women on the Federal Bench: A Comparative Profile." *Judicature* 65(6): 306–313.

——. 1987. "Gender and Judicial Selection: A Comparison of the Reagan and Carter Administrations." *Judicature* 71(3): 136–142.

——. 1991. "Judicial Gender and Judicial Choices." In *Gender and Policymaking: Studies of Women in Office,* ed. Debra L. Dodson. Brunswick, NJ: Eagleton Institute's Center for the American Woman and Politics, 91–108.

——. 1993a. "Women on the Bench: A Different Voice?" *Judicature* 77(3): 126–128.

——. 1993b. "The Representative Role of Women Judges." *Judicature* 77(3): 166–173.

——. 2004. "Gender and Presidential Judicial Selection." *Women & Politics* 26(3–4): 109–129.

Martin, Elaine, and Barry Pyle. 2002. "Gender and Racial Diversification of State Supreme Courts." *Women & Politics* 24(2): 35–52.

——. 2005. "State High Courts and Divorce: The Impact of Judicial Gender." *University of Toledo Law Review* 36(4): 923–948.

Martin, Mart. 1999. *The Almanac of Women and Minorities in American Politics.* Boulder, CO: Westview Press.

Matland, Richard E. 1994. "Putting Scandinavian Equality to the Test: An Experimental Evaluation of Gender Stereotyping of Political Candidates in a Sample of Norwegian Voters." *British Journal of Political Science* 24(2): 273–292.

——. 1998. "Women's Representation in National Legislatures: Developed and Developing Countries." *Legislative Studies Quarterly* 23(1): 109–125.

Matland, Richard E., and Deborah Dwight Brown. 1992. "District Magnitude's Effect on Female Representation in U.S. State Legislatures." *Legislative Studies Quarterly* 17: 469–492.

Matland, Richard E., and David King. 2002. "Women as Candidates in Congressional Elections." In *Women Transforming Congress,* ed. Cindy Simon Rosenthal. Norman: University of Oklahoma Press, 119–145.

Matland, Richard E., and K. Montgomery, eds. 2003. *Women's Access to Political Power in Post-Communist Europe.* Oxford: Oxford University Press.

Matland, Richard E., and Donley T. Studlar. 1996. "The Contagion of Women Candidates in Single-Member District and Proportional Representation Electoral Systems: Canada and Norway." *Journal of Politics* 58(3): 707–733.

——. 2004. "Determinants of legislative turnover: A Cross-national Analysis." *British Journal of Political Science* 34(1): 87–108.

Matsui, Amy K. 2012. "Women in the Federal Judiciary: Taking Stock." *National Women's Law Center Blog.* March 14. http://www.nwlc.org/our-blog/women-federal-judiciary-taking-stock (accessed November 15, 2012).

Mayes, G. 2003. "Beyond the Examining Room: Election 2004: Will Electing More Women State Legislators Advance Women's Health Policy?" *Medscape Ob/Gyn & Women's Health* 8(2). http://www.medscape.com/viewarticle/466268 (accessed February 20, 2010).

Mayhew, David. 1974. *Congress: The Electoral Connection.* New Haven, CT: Yale University Press.

Mayhew, David R. 1986. *Placing Parties in American Politics.* Princeton, NJ: Princeton University Press.

Mayhead, Molly A., and Brenda Devore Marshall. 2000. "Re-visioning and Re-framing Political Boundaries: Barbara Roberts' Response to Oregon's Budget Crisis." In *Navigating Boundaries: The Rhetoric of Women Governors,* eds. B. Devore Marshall and M. A. Mayhead. Westport, CT: Praeger Publishers, 125–140.

McCarthy, Meghan. 2012a. "Hill Squares Off over Contraception." *National Journal*, February 9.

———. 2012b. "Democrats Gin Up Money Ahead of Contraceptive Votes." *National Journal Daily*, March 1.

———. 2012c. "How Contraception Became a Train Wreck for Republicans." *National Journal*, March 5.

McCarty, Nolan, Keith T. Poole, and Howard Rosenthal. 2006. *Polarized America: The Dance of Ideology and Unequal Riches*. Cambridge, MA: MIT Press.

McCombs, Maxwell E. 1993. "The Evolution of Agenda-setting Research: Twenty-Five Years in the Marketplace of Ideas." *Journal of Communication* 43(1): 58–67.

McCormack, John. 2012. "Kelly Ayotte: Democrats Falsely Claim Women Will Lose Access to Contraception." *Weekly Standard*, February 29. http://www.weeklystandard.com/blogs/kelly-ayotte-democrats-falsely-claim-women-will-lose-access-contraception_633006.html (accessed July 26, 2013).

McDermott, Monika. 1998. "Voting Cues in Low-Information Elections: Candidate Gender as a Social Information Variable in Contemporary United States Elections." *American Journal of Political Science* 41: 270–283.

———. 1997. "Voting Cues in Low-Information Elections: Candidate Gender as a Social Information Variable in Contemporary US Elections." *American Journal of Political Science* 41(1): 270–283.

McGinley, Anne C. 2009. "Hillary Clinton, Sarah Palin, and Michelle Obama: Performing Gender, Race and Class on the Campaign Trail." *Denver University Law Review* 86(Special Issue): 709–725.

McManus, Doyle. 2010. "2010: The Year of the Conservative Woman?" *Los Angeles Times*. June 10. http://articles.latimes.com/2010/jun/10/opinion/la-oe-mcmanus-20100610 (accessed July 23, 2013).

Medoff, Marshall H. 2002. "The Determinants and Impact of State Abortion Restrictions." *American Journal of Economics and Sociology* 61: 481–493.

Meeks, Lindsey. 2012. "Is She "Man Enough"? Women Candidates, Executive Political Offices, and News Coverage." *Journal of Communication* 62(1): 175–193.

Meier, Petra. 2004. "The Mutual Contagion Effect of Legal and Party Quotas: A Belgian Perspective." *Party Politics* 10(5): 583–600.

Mendelberg, Tali, and Christopher F. Karpowitz. 2012. "More Women, but Not Nearly Enough." *New York Times*. November 8. http://campaignstops.blogs.nytimes.com/2012/11/08/more-women-but-not-nearly-enough/?ref=opinion (accessed July 23, 2013).

Merolla, Jennifer, Jean Reith Schroedel, and Mirya Rose Holman. 2007. "The Paradox of Protestantism and Women in Elected Office in the United States." *Journal of Women, Politics and Policy* 29(1): 77–100.

Medsger, Betty. 1983. *Framed: The New Right Attack on Chief Justice Rose Bird and the Courts*. New York: Pilgrim Press.

Mezey, Susan Gluck. 1978. "Women and Representation: The Case of Hawaii." *Journal of Politics* 40: 369–385.

———. 2000. "Gender and the Federal Judiciary." In *Gender and American Politics: Women, Men, and the Political Process*, eds. Sue Tolleson-Rinehart and Jyl Josephson. New York: M.E. Sharpe, 205–226.

Milyo, Jeffrey, and Samantha Schosberg. 2000. "Gender Bias and Selection Bias in House Elections." *Public Choice* 105(1–2): 41–59.

Minta, Michael D. 2012. "Gender, Race, Ethnicity, and Political Representation in the United States." *Politics & Gender* 8(4): 541–547.

Moncrief, Gary F., Peverill Squire, and Malcolm E. Jewell. 2001. *Who Runs the Legislature?* Upper Saddle River, NJ: Prentice Hall.

Montgomery, Lori. 2008a. "White House Threatens to Veto Discrimination Bill." *Washington Post*, April 23. http://www.washingtonpost.com/wp-dyn/content/article/2008/04/22/AR2008042202696.html (accessed July 26, 2013).

——. 2008b. "Senate Republicans Block Pay Disparity Measure." *Washington Post*, April 24. http://articles.washingtonpost.com/2008-04-24/politics/36770492_1_senate-republicans-f all-presidential-campaign-procedural-vote (accessed July 26, 2013).

Montoya, Lisa J., Carol Hardy-Fanta, and Sonia Garciá. 2000. "Latina Politics: Gender, Participation and Leadership." *PS: Political Science and Politics* 33: 555–561.

Morello, Karen Berger. 1986. *The Invisible Bar: The Woman Lawyer in America: 1638 to the Present*. New York: Random House.

Morris, Celia. 1992. *Storming the Statehouse*. New York: MacMillan Publishing Company.

Mossman, Mary Jane. 2006. *The First Women Lawyers: A Comparative Study of Gender, Law and the Legal Professions*. Oxford: Hart.

Moyer, Laura. 2013. "Rethinking Critical Mass in the Federal Appellate Courts." *Journal of Women, Politics & Policy* 34: 49–71.

Mullenbach, Cheryl. 2007. "The Election of Julia Addington: An Accidental Milestone in Iowa Politics." *Iowa Heritage Illustrated* (Fall): 1–8.

Murray, Rainbow. 2010. "Second among Unequals? A Study of Whether France's 'Quota Women' Are Up to the Job." *Politics & Gender* 6(1): 93–118.

Moser, R. G. 2001. "The Effects of Electoral Systems on Women's Representation in Post-Communist States." *Electoral Studies* 20(3): 353–369.

Mucciaroni, Gary. 2008. *Same Sex, Different Politics: Success & Failure in the Struggles over Gay Rights*. Chicago: University of Chicago Press.

Murray, Rainbow. 2004. "Why Didn't Parity Work? A Closer Examination of the 2002 Election Results." *French Politics* 2(4): 347–362.

——. 2008. "The Power of Sex and Incumbency: A Longitudinal Study of Electoral Performance in France." *Party Politics* 14(5): 539–554.

Nance, Peggy. 2010. "'Mama Grizzly' Sightings Increase!" http://www.grassrootsaction.com/705/Grizzly.asp?rid=&Ref_ID=500064 (accessed July 23, 2013).

National Archives and Records Administration. 1994. "Hillary Rodham Clinton." http://clinton2.nara.gov/WH/glimpse/firstladies/html/hc42.html (accessed July 23, 2013).

National Association of Latino Elected and Appointed Officials (NALEO). 2004. *National Directory of Latino Elected Officials*. Washington, DC: NALEO.

National Association of School Boards of Education. 2009. "Selection of Local School Boards, 2009." http://www.nsba.org/SchoolLaw/Issues/Governance/electionschart.pdf (accessed November 11, 2012).

National Association of Women Judges (NAWJ). 2012. "Representation of United States State Supreme Court Women Judges." http://www.nawj.org/us_state_court_statistics_2012.asp (accessed November 15, 2012).

National Conference of State Legislatures. 1999. Redistricting Task Force. "Multimember Districts." Chapter 5. http://www.senate.leg.state.mn.us/departments/scr/redist/red2000/ch4multi.htm (accessed February 22, 2013).

National Election Pool. 2004. *National Election Pool General Election Exit Polls, 2004* [Computer file]. ICPSR version. Somerville, NJ: Edison Media Research/New York, NY: Mitofsky International [producers], 2004. Ann Arbor, MI: Inter-university Consortium for Political and Social Research [distributor], 2005.

National Election Pool. 2008. *National Election Pool Poll General Election Exit Polls, 2008* [Computer file]. Somerville, NJ: Edison Media Research/New York, NY: Mitofsky International [producers], 2004. Roper Center for Public Opinion [distributor].

National Governors Association. 2011. "Governors." Washington, DC: Hall of States. www.nga.org/cms/home.html (accessed July 23, 2013).

*National Journal*. 2002. "Governor Jane Dee Hull." http://www3.nationaljournal.com/pubs/almanac/2002/people/az/azgv.htm# (accessed July 23, 2013).

National League of Cities. 2012. "City Councils." http://www.nlc.org/build-skill-and-networks/resources/cities-101/city-officials/city-councils (accessed July 23, 2013).

Nechemias, Carol. 1985. "Geographic Mobility and Women's Access to State Legislatures." *Western Political Quarterly* 28: 119–131.

Neff, Lisa. 2002. "Elaine Noble November 1974: A Progressive Massachusetts Candidate Becomes the First Openly Gay Person Elected to State Office." *The Free Library.* November 12. http://www.thefreelibrary.com/Elaine+Noble+November+1974%3a+a+progressive+Massachusetts+candidate...-a094598267 (accessed July 23, 2013).

Ness, Susan. 1978. "A Sexist Selection Process Keeps Qualified Women Off the Bench." *Washington Post,* March 26.

Ness, Susan, and Fredrica Wechsler. 1979. "Women Judges—Why So Few?" *Graduate Woman* 73(6): 10–12, 46–49.

Neuendorf, Kimberly. 2002. *The Content Analysis Guidebook.* Newbury Park, CA: SAGE.

Newman, Jody. 1994. "Perception and Reality: A Study Comparing the Success of Men and Women Candidates." A Report for the National Women's Political Caucus. Washington, DC.

Nichols, Larry. 2007. "A Talk with Elaine Noble." *Windy City Times,* October 10. http://www.windycitymediagroup.com/gay/lesbian/news/ARTICLE.php?AID=16288 (accessed July 26, 2013).

Nickerson, Michelle M. 2012. *Mothers of Conservatism: Women and the Postwar Right.* Princeton, NJ: Princeton University Press.

Niemi, Richard G., Jeffrey S. Hill, and Bernard Grofman. 1985. "The Impact of Multimember Districts on Party Representation in U.S. State Legislatures." *Legislative Studies Quarterly* 10: 441–455.

Niven, David. 1998. *The Missing Majority: The Recruitment of Women as State Legislative Candidates.* Westport, CT: Praeger.

——. 2005. "Gender Bias? Media Coverage of Women and Men in Congress." In *Gender and American Politics: Women, Men, and the Political Process,* eds. Sue Tolleson-Rinehart and Jyl Josephson. New York: M.E. Sharpe, 264–280.

Niven, David, and Jeremy Zilber. 2001. "How Does She Have Time for Kids and Congress? Views on Gender and Media Coverage from House Offices." In *Women and Congress: Running, Winning and Ruling,* ed. Karen O'Connor. New York: Haworth Press, 147–166.

Nixon, David L., and R. Darcy. 1996. "Special Elections and the Growth of Women's Representation in the House of Representatives." *Women & Politics* 16(Winter): 96–107.

Norrander, Barbara. 2008. "The History of the Gender Gaps." In *Voting the Gender Gap,* ed. Lois Duke Whitaker. Urbana: University of Illinois Press, 9–32.

Norrander, Barbara, and Clyde Wilcox. 1998. "The Geography of Gender Power: Women in State Legislatures." In *Women and Elective Office: Past, Present, and Future,* eds. Sue Thomas and Clyde Wilcox. New York: Oxford University Press, 103–117.

——. 1999. "Public Opinion and Policymaking in the States: The Case of Post-Roe Abortion Policy." *Policy Studies Journal* 27(4): 707–722.

——. 2005. "Change in Continuity in Geography of Women State Legislators." In *Women and Elective Office: Past, Present, and Future,* 2nd ed., eds. Sue Thomas and Clyde Wilcox. New York: Oxford University Press, 176–196.

Norrander, Barbara, and Sylvia Manzano. 2010. "Minority Group Opinion in the U.S. States." *State Politics and Policy Quarterly* 10: 446–483.

Norris, Pippa. 1985. "Women in European Legislative Elites." *West European Politics* 8(4): 90–101.

——, ed. 1997. *Pathways to Power.* New York: Cambridge University Press.

——. 2007. "Opening the Door: Women Leaders and Constitution Building in Iraq and Afghanistan." In *Women Who Lead,* ed. Barbara Kellerman. New York: Jossey Bass, 197–226.

Norris, Pippa, Elizabeth Vallance, and Joni Lovenduski. 1992. "Do Candidates Make a Difference? Race, Gender, Ideology, and Incumbency." *Parliamentary Affairs* 45(4): 496–547.

Norris, Pippa, and Joni Lovenduski. 1995. *Political Recruitment: Gender, Race and Class in the British Parliament.* Cambridge: Cambridge University Press.

Norris, Pippa, and Mona Lena Krook. 2011. *Gender Equality in Elected Office: A Six Step Action Plan.* Warsaw: OSCE. http://www.osce.org/odihr/78432 (accessed July 23, 2013).

Northpoth, Helmut. 2009. "From Eisenhower to Bush: Perceptions of Candidates and Parties." *Electoral Studies* 28(4): 523–532.

Norton, Noelle H. 1995. "Women, It's Not Enough To Be Elected: Committee Position Makes a Difference in Georgia." In *Gender Power, Leadership, and Governance*, eds. Duerst-Lahti and Rita M. Kelly. Ann Arbor: University of Michigan Press, 115–140.

——. 2002. "Transforming Congress from the Inside: Women in Committee." In *Women Transforming Congress*, ed. Cindy Simon Rosenthal. Norman: University of Oklahoma Press, 316–340.

Okin, Susan Moller. 1989. *Justice, Gender, and the Family.* New York: Basic Books.

Oklahoma Secretary of State. 2010. "Election Returns." http://www.ok.gov/elections/ Candidates_&_Elections/Election_Results.html (accessed July 23, 2013).

Omatsu, Maryka. 1997. "The Fiction of Judicial Impartiality." *Canadian Journal of Women and the Law* 9(1): 1–16.

Ondercin, Heather L., and Susan Welch. 2005. "Women Candidates for Congress." In *Women and Elective Office: Past, Present, and Future*, eds. Susan Thomas and Clyde Wilcox. New York: Oxford University Press, 60–80.

——. 2009. "Comparing Predictors of Women's Congressional Election Success: Candidates, Primaries, and the General Election." *American Politics Research* 37(4): 593–613.

O'Neill, Olivia A., and Charles A. O'Reilly III. 2011. "Overcoming the Backlash Effect: Self-Monitoring and Women's Promotions." *Journal of Occupational and Organizational Psychology* 84(4): 825–832.

O'Regan, Valerie R., and Stephen J. Stambough. 2002. "Female Candidates for Executive Office: The Road to the Governor's Mansion." *White House Studies* 2(3): 299–313.

——. 2011. "The Novelty Impact: The Politics of Trailblazing women in Gubernatorial Elections." *Journal of Women, Politics & Policy* 32(2): 96–113.

Organ, Joan Ellen. 1998. "Sexuality as a Category of Historical Analysis: A Study of Judge Florence E. Allen, 1884–1966." Ph.D. diss., Case Western Reserve University.

Orey, Byron D'Andra Orey, Wendy Smooth, Kimberly S. Adams, and Kisha Harris-Clark. 2006. "Race and Gender Matter: Refining Models of Legislative Policy Making in State Legislatures." In *Intersectionality and Politics: Recent Research on Gender, Race, and Political Representation in the United States*, ed. Carol Hardy-Fanta New York: Haworth Press, 97–120.

Osborn, Tracy L. 2012. *How Women Represent Women: Political Parties, Gender, and Representation in State Legislatures.* New York: Oxford University Press.

Osborn, Tracy L., and Jeanette Morehouse Mendez. 2010. "Speaking as Women: Women and Floor Speeches in the Senate." *Journal of Women, Politics, & Policy* 31: 1–21.

Pacelle, Richard L., Jr. 1997. "A President's Legacy: Gender and Appointment to the Federal Courts." In *The Other Elites: Women, Politics, and Power in the Executive Branch*, eds. MaryAnne Borrelli and Janet M. Martin. Boulder, CO: Lynne Rienner, 147–166.

Palin, Sarah. 2008. "Remarks Accepting Senator McCain's Nomination as the Republican Nominee for Vice President in Dayton, Ohio." *The American Presidency Project.* www.presidency.ucsb. edu/ws/index.php?pid=78574&st=hillary+clinton&st1= (accessed July 23, 2013).

——. 2009. *Going Rogue: An American Life.* New York: Harper Collins Publishers.

Palley, Marian Lief. 2001. "Women's Policy Leadership in the United Sates." *PS: Political Science and Politics.* 34(June): 247–250.

Palmer, Barbara. 2001a. "Women in the American Judiciary: Their Influence and Impact." *Women & Politics* 23(3): 91–101.

——. 2001b. "'To Do Justly:" The Integration of Women into the American Judiciary." *P/S: Political Science and Politics* 34(2): 235–239.

Palmer, Barbara, and Dennis Simon. 2003. "Political Ambition and Women in the U.S. House of Representatives, 1916–2000." *Political Research Quarterly* 56: 127–138.

———. 2006. *Breaking the Political Glass Ceiling: Women and Congressional Elections.* New York: Routledge.

———. 2008. *Breaking the Political Glass Ceiling: Women and Congressional Elections.* 2nd ed. New York: Routledge.

———, and ———. 2012. *Women & Congressional Elections: A Century of Change.* Boulder, CO: Lynne Rienner.

Panagopoulos, Costas. 2004. "Boy Talk/Girl Talk: Gender Differences in Campaign Communications Strategies." *Women & Politics* 26(4): 131–155.

Paolino, Phillip. 1995. "Group-Salient Issues and Group Representation: Support for Women Candidates in the 1992 Senate Elections." *American Journal of Political Science* 39: 294–313.

Paterson, Alan. 2006. "The Scottish Judicial Appointments Board: New Wine in Old Bottles?" In *Appointing Judges in an Age of Judicial Power: Critical Perspectives from around the World*, eds. Kate Malleson and Peter H. Russell. Toronto: University of Toronto Press, 13–38.

Pear, Robert. 2009. "House Passes 2 Measures on Job Bias." *New York Times*, January 9. http://www.nytimes.com/2009/01/10/us/10rights.html (accessed July 26, 2013).

Pearson, Kathryn, and Logan Dancey. 2011a. "Elevating Women's Voice in Congress: Speech Participation in the House of Representatives." *Political Research Quarterly* 64: 910–923.

———. 2011b. "Speaking for the Underrepresented in the House of Representatives: Voicing Women's Interests in a Partisan Era." *Politics & Gender* 7: 493–519.

Peresie, Jennifer. 2005. "Female Judges Matter: Gender and Collegial Decisionmaking in the Federal Appellate Courts." *Yale Law Journal* 114(7): 1759–1790.

Perkins, Jerry. 1986. "Political Ambition among Black and White Women: An Intragender Test of the Socialization Model." *Women & Politics* 6: 27–40.

Peters, Ronald M., Jr., and Cindy Simon Rosenthal. 2010. *Speaker Nancy Pelosi and the New American Politics.* New York: Oxford University Press.

Petrocik, John R. 1996. "Issue Ownership in Presidential Elections, with a 1980 Case Study." *American Journal of Political Science* 40: 825–850.

Petrocik, R. John, William L. Benoit, and Glenn J. Hansen. 2003. "Issue Ownership and Presidential Campaigning, 1952–2000." *Political Science Quarterly* 118(4): 599–626.

Phillips, Anne. 1991. *Engendering Democracy.* University Park: Pennsylvania State University Press.

———. 1995. *The Politics of Presence.* New York: Oxford University Press.

———. 2012. "Representation and Inclusion." *Politics & Gender* 8(4): 512–517.

Philpot, Tasha, and Haynes Walton. 2007. "One of Our Own: Black Female Candidates and the Voters Who Support Them." *American Journal of Political Science* 51: 49–62.

Pitkin, Hanna F. 1967/1972. *The Concept of Representation.* Berkeley: University of California.

Pitney, Nico. 2008. "Palin Misquotes Albright: 'Place in Hell Reserved for Women Who Don't Support Other Women.'" *Huffington Post.* October 5. www.huffingtonpost.com/2008/10/05/palin-misquotes-albright_n_131967.html?view=print (accessed July 23, 2013).

Plutzer, Eric, and John Zipp. 1996. "Identity Politics, Partisanship, and Voting for Women Candidates." *Public Opinion Quarterly* 60: 30–57.

Poggione, Sarah. 2004. "Exploring Gender Differences in State Legislators' Policy Preferences." *Political Research Quarterly* 57(2): 305–314.

Poole, Keith T., and Howard Rosenthal. 2007. *Ideology and Congress.* Piscataway, NJ: Transaction Publishers.

Poole, Keith T., and L. Harmon Zeigler. 1985. *Women, Public Opinion, and Politics—The Changing Political Attitudes of American Women.* New York: Longman.

Poole, Keith T. and Howard L. Rosenthal. 2007. *Ideology and Congress.* 2nd ed. Piscataway, NJ: Transaction Publishers.

Pope, Jeremy, and Jonathan Woon. 2009. "Measuring Changes in American Party Reputations, 1939–2004." *Political Research Quarterly* 62: 653–661.

Prestage, Jewel L. 1991. "In Quest of African-American Political Woman." *Annals* 515: 88–103.

Preston, Mark, 2006. "Analysts: Discontent Over Iraq May Favor Dems." *CNN.* November 7. http://www.cnn.com/2006/POLITICS/11/06/election.issues/ (accessed July 18, 2013).

Prindeville, Diane-Michele, and Teresa Braley Gomez. 1999. "American Indian Women Leaders, Public Policy, and the Importance of Gender and Ethnic Identity." *Women & Politics* 20: 17–32.

Project for Excellence in Journalism. 2005. *The State of the News 2005*. Washington, DC: Project for Excellence in Journalism.

———. 2006. *The State of the News Media 2006*. Washington, DC: Project for Excellence in Journalism.

———. 2010. *The State of the News Media: An Annual Report on American Journalism*. Washington, DC: Project for Excellence in Journalism.

Quist, Peter. 2010. "The Role of Money & Incumbency in 2007–2008 State Legislative Elections." *FollowTheMoney.org*, National Institute on Money in State Politics. http://www.followthe-money.org/press/PrintReportView.phtml?r=423 (accessed June 12, 2013).

Rahat, Gideon, and Reuven Hazan. 2001. "Candidate Selection Methods." *Party Politics* 7(3): 297–322.

Rahn, Wendy. 1993. "The Role of Partisan Stereotypes in Information Processing about Political Candidates." *American Journal of Political Science* 37(2): 472–496.

Raju, Manu, and Jake Sherman. 2012. "Few GOP Women Picked for Leadership Spots." *Politico*. November 14. http://www.politico.com/news/stories/1112/83888.html (accessed July 23, 2013).

Rausch, John David, Jr., and Mary S. Rausch. 1997. "Why Did West Virginia Voters Not Elect a Woman Governor?" *Comparative State Politics* 18(3): 1–12.

Rausch, John David, Jr., Mark J. Rozell, and Harry L. Wilson. 1999. "When Women Lose: A Study of Media Coverage of Two Gubernatorial Campaigns." *Women & Politics* 20(4): 1–21.

Rayside, David Morton. 1998. *On the Fringe: Gays and Lesbians in Politics*. Ithaca, NY: Cornell University Press.

Reddick, Malia, Michael J. Nelson, and Rachel Paine Caufield. 2009. "Explaining Diversity on State Courts." Presented at the annual meeting of the Midwest Political Science Association, April 2–5, Chicago.

Reed, W. Robert, and D. Eric Schansberg. 1995. "The House under Term Limits: What Would It Look Like?" *Social Science Quarterly* 76: 698–719.

Reeves, Keith. 1997. *Voting Hopes or Fears? White Voters, Black Candidates & Racial Politics in America*. New York: Oxford University Press.

Reid, Traciel. 2004. "The Competitiveness of Female Candidates in Judicial Elections: An Analysis of the North Carolina Trial Court Races." *Albany Law Review* 67(3): 829–842.

———. 2010. "Women Candidates and Judicial Elections: Telling an Untold Story." *Politics & Gender* 6(3): 465–474.

Reingold, Beth. 1996. "Conflict and Cooperation: Legislative Strategies and Concepts of Power among Female and Male State Legislators." *Journal of Politics* 58(2): 464–485.

———. 2000. *Representing Women: Sex Gender, and Legislative Behavior in Arizona and California*. Chapel Hill: University of North Carolina Press.

———. 2008. "Women as Office Holders: Linking Descriptive and Substantive Representation." In *Political Women and American Democracy*, eds. Christina Wolbrecht, Karen Beckwith, and Lisa Baldez. New York: University of Cambridge Press, 128–147.

Reingold, Beth, and Adrienne R. Smith. 2012. "Welfare Policymaking and Intersections of Race, Ethnicity, and Gender in US State Legislatures." *American Journal of Political Science* 56(1): 131–147.

*Republican Party of Minnesota v. White*, 536 U.S. 765 (2002).

Resnik, Judith. 1996. "Asking about Gender in Courts." *Signs* 21(4): 952–990.

Reynolds, Andrew. 1999. "Women in the Legislatures and Executives of the World: Knocking at the Highest Glass Ceiling." *World Politics* 51(4): 547–572.

Riccucci, Norma M., and Judith R. Saidel. 2005. "The Demographics of Gubernatorial Appointees: Towards and Explanation of Variation." *Policy Studies Journal* 29(1): 11–22.

Richards, Ann, with Peter Knobler. 1989. *Straight for the Heart*. New York: Simon and Schuster.

Richardson, Lilliard E., Jr., and Patricia K. Freeman. 1995. "Gender Differences in Constituency Service among State Legislators." *Political Research Quarterly* 48(1): 169–179.

Roberts, Barbara. 2011. *Up the Capitol Steps: A Woman's March to the Governorship*. Corvallis: Oregon State University Press.

Robertson, Terry, Kristin Froemling, Scott Wells, and Shannon McGraw. 1999. "Sex, Lies, and Videotape: An Analysis of Gender in Campaign Advertisements." *Communication Quarterly* 47(3): 333–341.

Rodgers, Shelly, Esther Thorson, and Michael Antecol. 2001. "'Reality' in the St. Louis Post-Dispatch." *Newspaper Research Journal* 21(3): 51–68.

Rogers, David. 2012. "Why Nancy Pelosi Stayed." *Politico*, November 14. http://www.politico.com/news/stories/1112/83880.html (accessed July 23, 2013).

Rose, Melody, ed. 2013. *Executive Women: Pathways and Performance*. Boulder, CO: Lynne Rienner Publishers.

Rosen, Jeffrey. 2009. "The Case Against Sotomayor: Indictments of Obama's Frontrunner to Replace Souter." *New Republic*. May 4. http://www.tnr.com/article/politics/the-case-against-sotomayor?id=45d56e6f-f497-4b19-9c63-04e10199a085 (accessed July 10, 2010).

Rosenthal, Brian M. 2012. "In Contrast to Congress, Diversity Diminishes in Washington Legislature." *Seattle Times*. November 26. http://seattletimes.com/avantgo/2019758561.html (accessed March 4, 2013).

Rosenthal, Cindy Simon. 1995. "The Role of Gender in Descriptive Representation." *Political Research Quarterly* 48: 599–611.

——. 1998. *When Women Lead: Integrative Leadership in State Legislatures*. New York: Oxford University Press.

——. 2000. "Gender Styles in State Legislative Committees: Raising Their Voices in Resolving Conflict." *Women and Politics* 22(1): 21–34.

——. 2005 "Women Leading Legislatures." In *Women and Elective Office*, 2nd ed., eds. Sue Thomas and Clyde Wilcox. New York: Oxford University Press, 197–212.

——. 2008. "Climbing Higher: Opportunities and Obstacles within the Party System." In *Legislative Women: Getting Elected, Getting Ahead*, ed. Beth Reingold. Boulder, CO: Lynne Rienner Publishers, 197–222.

Rosenwasser, Shirley, and Norma Dean. 1989. "Gender Role and Political Office: Effects of Perceived Masculinity/Femininity of Candidate and Political Office." *Psychology of Women Quarterly* 13: 77–85.

Rosette, Ashleigh Shelby, and Leigh Plunkett Tost. 2010. "Agentic Women and Communal Leadership: How Role Prescriptions Confer Advantages to Top Women Leaders." *Journal of Applied Psychology* 95(2): 221–235.

Rule, Wilma. 1981. "Why Women Don't Run: The Critical Contextual Factors in Women's Legislative Recruitment." *Western Political Quarterly* 34: 60–77.

——. 1987. "Electoral Systems, Contextual Factors and Women's Opportunity for Election to Parliament in Twenty Three Democracies." *Western Political Quarterly* 40(3): 477–498.

——. 1988. "Why Women Don't Run: The Critical Contextual Factors in Women's Legislative Recruitment." *Western Political Quarterly* 34: 60–77.

Rule, Wilma, and Joseph F. Zimmerman. 1994. *Electoral Systems in Comparative Perspective: Their Impact on Women and Minorities*. Westport, CT: Greenwood Press.

Russell, Peter H. 1990. *Interim Report: Judicial Appointments Advisory Committee*. Toronto: Judicial Appointments Advisory Committee.

Rymph, Catherine. 2006. *Republican Women: Feminism and Conservatism from Suffrage through the Rise of the New Right*. Chapel Hill: University of North Carolina Press.

Sachs, Albie, and Joan Hoff Wilson. 1978. *Sexism and the Law: A Study of Male Beliefs and Judicial Bias*. Oxford: Martin Robertson.

Saine, Cindy. 2010. "Republican Women Play Key Role in US Elections." http://www.voanews.com/english/news/usa/Republican-Women-Play-Key-Role-in-US-Elections-105888293.html (accessed July 23, 2013).

Saint-Germain, Michelle. 1989. "Does Their Difference Make a Difference? The Impact of Women on Public Policy in the Arizona Legislature." *Social Science Quarterly* 70: 956–968.

Sanbonmatsu, Kira. 2002. *Gender Equality, Political Parties, and the Politics of Women's Place*. Ann Arbor: University of Michigan Press.

———. 2002. "Political Parties and the Recruitment of Women to State Legislatures." *Journal of Politics* 64: 791–809.

———. 2006a. *Where Women Run: Gender and Party in the American States*. Ann Arbor: University of Michigan.

———. 2006b. "Do Parties Know that 'Women Win'? Party Leader Beliefs about Women's Electoral Chances." *Politics & Gender* 2(4): 431–450.

———. 2006c. "Gender Pools and Puzzles: Charting a 'Women's Path' to the Legislature." *Politics & Gender* 2(3): 387–399.

Sanbonmastu, Kira, Susan J. Carroll, and Debbie Walsh. 2009. *Poised to Run: Women's Pathways to State Legislatures*. http://www.cawp.rutgers.edu/research/reports/PoisedtoRun.pdf (accessed July 23, 2013).

Sanbonmatsu, Kira, and Kathleen Dolan. 2009. "Do Gender Stereotypes Transcend Party?" *Political Research Quarterly* 62(3): 485–494.

Sanchez, Linda, and Loretta Sanchez with Richard Buskin. 2008. *Dream in Color: How the Sanchez Sisters Are Making History in Congress*. New York: Grand Central Publishing.

Sanger-Katz, Margot. 2012. "Retreat!" *National Journal*, March 1.

Sapiro, Virginia. 1981–82. "If Senator Baker Were a Women: An Experimental Study of Candidate Images." *Political Psychology* 2: 61–83.

Sapiro, Virginia. 1982. "Private Costs of Public Commitments or Public Costs of Private Commitments? Family Roles versus Political Ambition." *American Journal of Political Science* 26: 265–279.

Sapiro, Virginia, and Barbara Farah. 1980. "New Pride and Old Prejudice: Political Ambition and Role Orientations among Female Partisan Elites." *Women & Politics* 1: 13–36.

Sapiro, Virginia, Katherine Cramer Walsh, Patricia Strach, and Valerie Hennings. 2011. "Gender, Context, and Television Advertising: A Comprehensive Analysis of 2000 and 2002 House Races." *Political Research Quarterly* 64(1): 107–119.

Sargent, Greg. 2012. "The Next Big Battle in the War Over Women, Ctd." *Washington Post*, May 29. http://www.washingtonpost.com/blogs/plum-line/post/the-next-big-battle-in-the-war-over-women-ctd/2012/05/01/gIQAWSVYuT_blog.html (accessed July 26, 2013).

Saxonberg, S. 2000. "Women in East European Parliaments." *Journal of Democracy* 11(2): 145–158.

Schlafly, Phyllis. 1972. "What's Wrong with Equal Rights for Women?" *Phyllis Schlafly Report* 5(7).

Schaffner, Brian F. 2005. "Priming Gender: Campaigning on Women's Issues in U.S. Senate Elections." *American Journal of Political Science* 49: 803–817.

———. 2006. "Local News Coverage and the Incumbency Advantage in the U.S." *Legislative Studies Quarterly* 31(4): 491–511.

Scheer, Teva J. 2005. *Governor Lady: The Life and Times of Nellie Tayloe Ross*. Columbia: University of Missouri Press.

Scherer, Nancy. 2003. "The Judicial Confirmation Process: Mobilizing Elites, Mobilizing Masses." *Judicature* 86(5): 240–250.

———. 2005. *Scoring Points: Politicians, Activists, and the Lower Federal Court Appointment Process*. Stanford, CA: Stanford University Press.

Schnepf, S. V. "Gender Differences in Subjective Well-Being in Central and Eastern Europe." *Journal of European Social Policy* 20(1): 74–85.

Schreiber, Ronnee. 2011. "Palin as Supermom: Conservative Ideology, Motherhood and Running for Elective Office." Presented at the annual meeting of the Western Political Science Association, San Antonio. http://ssrn.com/abstract=1808302 (accessed July 23, 2013).

———. 2012a. *Righting Feminism: Conservative Women and American Politics with New Epilogue*. New York: Oxford University Press.

———. 2012b. "Dilemmas of Representation: Conservative and Feminist Women's Organizations React to Sarah Palin." In *Women of the Right: Comparison and Interplay across Borders*, eds. Kathleen M. Blee and Sandra McGee Deutsch. University Park: Pennsylvania University Press, 273–290.

——. 2012c. "Mama Grizzlies Compete for Office." *New Political Science* 34(4): 549–563.

Schroedel, Jean Reith, Michelle Bligh, Jennifer Merolla, and Randall Gonzalez. 2013. "Charismatic Rhetoric in the 2008 Presidential Campaign: Commonalities and Differences." *Presidential Studies Quarterly* 43: 101–128.

Schultz, Ulrike, and Gisela Shaw. 2003. *Women in the World's Legal Professions.* Oxford: Hart.

Schumaker, Paul, and Nancy E. Burns. 1988. "Gender Cleavages and the Resolution of Local Policy Issues." *American Journal of Political Science* 32(4): 1070–1095.

Schwindt-Bayer, L. A. 2005. "The Incumbency Disadvantage and Women's Election to Legislative Office." *Electoral Studies* 24(2): 227–244.

Scola, Becky. 2006. "Women of Color in State Legislatures: Gender, Race, Ethnicity and Legislative Office Holding." *Journal of Women, Politics & Policy* 28(3–4): 43–70.

Seelye, Katharine Q. 2012. "Crucial Subset: Female Voters Still Deciding." *New York Times,* October 24. http://www.nytimes.com/2012/10/25/us/politics/female-swing-voters-a-coveted-demographic.html?pagewanted=all (accessed July 26, 2013).

Sellers, Patrick. 2010. *Cycles of Spin: Strategic Communication in the U.S. Congress.* New York: Cambridge University Press.

Seltzer, Richard, Jody Newman, and Melissa Leighton. 1997. *Sex as a Political Variable: Women as Candidates and Voters in U.S. Elections.* Boulder, CO: Lynne Rienner.

Seyranian, Viviane, and Michelle Bligh. 2008. "Presidential Charismatic Leadership: Exploring the Rhetoric of Social Change." *Leadership Quarterly* 19(1): 54–76.

Shaheen, Jeanne, Barbara Boxer, and Patty Murray. 2012. "Why the Birth-Control Mandate Makes Sense." *Wall Street Journal,* February 7. http://online.wsj.com/article/SB10001424052970204136404577207482497075436.html (accessed July 26, 2013).

Shamir, Boaz. 1995. "Social Distance and Charisma: Theoretical Notes and an Exploratory Study." *Leadership Quarterly* 6(1): 19–47.

Shamir, Boaz, Robert House, and Michael B. Arthur. 1993. "The Motivational Effects of Charismatic Leadership: A Self-Concept Based Theory." *Organizational Sciences* 4(4): 577–594.

Sheehy, Gail. 2008. "Hillaryland at War." *Vanity Fair.* August. http://www.vanityfair.com/politics/features/2008/08/clinton200808?currentPage=1 (accessed July 23, 2013).

Shepsle, Kenneth A. 1972. "The Strategy of Ambiguity: Uncertainty and Electoral Competition." *American Political Science Review* 66(2): 555–568.

Shogan, Colleen. 2001. "Speaking Out: An Analysis of Democratic and Republican Women-Invoked Rhetoric of the 105th Congress." *Women & Politics* 23: 129–146.

Shor, Boris, Christopher Berry, and Nolan McCarty. 2010. "A Bridge to Somewhere: Mapping State and Congressional Ideology on a Cross-Institutional Common Space." *Legislative Studies Quarterly* 35(3): 417–448.

Siaroff, A. 2000. "Women's Representation in Legislatures and Cabinets in Industrial Democracies." *International Political Science Review* 21(2): 197–215.

Sierra, Christine, and Adaliza Sosa-Riddell. 1994. "Chicanas as Political Actors: Rare Literature, Complex Practice." *National Political Science Review* 4: 297–317.

Sigelman, Lee, and Susan Welch. 1984. "Race, Gender, and Opinion toward Black and Female Candidates." *Public Opinion Quarterly* 48: 467–475.

Simiem, Evelyn M. 2005 "Race, Gender, and Linked Fate." *Journal of Black Studies* 35(5): 529–550.

Simmons, Wendy. 2001. "A Majority of Americans Say More Women in Political Office Would Be Positive for the Country." *Gallup Poll Monthly,* January.

Singh, Robert. 1998. *The Congressional Black Caucus: Racial Politics in the U.S. Congress.* Thousand Oaks, CA: SAGE.

Slotnick, Elliot E. 1979. "The Changing Role of the Senate Judiciary Committee in Judicial Selection." *Judicature* 62(10): 502–510.

——. 1988. "Federal Judicial Recruitment and Selection Research: A Review Essay." *Judicature* 71(6): 317–324.

——. 2002. "A Historical Perspective on Judicial Selection." *Judicature* 86(1): 13–16.

Sloviter, Dolores Korman. 2005. "Personal Reflections." *University of Toledo Law Review* 36(4): 855–861.

Smith, Aaron. 2011. "The Internet and Campaign 2010." http://pewresearch.org/pubs/1931/online-political-use-2010-over-half-us-adults (accessed March 17, 2013).

Smith, Ben. 2008. "As Campaign Ends, Was Clinton to Blame?" *Politico.com*. June 7. http://www.politico.com/news/stories/0608/10910.html (accessed July 23, 2013).

Smith, Eric R. A. N., and Richard Fox. 2001. "The Electoral Fortunes of Women Candidates for Congress." *Political Research Quarterly* 54: 205–221.

Smith, Jessi L., David Paul, and Rachel Paul. 2007. "No Place for a Woman: Evidence for Gender Bias in Evaluations of Presidential Candidates." *Basic and Applied Social Psychology* 29(3): 225–233.

Smith, Kevin B. 1997. "When All's Fair: Signs of Parity in Media Coverage of Female Candidates." *Political Communication* 14: 71–82.

Smith, Raymond A., and Donald P. Haider-Markel. 2002. *Gay and Lesbian Americans and Political Participation.* Denver: ABC-CLIO Publishers.

Smith, Tom. 1975. "A Study of Trends in the Political Role of Women, 1936–1974." May. Social Change Report, Chicago, NORC.

Smolowe, J., and W. Cole. 1992. "Politics: The Feminist Machine." *Time* 139(18): 34–36.

Smooth, Wendy. 2001a. "African American Women State Legislators: The Impact of Gender and Race on Legislative Influence." Ph.D. diss., University of Maryland.

Smooth, Wendy. 2001b. "African American Women State Legislators and the Politics of Legislative Incorporation." Monograph. Prepared for the Center for the American Woman and Politics Forum for Women State Legislators, November 15–18.

Smooth, Wendy. 2006. "Intersectionality in Electoral Politics: A Mess Worth Making." *Politics & Gender* 2(3): 400–414.

Sobotka, T. 2003. "Re-Emerging Diversity: Rapid Fertility Changes in Central and Eastern Europe after the Collapse of the Communist Regimes." *Population* 58(4–5): 511–547.

Solowiej, Lisa A., Wendy L. Martinek, and Thomas L. Brunell. 2005. "Partisan Politics: The Impact of Party in the Confirmation of Minority and Female Federal Court Nominees." *Party Politics* 11: 557–577.

Somit, A., R. Wildenmann, B. Boll, and A. Rommele, eds. 1994. *The Victorious Incumbent: A Threat to Democracy?* Aldershot, UK: Dartmouth.

SoonerPoll. 2010. "Oklahoma Poll." *Shepard Research*, October.

Squire, Peverill. 1992. "Legislative Professionalization and Membership Diversity in State Legislatures." *Legislative Studies Quarterly* 17: 69–82.

———. 2007. "Measuring State Legislative Professionalism: The Squire Index Revisted." *State Politics and Policy Quarterly* 7: 211–227.

Stalsburg, Brittany. 2010. "Voting for Mom: The Political Consequences of Being a Parent for Male and Female Candidates." *Politics & Gender* 6: 373–404.

Stambough, Stephen J., and Valerie R. O'Regan. 2007. "Republican Lambs and the Democratic Pipeline: Partisan Differences in the Nomination of Female Gubernatorial Candidates." *Politics & Gender* 3: 349–368.

Stanton, Ryan J. 2012. "'West Wing' Cast Reunites to Make Campaign Video for Ann Arbor's Bridget Mary McCormack." *AnnArbor.com*. September 21. http://www.annarbor.com/news/west-wing-cast-reunites-to-make-campaign-video-for-ann-arbors-bridget-mary-mccormack/ (accessed November 14, 2012).

Steigerwalt, Amy. 2010. *Battle over the Bench: Senators, Interest Groups, and Lower Court Confirmations.* Charlottesville: University of Virginia Press.

Stolberg, Sheryl Gay. 2009. "Obama Signs Equal-Pay Legislation." *New York Times*, January 29.

———. 2011. "When It Comes to Scandals, Girls Won't Be Boys." *New York Times*. June 11. http://www.nytimes.com/2011/06/12/weekinreview/12women.html?_r=3 (accessed March 26, 2013).

Stone, Matthew. 2012. "What's Olympia Snow Going to Do with Her Campaign Money?" *Bangor Daily News*. July 13. http://bangordailynews.com/2012/07/13/politics/whats-olympia-snowe-going-to-do-with-her-campaign-money/ (accessed March 24, 2013).

Stoper, Emily. 1977. "Wife and Politician: Role Strain among Women in Public Office." In *Portrait of Marginality: The Political Behavior of the American Woman*, eds. M. Githens and J. Prestage. New York: McKay, 320–337.

Stout, Christopher T., and Reuben Kline. 2011. "I'm Not Voting for Her: Polling Discrepancies and Female Candidates." *Political Behavior* 33: 479–503.

Streb, Matthew, Barbara Burrell, Brian Frederick, and Michael Genovese. 2008. "Social Desirability Effects and Support for a Female American President." *Public Opinion Quarterly* 72: 76–89.

Studlar, Donley, and Susan Welch. 1996. "The Opportunity Structure for Women's Candidacies and Electability in Britain and the United States." *Political Research Quarterly* 49: 861–874.

Swain, Carol M. *Black Faces, Black Interests: The Representation of African Americans in Congress.* Cambridge: Harvard University Press 1995.

Swers, Michele L. 1998. "Are Congresswomen More Likely to Vote for Women's Issue Bills than Their Male Colleagues?" *Legislative Studies Quarterly* 23(3): 435–448.

——. 2002. *The Difference Women Make: The Policy Impact of Women in Congress.* Chicago: University of Chicago Press.

——. 2007. "Building a Reputation on National Security: The Impact of Stereotypes Related to Gender and Military Experience." *Legislative Studies Quarterly* 32: 559–595.

——. 2008. "Policy Leadership beyond 'Women's' Issues." In *Legislative Women: Getting Elected, Getting Ahead*, ed. Beth Reingold. Boulder, CO: Lynne Rienner Publishers, Inc., 117–134.

——. 2013. *Women in the Club: Gender and Policy Making in the Senate.* Chicago: University of Chicago Press.

Swers, Michele L., and Christine C. Kim. Forthcoming. "Replacing Sandra Day O'Connor: Gender and the Politics of Supreme Court Nominations." *Journal of Women, Politics & Policy.*

Swers, Michele, and Carin Larson. 2005. "Women and Congress: Do They Act as Advocates for Women's Issues." In *Women and Elective Office: Past, Present, and Future*, 2nd ed., eds. Sue Thomas and Clyde Wilcox. New York: Oxford University Press, 110–128.

Tadlock, Barry L., and Ann Gordon. 2003. "Political Evaluations of Lesbian and Gay Candidates: The Impact of Stereotypic Biases in Press Coverage." Presented at the annual meeting of the American Political Science Association, August 28–31, Philadelphia.

Takash, Paule Cruz. 1997. "Breaking Barriers to Representation: Chicana/Latina Elected Officials in California." In *Women Transforming Politics: An Alternative Reader*, eds. Cathy J. Cohen, Kathleen B. Jones, and Joan C. Toronto. New York: New York University Press, 412–433.

Tamerius, Karin. 1995. "Sex, Gender, and Leadership in the Representation of Women." In *Gender Power, Leadership, and Governance*, eds. Georgia Duerst-Lahti and Rita Mae Kelly. Ann Arbor: University of Michigan Press, 93–112.

Tarr, G. Alan. 2012. *Without Fear or Favor: Judicial Independence and Judicial Accountability in the States.* Stanford, CA: Stanford University Press.

Tate, Katherine. 1997. "African American Female Senatorial Candidates: Twin Assets or Double Liabilities?" In *African American Power and Politics*, ed. Hanes Walton Jr. New York: Columbia University Press, 264–281.

——. 2003. *Black Faces in the Mirror, African Americans and Their Representatives in the U.S. Congress.* Princeton, NJ: Princeton University Press.

——. 2011. "Introduction." In *Black Power in Black Presidential Bids from Jackson to Obama*, eds. Michael Mitchell and David Covin. Piscataway, NJ: Transaction Publishers, 3–22.

——. 2013. *Concordance: Black Lawmaking in the U.S. Congress from Carter to Obama.* Ann Arbor: University of Michigan Press.

Thomas, Sue. 1990. "Voting Patterns in the California Assembly: The Role of Gender." *Women & Politics* 9: 43–56.

——. 1991. "The Impact of Women on State Legislative Policies." *Journal of Politics* 53(4): 958–976.

——. 1992. "The Effects of Race and Gender on Constituency Service." *Western Political Quarterly* 45: 169–180.

——. 1994. *How Women Legislate.* New York: Oxford University Press.

———. 1997. "Why Gender Matters: The Perceptions of Women Officeholders." *Women & Politics* 17: 27–53.

———. 1998. "Introduction: Women and Elective Office: Past, Present, and Future." In *Women and Elective Office*, eds. S. Thomas and C. Wilcox. New York: Oxford University Press, 1–14.

———. 2002. "The Personal is Political: Antecedents of Gendered Choices of Elected Representatives." *Sex Roles: A Journal of Research* 47: 343–353.

Thomas, Sue, Rebekah Herrick, and Matthew Braunstein. 2002. "Legislative Careers: The Personal and the Political." In *Women Transforming Congress*, ed. Cindy Simon Rosenthal. Norman: University of Oklahoma Press, 397–421.

Thomas, Sue, Lisa Rickert, and Carole Cannon. 2006. "The Meaning, Status and Future of Reproductive Autonomy: The Case of Alcohol Use during Pregnancy." *UCLA Women's Law Journal* 15(1): 1–43.

Thomas, Sue, and Susan Welch. 1991. "The Impact of Gender on Activities and Priorities of State Legislators." *Western Political Quarterly* 44(2): 445–456.

Thompson, Joel A., and Gary F. Moncrief. 1993. "The Implications of Term Limits for Women and Minorities: Some Evidence from the States." *Social Science Quarterly* 74: 300–309.

Thomsen, Danielle M. 2012. "Partisan Polarization and the Representation of Women in the U.S. Congress." Presented at the annual meeting of the 2012 American Political Science Association. http://ssrn.com/abstract=2108017 (accessed July 23, 2013).

Todorov, Alexander, Anesu N. Mandisodza, Amir Goren, and Crystal C. Hall. 2005. "Inferences of Competence from Faces Predict Election Outcomes." *Science* 308(10): 1623–1626.

Tokarz, Karen L. 1986. "Women Judges and Merit Selection under the Missouri Plan." *Washington University Law Quarterly* 64(3): 903–951.

Tolbert Caroline J., and Gertrude A. Steuernagel. 2001. "Women Lawmakers, State Mandates and Women's Health." *Women & Politics* 22: 1–39.

Tolchin, Susan, and Martin Tolchin. 1973. *Clout: Womanpower and Politics*. New York: Coward, McCann, & Geoghegan, Inc.

Tolleson Rinehart, Sue. 1991. "Do Women Leaders Make a Difference? Substance, Style, and Perceptions." In *Gender and Policymaking: Studies of Women in Office*, ed. Debra Dodson. New Brunswick: Rutgers University.

———. 2001. "Do Women Leaders Make a Difference: Substance, Style, and Perceptions." In *The Impact of Women in Public Office*, ed. Susan J. Carroll. Bloomington: Indiana University Press, 149–165.

Tolleson-Rinehart, Sue, and Jeanie R. Stanley. 1994. *Claytie and the Lady: Ann Richards, Gender, and Politics in Texas*. Austin: University of Texas Press.

Toner, Robin. 2008. "Mining the Gender Gap for Answers." *New York Times*, March 2.

Toobin, Jeffrey. 2007. *The Nine: Inside the Secret World of the Supreme Court*. New York: Doubleday.

Torres-Spelliscy, Ciara, Monique Chase, and Emma Greenman. 2008. "Improving Judicial Diversity." Brennan Center for Justice. http://brennan.3cdn.net/31e6c0fa3c2e920910_ppm6ibehe.pdf (accessed November 23, 2011).

Totenberg, Nina. 2010. "Should Kagan's Lack of Judicial Experience Matter?" *National Public Radio*. May 12. http://www.npr.org/templates/story/story.php?storyId=126764692 (accessed September 6, 2010).

Towns, Ann. 2010. *Women and States: Norms and Hierarchies in International Society*. New York: Cambridge University Press.

Tuve, Jeanette E. 1984. *First Lady of the Law: Florence Ellinwood Allen*. Lanham, MD: University Press of America.

United Nations. 1995. "Platform Strategic Objective G1." Fourth World Conference on Women, Beijing, China. http://www.un.org/womenwatch/daw/beijing/platform/decision.htm (accessed July 23, 2013).

U.S. Census Bureau. 2012. "Census of Governments: Organization Component Preliminary Estimates." http://www.census.gov/govs/cog2012 (accessed October 19, 2012).

U.S. Conference of Mayors. 2012. "Women Mayors' Group." http://www.usmayors.org/about/women.asp (accessed November 11, 2012).

U.S. Senate Democratic Steering and Outreach Committee. 2008. "Congressional Women Rally for Fair Pay." July 17. http://democrats.senate.gov/checklistforchange/newsroom.cfm (accessed July 23, 2013).

Uscinski, Joseph E., and Lilly J. Goren. 2011. "What's in a Name? Coverage of Senator Hillary Clinton during the 2008 Democratic Primary." *Political Research Quarterly* 64(4): 884–896.

van Assendelft, Laura, and Karen O'Connor. 1994. "Backgrounds, Motivations and Interests: A Comparison of Male and Female Local Party Activists." *Women & Politics* 14: 77–92.

van Assendelft, Laura, and Cytha Stottlemyer. 2009. "Women in Local Government: A Case Study of Southwest/Western Virginia." *Virginia Social Sciences Journal* 44: 1–21.

Van Der Lippe, T., and E. Fodor. 1998. "Changes in Gender Inequality in Six Eastern European countries." *Acta Sociologica* 41(2): 131–149.

Van Hightower, Nikki R. 1977. "The Recruitment of Women for Public Office." *American Politics Quarterly* 5(3): 301–314.

Vega, Arturo, and Juanita M. Firestone. 1995. "The Effects of Gender on Congressional Behavior and Substantive Representation of Women." *Legislative Studies Quarterly* 20: 213–222.

Vinson, Danielle C. 2003. *Through Local Eyes: Local Media Coverage of Congress and Its Members.* Cresskill, NJ: Hampton Press.

Volden, Craig, Alan E. Wiseman, and Dana E. Wittmer. 2013. "When Are Women More Effective Lawmakers than Men?" *American Journal of Political Science.* Online version. Doi: 10.1111/ajps.12010.

Wahlke, John C. 1971. "Policy Demands and System Support: The Role of the Represented." *British Journal of Political Science* 1(3): 271–290.

Walton, Don. 2012. "Palin Endorses Fischer, Stenberg Says He's the Conservative." *Lincoln Journal Star,* May 9.

Warren, Jenifer. 2001. "Capitol Gains for Gay Pols; Legislature's Four Lesbians Help Push California to the Forefront in the Fight for Equal Rights." *Los Angeles Times,* December 10.

Wasson, Erik. 2012. "Lowey, Kaptur Fight for Democrats' Top Spending Panel Slot Heats Up." *The Hill,* November 18.

Weber, Max. 1947. *The Theory of Social and Economic Organization.* New York: Oxford University Press.

Weikart, Lynn A., Greg Chen, Daniel Williams, and Haris Hromic. 2006. "The Democratic Sex: Gender Differences and the Exercise of Power." *Journal of Women, Politics, & Policy* 28(1): 119–140.

Weisman, Jonathan. 2012. "Women Figure Anew in Senate's Latest Battle." *New York Times,* March 14. http://www.nytimes.com/2012/03/15/us/politics/violence-against-women-act-divides-senate.html?_r=0&gwh=3B3059CE0CFD05C27A9AAC743CA2E1B2 (accessed July 26, 2013).

Weissman, Art. 1996. *Christine Todd Whitman: The Making of a National Political Player.* New York: Carol Publishing Group.

Welch, Susan. 1985. "Are Women More Liberal than Men in the U.S. Congress." *Legislative Studies Quarterly* 10(1): 125–134.

Welch, Susan, and Donley Studlar. 1990. "Multimember Districts and the Representation of Women: Evidence from Britain and the United States." *Journal of Politics* 52: 391–412.

Weldon, S. Laurel. 2006. "Women's Movements, Identity Politics and Policy Impact: A Study of Policies on Violence Against Women in the 50 U.S. States." *Political Research Quarterly* 58(1): 111–122.

Werner, Emmy E. 1968. "Women in the State Legislatures." *Western Political Quarterly* 21: 40–50.

Whicker, Marcia Lynn, and Malcolm Jewell. 1998. "The Feminization of Leadership in State Legislatures." In *Women and Elective Office: Past, Present, and Future*, eds. Sue Thomas and Clyde Wilcox. New York: Oxford University Press, 163–174.

Whistler, Donald E., and Mark C. Ellickson. 1999. "The Incorporation of Women in State Legislatures: A Description." *Women and Politics* 20(3): 81–97.

Whitby, Kenny J. 1998. *The Color of Representation: Congressional Behavior and Black Constituents.* Ann Arbor: University of Michigan Press.

Wilcox, Clyde. 1994. "Why Was 1992 the 'Year of the Woman'? Explaining Women's Gains in 1992." In *The Year of the Woman: Myths & Realities*, eds. E.A. Cook, Sue Thomas, and Clyde Wilcox. Boulder, CO: Westview Press, 1–24.

Williams, John, and Deborah Best. 1990. *Measuring Sex Stereotypes: A Multination Study.* Newbury Park, CA: SAGE.

Williams, Margaret. 2006. "In a Different Path: The Process of Becoming a Judge for Women and Men." *Judicature* 90(3): 104–113.

——. 2007. "Women's Representation on State Trial and Appellate Courts." *Social Science Quarterly* 88(5): 1192–1204.

Williamson, Vanessa, Theda Skocpol, and John Coggin. 2011. "The Tea Party and the Remaking of Republican Conservatism." *Perspectives on Politics* 9(1): 25–43.

Wills, Garry. 1992. "H.R Clinton's Case." *New York Review of Books*, March 5. http://www.nybooks.com/articles/archives/1992/mar/05/hr-clintons-case/?pagination=false (accessed July 26, 2013).

Wilson, Angelia, and Cynthia Burack. 2012. "'Where Liberty Reigns and God Is Supreme': The Christian Right and the Tea Party Movement." *New Political Science* 34(2): 172–190.

Wilson, Sarah. 1995. "Interview with Professor Barbara Babcock." *Diversifying the Judiciary: An Oral History of Women Federal Judges.* Federal Judicial Center. May 19.

Windett, Jason Harold. 2011. "State Effects and the Emergence and Success of Female Gubernatorial Candidates." *State Politics & Policy Quarterly* 11(4): 460–482.

Winter, Nicholas J. G. 2010. "Masculine Republicans and Feminine Democrats: Gender and Americans' Explicit and Implicit Images of the Political Parties." *Political Behavior* 32: 587–618.

Wistrand, Birgitta. 1981. *Swedish Women on the Move.* Stockholm: Swedish Institute.

Witt, Linda, Karen Paget, and Glenna Matthews. 1994. *Running as a Woman.* New York: Free Press.

Wolbrecht, Christina. 2000. *The Politics of Women's Rights: Parties, Positions, and Change.* Princeton, NJ: Princeton University Press.

Wolbrecht, Christina. 2002. "Female Legislators and the Women's Rights Agenda: From Feminine Mystique to Feminist Era." In *Women Transforming Congress*, ed. Cindy Simon Rosenthal. Norman: University of Oklahoma Press, 170–239.

Wolfson, Charles. 2009. "Hillary Clinton's 6-Month Checkup." *CBS News*, August 14. http://www.cbsnews.com/2100-18568_162-5169849.html (accessed July 26, 2013).

*Women's e-news.* 2013. "State Court Tips Genderwise; Asian Poll Says Rape Ok." January 19. http://womensenews.org/story/cheers-and-jeers/130118/state-court-tips-genderwise-asian-pol-says-rape-ok (accessed March 24, 2013).

Wong, Scott. 2012. "Patty Murray: I Will Chair Senate Budget Committee." *Politico.* November 15. http://www.politico.com/news/stories/1112/83902.html (accessed July 23, 2013).

Woods, Harriet. 2000. *Stepping Up to Power: The Political Journey of American Women.* Boulder, CO: Westview Press.

World Bank. 2012. *The World Development Report 2012: Gender Equality and Development.* Washington, DC: World Bank.

Wright, Gerald, Tracy Osborn, and Jonathan Winburn. 2009. "Patterns of Roll Call Voting in America's Legislatures." Presented at the annual State Politics and Policy Conference, May 22–23, Chapel Hill, NC.

Wright, Gerald, and Brian Schaffner. 2002. "The Influence of Party: Evidence from the State Legislatures." *American Political Science Review* 96(2): 367–380.

Yiannakis, Diana E. 1982. "House Members' Communication Styles: Newsletters and Press Releases." *Journal of Politics* 44(4): 1049–1071.

Zernike, Kate. 2008. "She Just Might Be President Someday." *New York Times*. May 18. http://www.nytimes.com/2008/05/18/weekinreview/18zernike/html?_r=2&hp&oref=slogin&oref=slogin (accessed July 23, 2013).

—. 2012. "In Act of Defiance, Democrat Stalls Obama Choice for Court." *New York Times*. January 5. http://www.nytimes.com/2012/01/06/nyregion/senator-robert-menendez-stalls-obama-move-to-promote-judge-patty-shwartz.html (accessed May 28, 2012).

# INDEX

2000 Millennium Declaration, 291
Abrahamson, Shirley, 230
affinity effect, 62–65
Affordable Care Act, 15, 83, 121, 124
Afghanistan, 31, 58, 60
Aguirre, Alicia, 19
Akers, Dolly Smith, 4
Allen, Florence Ellinwood, 5
Allen, Susan, 5
American College of Trial Lawyers, 219
American Judicature Society, 232
American National Election Studies (ANES), 47
Anderson, Cora Belle Reynolds, 4
Arab Spring, 85
Aristotle, 1, 23
Askins, Jari, 147, 158

Bachmann, Michele, 27
Bailey, Consuelo Northrup, 5
Baitinger, Gail, 7
Baldwin, Tammy, 1, 164, 253, 257
Barrette, John, 149
baseline gender preference, 53
Bass, Karen, 5, 12
Beutler, Jaime Herrera, 238
Biden, Joe, 123
bipartisan, 9, 20, 167, 300
Bird, Rose, 218, 230
Blackburn, Marsha, 175
"Blue slip," 218, 233–234
Bolin, Jane Matilda, 6
Boosalis, Helen, 147, 149
Born, Brooksley Elizabeth, 219
Boxer, Barbara, 25, 171, 180
Branstad, Terry, 218
Brewer, Jan, 11, 146, 154, 156
Breyer, Stephen, 224
Bright, Chelsie Moore, 8

Brown, Corrine, 239
Brown, Janice Rogers, 169
Brown, Kate, 20, 255
Brown, Scott, 174
Buhl, Angie, 255
Burke, Edmond, 207
Burstein, Karen, 256–257

campaign finance, 105, 110
Cannon, Martha Hughes, 4
Cantwell, Maria, 171, 180
Carter, Jimmy, 82, 148, 169, 219
CEDAW, 291
Census of Governments, 199
Chafee, Lincoln, 170
character traits, 86–88, 93
Chisholm, Shirley, 3, 237, 239
Christian Right, 285, 287
Chu, Judy, 241, 252
Clare Boothe Luce Policy Institute, 114, 116
Clinton, Bill, 82, 148, 220, 242, 272
Clinton, Chelsea, 74
Clinton, Hillary Rodham, 1, 5, 7, 27, 31, 43, 50,
    67–80, 85, 96, 171, 180, 216
Collins, Barbara-Rose, 239, 246
Collins, Cardiss, 239, 250
Collins, Susan, 170
Committee on the Federal Judiciary, 219
Concerned Women for America (CWA), 116,
    118
Congressional Black Caucus (CBC), 237, 246
Constituency service, 127, 144, 207–208, 211,
    214
Convention on the Elimination of All Forms of
    Discrimination against Women, 291
Cook Report, 105, 109
Cook, Beverly Blair, 221, 225
Cordova, Alyssa, 114

council-manager, 202–203
Craig, Minnie Davenport, 5
Cressingham, Clara, 4
critical mass, 17, 184
Crosby, Susan, 17

Dannenfelser, Marjorie, 114
Daughters of the Confederacy, 250
De Priest, Oscar, 238
Dellums, Ron, 237
Dillon, John, 202
Dillon's Rule, 202
district magnitude, 294
Dolan, Kathleen, 7, 70
Dole, Elizabeth, 170
double quotas, 297
Duckworth, Tammy, 4, 241
Dunn, Jennifer, 152
Dunn, Jennifer, 152

Earhart, Amelia, 3
Edmondson, Drew, 158
Eisenhower, Dwight, 222
electoral formula, 294
electoral systems, 227, 289–297
electoral threshold, 294
eligibility pool theory, 199
Emerge America, 38
EMILY's List, 9, 43, 224, 303
EMILY's List Political Opportunity Program,
    24, 38
Equal Rights Amendment, 43, 113
Estrada, Miguel, 169

Fabe, Dana, 229
Fallin, Mary, 11, 147, 153, 155–156
Family and Medical Leave Act (FMLA), 194
family planning programs, 195
Fauset, Crystal Dreda Bird, 4
Feinstein, Dianne, 149, 171, 180
Felton, Rebecca Latimer, 3
Ferraro, Geraldine, 5, 150
Finney, Joan, 146
Fisher, Jimmie Lou, 150
Fong, Hiram, 242
Ford, Gerald, 222
Foster, Vincent, 83
France, 289, 296
Fridkin, Kim, 8

Gabbard, Tulsi, 4, 241
Gallegos, Fedelina Lucero, 4
gender consciousness, 43, 62
gender diversity, 2, 222
gender gap in political ambition, 27, 29, 32, 34,
    42–43, 201

gender gap, 7, 21–45, 155, 166, 178, 201
gender quotas, 290, 293, 295, 299–302, 305
gender stereotyping, 8
gender strategies, 70
gender-office congruency, 68, 71, 76, 78
General Social Survey (GSS), 47
Georgia, 3, 10, 45, 99, 188, 237, 239, 276, 279
Germany, 289, 296
Gill, LaVerne McCain, 250
Ginsburg, Ruth Bader, 5, 219
Glass ceiling, 22, 76, 152, 217
Global Database of Quotas for Women, 303
*Goodridge v. Department of Public Health*, 269–270
Graham, Lindsey, 84
Granholm, Jennifer, 147
Grasso, Ella, 5, 27, 146, 150
Gregoire, Christine, 146–147
GSS, 47, 50

Haley, Nikki, 5, 11, 153, 156
Hanabusa, Colleen, 5, 241
Harding, Warren, 158
Harper, Minnie Buckingham, 4
Hassan, Maggie, 6, 11
Helms, Jesse, 248
Henry, Brad, 158
Herrick, Rebekah, 8
Hirono, Mazie, 2, 147, 153, 237, 241
Hispanic Caucus, 238, 251–252
Hogan, Kate, 270
Holly, Carrie Clyde, 4
Holmes, Alvin, 267
Honda, Mike, 243
Huckabee, Mike, 150
Hull, Jane, 146, 154

incumbency advantage, 30, 295
incumbency, 7, 30, 62–66, 104–105, 116, 122,
    205, 211, 228–231, 295, 305
Independent Women's Forum, 116, 118
individualistic political culture, 279
Infinity Project, 224
Inouye, Daniel, 242
institutional gendering, 21–22
International Institute for Democracy, 303
International Knowledge Network of Women in
    Politics (iKNOW), 303
Inter-parliamentary Union (IPU), 11, 288
Iraq, 31, 134, 244

Jackson, Jesse, 237
Jacques, Cheryl, 270
Jenkins, Lynn, 25, 179
Johnson, Lyndon, 221
Jones, Stephanie Tubbs, 4
Jordan, Barbara Charline, 237

Judicial Selection Project, 223
Justice at Stake, 232

Kagan, Elena, 5, 216
Kassebaum, Nancy Landon, 3–4
Kaufmann, Christine, 267
Kelly, Jane, 224
Kennedy, John F., 222
Kilpatrick, Carolyn Cheeks, 251
Klock, Frances S., 4
Kotek, Tina, 2
Krook, Mona Lena, 10
Kuehl, Sheila, 267
Kuhl, Carolyn, 169

La Guardia, Fiorello H., 221
Landrieu, Mary, 172, 180
Larsen, Sylvia, 7
Lawless, Jennifer, 7
Lawrence, Regina, 8
leadership style, 94, 166, 200, 205, 207, 214
Ledbetter, Lilly, 162, 168, 172–175, 180
Lee, Barbara, 24
lesbian legislators, 268
Lesbian Political Action Committee (LPAC), 9
Lewis, Rhoda, 218
Lilly Ledbetter Fair Pay Act, 162, 168,
    172–176, 180
Lincoln, Blanche, 180
Lingle, Linda, 146–147, 153
Lockwood, Lorna, 6
Lomen, Lucille, 224
Lowey, Nita, 178

Madsen, Susan R., 149
Maggie's List, 25
Malia, Elizabeth, 269
Mama Grizzlies, 111, 114, 117–118, 120, 122
mammograms, 15
Mansfield, Belle Babb, 217
marital status, 239–240
Marshall, Brenda DeVore, 149
Martinez, Susana, 5, 11, 147, 156–157
Maryland Nominating Commission, 227
Matsui, Doris, 241
Mayhead, Molly A., 149
Mayor-council system, 202
McCain, John, 69, 76, 92, 123, 156, 174
McCloud, Sheryl Gordon, 6
McCormack, Bridget Mary, 216
McCullough, Catherine, 5
McKenna, Margaret, 222
media treatment, 7, 9, 24
Medicaid, 96, 288
Meek, Carrie, 239, 249
Mendez, Jeanette Morehouse, 8

Meng, Grace, 241
Mexico, 4–5, 11, 99, 147, 156–158, 238, 252, 276
Middle East, 85, 292, 296
Miers, Harriet, 219
Migden, Carol, 268
Mikulski, Barbara, 3–4, 15, 173, 178, 180
Milk, Harvey, 269
Millender-McDonald, Juanita, 4
Mink, Patsy Takemoto, 4, 236
Minner, Ruth Ann, 146
moralistic political culture, 281
Morris, Celia, 149
Moseley Braun, Carol, 3, 237, 248
Motley, Constance Baker, 221
Moua, Mee, 248
multimember districts, 279–285, 294
Murkowski, Lisa, 176
Murphy, Diana, 224
Murray, Patty, 4, 25, 178, 180

Napolitano, Janet, 146, 154
NARAL Pro-Choice America, 43
National Association of Latino Elected and
    Appointed Officials (NALEO), 246
National Association of Women Judges, 223, 233
National Democratic Institute for International
    Affairs, 303
National Organization for Women (NOW), 125,
    237
National Political Awareness Test (NPAT), 186
National Women's Political Caucus (NWPC),
    44, 62, 223
Neuman, Linda Kinney, 218
Nixon, Richard, 82, 219
Noble, Elaine, 5, 254, 269
Norrander, Barbara, 10
Norris, Pippa, 10
Norton, Eleanor Holmes, 246, 250

O'Connor, Sandra Day, 5, 219, 232
O'Regan, Valerie, 9
Obama, Barack, 31, 74, 83, 92, 123, 162, 172,
    219, 272
Office of Public Liaison, 244
Office of Women's Health, 164
opportunity structure, 78, 289–290
Orr, Kay, 147, 149
Owen, Priscilla, 169

Palin, Sarah, 1, 5, 7, 10, 27, 31, 50, 67, 70–78, 111,
    118, 123–124, 150, 156, 165
Parker, Annise, 203, 254–255
party list, 290, 294–299, 305
Peake, Sarah K., 270
Pelosi, Nancy, 1, 6, 21, 25, 27, 31, 152, 162,
    168, 216

"Pipeline" explanation, 233
Pitkin, Hannah, 61
Planned Parenthood, 43, 167, 178
Planned Parenthood Action Fund, 43
plateau effect, 150
political action committees, 9, 111
political ambition, 14, 23, 29, 30–31, 40, 42, 72,
   97, 199–201, 207, 215, 245, 281
political ideology, 56, 198
power over, 19, 72, 86
power to, 16, 19, 85
principle of alternation (zippering), 299
Project Vote Smart, 186
proportional representation, 226, 290
Pryor, William, 169

Quadrennial Diplomacy and Development
   Review, 85
Quan, Jean, 11, 203–204
quotas, 296–298, 303

Rankin, Jeanette, 3
Rawlings-Blake, Stephanie, 11, 204
Ray, Dixie Lee, 27
Reagan, Ronald, 148, 176, 219
Rell, Jodi, 146, 154
Representation in American Legislatures (RAL)
   Project, 189, 198
Resnick, Alice Robie, 229
Richards, Ann, 146, 149
Roberts, Barbara, 149
Roby, Martha, 20
Rodgers, Cathy McMorris, 25, 179
Rodham, Dorothy, 74
Roe v. Wade, 169–170
Romney, Mitt, 92, 174
Roosevelt, Franklin D., 218
Rose, Melody, 8
Ros-Lehtinen, Ileana, 3, 175, 237
Ross, Nellie T., 5
Roy, Vesta, 146
Roybal-Allard, Lucille, 238

Saiki, Patricia Fukuda, 237
Saiz, Porfirria Hidalgo, 4
Salazar, Ken, 172
Salter, Susanna Medora, 5
Sánchez, Linda, 238
Sánchez, Loretta, 238, 240
Saund, Dalip Singh, 242
Scalia, Antonin, 224
Schakowsky, Jan, 25
Schreiber, Ronnee, 8
Schroedel, Jean Reith, 8
Schultz, Debbie Wasserman, 25, 178
Schumer, Charles, 84

Sebelius, Kathleen, 146
security moms, 166
Senate Judiciary Committee, 218, 223, 233
seniority, 132–138, 141, 144, 178, 248
September 11, 31, 57, 84
Sewell, Terri, 15, 20
Shaheen, Jeanne, 25, 146, 152, 180
single-member plurality, 290
Smart Girl Politics, 115
Smith, Margaret Chase, 9
Snowe, Olympia, 26, 152, 170
soccer moms, 166
Solís, Hilda, 251–252
Sotomayor, Sonia, 5, 216
Spencer, John, 84
Stabenow, Debbie, 25, 171, 180
stereotype, 58, 87, 97, 104, 107, 256, 259
Stokes, Louis, 239
strategic politicians, 98
Susan B. Anthony List, 114, 116
Sweden, 299, 301, 304
Swers, Michele, 16
Switzerland, 293

Takash, Cruz, 245–247
Tate, Katherine, 10
Tea Party, 31, 115, 117, 124, 143, 165, 197, 257
Temporary Assistance for Needy Families, 286
term limits, 24, 240, 247, 281–285
Thomas, Clarence, 43
Title IX, 9, 75, 91, 194, 250
Title VII of the Civil Rights Act, 173
Todd, Patricia, 267
traditional political culture, 279–280, 285
Truman, Harry, 222

U.N. Millennium Development Goals, 288, 291, 304
U.S. Court of Appeals, 218, 226, 230
U.S. Department of Justice, 219
UN Development Fund for Women, 303
UN Security Council Resolution 1325, 291
unicameral, 182, 185, 279–280
United Kingdom, 289, 299, 303
United Nations Conference on Women in Beijing,
   83
United Nations Development Programme, 303
United Nations Human Rights Council, 85
United Nations, 83, 85, 288, 291, 303, 305
Universal Declaration of Human Rights, 291–293,
   301
University of Arkansas, 82

Vercoe, Moana, 8
Vietnam War, 237
Violence Against Women Act, 16, 164
Voices of Conservative Women, 115

Wahl, Rosalie, 218, 229
Wald, Patricia, 17
Wal-Mart moms, 166
war on women, 1, 16, 162, 167–168, 178–179
Washington Women's Network, 223
Waters, Maxine, 25, 239, 246, 250
Watson, Diane Edith, 246
welfare reform, 16, 164, 249
Wellesley College, 80–81, 89
White House Counsel's office, 219, 222
White, Penny, 218, 230
Whitewater, 83
Whitman, Christie Todd, 156

Whitman, Meg, 148, 156
Wiggins, David, 216
Wilcox, Clyde, 10
Winfrey, Oprah, 74
women-friendly, 12, 16, 98, 101–102, 295
women-friendly policy, 17, 25
Women's Suffrage Amendment, 111
Wong, Janelle, 10

Year of the Woman, 121, 150, 155

Zamarripa, JoCasta, 255